Finding Me
Finding You

LAURIE SMALE

Acknowledgements

I would like to extend a heartfelt thank you to the myriad interesting people I've met along the way who have inspired and influenced this book.

I would also like to thank my friends and colleagues who so diligently read my manuscript. I valued your insightful feedback; it really helped sharpen my focus in the writing of this book.

Four special mentions are also necessary: Dr Heinz Dreher for his meticulous annotated study of the manuscript; established editor Andrea Hanke, for her astute evaluation of the narrative and in-depth comments on purpose and direction; and Mark Smale for his endless weeks of proofreading and analysis. Thank you. Your devotion of time and effort made a significant difference to my thinking and bringing this book to its conclusion.

Thank you to the team at Michael Hanrahan Publishing, for their unsurpassed publishing expertise in helping me bring this book to life.

Finally, thank you to my three grown-up children who were somewhat apprehensive about what their dad had been writing for the past two years! Thanks for putting up with my years of *ordinariness* and imperfections. The truth is, before you guys came along I'd lived a string of incredible experiences as I tried to find my way in life … many of which I find hard to believe really happened!

Some names have been changed throughout the book to protect some people's privacy.

First published in 2020 by Laurie Smale

A catalogue entry for this book is available from the National Library of Australia.

ISBN: 978-1-922391-00-1

Project management and text design by Michael Hanrahan Publishing
Cover design by Peter Reardon

Contents

INTRODUCTION

Getting you right first!

Don't skip this introduction: it's an essential part of your mind-opening journey. Read every word to get the most out of this book.

My story is *your* story

Have you ever fallen into conversation with a complete stranger and soon realised how much we all have in common? The interesting thing is, in many ways *my* story is *your* story and *your* story is *my* story. Our lives are an uncanny compilation of these similarities as we travel life's journey. Your stories will be different to mine but the *life principles* within them are the same. Sometimes these happenings can be momentous; others can be of a 'sliding door' nature where our choice of paths could have gone in different directions; and still others are the simple, everyday things we do on a regular basis ... which are enjoyable when revisited. The only difference in the way you share your daily happenings in a conversational setting and the way I recount them in a book like this is I've learned a few writing skills along the way to ensure what I'm saying is expressed in an *interesting* way. Other than that, our everyday conversational stories of trials, tribulations, happiness and tears remain the same; they embody the essence of being a fallible, interesting human being; they reflect how much we really do have in common, and they ring true to us.

So as you read what I've experienced and how I've interacted with others, reflect on *your life* and how the things that have happened to me embody universal principles that also *relate to you*. You'll see how my thinking changes and how I now accept that the paths I've travelled have not been meaningless or of little interest to anyone. I now know that life's ups and downs are a normal part of my experiences and common to us all. If you glean one idea from this book that *shifts your thinking* and takes you to a better understanding of *you*, it will have been all worthwhile.

How to get the most out of this book

As you mentally travel with me through this book, related happenings from your own experiences will magically appear in your mind. Have a pen handy to jot these priceless stories down as headings or topics so you'll remember them. Then list these precious notes in sequence in an exercise book or electronic device to contemplate later. Leave space between them so you can add other happenings that come to mind.

Take your time as you reflect on these things, for this narrative is no ordinary book; it was written with the specific objective of *getting you right first*. Who knows? You might be able to cast off some of your unwanted baggage too as you see me do the same with mine. You'll now have a timeline of your personal journey for future reference for speeches, a book, your memoirs – a bank of irrefutable evidence that you're not an empty vessel; you've earned the right to have something to say on many aspects of life and are certainly no shallow fake or fraud!

Oh, and keep your eyes open for my 'proverbial hindsights' *written in this special font*. These words of hard-earned wisdom not only embody the universal lessons life has taught me, they keep reminding me of how to make the most of the *imperfect* person I am!

So make sure that pen is handy and let's get cracking on this mind-opening journey of *getting you right first* by taking you back to the beginning of my story …

Laurie Smale
April 2020

Part I
Donald: the early years

(1946 to 1960)

CHAPTER 1

Donald: the early years

"Here goes!" I said to myself and nervously walked through the door of the old Donald pub. But there was no eager face looking out for me; no warm person moving forward to greet me… which threw me somewhat: *am I in the right place?* I asked myself. *Have I got the date wrong?* A familiar fear of uneasiness swept over me as I stood there wondering what to do next.

It had been sixty-eight years since I'd set foot in this country town in Victoria's Mallee wheat belt. Still ill at ease, I scanned the room for some sign of my long-lost contact, for I had no idea what Des Mortlock now looked like. Yet the room was buzzing with ex–Donald Secondary School students and their old teachers comfortably chatting away because they all knew one another. Not a soul knew me because I had not gone to the Donald Secondary School. I had only been to prep and grade one of the Donald *Primary* School. This was *their* reunion and it was *them* who had something in common to reminisce about. Not knowing which of these people used to be my little playmate, and perplexed as to why he hadn't sought me out, I had to do something. So I did what I always do when assailed with these feelings of uneasiness in a room full of people I don't know.

I go and talk to somebody. I spied an officious looking man sitting prominently at a card table and I introduced myself to Jeff (Woofa) Guild, chairperson of the night, as a true 'Donaldite' from times gone by and a guest of Desi Mortlocks.

"Oh, Desi's plane was delayed and he won't be here till tomorrow," Jeff said. "I might get you up after dinner to introduce yourself and tell us a bit about your connection with Donald."

Great! I thought, *Desi's not here and I have to give a speech to a room full of strangers!*

Although I've travelled far amid life's twists and turns, and am quite happy where I now am in my life, it's been a *very* interesting, and at times, *more* than interesting journey. But here I was in a room full of people I didn't know with nowhere to run, trying to fill in the one gap I'd often wondered about: "what *is* the story about my very early days in Donald?"... The little Victorian country town, situated between St Arnaud and Birchip along the main route that links Ballarat and Mildura. The place where I was born. All I had to go on for the five years I was there were the disjointed snippets I'd heard from my mother and my own scarce memories from long, long ago ...

But now I'd been called on to give an impromptu speech to a room full of strangers who had no idea who I was or why I was there... I was totally unprepared for this! I was relying on Desi to shore me up and help me break the ice and meet people. Now I was all alone and found myself having to speak before a roomful of folk who knew nothing of my existence and who I'd never been to school with!

"Fine," I said to 'Woofa', feeling very uneasy for I hate being unprepared... I nervously asked myself: *what am I going to say to these people for I know absolutely nothing about the Donald Secondary School?*

My mind was racing. Drawing on my skills as an experienced speaker and speaking coach I took control of my erratic thinking and began formulating a strategy to get me through. With nowhere to go I decided to speak from the heart about my short existence in Donald and what it meant to me.

The layout was three long trestle tables with about 20 people seated at each; 'Woofa', as organiser and chairman of the evening, was seated to the side at his own card table. A large and portly ex-champion Donald footballer – and their current coach – he kept everything under control. But he left them to talk over old times for two more hours, which did little to settle my nerves. When it was time for me to get up and speak, 'Woofa' put on his coach's hat and commanded their attention. His simple introduction left the audience none the wiser about who I was and what I was doing there. With a racing heart ... I took a deep breath and stood up.

To help calm my nerves and come across as more confident than I actually felt, my first words were a little louder than I normally speak: what's more, to grab their attention, get them involved, and take all the pressure off me I opened with a question about something they all had in common and couldn't help but agree with!

"In 1946 Dr Calhoun brought me into the world in the little Donald hospital a few doors from here ... Can anyone remember him?"

Lots of people warmly responded to this and a sea of hands went up. Phew! Something in common! Most of them were around my age, after all. I began to feel a little better.

I went on to tell them that Desi Mortlock's mother, Irene, and my mother, Jean Smale, were the best of friends, and that we three Smale kids used to play with Johnny and Desi Mortlock. This struck another chord with my listeners, for they all knew the Mortlocks and Johnny had been the Donald postman for decades. More things in common! I was starting to feel in the company of friends.

I told them of my memories of likeable Ron Bignall, Irene Mortlock's partner. I shared how I remembered his big red truck and how tall he was. They all responded warmly to the mention of Ron Bignall, the larger-than-life town truckie; now I was feeling at home.

I told them about the ramshackle house we used to live in on the corner of Woods Street and the little dirt road that led down to the river. I told them about the glass kerosene lamps we had for lighting; our Coolgardie safe in the kitchen; and the old rusty tank which sat askew on its stand for our water supply.

I shared that the reason we were living in Donald was my dad had tuberculosis and it was believed that a warmer climate would help him – but he died when I was three … all my memories of Donald are from around the four-year-old mark. At this stage we were enjoying a *two-way* conversation, for my listeners had comfortably settled in for more of my story … and herein lies one of the best kept secrets of *panic-free* public speaking: always chat with your listeners as if they're your friends.

Then something flashed into my mind: "Who went to the Donald Primary School?" I asked. Of course almost everyone put their hand up.

I went on to share the day an enraged bull terrorised us preppies in the shelter shed while we were being read a story by our young student teacher. I told them how frightened we were; how the angry bull was snorting and butting the corner support post; how the shed was swaying; the shouting stockmen and galloping horses that were giving chase; and finally our desperate dash to the safety of the school house.

I could feel they were all with me.

Then, and I don't know why, I asked: "Was anyone there that day?" And to my pleasant amazement a lady said, "Yes, I was there and I remember it clearly," which really helped validate my authenticity.

And finally I came to 'Georgie the Chinaman': a kind and humble man whose homegrown vegetables had nurtured three generations of the people of Donald. (Of course, nobody would call him that these days, but that's the way things were then.) Everybody loved him – especially the children. I asked, "Who remembers Georgie?" The response was animated and universal. Not a person remained silent. Such was this revered man's effect on the people of Donald.

I shared how he called my mother 'Little Missy' and how we kids rushed to him the moment we herd his cart creak to a stop outside our house. I shared how he'd turn a blind eye to us kids appropriating an apple from a case purposely placed within our reach. I shared how he let us pat his beloved horse. I shared how he'd give my mum her vegetables even if she was battling for money that week (she had told me this later). I shared how he'd proudly sit on his cart with his friendly stumpy-tooth smile beaming out from under his big hat.

"Georgie," I told them, "was the highlight of our day and we all adored him."

I kept my final words crisp, clear, and deliberate: "I was born here; I went to primary school here; I lived here on the corner of Woods Street; we had friends here; I've experienced the kindness of Georgie the Chinaman; and I feel I've earned the right to be here tonight as a proud Donaldite... Thank you for your welcome home."

Their warm applause filled a gap I'd been yearning to fill for years. At long last the Donald part of my life was complete – well, almost ... There were still a couple of loose ends that needed attending to: I wanted to walk down near the river where the back of our house used to be to see what I remembered, and I wanted to visit the little weatherboard bush hospital where I was born. I also wanted to visit Georgie the Chinaman's hut. But all this would have to wait till Desi Mortlock arrived in the morning.

Before we pick up with Desi Mortlock, allow me to introduce my mother, who was something else. She felt completely at home in this tough rural setting of the 1940s, which was strange for she grew up as an only child in Murrumbeena, a well-to-do suburb in Melbourne's south east. This was something we knew next to nothing about till the twilight years of her life, because her down-to-earth behaviour reflected none of this. We simply didn't believe half the stuff she told us – which turned out to be true.

The only time I got an inkling of her living a different life to the rough-edged mother I knew was the time I saw her competently playing tennis in a nice white dress at the Donald tennis courts – a vision I was never to see again.

Although pretty in her own way, I've only ever known her as a down-to-earth, no-nonsense person who swore like a trooper, though there were times when butter wouldn't melt in her mouth. In short, she could do anything and everything, and in my view she was Australia's answer to that all-round hillbilly Mrs fix-it, Ma Kettle of 1940s and '50s film fame!

Desi and I organised to meet at my hotel at 10 am that morning, and right on the dot there he was. He certainly wasn't the tall, dark, weather-beaten country-type character I'd envisioned. On the contrary, he was short of stature, rather distinguished with silver hair and moustache to match, a little ruddy of complexion and wearing a white short-sleeved shirt. But the dead giveaway was the mischievous twinkle in his eye. This was the little Desi I knew sixty-eight years ago!

"What would you like to do first?" he asked.

"We'll, if it's still there I'd like to see my old house and the little road beside it that led down to the river."

"Your house is no longer there, but the gravel road and the river are," he said. We drove about 200 metres down Woods Street and he pulled up. I'd forgotten I was so young at the time and my whole universe would have existed within a 500-metre radius of where we now were. (My ever-eccentric mother expanded this range somewhat, with me and my two brothers hurtling around the streets of Donald with her on her old man's bike, fitted out with three child seats: one attached to the handlebars, one on the cross bar, and one on the rack behind her. I am not sure where I sat in the scheme of things, but I do have faint memories of being lifted on and off this innovative conveyance.)

As we walked down the gravel road, Desi pointed out where my back yard would have been in relation to the river, which at the time was nothing more than a glorified stream …

My mind drifted off to a different day by the river.

This day the Richardson River was in full flood, its murky yellow waters treacherously wide and swirling before us. I forget which boys were with me at the time, but I desperately wanted to do what they were doing because it looked like they were having so much fun. The raging waters had pushed a massive palm tree up against the bank and these boys were pulling the fronds off it and making hula dresses out of them. It looked so easy. So with my little legs, I waded into the swirling waters to do the same.

The next instant my whole world turned upside down. My body was pulled every which way, and there was an unbearable stinging pain in my legs and arms. Something ripped at my hair and the pain was excruciating. Then my mind came into focus. I was wobbling unsteadily on the slippery bank with the imposing figure of Mrs Mortlock screaming over me. She looked fierce, with her face framed in her basin-trimmed hair cut. Although short and stocky, she had the forearms of a woodcutter and had hold of my arm in a vice-like grip. Then I twigged where the awful pain was coming from. She was slapping me as hard as she could: one, to bring me round, and two because she was so angry! Apparently she had been watching from her kitchen window, and raced down and grabbed me by the hair just as I'd gone under those swirling waters near the palm tree for a third time.

"Get on home!" she bellowed. "And never come down to the river again! … And I'll be telling your mother all about this too! Now get going!"

Although I was very young, I clearly remember her saying this. She was formidable. I just ran. But now there was a new fear: my mother.

When I got home all wet and dishevelled, I told my mother that I'd fallen in a drain and she believed me. But when Mrs Mortlock caught up with her later that day and told her what had really happened, I got another hiding from my mother for telling lies. That's how it was in those days.

This event was so traumatic it put a stop to us visiting the river for a while. My poor mother must have been at the end of her tether. She enlisted the help of the local butcher to help scare us boys away by saying there were lots of nasty crocodiles in the river. "There's a big bugger climbing up onto the bridge right now!" he'd say, supposedly pointing it out to my concerned mother. "He looks a really nasty one. I'd hate to ever meet him!"

This terrifying image put the fear of God into us. I can see him standing at our back door now, a giant of a man towering over my little brother and me in his blue-striped butcher's apron. This worked for a while, but with the passage of time it slipped from our minds.

Some weeks later the river again beckoned my younger brother Brian and me to venture once more into the stinking black mud among the reeds to see what other exciting things we might discover. It was heavy going as each of our skinny legs had to be pulled out with both hands after each laborious step. The viscous ooze was like squelching through knee-high glue. Because the reeds were high above our heads they gave us the sense of being in the jungle. It took us a good fifteen minutes before we breached the final barrier of reeds and burst through to the water's edge. It was quite an achievement! There we stood, two intrepid explorers surveying our vast domain, at peace with the tranquil scene of this meandering river as it flowed through the dense jungle.

While all this was going on, someone upstream must have been doing a bit of gardening or a farm yard tidy-up and emptied a heap of grass clippings into the river. By the time this floating pile of green off-cuts reached us, its form had dramatically morphed into something long and sinister with two beady eyes and a snout. At first mesmerised by this elongated form heading towards us with apparent purpose, it soon dawned on us exactly what we were looking at.

"Hey! The butcher was right! This is probably the bugger that was climbing over the bridge!"

We ploughed back through the mud and reeds as if they weren't there, running for our lives.

I have no recollections of river adventures after that.

Desi broke my reverie: " … and the river is sometimes prone to floods," he was saying.

"I know," I said. "Your mum once pulled me out … saved my life!"

He nodded knowingly.

Mentioning my younger brother Brian in this incident brings to mind another quirky occurrence: to this day he swears that once while sitting beside the gravel road next to our house, our little fox terrier Diggy *spoke* to him. Well, who am I to say he didn't? Even today Brian smiles when I bring this up – he still won't deny it happened.

Desi then took me down another side street for a different view of the meandering river. "A guy used to have a Jersey cow over there," he said, "and sold everyone its milk."

"Hey, I know that cow!" I exclaimed. "It once held me hostage and traumatised me!"

Desi smiled. He was enjoying this.

My mother believed we should start learning to be independent at an early age. This particular morning she decided to expand my worldly experience by sending me on an errand to get the day's milk from Mr Jones' milking shed a couple of houses down the road.

"Here, Lozzy Boo." That was my mother's nickname for me; we all had one. "Take this billy can, and when you get to the old milk shed on the corner, go in there and Mr Jones will fill your billy with the milk for mummy."

At this tender age I had little understanding that cows and milk were somehow connected. Filled with importance, I proudly strode off with my billy can. All was going well, for the milking shed soon came into view. But, then I nearly died! Without warning, a monstrous Jersey cow thrust her head over the low railing and fixed me with her big menacing eyes. I froze. All I could see were two nasty horns, a mouth full of shiny square teeth, and a big blue tongue lolling all over the place. Fixed to the spot and unable to move, I was crying at the top of my lungs, for this frightening beast, a hundred times my size, wouldn't get out of my way. Perplexed at all this noise, the cow let out an inquisitive moo from its big drooling mouth.

This was enough for me. Clutching my mum's precious billy, I turned tail and fled home.

"Mummy," I sobbed as I burst into the kitchen. "It's there, near the fence!"

"It's just a nice friendly moo cow," my mother soothed in a reassuring tone. "She won't hurt you at all. Come on, let's go and get the milk together!" And that's exactly what we did. To my absolute astonishment she even patted this frightening beast on the head, and it just looked at her with loving eyes!

We then went into the milking shed, had our billy filled with milk by friendly Mr Jones, and I saw my first stainless steel milk separator in action. And most important of all, I made my first rudimentary connection between a cow and milk.

Like I said, even at a very young age my mother believed in hands-on learning.

"Where to now?" Desi asked.

"What about my old school?" We didn't have far to go – it was just down the road. The old cream weatherboards were exactly as I'd remembered them. I walked over and gently laid my hand on the wall and held it there a moment. I then put my face to a window and looked through. But what I saw was years ago in the prep-school farm yard play …

I remember this being a big deal with a great build up to it. All the kids were fitted out as different farm yard animals and went to a lot of trouble to make their costumes with their families. I was a big white duck. I can see myself now, sporting the huge paper duck head my mother made with its hinged, oversized yellow bill, which, for some reason, stayed wide open and people could see half my face. This didn't worry me at all. My mother told me later: "You quacked the loudest and were the most animated of the whole farm yard!" Typical.

Right next to the school was a massive black steam locomotive in a park for children to play on. Probably just like the ones that used to transport all the wheat and barley of the region to the distant ports in Melbourne and Geelong. This switched my memory to something a little more challenging …

"Do you remember a big train turntable being somewhere around here?" I asked Desi.

"Oh yes, it was right over there," he said, pointing to the edge of the playground, "but it was filled in years ago."

Now a train turntable is like an enormous 'Lazy Susan'; the train engine rolls out over this gigantic pit atop a moveable turntable; then, by cleverly geared human power, the engine is turned around to face the other way for the return journey. I clearly remember standing on the edge of that scary pit and looking down into it.

It's important to keep in mind that my elder brother Darryl was eighteen months older than me, which is a lifetime when considering how siblings can treat each other. He certainly didn't want his troublesome mite of a brother joining in with the 'grown up' things he was involved in. But one day he somehow didn't notice his annoying little brother hanging in there behind him as he and his mates made their way to the train turntable. I've never forgotten the unbelievable things I saw that day.

A hand-powered railway trolley was parked on the tracks about 30 metres from the cavernous turntable pit. About three metres from the perilous drop was a large pile of ballast stones and bricks put on the rails by the boys to act as a brake to stop the trolley hurtling into the abyss.

They were all ready for action.

It was thrilling to see them running beside, and sitting *astride*, the trolley, enthusiastically pushing and pumping the handle as it gained speed, only to buck violently as it crashed into the pile of 'safety' stones at the last second, avoiding that deathly plunge. How exciting it all was. The whole operation smelled of railway ballast and oil, which added a level of danger to it all.

It was all hands on deck to push the trolley back to the start, ready for its next thrilling run. I was just getting ready to wheedle my way on board to be a part of the next bout of thrills and spills when the worst possible thing happened; my enraged mother appeared on the scene. She had sensed us being up to no good and had tracked us down.

"Right – you two! Get here!" she roared.

The rest of the kids scattered. You didn't mess with Mrs Smale. Darryl and I were marched home to face the music.

Desi smiled and said, "I was probably there – we did that often." Sometimes I wonder at the things we put our poor mother through and how we ever survived!

"It would be nice to see the old hospital," I said.

"You mean ... what's left of it."

"What do you mean?" I'd thought it was still there.

"I mean, it's been left to ruin, and squatters have been living in it for years."

We drove down the road a hundred metres or so and he stopped the car. He nodded towards a tiny dilapidated weatherboard house, overgrown with bushes and covered in rubbish.

"Here's the hospital," he said.

I was taken aback: "Was *this* really the place I was born? ... Can I go in and have a look?"

"Yeah, but there's not much to see!"

I tentatively made my way through the overgrown junk and discards of yesteryear to what was once the front porch. The pitiful scene that greeted me was a real let down, and I just stood there trying to remember anything about the place ... then it all came back to me.

I'd been brought here once as a youngster. I saw my tiny self, a blood-drenched towel wrapped around my hand and arm, being hurried through the door by my distraught mother. A stabbing pain was beginning to kick in, but my mind was clear enough to register a clean surgery with a definite 'hospital' smell about it.

So what had happened to bring me there?

I clearly remember running around with the Mortlocks and my younger brother Brian on a vacant block of land with one of our ankles tied together, when I fell heavily on a broken bottle and severely sliced my wrist. I remember a bolt of pain shooting through my body; then I must have gone into shock.

"I've cut myself," I told the others, and instinctively covered my hanging wrist with my good hand. They quickly untied me and I took off for home.

"Look what I did mummy," I casually said to my astonished mother, uncovering my partially severed hand. By now I was drenched in blood. She snapped into action, threw a makeshift bandage over my gaping wound, and off we rushed down the road to the quaint Donald Hospital.

The legendary Dr Calhoun, and his no-nonsense matronly nurse, met us in the foyer and quickly assessed the gravity of the situation.

"We'd better get him into the surgery!" declared the concerned doctor.

"No! No one can touch my hand!" I defiantly announced, holding my damaged arm as tight as I could.

"That's fine," purred the nurse. "Let's go down and see where all the little babies are born."

Somewhat distracted, but still on my guard, I followed her. I remember the hallway walls were a calming sky blue with yellow and green fairyland pictures all over them.

This is more like it, I thought.

All the while, the by now 'friendly' nurse, was telling me about the cute little babies we were about to see. I felt a lot better and looked forward to her surprise.

Without warning, the nurse transformed into the negative being I'd first sensed in the foyer. She unceremoniously grabbed me around the waist and whisked me onto a table and pinned me down. I tried my best to get free, but struggling against her was useless. I do recall a funnel contraption being put over my face, a glimpse of white cotton-wool, and hearing the glug, glug, glug of liquid chloroform being poured over it. I then found myself in a horrifying world of witches, goblins and other nasty creatures. Thankfully, right at the worst part, I woke up.

"See! No one touched my hand!" I defiantly proclaimed.

"It's all mended now," smiled the kindly nurse.

I contemplated my bandaged arm with wonder.

The noisy air brakes of a passing wheat truck jolted me back to reality … still trying to make sense of the sad ruins before me and what I remembered of the Donald Hospital. Gone was the spick-and-span cleanliness of the foyer and the nice hospital smell. It was now all dark, dank and mouldy. The windows were broken and the front door was askew on one of its hinges. I wedged myself through the gap, and what I saw was dismal. Most of the floorboards were missing, as were the internal walls. Dust and dirt was inches thick on everything, mixed with the refuse of long-gone human habitation. Notwithstanding this miserable scene, I felt compelled to venture into the hallway the 'kindly' nurse had walked me down 'to see the little babies' all those sixty-eight years ago.

But there was nothing there. No hallway; no calming sky blue on the walls and ceilings; no fairy frescoes. All gone. Just stark beams, empty floor joists, and holes in the roof.

I'd had enough. I carefully sidestepped my way back to safety, trying to come to terms with the impact of it all. But all was not lost. Thanks to the telling scar on my left wrist, I have a vivid reminder of what a nice little health centre the Donald Hospital was. The place where I was born.

At lunchtime Desi and I stopped at the time-honoured Royal Hotel, which was certainly there when I was little, for a hearty country-style counter lunch. Everyone nodded their acknowledgement to Desi and the respected Mortlocks. As we drove around the streets and visited the various establishments, everyone new Desi and stopped to say hello. Even the old school mates he bumped into as we travelled around remembered him too. I was beginning to feel a bit left out. After all, I too was born in the Donald Hospital like a majority of the locals, and indeed, I also went to the Donald Primary School, albeit only prep school and a few months of grade one. Yet not one of these people remembered the Smale children, my dad Ron, or my mother Jean.

The only person who could legitimise my existence of having ever been there was Des Mortlock. His brother Johnny, the town postman for years, had died; Irene Mortlock, to whom I owe my life, had gone; as had Ron Bignell, her beloved partner who always had time for us kids; they'd all gone. Only Desi was left. In this somewhat deflated state, I followed Desi into the Heritage Society's old building in Woods Street for some more general information, when something magic happened!

As we were chatting to the elderly archivist, the name Jim Murray came up.

"I know him!" I exclaimed. "My mother used to take us kids to visit him regularly. He used to be in a wheelchair and always wore a checked dressing gown and slippers. I even remember we had to walk through a white picket gate to get to the front door."

"That was Jim Murray senior," the old lady said. "But the Jim Murray we're talking about is his son, and would have been one of the kids you'd seen during those visits with your mother."

That made sense. My mother used to correspond with the old Jimmy Murray for years by mail.

Fortune had it that we bumped into the young Jimmy Murray an hour later as he was opening his hardware store. When Jimmy found out who I was, he spoke warmly of our visits to his invalid dad.

"I can clearly remember your mother and you guys paying us regular visits – in fact your mother wrote to us for years … after that, we often wondered what had happened to her." At last I had another person who could verify my existence in Donald as well as Desi Mortlock and the lady from the raging bull episode.

Georgie the Chinese market gardener

Georgie Ah Ling came out to Australia – as did tens of thousands of other Chinese adventurers – during the mid to late 1800s to seek their fortune on the goldfields. But many Chinese discovered that feeding the gold diggers and growing vegetables for them was more lucrative than sweating it out digging for gold that rarely came your way. Supplying the gold diggers with food and vegetables was a much more profitable and dependable income than risking all on the fickle gold fields. And that's how Georgie the market gardener ended up with his half acre vegetable plot on the outskirts of the tiny frontier town of Donald. But his iconic presence became much more than that of a friendly market gardener; he became the very *essence* of Donald. More than three generations of Donald folk grew up with him, for he lived to over one hundred – and everybody loved him.

Reflecting on this, I said to Desi, "Where exactly is Georgie's Hut that everyone talks about?"

"Get in," he said. "I'm saving the best to last."

We drove to the edge of town and turned right towards the racecourse. A couple of kilometres further on, Desi pulled over.

"There you are," he said, pointing. "That's Georgie's shack."

All I could see was a forlorn and tumbledown hut that hadn't been touched for years. It looked sad and forgotten, left to rack and ruin beside a dried-out water hole. Georgie's once lovingly tended and prized market garden was now a tangle of overgrown weeds, abandoned and unrecognisable.

How could this be? I wondered. *Poor Georgie! Had his revered plot of land and humble abode really been forsaken and left to ruin by a population who once loved him?*

The truth is, the good folk of Donald have left things just as they were in deference to this special place Georgie considered his adopted home. Although it encroaches on a tiny bit of adjacent farmers' land, they won't touch it. So here it remains, a heartfelt memorial to the memory of a very special person we all loved and appreciated.

"Desi," I said, "I just want to go for a bit of a walk and contemplate what's before me ... I won't be long."

I made my way over an old culvert full of weeds and rubble and stood by the barbed-wire fence looking over the overgrown remnants of Georgie's beloved home and garden. I could just make out the very furrows that Georgie would have walked along tending his garden beds with so much love and care. I pictured him cheerfully walking along these neat garden rows with his long bamboo pole across his shoulders, two oversize watering cans on each end, watering his fruit trees and vegetables. Plants get very thirsty here in Donald.

As I contemplated the ruins of his dilapidated little home, I imagined Georgie coming in from a hard day's toil under the scorching Mallee sun; I can see him relaxing in his solitary wooden chair and smoking his homemade cherry-wood pipe by the light of his kerosene lamp. I also see his few cherished bits and pieces that mean so much to him, all neatly in their place. But most of all, I visualise Georgie leaving his little market garden just as I – and following generations – remember him: his cart is laden with healthy vegetables nurtured by his own hands; he whispers something to his beloved horse, and they both turn into Racecourse Road and intuitively set off on their well-trod path. A path that is much more than a local greengrocer delivery run; it is a path that nurtures life-long relationships and respect; it is a path where Georgie looks forward to sharing his prized produce with his adoring extended family – the friendly people of Donald.

One thing is for sure, the people of Donald will never relinquish the rich heritage their Georgie has bequeathed them. And as someone who was born and spent the first five years of his life there, I share in this heritage too.

Even though I had to wait a lifetime before I returned to my birthplace, and my early days in Donald were but fleeting, it was important for me to retrace my roots and re-establish myself as a true Donaldite. The fact is, I used to be, and will always remain, a proud part of Donald.

The following day Desi Mortlock and I embraced like newfound brothers as we said our goodbyes. I thanked him for helping me find that unfinished 'Donald' part of me that had eluded me for so long. It was an unwritten pact that our friendship would continue and go on from here. In fact, we parted with the promise that we'd soon meet again in Rockhampton where he now lived, but this time it would be me making the long trip up north!

"Great!" he said, "I look forward to it!"

Sadly, I would never see Desi Mortlock again. Our enjoyable stroll down memory lane was to be our first and last time together as adults. Twelve weeks later, my long-lost friend died from an unexpected manifestation of cancer.

Rest in peace Desi. Our Donald tour of self-discovery meant a lot to me.

My father

Before we turn the page on a new chapter in my journey, there are a couple of small but important things that tie us back to Donald before we move on. The first is, how did my father contact tuberculosis? And why live in faraway Donald? And what, if anything, do I remember of him?

When my father was seventeen he contracted tuberculosis during the war while serving as a young recruit in New Guinea, so he was repatriated back to Australia for treatment. As a consequence, my future parents sought out a warmer climate, for in those days this was considered beneficial in fighting this insidious disease. Antibiotics were relatively new at the time, apart from penicillin, and were yet unproven and still being tested. So, full of hope, to Donald they moved.

Sadly their time together was cut short, for in spite of the climate, the disease steadily progressed from his lungs to his arm. He had to be moved to the Caulfield Military Hospital for specialised care, unaware he would never hold his little boys again. My mother told me he always believed he was going to get better.

Visiting dad now meant an all-day trip by train and bus for my mum and us boys to visit him when we could. I have no memory of these journeys; but there is one thing that remains indelibly etched in my mind: the day I saw my dad on the hospital veranda.

A lifetime later, I was driving along Kooyong Road in Caulfield, and there, after all these decades, was a sign set back from the road saying, 'Caulfield Hospital'. I pulled over thinking, *I wonder if that's it? I wonder if the veranda is still there?* I tentatively walked across the road, for all the buildings seemed very modern and not of the era that was in my mind. Then my heart began to quicken, for there, tucked away to the side among the trees, was a lower, older 1940s building – still with the veranda I remembered!

Why was the veranda so important? Well, tuberculosis is so contagious I was never allowed to go into the ward to visit my father, so they would wheel him out onto this veranda in his hospital bed. Even there, my mother told me, I had to stay on the other side of the railing because it was too dangerous for me to get near him. So I really only ever knew my dad as 'the man who waved to me'.

Getting back to this one indelible image I have of my father (which is more a moving scenario than a still picture); if he died when I was three, this vivid recollection must have happened just before then, and this scenario is as clear as if he were before me now. The only way I can share this little tableau with you is the way it starkly remains in my mind; a sort of out-of-body experience where I am an onlooker at what is happening. I clearly see my mother in a brownish tartan tweed skirt lifting little Laurie up beyond the veranda balcony; I see my fattish toddler legs and shiny going-out shoes; I see my wispy snow-white hair; and most of all I *feel* all this at the same time. There are plenty of coloured flowers in the garden, it's sunny and warm, and everything is green.

"Wave to Daddy," my mother is saying, and I innocently wave in the general direction of this man. He is sitting up in a white hospital bed on the veranda. He is wearing blue-and-white striped pyjamas. His shiny dark hair is slicked back and he is wearing big black sunglasses which stare straight ahead beyond me. But unlike other times, he is not waving back.

My father was only twenty-five when he died.

So, there was my twenty-two-year-old mother, now a war widow with three little boys under four to care for, while facing an uncertain future in faraway Donald.

One thing I do regret is I never did sit down with my mother and ask her about my father. The only thing I know about him is what's written on my birth certificate: 'fibrous plasterer'. That's the extent of my knowledge of him.

I would have asked her what he sounded like. What his personality was like. Where they first met. How old they were. What sort of courtship they had during wartime. What pleasant memories she had of them together. How she coped when he died. Where his funeral was and who was there.

So many questions, but none of them asked. If only I had known how to do this, both our loads would have been lightened.

A postscript on my father

Not long after my enlightening pilgrimage to Donald, I decided to visit my second cousin Ken Smale, a person I'd never met, in Warracknabeal, a five-hour trip from Melbourne. It was great to spend some time with the son of my father's father's brother and fill in a few more gaps in my family history. Ken also happened to be a famous Collingwood footballer, who'll go down in history for his memorable eight-goal performance which kicked his team into the 1956 Aussie Rules Grand Final.

A few days after this I received a phone call from a lady called Eileen Bremmer: "You don't know me," she said, "but I did know your father Ron. I'm also one of your cousins. My dear friend Jean Smale, Ken's wife, from Warracknabeal rang and told me about your visit."

"This is a surprise!" was all I could say.

"Oh, yes," she said, 'I clearly remember your father, he really was a tall, dark, and handsome man!" She then told me a story: "One day he rode all the way from Donald to our place in Mt Eliza on his big Indian motorbike with little Darryl in the sidecar ... You and your smaller brother Brian wouldn't have been born then. What I remember about this is Ron apparently started the journey with his favourite broad-brimmed hat on, but after a while decided to take it off and tuck it in the sidecar with his little boy. When he arrived at our place I remember him saying to Darryl, 'Where is Daddy's hat?' And little Darryl saying, 'Hat blow away!'"

This was the first time anybody had ever replayed to me an actual conversation that had fallen from my father's lips. Amazing the nice things that can happen when we go out of our way to say hello to people.

Disjointed early memories

Apart from my mother's grieving and the demands of a young family, the next couple of years must have been really tough financially for her. The Australian Government reneged on giving her a war widow's pension because my dad hadn't actually been in combat. But he was stationed and trained in New Guinea and right in line to fight the Japanese to defend his country. He contracted tuberculosis while in service there and ended up dying from it. But they met their match when they came up against my mother – she was a real fighter. In the end, she got her rightful way.

My memories from this shadowy, transitory period from Donald to the next phase of my life are very disjointed and scattered, but they're important in the overall scheme of where I stem from. The following things must have happened not long after my father's death for they persist in my distant memory …

My mum once said she was standing at the counter of the Office of Veterans Affairs in Melbourne desperately trying to organise the clearance of her pension, with the added weight on her mind of having to go into hospital herself. My two brothers, Brian and Darryl, were being minded but she had no one to look after me.

"What am I going to do with my little boy?" she pleaded to the unfeeling official.

Fortunately a kind stranger in the foyer overheard this conversation and said, "Our family will look after him till you are better." What kindness! And that's exactly what they did, at no cost to my mother. All I know is their surname was Morris and they lived in the bayside suburb of Beaumaris. What I do clearly remember is luxuriating in a big yellow bathtub while this loving family pampered me and gave me a nice warm bath. A far cry from what I'd been used to in Donald – all we had there was a tin tub you sat up in!

Another of these disjointed recollections stems from my mother's association with Blamey House as a cleaner, some sort of halfway refuge of the time. My mother had mentioned this dismal place, which helps me remember it. I would have had to be just over three but I have no idea where we were living. However, my memory of what happened that day is very stark and illustrates what she must have been going through; it is very painful, both physically and emotionally, yet I am completely helpless to do anything about it. I am tightly strapped into a cot with a leather harness secured crossways to each corner; I am screaming and struggling to stand up because the red spots of my measles are excruciatingly itchy and stinging; and I can see my poor mother scrubbing the floor on her hands and knees in a white dress with blue flowers. She is not allowed to comfort me, and I was too young to understand why. An image not easy to shake.

Some time after this, my mother had to go to hospital yet again, and needed to farm us kids out till she got well enough to come and get us – which she always did. My luck of the draw was a sad six-month stay in a cold, loveless boys' home in Box Hill. My poor mother had no choice but to hand her distraught little boy over to a complete stranger on the large blue-stone steps of this forbidding place. Bravely holding back her tears, she said, "Mummy loves you, and it won't be long before I'm better and come back to get you."

Overcome with a mixture of sadness and fear, I do remember how terrified I felt as I was dragged away from my crying mother into that cold, cavernous entrance hall. From then on I was kept isolated because of my age.

I hated that awful place.

Although my mother did visit me when she could, it was sporadic. I always felt lost, lonely and sad because I was treated like a number and not allowed to interact with the other boys. As dismal days turned into weeks, and then months, I sank deeper and deeper into dark despair.

Just when I thought all hope was gone, my mother returned with my two brothers to take me away from there. We were all together again. What's more, my mother had magically procured a brand new Housing Commission house in Victoria's Latrobe Valley for us to live in.

A new chapter in our lives was about to begin. So it was all aboard for the little town of Moe!

CHAPTER 2

Off to Moe

So we arrived in Harold Street Moe to rent our nice new Housing Commission home with running water, lights you could have by a flick of a switch, and a real refrigerator! Our stay in Moe was brief, barely a year, but it helped settle us into a more sedate, predictable way of life.

But there was something extra as well … there was a new man in my mother's life! His name was John Forrest, and she had met him in a returned serviceman's hospital because he had some sort of war neurosis problem, as do many returned soldiers. He was not really a father figure to me or my brothers; he was just there in the background, so he doesn't figure prominently in my memory as such. He was to stay with my mother for four years then fade out of our lives. Towards the end I do recall their relationship did get a bit tumultuous because he found it hard to hold down a job. The good thing is we boys got a wonderful brother and sister, Leanne and Mark, out of this union when I was nine. I was not to know I would take on the role of older guardian for these vulnerable little children in their formative years. The last I heard of John Forrest is that he died as a jackaroo somewhere in outback Australia. I hope he ended up finding some sort of peace.

Even though our stay in Moe was a less disruptive existence than Donald, I recall a couple of stand-out exceptions. Like the time my beloved little black dog Sophie ran across the road and got hit by a car. Her ear-splitting yelps as the car struck were more than I could bear, and blood was pouring out of her mouth. It was the first time I had ever seen anything like this; it was heart-wrenching. Little Sophie must have been in deep shock because although she appeared terribly damaged, she was looking up at me from the side of the road with her loving eyes as if trying to say, "Don't worry, it's not your fault." The kind driver somehow managed to carry her inside and lay her down in her basket in the laundry. Her little jaw was broken so she wouldn't be able to eat. Later my mum called a nice policeman and told me, "He would put her to sleep so she wouldn't hurt anymore."

I really loved Sophie.

I hadn't been in Moe long when I found my way to the local public swimming hole on the edge of the State Forest at the top of Wirraway Street. It was pretty big, and even had its own high-diving board and wooden jetty. One day I was standing on the jetty watching the high divers defy gravity with their swallow dives and clever somersaults. I'd never seen anything like it! I was standing there thinking, *I'll be able to do that when I grow up.*

I started to feel nice and relaxed and see my own images of things flashing past; in fact, a lot of what I was seeing was back in Donald and I was really enjoying it! The next thing I know, someone was rudely interrupting this pleasant state of affairs by shaking me violently and yelling, "Quick grab him! Help me get him out!"

Totally absorbed by the awesome display of aerial dynamics I'd been watching, I'd stepped off the jetty into four metres of murky water and went straight to the bottom. I still couldn't swim! Thankfully some guy saw this happen and went in after me. One thing I can attest to is, you actually *do* see pictures of your life flashing past when you are dying, because that's exactly what I saw.

Elmer Fudd

During our stay in Moe a slight speech impediment began to creep up on me. I had trouble saying my 'Rs', and sounded like the Warner Brothers cartoon character Elmer Fudd when he refers to Buggs Bunny as "that Wascally Wittle Wabbit!", but I was totally unaware of it.

Now Mr Russell, our next-door neighbour, had a little brown bitzer dog called Rusty who we all loved. And this day Mr Russell and my mum were talking at the front gate when I ran up and said, "Hey, Wusty Wussell Wan accWoss the Woad!" How they both laughed and kept repeating what I'd said, which made me feel bad. But I could see what was amusing about it because it did sound funny when they good-naturedly mimicked what I sounded like. There was no way I wanted to go on sounding like Elmer Fudd, so for the next few days I practised the 'Rs' in 'Rusty Russell' over and over till it sounded like everyone else. Nobody laughed about the way I pronounced my 'Rs' ever again.

One thing we did do for the next decade or so was make a yearly pilgrimage to the TB Clinic in Latrobe St Melbourne for our obligatory TB vaccinations. The first of these annual journeys was to be from Moe. To do this from Moe, the first leg of our all-day journey had to be in an old steam train to Warragul. And how exciting that was! To see that massive steaming, smoking, clanking steam engine with wheels towering far above me storm into the station effortlessly pulling its carriages was a sight to behold. I still see the oil-covered train driver leaning out of the engine to pass the special cane ring over the Station Master's arm for safety. It was awesome! We wasted no time in getting a good window seat but were not allowed to open the window because our good clothes would get covered in soot. We could only do that once we'd changed to an electric train in Warragul.

Our reward for good behaviour was our traditional lunch in Coles cafeteria in Bourke Street in Melbourne, something we really looked forward to. My mother would *always* ask the long-suffering girl in blue to help fill our trays with our pies, custard tarts and drinks. We'd talk about how wonderful this special treat was for weeks.

One of our neighbours in Moe was Edie Davidson who lived behind us, and I remember she would always talk to me and say hello. Once I noticed she had a full-sized men's bike in the shed and decided I'd ask her could I have a ride on it. It had a cross bar and was much higher than me, but I thought, *I can ride it from under the bar.* I plucked up the courage to ask her.

"Could I have a ride on your bike in the shed?" I tentatively enquired. I could see her sizing me up and trying to figure out how I could do this. In the end she said, "Okay, but be careful!"

I wheeled it a couple of doors down out of sight before I attempted my fateful ride. I had a feeling this wasn't going to be easy. I got in under the bar slant-wise and somehow managed to get my arms back to the handlebars with the bike tilted at an acute angle … then away I went down the hill!

I was moving fast. But I hadn't given any thought to how I was going to steer the thing, let alone stop. I was now careening out of control, and crashed at a fair pelt into Mr Russell's brick fence. I was grazed but none the worse for wear. What I was really worried about was Edie's bike, for I noticed the wheel was wobbling as I wheeled it back. But she was lovely. "Don't worry about it," she said. "Les will fix it up. I think we'll wait till you're a bit older till you have another go!"

I still tend to rush into things like a bull at a gate, which often gets me into trouble.

All in all, Moe was a pleasant country town full of nice people – but Seaford was a veritable land of adventure!

CHAPTER 3

Seaford: a whole new adventure

After a year my mum must have been thinking about something more permanent for us than a rented Housing Commission home; she wanted us to have our very own place to live in. One day she announced, "Mummy has bought us a new house and we're moving to Seaford!" Wow! How she did that on her meagre widow's pension I still don't know, but she did! For us this was a great adventure – we had no idea where Seaford was.

Mr Kestle, who lived a few doors away, kindly offered to take us there on his red Ford tray truck. So like the pictures you see of the destitute okies loading all their belongings onto their old jalopies to escape the lifeless dust bowls of America's mid-west of the 1920s; that's just how Mr Kestle's overloaded truck looked, chock-a-block with everything we owned and mum and all us kids crammed on board as we waved goodbye to Moe. So it was off to Seaford, the place where I grew up. I was now six years old.

I don't remember John Forrest coming on the trip with us, but I know he joined us later. He must have been away seeking work or getting war neurosis treatment.

The trip to Seaford was uneventful as we trundled along with the wind blowing in our faces till finally we arrived. Our little two-bedroom house, although new, was in the middle of nowhere on a dirt road. Lot 12 Wells Road, Seaford (now a part of the Frankston freeway). We all piled out to explore, as was our nature, while mum and Mr Kestle unloaded all our belongings inside as best they could.

We were so excited. This was a real palace – and it was ours! We rushed around the back to have a look and couldn't believe our eyes: an endless expanse of mirror-smooth sheets of inviting blue water with bank upon bank of high reeds bordering it. It reminded us of the Richardson River, only bigger! My mum was right behind us, and I heard her say, "Oh, no! They've seen it!"

"You're not allowed to go there," she said. "It's dangerous!"

But we'd already made a note of it for future adventures.

While Mr Kestle and mum were unloading and organising things into some semblance of order, we wandered across the road to see what lay beyond a large stand of gigantic cypress pines. And what a sight we found! There before our eyes was a disused reddish-orange quarry, full of crystal clear water, lilies, and large, shiny yellow-and-green frogs. We made a note of this too. All of us had the same thought: *we were going to enjoy this place!*

We were yet to discover the massive flocks of black swans and hundreds of other waterbirds that inhabited the nearby wetlands. And even more exciting … we were yet to discover that we were only twenty minutes' walk from one of Melbourne's most popular beaches.

After offering the kind Mr Kestle a cup of tea, brewed on a little camp primus, and a pre-prepared sandwich, we thanked him and he was on his way back to Moe. Now it was time to explore our new house.

Our new house

The living space was small with a basic living plan. A front porch opening on to a small entrance hall; directly opposite this was our lounge room, equipped with an open hearth fireplace for heating; further back, one behind the other, were the small bedrooms – our mum would have the bigger of the two while we boys had our bunk beds in the other; the kitchen was on the other side to the bedrooms with its own wood-fire stove; and rounding off the layout in the rear was the laundry and a small back-entry porch with a wooden ramp and rails leading up to it. And of course the proverbial dunny found itself down the back yard.

As for essentials, it really was back to Donald, for we had no electricity and no running water. Our water supply depended on two 1000-gallon tanks sitting up on very high tank stands at the back of the house. If this ran out, that was it, so we had to supplement our water supply with buckets from the old quarry over the road for our baths and the washing. With the open fireplace most of the heat went up the chimney, but it did warm those sitting around it; these were the sort of things you had to do if you had no electricity. And it was the same with the kitchen fire. If you didn't clean it out each day and set it with kindling, you had nothing to cook on or to get warm by. It was nothing for my mother to have half a tree stump stuck in the open fire burning happily for half the night, while the kitchen fire had a length of old floorboard she'd scrounged somewhere feeding the fire while supported on the back of a chair.

By now most of these chores were done by us boys, for we knew if we had a good fire going, mum would be cooking us a great breakfast or hearty dinner and we'd have hot water for a nice hot bath. Even if we'd have to pile in one after the other to save water. And John Forrest did his bit in this regard, for I recall a great stack of wood he'd chopped for my mum.

We were always on the lookout for any old timber or fallen branches to drag home for our fires. As we used to do in Donald before we had electricity, mum boiled the washing in an outside copper tub, as did most people of the day. And likewise without electric lighting, we again had to rely on the dim kerosene lamps of the 1800s to get by of a night. When mum acquired a WWII Tilley lamp that lit up the whole room with its super-bright light we couldn't believe it!

Then there was the outside toilet, otherwise known as the 'dunny'. There were no sewerage services out there for years. So the nightman had to exchange a clean new pan twice weekly by way of the service flap at the back of the dunny. The night cart was a big red truck with three shelves of lidded pans, all of which the nightman would happily carry on his shoulder whistling as he went about his work. No one really knew who he was or who he belonged to, but on occasion we did get glimpses of him in his baggy, stained work clothes and floppy brimmed hat.

The man trap

It didn't take long for us three boys to settle into the environment, which wasn't the rock hard ground and stifling heat of Donald – it was milder and the soil was very sandy and easy to dig. One day we decided to have a bit of fun and build a 'man trap', which consisted of a fairly large pit, about two feet deep, covered with a false top of sticks, light twigs and newspaper, and finished off with a sprinkle of dirt, leaves and grass. It took us hours to build, but when we stood back to admire our creation you couldn't see a thing ... a real work of art! We three boys were quietly admiring our handiwork when our mum called out, "Dinner time! Come in and wash your hands!"

We downed tools and headed for the table, for our mother always managed a bountiful meal! In fact, so delicious was mum's home-cooked meal, and so warm was the kitchen, we completely forgot about the 'man trap' we'd so assiduously constructed on the garden path at the side of our house.

In the depths of that night while we were sound asleep in our cosy beds, the cheerful nightman was doing his rounds and pulled up in front of our place. All was fine on his way down to the dunny in the back yard, for he fortuitously stuck to the *right* of the path. It was on his way back where he kept to the *left* that disaster struck!

I've since tried to imagine what must have happened: there he was, full pan on his shoulder, about to make the return trip he'd routinely done so many times. It's pitch black, but he intuitively knows his well-trodden way.

Suddenly the earth gives way from under him and down he goes, full pan sailing through the air ... He must have dragged himself out of that messy pit thinking he had stumbled upon some half-dug garden or trench, and that it was half his fault for not looking where he was going. The darkness of the night was on our side, for it was too hard for him to discern the carefully dug pit we'd constructed for passing quarry.

Luckily we boys usually got up earlier than our mother, so we came across the aftermath of the night's events first. We quickly got a shovel and scraped all the evidence into the hole, covered it with sandy soil, threw a couple of buckets of water over it, and you'd never know we'd been there.

We never heard another word about it.

The Smale boys were beginning to make their mark.

As fresh bread was scarce, one treat we did have was the occasional Australian damper in the back yard. My mum would dig a small hole, set a fire, mix some flour, a pinch of salt, a hand-full of raisins and water, and bake it in a cast-iron camp oven. We'd eat our freshly baked damper with butter and jam ... absolutely delicious! When we did have bread it was delivered by Clem Cuddy in the horse-drawn baker's cart.

Once I had to go and help the baker's son Peter Furness 'bring in the horses' from a distant paddock. Now when I say 'bring in the horses', I mean gigantic Clydesdales that towered far above me with feet the size of dinner-plates. "You'll be okay," said Peter. "You can climb a tree then drop down onto it and it'll safely walk you back to the bakery." So that's what I did. Only Dolly the big grey took off at break-neck speed, leaving me bumping around and clinging to her neck for grim life.

"Hold on tight!" yelled Peter, as the powerful beast surged ahead. It was only when he caught up to me on his chestnut that Dolly quieted down to a fast walk. Stricken with fear, I couldn't talk – I was so high up and had no saddle to hold me on. I was so relieved when Dolly finally lumbered into the stables. It took me a good week to get over this traumatic ordeal, and I never helped Peter 'bring in the horses' again.

Fishing for eels

During the summer the vast swamplands tended to dry up. One day we three boys saw a young guy fishing in what was left of the shallow water. It turned out to be Keithie Dowler, who lived on a farm across the way. Intrigued, we asked, "What are you fishing for?"

"Eels," he said. "There's tons of them in there. See that little ripple? ... Well that's an eel."

No sooner had he said this than he pulled a big one out – all writhing, slippery and slimy.

"What do you do with it?"

"You eat it," he said. "It's just like fish. But to skin it you've got to nail its head to a post, cut the skin around it, then pull it off with pliers ... To cook it, cut it in sections, roll it in flour, and eat it with chips."

That said, Keithie finished the eel off with his knife, put it in a sack and said goodbye. "See you later," we said, and stood there trying to absorb what we'd just experienced.

It sounded worth a try, but we didn't have any fishing gear. Then Darryl had a brilliant idea: "Hey, if those ripples are eels and the water is only a few inches deep, why don't we go and get the rake and whack the ripples?" We all thought this was very clever, and Brian and I ran back to get the rake, a knife and an old bag in case we managed to get one. When we got back, Darryl – being the oldest – was eagerly waiting for us, so we let him test our eel-hunting theory out first.

In he strode with purpose, whacking down on the first ripple he saw. The result was extraordinary, for up came a stunned eel which Darryl flicked to the bank with the rake. I then quickly dispatched it with our knife, just as Keithie had done, and pushed it into our bag. I got Brian to keep his foot on it just in case it got away. For a good hour the three of us hunted eels like this till we had six big, fat juicy ones in the bag. We were covered from head to toe in black swamp mud, and all you could see was the whites of our eyes. Then we headed for home to show our mum what we'd caught for tea.

To say she was surprised to see us is an understatement: "Leave the eels on the step and run over the road to the quarry with the bucket and rinse yourselves down, then we'll see what to do with them."

"You've got to nail their heads down and skin them with pliers," we told her. "That's what Keithie Dowler told us," and off we ran to the quarry for a quick rinse down, then we changed into some clean clothes.

When we got back, we again told her how we were supposed to skin them, cook them, and eat them with chips. At the time we only had an old make-shift table, so our mother let us nail the eels to this so we could get at them easily with the pliers. While all this was going on, we had a surprise visit from Uncle Peter and Auntie Jean and all their kids; our long-time friends from Moe. They couldn't believe the incredible scene that greeted them in the kitchen. Years later they still spoke of the day they found us kids skinning eels nailed to the kitchen table.

Once skinned and all rinsed clean, the flesh looked as white as fish. And when cut into sections and rolled in flour, the segments looked and smelt even more like fresh fish. Then, keeping to Keithie Dowler's suggestion, mum cooked a massive heap of her homemade chips to go with the 'fish'. After a tentative taste, we all agreed that fried eel *really did* taste like fried fish and wasn't bad at all. There wasn't much left of the eels or the chips when we were finished.

My mother's version of this story varies slightly, for she says there was a tiger snake mixed in with the eels that we brought home. Which is ridiculous, for being country boys we clearly knew what a snake was. But my mother was never one to let a fact or two get in the way of a good story.

Mushrooms and snakes

Talking about snakes, one day I really did do something silly. Darryl, Brian and I were out mushrooming in the fields behind the swamp lands in the days when you could quite easily pick a bucket-full of beautiful field mushrooms in next to no time. We'd just entered a small meadow surrounded by low bracken fern, with scrubby woodlands further back. The perfect place for mushrooms. I was carrying a large perforated sheet-steel basket in which to carry them home. Then something caught my attention: a magnificent copperhead snake was curled up asleep on the edge of the bracken fern. Its burnished copper colour glistened in the sunlight, and it moved slightly as it sensed our approach.

Now anyone with a brain would have left the creature alone and continued gathering mushrooms in the meadow. But not me! For some unknown reason, I decided to play the hero and push my steel basket down upon it. Very dumb move. This particular copperhead was as thick as my wrist, and its head was bigger still. What's more, its fangs harboured a deadly poison. The moment I did this I knew I was in big trouble – this snake was almost as strong as me. It literally was now a battle of life and death. I panicked as it wrapped its strong tail around my skinny leg for leverage and began to pull itself out from under the basket. I pressed downwards with all my might.

"Quick, go and get a stick!" I screamed at my brothers. "It's getting out!"

The more I pushed the basket down into the giving grassland, the more the desperate snake edged itself out. I was losing the battle – the snake was halfway out. A fateful notion swept over me … not long back a classmate of mine, Owen Bourke, had been killed by a copperhead – and I was about to be next.

"Hurry up! It's nearly out!" I screamed to my brothers, who'd been away for what seemed like an eternity. By now most of the snake was out from under the basket and wrapped around my ankle, and I could feel its constrictions.

"Help!" I desperately screamed again, hope almost gone. Only a third of the snake – and its deadly head – remained precariously under the basket. I was beside myself with terror when my brothers finally returned with a branch.

My spindly young legs were now wide apart, the tail end of the snake securely wrapped around my ankle and its business end about to get free and strike to defend itself. There wasn't a moment to lose.

"Quick, hit it while it's stretched out!" I yelled. Then, right when every second counted, Brian and Darryl began to argue about who would do the hitting. An ice-cold sweat took hold. My end was near … I let out one last scream, "Anybody do it, its head's almost out!" And indeed just as the snake's huge head wriggled itself free from under the basket, the branch came down on its back and I was saved.

I was left to recover from this ordeal and reflect on the stupidity of my dangerous action that ended up jeopardising us all, while my brothers made sure the snake was really dead. The whole thing was unnecessary and without reason. I should have simply left this beautiful creature to bask in the sun and gone on with our mushrooming.

You live and learn.

A load of old tripe!

Regarding my mother's meals, she never followed any set recipe or measured anything, yet they were always hearty and mouth-watering despite her slap-happy approach to it all. But there was one of her regular dishes that still traumatises me to this day … and that was her pressure-cooked tripe in white sauce. It was nothing short of vile, and makes me nauseous even writing about it.

"There's nothing wrong with it … it's good, wholesome food and you'll sit there till it's eaten," she'd say to us boys, and she meant it! Many's the night I found myself staring at my plate of inedible chunks of chewy cold tripe for an hour or so … which to my mind tasted like regurgitated sick!

Mercifully, on occasion our mother would have to leave the room, and in one smooth operation we'd have that kitchen window open and our plates scooped clean in seconds before she got back. If this wasn't possible, we'd put our plan B into action: we'd fill our pockets with our detested tripe and white sauce, to be dealt with later. Strangely, our mother never caught us in these sneaky acts of 'tripe in white sauce disposal', so it was something we had to live with and devise ever-more creative ways to avoid. The result is the mere mention of the word 'tripe' still makes me shudder; I only have to find myself anywhere near the stuff and I've got to get away from it fast before I start gagging.

When I tell others this story, I'll often hear, "Oh, but you haven't tried *mine*, it really is delicious." And I say, "No amount of cooking, no amount of fancy sauces and spices can disguise the unmistakable smell and taste of tripe!"

Now, I'm not one to refuse lovingly prepared food and hurt the feelings of others, for I can enjoy just about anything; but I do draw the line at the spongy lining of the main stomach of a cow – the one pet hate in my life. Such is my aversion to this loathsome food that I swore I'd never put my kids through the traumatic experience I had to go through when I was young, and they've blissfully lived their lives not even knowing what tripe is.

Seaford State School

The Seaford State School was a good mile walk from our place across the elevated back lane that spanned the swamplands. We boys traversed this walkway for six years through rain, hail and shine. I can remember some frosty mornings being so cold it made us cry. But most of the time the weather was fine. Summer, however, could get very hot indeed.

I started school in the first grade, and my first day was at the school fete. I recall it was a very hot day. As I had not made any friends yet, my mother thought it a good idea to enter me in the Mad Hatters competition for some 'social' experience and to get to know people. My Mad Hatters hat comprised an empty Wheaties packet with a head-hole in the side of it, a bunch of silver beet, and six sausages attached to it. I kid you not! But looking at it logically, my mother was right; you'd be battling to think up anything *madder* than this! So, off I proudly trotted across the back lane adorned with my funny hat to the fete.

Round and round the school in that blazing sun I walked, feeling very important. Hour after hour I wandered among the myriad stalls, and I began to feel tired – as did my wilting silver beet and sagging sausages! I heard one lady disparagingly say: "The poor little thing, it's a wonder they don't start to smell!" This dented my feeling of importance somewhat. As the day went on I felt more and more deflated, and my 'hat' was getting very heavy and uncomfortable. Finally, when the winner of the Mad Hatters competition was announced, my mum's work of art wasn't even mentioned. I just faded into the crowd, and secretly pushed my now-ridiculed hat into a rubbish bin. The long walk home across the swamp lifted my spirits, for I knew my mum would have a big meal waiting for me. That was the last time I ever let her make school costumes for me.

Interestingly, it was very rare that my mother attended school activities, or was a part of the school community. I recall only two: me as that duck in the farm yard scene at the Donald Primary; and me, all dressed up in a fancy Chinese costume and singing in the Seaford Hall when I was in grade two.

And then there were the Seaford school teachers: overall they were memorable and inspirational; apart from grade one's Miss Sheddon. A stern, matronly figure who wore button-up boots, small round granny spectacles and sported prominent buck teeth. She was deadly. The only thing I remember her for is the way she constantly wrapped us innocent little first graders over the knuckles with her ruler for making any mistake whatsoever. "Hold out your hand," she would screech in her high-pitched voice. And it really hurt! I was more than relieved when I finally moved on to grade two and left the frightening Miss Sheddon behind.

A touch of kindness

Other teachers, like Mr Lipscombe, were kind and lovable, and I had him for grades three and four. I'd say he was about forty, with dark hair slightly greying at the temples. He always wore a grey dust coat over his shiny black shoes. Every year Melbourne has its Royal Melbourne Show, and Show Day was a big, *big* deal for children. Most kids end up getting there somehow and would come home with their prized showbags. But we never did because we couldn't afford it. All we could do was wistfully look at what the other kids got when they returned to school the following day. Perceptive Mr Lipscombe got wind of this, and at the end of the day after Show Day he said, "Smale, remain back after class," which I dutifully did.

Thinking I was in some kind of trouble as was my wont, I nervously waited while he packed his things up. Then he bent down behind his desk and picked something up. Three big showbags! Just to see these revered things was a joy for me. *He probably didn't have a chance to take them home with him because of school*, was the first thing that came to mind.

"You boys couldn't go to The Show," he said, "so I've brought something for you."

I just stood there, astonished. "Showbags ... for me?!" I blurted out. "Oh ... thank you Mr Lipscombe!" I could see that one of them was a Tongala Milk showbag, which I knew had chocolates and other yummy things in it. I couldn't wait to get outside to have a peak at what other wonders lay within.

That day I learnt a little about reaching out to others in need - simply for the joy of giving.

The Scotchie way

One day after school my third-grade school mate Milosh Nachman and I found ourselves down behind Bobby Lee's place by the Kananook Creek ... its dank undergrowth and swampy saplings always a good place for an adventure. This day, spying some washed-up bottles among the swampy tea trees, I suggested to the others, "Why don't we smash some bottles the Scotchie way?"

Now, smashing bottles 'the Scotchie way' was a mythical belief we'd picked up that this is what they did in Scotland. How it works is two people face each other about twenty paces apart then lob their bottles into the air in the direction of the other person, with the objective of the bottles smashing mid-air between them and falling harmlessly to the ground. It was all so simple. Milosh and I would go first while Bobby watched on.

Milosh was small of stature, around the same size as me, so we were evenly matched, whereas Bobby was taller and always wore a white patch on his glasses over one of his eyes, so he was to officiate. I distinctly remember Milosh selecting a flat-sided sauce bottle, but I don't remember mine. Anyway, we found a bit of a clearing and faced each other at a suitable distance, bottles at the ready. Bobby shouted "Throw!" and our bottles went spinning majestically through the air.

It was a chance in a million; there was a glassy crash as our bottles clipped each other mid-way along their curved trajectory, splintering the stem of Milosh's sauce bottle, just as the Scotchies do in Scotland. It was mid summer, very humid. I'd discarded my shirt, and all I had on was a pair of shorts. His sauce bottle, now a jagged, lethal missile, continued on its way.

Now if a broken sauce bottle is spinning through the air, one has the chance of being hit by the bottom of it; its flat side; or its jagged stem. It was the third option that I copped full in the midriff. I felt my stomach split apart and my insides spill out. Instinctively my hands went up to hold it all against me, and I fell to my knees. Bobby Lee thought I was feigning a wound as if in battle, and pushed me with his foot. "Get up," he said, "and stop mucking around."

"I'm really hurt," I said. Shocked into action, Bobby and Milosh carried me inside and lay me on the couch. I remember a poor Mrs Lee putting her head in her hands, taking a breath, then decisively straightening up and speaking on the telephone. Like Sophie the dog had reached out to me with her loving eyes when she was critically injured, I reassured a distraught Milosh with the words: "It's alright, it wasn't your fault."

After that my memory of the event is hazy; the sounds of the ambulance siren; eerie blue and red lights flashing through the windows; and the rocking and swerving of the ambulance as it sped me to the Frankston Hospital. I do remember being wheeled on a trolley and trying to swallow, but I couldn't because everything was outside of me. The last thing I remember was warm flannels being put over my exposed insides, which gave me comfort.

They say I spent five hours in the operating theatre and Dr Ready saved my life. I awoke the following day very groggy and sore, and there was my mum beside me with another fishing rod and twelve bottles of lemonade, which cheered me up. It took weeks before I could straighten up and walk again, and three months before I had the strength to go back to school. This critical loss of learning – especially arithmetic – would hold me back for years.

Maths rears its ugly head

In my absence, Mr Lipscombe had been gently leading the grade three children along a path of 'arithmetic understanding' to confidently empower them to add up, subtract and divide. I missed out on all of this, and walked into a full exposé of long division set out on the board. No matter how hard I tried, I couldn't understand it. As a consequence, I had to repeat grade three, which I didn't really mind for I spent my final four years of primary school with my younger brother Brian in the same class.

But my crippling fear of arithmetic never went away. In fact, from that moment my brain completely switched off from anything to do with it, and stayed switched off for the next forty years. I would come out in a cold sweat whenever confronted with anything even the slightest bit mathematical. I became the clown of the class to help me survive this torment. In time, this debilitating state of mind virtually ran my life, so I only worked in menial jobs where things were simply black and white and I didn't have to mathematically figure things out.

Reading

Another thing I struggled with was reading. For some reason my mother never encouraged us to do homework, nor did she read to us when we were little, so when confronted with even the simplest of books I had trouble. But in grade three there was one book on the class library shelf I kept going back to; an old, frayed, nondescript, plain-covered pink book about the Pawnee Indians. Why? No particular reason. I'd just selected it at random because we were told to do so by our teacher. I absolutely loved it. Whenever I got my hands on it you wouldn't hear a peep out of me. I was a real plodder and could only savour one page at each sitting. I would learn incredible things about them like how they could make themselves invisible in the long prairie grass of the great plains. I stayed with this book for the two years I was with Mr Lipscombe in grades three and four. When I say 'stayed with it', I probably went over the same pages a few times and then moved on to a few more. But I had made a positive start.

It wasn't until I was twenty-two that I actually read my first book. Prior to this I would proudly announce, "I've never read a book in my life!" How sad. I happened to be staying with some friends in Brisbane, and while they were at work I picked up a book from their coffee table, attracted by the jungle scene pictured on the cover. I glanced at the title and author: *Hold My Hand I'm Dying* by John Gordon Davis. With nothing else to do, I slumped into an armchair and began to read.

The next time I looked at my watch two hours had gone by. This book was *interesting*, and I didn't want to put it down! For three days I lived with the characters and their conflicts. I now love reading, but I'm still a plodder; I enjoy stopping to ponder and reflect over what I've read. I'm now aware that any book is a font of mind-expanding wisdom and I just love to soak it in. It takes me a long time to read a book.

The magic man

I remember once in Mr Lipscombe's grade four class we had a professional magician visit our class. I was eagerly looking forward to it for I had been practising my disappearing egg trick I'd learnt on my first ever holiday with Legacy. And what a treat his show was. We were spellbound. I was especially transfixed by the solid rings he could push together without breaking them! So intrigued was I that I badgered him all the way to the Seaford station to find out how he did it! But of course he wouldn't tell me. (Later on in our journey we'll be meeting this particular individual again – but with an unexpected twist!)

A talent emerges

One thing that emerged from within me at Seaford Primary School was a natural talent to draw and colour things in. I recall one day in the first grade the teacher wheeled a girl's bicycle to the front of the class and got us to draw it. All the drawings were what was to be expected from a grade one competence – except mine. My image was a credible duplicate of what was before me, a bike. I remember a group of teachers discussing what I'd done with wonder. This made me feel that with my drawings, there was something special about me, and I looked forward to that part of my day.

In grade three, the one and only time my mother ever came to my primary school in Seaford was to see me awarded first prize in an art competition for a coloured drawing of three men working in a steel foundry manipulating a cauldron of molten metal. I'm not sure where I got the idea for such a challenging subject, but I quietly basked in all the attention. Never during an art assignment did I need to be the class clown, for I derived recognition through my artistic 'cleverness'. It was very powerful, and I knew it.

Pretty quickly, I discovered that being able to shine in the magical world of artistic creation worked as an effective counterpoint to my abject fear of maths. One day my grade five teacher, old Mr Dickson, a hunched-over older Scotsman around the age of sixty, reinforced this with an observation I will never forget. He was walking down the aisle between our desks when he stopped and looked at what I was doing: I was sketching a picture of two seagulls standing on a cliff among the sword grass looking out to sea. "Aye," said Mr Dickson in his broad Scottish accent, "tis a gift."

I was to tenuously cling to my artistic endeavours for a few more months at Frankston Tech, but in the end my paranoia of maths, the pressures of social circumstance, and the need to survive were much too powerful a force to contend with, and this wonderful confidence-boosting experience lost its place in my life and simply fell away. But I never completely gave up on it. I always had the intention of taking it up again some time in the future. Mr Dickson's prophetic words never went away, and were ever quietly reverberating in the recesses of my mind. Fifty-one years later I plucked up the courage to join a painting class with Melbourne water colourist Velda Ellis, and pretty well picked up where I left off. Amazing.

Sometimes all that's needed is the courage to take that first tentative step.

Lolly wonderland

In Mr Dickson's grade five class I was around ten years old and distinctly remember the first time I ever set foot in the newfangled concept of a supermarket. It was Ritchies of Frankston. Prior to this, I'd only ever experienced the traditional grocery store in Seaford's main street, where you'd be served everything from behind the counter with that reassuring old-worldly smell of cheese, ham, pickles, and biscuits wafting over you. I can still see old Mr Quilliam with his grey apron on, pencil behind his ear, diligently serving each customer in turn. It had always been this way.

So it was a real shock to the system when Ritchies of Frankston appeared on the scene, a train stop away from where we lived. This day my mate Peter Furness and I decided to go and check it out. By today's standards it was pretty small, but to our unaccustomed eyes it was a veritable wonderland! Row upon row of every lolly and chocolate bar you could think of assailed our senses. We simply couldn't believe it. And not seeing anyone manning these free-standing displays, I said to Pete, "What are you supposed to do?"

"I don't know," he said, still spellbound by this tempting array of everything a boy could ever dream of laid out before him; as indeed was I. In the end, it was all too much: "Let's just take some," I said, for we'd assumed that this was what a 'supermarket' was all about … you just came in and helped yourself. Comfortable with this simple logic, we unashamedly began to load up with a mixture of every tantalising morsel we could lay our hands on.

How easy was this supermarket lark? we both agreed as we walked out the door quite pleased with ourselves and making plans to be back again next week for another load. We'd travelled but a few metres outside the store when two massive hands grabbed both of us behind the neck and a deep, resonant voice said: "Hold it right there boys and come along with me!" … We froze, for we knew we were in for it … it was all too good to be true! You had to *somehow* pay for these things. Those fearsome hands were now propelling us towards the back of the store. They belonged to a giant of a man who was now striding before us, beckoning us to stay with him. Terrified, all we could do was follow.

It was akin to what walking the plank must have felt like, for there was nowhere to go but over the edge to the sharks: *I've got to get out of this*, I thought, and deftly unloaded my pockets into other displays and shelving as we dragged our feet to who-knows-what awful fate.

Once in his office, he sternly looked at us and said in that deep, grave voice, which again sent shivers down our spines: "You know what you've done is stealing." He turned to me: "What have you got in your pockets?" I pulled out one solitary packet of Fruit Tingles, for I had safely unburdened myself of all incriminating booty.

"And what about you?" he said to a petrified Peter.

"I haven't got anything."

"Lift your jumper."

Peter slowly complied, and a bonanza of multi-coloured lollies and chocolate bars spilled out onto the floor around him. The whole array was there, including all the favourites! Poor Peter, if only he had thought to get rid of them! Though this may have achieved little, for in this guy's eyes we were both guilty. After he took down our addresses we knew we were done for. He fixed both of us with a fearsome gaze to reinforce he meant business: "What you did was thieving," he repeated, "and you can expect the police to come to your place sometime within the next three weeks ... Now get out of here!"

This was the worst of all. For the next twenty-one days Peter and I lived in absolute hell waiting for the police to come knocking on our doors to take us to jail ... as well as the inevitable hiding I would have got from my mother if she ever came to know about it. Day after painful day the interminable waiting for fate to play its merciless hand was unbearable. But the police never did turn up. I'd learnt my lesson. From then on I stuck to collecting the deposits on lemonade bottles and scrap-metal scrounging to finance special treats like lollies and fish and chips.

The wonderful Mr Jackman

Then it was time for me to move into the last class of Seaford Primary School. Mr Jackman was our grade six teacher, and what a teacher he was. In our eyes he could do anything. A very tall, ram-rod straight man, he carried himself with the certainty that he was in control, and that his charges totally respected him and that control. He would have been in his early fifties, had curly black hair, a rather ruddy face, and squarish teeth with gaps in them. How we loved him!

Every Friday we would have a rollicking sing-along with him playing his fiddle; other times we would all do folk dancing with him playing the saxophone; and at other times he'd hold us enthralled by reading us stories. But Mr Jackman didn't just read them, he'd bring them to life by acting out all the characters with their different voices and mannerisms. Oh how we looked forward to his storytelling!

If we ever played up, one word from him that we'd miss out on one of these fun-filled activities and we'd instantly become a model classroom. And we knew he'd do it, because he once carried out his threat and we had to wait a whole week for the next instalment of a story he'd hooked us all into and were counting on.

Of course, interspersed with all this was the stuff we didn't like that much. But he even made this stuff interesting because he always had a few bribes in his pay-off bag, such as, "Do this well, and we'll finish off the day with a sing-along." Mr Jackman rarely had any disciplinary problems – even from a resident class clown like me!

The end-of-year concert

One year Mr Jackman organised an end-of-year concert for the whole school and put word out that he was looking for extra acts to complement what each class had already prepared. Now, ever since that magic man with the intriguing rings had put on his show at our school, I'd been working on my own act and my repertoire had expanded considerably. What's more, I'd already given a performance of these tricks to the neighbourhood children using our back yard dunny as a theatre, with one of mum's sheets draped in front of it for a curtain. So, my performance was tried and proven.

"I can put on a magic act in the concert," I said to Mr Jackman one morning before class.

"That'd be great," he said. "You can be the star act!"

Wow! I thought. *Now I'll have to get working and polish up all my tricks!*

I carefully thought it all through: I would have a 'magic' table up on the platform with me, upon which I'd perform my tricks: my disappearing egg in the bag trick; the Indian rope trick where I would tie big knots in it and they would disappear before your eyes; the 'vanishing' coin that everyone hears tinkling as it drops in a glass, yet it's not there when you whisk the magic silk away; and my floating silver ball which seems to defy gravity! I rehearsed my act over and over – I even had my lines between each trick memorised so everything would run smoothly. I was more than ready for the big day.

Well, the big day came and Mr Jackman was the Master of Ceremonies. I don't know much about what happened before I was on because I was in another room making sure all was where it should be. All I had to do was slip on my gold-sequinned cloak and wizard's hat and have my assistant, Peter Furness, help me carry my already set-up table onto the platform.

When it was my turn, out we went. And what a scene it was! The multi-purpose room was packed with the 300 students of our school, with teachers down each side to keep an eye on things and parents at the back of the room. The little preppies made up the two front rows.

Mr Jackman's rousing introduction built up great expectations of the magic to follow. A great cheer went up on my dramatic entrance, all decked out in my magic gold cloak and hat … a great boost to my confidence. My Indian rope trick engaged them from the start as I asked them questions about what they thought was happening. Then, with a flick of the wrist, all the knots disappeared!

So far, so good.

The disappearing egg in the bag had them enthralled! Then it was into the floating ball, which had them spellbound as it sailed away from my hands and then came back again. And I rounded off my act with my 'disappearing coin in the glass' trick – wonderful! Then, with a sweeping bow, I stimulated another great cheer from my appreciative audience, which was the cue for Peter to jump up onto the platform and help me off with my table.

Just as this was happening, a little pre-schooler in the front row yelled out, "Hey, he's got a drawer open!"

"I have not!" I yelled back.

"Yes, you have!" he retorted, standing up and pointing it out. "I can see it open round the back!" I began to panic. The magic aura of my whole act was about to go up in smoke … Then Mr Jackman stepped forward and said, "Let's give our wonderful Magician, Laurie Smale, another round of applause!"

Peter and I slammed the drawer shut and quickly made our escape through the side door. The good thing was no one really knew what the pre-schoolers were saying for Mr Jackman had deftly shifted the audience's attention back to the 'wonder' of my tricks – just in time.

People spoke about my magic show for weeks after that.

One thing I was good at, and closely related to this artistic bent I had, was my hand writing in my exercise books. Good writing was highly prized in the days of steel-nib pens and ink. Students would vie for the privilege of being invited to hold up the neatness of their writing before the whole class. Just like my drawing, this came easy to me, and I was always up the front feeling proud of my efforts. Not so with my deep, dark secret of not understanding anything about maths. The problem was that being clever at drawing, proficient at writing, great on the sports field, and by now pretty good at writing stories, no one would believe I harboured such a profound fear of maths. So I had to hide it.

Enter Cornelius Van Weezip.

Cornelius Van Weezip

Now Cornelius was as good at maths as I was at drawing, and could do the most complicated of equations without thinking, whereas I would hopelessly stare at my paper. In desperation, I connived to sit beside him and, becoming his best friend, he let me copy all his work. This of course was a double-edged sword, for although I now received good marks for maths, which was expected for it fit in with all my other achievements, my fear only got worse for I was living a shameful lie and I couldn't tell anybody about it.

One day Cornelius was away sick and I nearly freaked out. When it was time to open our maths books and get to work on the day's exercises, I came out in a cold sweat and began to tremble. My worst nightmare ran through my mind: *what if I'm found out ... I'll be humiliated in front of the whole class!*

"Are you feeling okay?" asked a concerned Mr Jackman.

Desperately afraid my cover was on the verge of being blown, I grasped my chance: "Yeah … I don't feel very well … " Which was indeed true.

"You had better take yourself to the sick room and lie down for a while." I nodded meekly, and gingerly left the classroom. The whole class could see there *was* something really wrong with me. On the sickbed I was safe from my secret being discovered, and by lunch time (when the dreaded maths lesson was over) I'd miraculously recovered.

How relieved I was when I saw Cornelius in assembly the following morning.

Another burden to carry

In addition to being weighed down by this debilitating burden, I'd developed a painful shyness of girls, notwithstanding the fact that I could impress them by effortlessly doing a magic show in front of the whole school and being the clown of the class. But in a face-to-face situation where I had to speak to a girl personally, no sensible words would come out, and I'd feel ashamed and lost. My only recourse was to play the clown, and a lonely one at that. (This paralysing shyness of females was to plague me for most of my life.)

The only times I had a reprieve from this debilitating social malaise, and could feel a measure of confidence with girls, were in the following scenarios: if the interaction with the girl was of a frivolous, non-threatening nature, without the slightest hint of intimacy, I was okay; but if I was keen on her, the girl had to feel confident enough in herself to put me at ease and carry me along with her forwardness, otherwise nothing would happen; the final scenario was when I had the opportunity to shine in front of an audience and the girl perceived this 'cleverness' as me being a confident person in *all* situations. All I had to do then was bask in the short-lived glow of my 'performance' and live this lie for a while.

Other than these three scenarios, my only recourse was to be a great achiever in anything I tackled and be noticed – which, in the overall scheme of things, didn't amount to much. ***I had yet to learn that to be an interesting person we've first got to be interested in others.***

For the whole of grade five and six I had a heart-rending crush on Pat Merton; but she loved my friend Graham Reynolds. So all I could do was hang in there on the periphery, being the funny man, for no one took me seriously. I did do something though. I bought myself a heart-shaped aluminium token and chain, got *Pat Merton* engraved on it, and secretly wore it round my neck till I moved to Frankston Tech the following year. Pat Merton never knew about this. Years later, I caught a glimpse of her getting on a train and wondered what she was doing with her life.

The 1956 Olympics comes to our school

Before we bring the curtain down on the Seaford Primary School, there is one more highlight to share: the day the 1956 Olympic Games came to our school. The connection is simple: to everyone's surprise, Mr Jackman's daughter, Lois Jackman, was Australia's Olympic champion discus thrower, and he invited her to visit us right at the time the 1956 Olympic Games were about to be held in Melbourne. And Lois Jackman said "yes"!

The whole school was abuzz the day she came. Mr Jackman proudly walked his daughter down to the lower oval surrounded by swarms of excited children. You might recall that Mr Jackman was a tall, stately man, well Lois Jackman was even taller! She had long blond hair, and her finely featured face had a Nordic air about it. Because the day was a mite chilly, she was wearing a fashionable light-grey, full-length coat. And her shiny black high-heeled shoes made her walk like a beautiful fashion model. I distinctly remember feeling, *she is like a Greek goddess!* We'd never seen anything like it.

Once on the oval we were all arranged in order behind a big white line so we could get a good view of Lois Jackman throwing the discus. We saw Mr Jackman take her coat from her, revealing the smart Olympic uniform she was wearing. We gasped. How handsome she looked with her muscular legs and arms. Lois then kneeled down and put on her special 'discus throwing' shoes with spikes in them to keep her firmly in place.

While Lois was warming up, Mr Jackman took the microphone and explained some history of the discus, the early Olympic games in ancient Greece, and how Lois would throw the discus. We then saw her firmly hold the discus down low in her outstretched arm, and then, like a giant sling shot, hurl the discus way up in the air as far as she could. You could hear the children's 'ooos' and 'ahhs' as it sailed through the air. The distance from where she was standing to where it landed was measured to see how it compared with the existing Olympic record. She had three goes, and with the help of our cheers, got closer to the record with each throw.

The whole school then rose as one and spontaneously thanked Lois Jackman, the 1956 Australian discus Olympian, with sustained and warm applause for the special effort she'd put into her visit. We were then given permission to personally say goodbye to this striking young Australian Olympian – which kept the teachers busy because it almost turned into a stampede by eager young fans trying to get her autograph.

Although there was still some unfinished business with *getting me right first*, my overall learning experience with the Seaford state primary school was a positive one.

CHAPTER 4

Melbourne Legacy

One thing I'll be forever grateful for is the dedicated care Melbourne Legacy afforded our family. Here is the charter of this wonderful organisation:

> The care of dependants of those who served the country; namely, veterans who gave their lives or health on operational service or subsequently, and Australian Defence Force members who die in service, afford a field for service. Safeguarding the interests of dependants, especially children, is a service worth rendering. Personal effort is the main essential. Inasmuch as these are the activities of Legacy, it is our privilege to accept the legacy of the fallen.

Our allocated Legatee was Mr Boyd, who unselfishly gave his time and assistance to the wellbeing of our family for years. He was a kind man, and I won't forget him. Mr Boyd was the embodiment of the spirit of Legacy and what it stands for, and would regularly visit us to see how we were getting on. He was a father figure we could look up to in our disrupted lives.

My first holiday

Because of Legacy I was able to go on my first ever holiday; have my first exciting experience at Luna Park; and attend the yearly Legacy Christmas party for children at Government House, during the Governorship of Sir Dallas Brooks.

This first ever holiday was with the Day family on their dairy farm in the Victorian country town of Boolarra; a life-changing experience. I was nine years old and it was a real eye-opener; I learnt how to milk cows, drive a tractor, and fish in the Morwell River. Mr and Mrs Day had a son Robert the same age as me, and we got on well and had a lot of fun together. They had an older daughter Elaine who didn't live on the farm but visited us on occasion with her boyfriend in their green Morris Minor. What I liked about her boyfriend was he did magic tricks, and I drove him crazy till he taught me one. (This happened to be the 'disappearing egg in the bag' I bamboozled the school with in Mr Jackman's concert.)

Then there was the day I nearly ran over Mr Day with the tractor. He had been pulling out the noxious weed ragwort from the paddocks and making little heaps of it to be picked up by the tractor.

"You can steer it," he said. "Drive towards me so I can throw it in the trailer." And what a thrill this was. So with the literal mind of a nine-year-old, I proudly followed his instructions and steered his massive Fordson tractor straight at him. He looked up to see his formidable farm machine bearing down on him and jumped aside just in time.

"What are you doing!" a shaken Mr Day yelled. "I meant *alongside* me not *at* me!"

Thoroughly chastened, I thought to myself, *well, that's not what you told me.*

Sticking to the high ground

And this wasn't the only time I missed the message by taking things literally. One morning after helping them milk their sixty cows and hose down all the cow manure from the milking shed, Mr Day sent me on an errand. I had to take a billy-can of milk to the house on the hill above our farm where his mother lived.

"Stick to the high ground," he said, "and you'll be fine." Now these wise words were meant to help me avoid the sea of ankle-deep sloshy cow pats we'd just hosed from the cow shed into the adjoining yards. This advice of *"sticking to the high ground" is all well and good,* I thought, wistfully looking at the nice grass-covered hill beyond me, *but I've got to get to the high ground first before I can stick to it!* So seeing no logic in these instructions at all, I set off through the ankle-deep cow shit to the safety of the high ground 100 metres beyond me. On my return trip I had to again wade through this mucky gauntlet to the relative cleanliness of the cow shed. When Mr Day saw me covered in cow dung I was a sight to behold: "Why didn't you stick to the high ground like I told you!" he said.

"I did," I said, "but I had to walk through all the muddy stuff to get to it."

"I meant for you to use the little island tufts of grassy high ground as stepping stones," Mr Day explained.

"Oh," was all I could say ... and then, for the first time I noticed them. My problem was I hadn't twigged to this strategy for I was focusing on the bigger picture before me; the high ground of the whole hill.

To this day I always repeat a request to make sure I get it right.

Surprise in the river

I had lots of wonderful experiences on the farm, like fishing for eels in the Morwell River with a chunk of meat tied to a piece of hay bale twine. The eels latch onto it and won't let go ... a different technique to our experience of whacking them with a rake! One day I was quietly sitting on the dark and gloomy roots of a big willow tree encroaching into the river ... I was miles away from the world in my thoughts. I had my length of hay twine dangling down into the dark placid water below me, when I felt something on the end of my line. My interest piqued for it didn't feel like an eel; there was no nibbling or tugging. I tentatively began pulling it in, but it was a dead weight. So I yanked it to the surface, eager to see what it was.

In an instant I thought my world had come to an end! A massive clawed monster with huge spindly legs the size of a frying pan broke the surface. I screamed, dropped the lot into the river, and ran to the safety of the farm house.

"A big spidery monster was on the end of my line!" I gasped breathlessly, to a bemused Mrs Day.

"Oh, that's only a fresh-water crayfish," she said. "He won't hurt you." I was relieved to hear this, but wasn't too eager to put her theory to the test and gave the river a wide berth from then on.

Home cooking

One thing I really looked forward to was Mrs Day's mouth-watering home cooking. Her Yorkshire pudding was something to die for: it looked like a scrumptious golden cake baked in the very juices of the roast itself, all served with mashed potatoes, vegetables and gravy. When dinner was ready she'd wave her tea-towel from the farmhouse verandah and in we'd come for a marvellous feast.

Another day we were baking a cake together and Mrs Day asked me to look at the clock and tell her what time it was. I looked at the clock ... but nothing happened. Mrs Day said, "You can't tell the time, can you."

"No," I softly said.

"Well, we're going to show you," she said with a flourish. And for the next forty minutes we sat at the table while the cake was cooking and she taught me how to tell the time! From that moment on I never had a problem with it.

Eight years later, I rode my racing bike the 100 kilometres all the way to their farm to thank them for the wonderful holiday they'd given me all those years ago. Now a young man, I walked into the cow shed and said to a surprised Mr Day, "Do you know who I am?" He looked at me a moment then said: "You're Laurie Smale."

It was like a welcome home.

Luna Park: tales of the unexpected

The other memorable treat that Melbourne Legacy gave me was my first ever trip to Luna Park. I was eight years old and I had absolutely no idea what it was all about.

We children all arrived on a dedicated bus, were given a handful of tickets, then let loose in this legendary amusement park for three hours. There are two things that stick in my mind from this experience: The Rotor, and the Jack and Jill. With no knowledge of how it all worked, all I could do was line up at things and learn as I went along.

My first ride happened to be The Rotor, so I followed the crowd like a lamb to the slaughter. I found myself in a huge cylindrical room wondering *what next*, when a voice commanded, "Stand flat against the wall!" I did what I was told. Then the room started to spin with amazing speed, which was frightening enough – but when the floor fell away and I was stuck to the wall whizzing around for a good five minutes! I was terrified! Thankfully the spinning did stop, the floor come back up, and on very wobbly legs I staggered out to safety.

After that I was very tentative about what to go on next. But I reasoned that nothing could be as bad as the horror I'd just been on. It wasn't long before I'd joined another queue.

"What is it?" I asked a tall man in front of me.

"It's the Jack and Jill," he said, which seemed pretty benign to me because I'd learnt that nursery rhyme in kindergarten. It was soon our turn, and the man in front of me was given a carpet and laid it flat in a two-seat bucket. "Get in," he said, "and hold the carpet handle tight!' I did what he said.

Up and up we clickety-clacked, higher and higher. Which was rather pleasant because we were going nice and slow. I could see the whole of the park below me, and I remember the sky was very placid and a nice pale blue. I knew we were going ever higher, and by now we were among the clouds … a twinge of fear crept into my mind: *how were we going to get down?* Suddenly the man beside me cried out: "Hold on tight!" Luckily I was already doing so, for our bucket unceremoniously tipped us out into the open sky … My heart stopped!

This is it! was my last thought … but in reality it was a giant slide. Down we raced at breakneck speed till soft buffers and a slight incline brought us to a stop. I was shaking all over – it took me a while to find my feet and calm down.

I spent the rest of the day on more gentle rides and eating fairy floss and ice-cream.

* * *

Simply because Melbourne Legacy was there for my mother to call on, it played an important part in stabilising my early life and keeping me on the straight and narrow. I'll be forever grateful to them and can't sing their praises highly enough.

Years later, when I was a grown man, I bumped into Mr Boyd and he still remembered me and was genuinely interested in what I was doing with my life. Luckily he'd never get to learn of some of the things I've shared in this book … all he knew was we were a rough-and-ready family who needed a helpful leg-up now and again; and as our Legatee he was always on call to help. (Later in our story, we have another unexpected connection with Mr Boyd which I'll flag when we come to it.)

CHAPTER 5

Finding my feet in Seaford

While all this was going on at Seaford Primary School, there were lots of other interesting things happening in my life, especially anything involving my ever-eccentric mother and her practical approach to life. One day I distinctly remember our neighbour Mrs Davidson running into our front yard screaming, "Mrs Smale! Mrs Smale! Help! My little boy is choking!"

Without hesitation, my mum took the blue-faced and by now limp toddler from her distraught mother's arms, grabbed him by the ankles, and began swinging him round and round in circles like a merry-go-round with him stretched out horizontally. Poor helpless Mrs Davidson; she just stood there wide-eyed and agape at what was happening to her defenceless little Ian.

Yet somehow the centrifugal force of this 'whirling' around dislodged half an egg shell from his throat, clearing his vital airways. This forced him to gulp a life-giving breath of air and he let out a scream. My mother gently laid him on the grass while he regained colour, opened his eyes, and found his tiny self again.

Unorthodox though this behaviour may have been – even dangerous – this little boy was dying before our eyes and something drastic had to be done. Nowadays, holding him upside down and giving him a firm thump in the middle of the back would probably be the way to go.

Mum's artistic flair

Once, when I was around nine years old, I arrived home from school and got a pleasant surprise as my mum had been displaying a spot of artistic flair I wasn't aware of. Not long before this, we boys had been throwing some left-over beetroot at each other for a bit of fun, and it left an awful stain on the wall of a small alcove beneath the kitchen window. One day while we were at school, my mother painted over the offending beetroot stains with some left-over pink paint. This done, she then 'flicked' darker green and grey colours over the pink with her brush for a pleasant speckled effect. I couldn't believe how wonderful it looked, and said so. Fatal mistake!

When I got home from school the following day, not only did we have the alcove decorated in this fanciful way, but the window frame; two of the kitchen walls; and the kitchen cabinet had copped it too! It was like looking at one of those illusory pictures where you've got to guess what's in the pattern by staring at it; for standing against the wall as it was, the kitchen cabinet had vanished!

Leanne and Mark arrive

So around the age of nine my new siblings Leanne and Mark arrived on the scene, and it wasn't long before our mum had us three boys changing nappies, bathing them, and making their bottles as a matter of course. We lived a very hands-on existence and you took part in everything. We had our fun moments though, like me making frightening lion growls through Leanne and Mark's bedroom door on a regular basis. While writing this book Mark told me: "That was bloody scary you bastard, but you wouldn't stop!"

The training session

In time my sister Leanne grew up to be a senior officer for home care for the elderly and those in need. In one of their regular professional development sessions the facilitator said, "I'm now going to show you a video of the extreme challenges we can face with some of our clients, yet we must remain professional at all times." She then pressed the button and a seventy-year-old lady in a bright red dress and equally bright red hair appeared who was laughing and chatting away about nothing in particular to the carer. Instantly Leanne burst out laughing. Somewhat taken aback, the facilitator said, "I'm not sure what's funny ... this is meant to be serious."

"She's my *mother*!" Leanne responded, "and I couldn't even *begin* to tell you the full story!"

For my part, never in my life have I known my mother to dye her hair bright red.

Like I said, my mother was something else: a totally unpredictable, practical, and wonderful person.

Guy Fawkes night

There was one event we really looked forward to – and that was fire cracker night! Families would gather round their traditional bonfires to let off their crackers and throw a few potatoes into the coals to eat with butter. But my mum's bonfire was always the biggest. I can see it now, an enormous heap of branches and old furniture to feed the roaring flames, which could leap a good ten metres into the air! For us kids it was all so exciting, each with our big bowl of crackers to let off. We older boys would light the spinning Catherine wheels on the back fence and send the sky rockets whooshing into the night sky before they spectacularly exploded. Little Leanne and Mark would just stand there wide-eyed at the wonder of it all.

One night a stray cracker landed in Mark's bowl and set of all his fireworks at once – he was heartbroken. With Tom Thumbs and penny bungers still going off around his feet, all he could do was look down at his shattered bowl and cry: "All my crackers are blowing up!" We quickly pooled in and replenished another bowl from our own supplies, and all was well.

Memories … those days are no more.

My magnificent obsessions

As my journey in life progressed, a recurring pattern of single-mindedness in the way I involved myself in things to the exclusion of all else began to take shape. In fact, at times, certain of my undertakings became a total obsession. Some of these 'projects' were short-lived, others went on for years. But my aim was always the same: I had to be the very best at whatever it was that I was doing – even if it unintentionally caused others pain. Being totally obsessed with something to the exclusion and detriment of others – I was to reflect on decades later – was very negative and in the end unrewarding. But that realisation was a long way off …

In deep water

So in Seaford right behind us we had these incredible swamplands that went for miles, full of all kinds of bird and animal life that we continued to explore. The swamp wasn't that deep, so you were unlikely to drown in it. But the Seaford beach on Port Phillip Bay was another matter. Here there was really deep water off the end of the pier, as well as dangerous rips between the sandbanks. At times there were even quite large waves – and I still couldn't swim! As we spent most of our time at the beach during summer, I had to learn to get myself out of trouble fast. But to this day I'm still not a strong swimmer.

Once, the Martin boys – two of the Seaford beach life-savers I really admired – took me and a couple of my young mates out beyond the end of the pier to the very deep, murky green water in the club row boat and threw us in for a joke so we could swim back to the boat. While my mates easily made it back on board, I panicked and went under. Realising what they'd done, the Martin boys dived straight in to pull me out, which they did with great difficulty for I was tearing Dave Martin's hair out by the roots in sheer terror. I can still see him going under too, with me desperately clawing at his head. The fear of that experience still lives with me, and I have avoided deep water at the beach ever since.

Hooked on fishing

I began to take an interest in the fishermen on the Seaford pier. I was fascinated in how they put the bait on the hook, cast their line in, and, on occasion, pulled in a nice fish. Pretty soon I decided I was going to be a part of this adventure. One kind old guy appreciated my interest and set me up with a fishing line, complete with hook and sinker wrapped around an old coke bottle – its wedged-shaped bottom made it perfect for casting.

I was hooked! For the next year or so, rain, hail or shine, I was down on the Seaford pier casting in my coke-bottle line. And I caught some beauties too. My biggest prize was a four-and-a-half-pound flathead that I had to wrestle with for a good ten minutes before I could haul it up onto the pier; it was almost as tall as me! I was so proud when I showed it to my astonished, cash-strapped mum. That night we had it for tea with heaps of mum's legendary homemade chips.

From then on I regularly brought home an old pillow-slip full of sweet-tasting bay trout and garfish. Only now do I realise how grateful my mother must have been for this bountiful supplement to our diet.

A magic fishing rod

One day my mother somehow managed to buy me a brand new cane fishing rod for my birthday out of her meagre pension. I was overjoyed and couldn't wait to get down to the pier to test it out. That very evening straight after school, down to the pier I ran with my prized fishing rod. Barely had I cast my baited line in than I got a tremendous bite, and hooked a decent sized trout! Amazing! *This rod has gotta be magic*, I thought. That was it. I couldn't wait to tell my mum I'd caught this beautiful fish on my *first* cast! With my one-pound bay trout safely in my pillow-slip, I hurried for home across the back lane that straddled the swamp.

That night, my new fishing rod securely within reach beside my bed, I found it hard to sleep for two reasons: I kept dreaming about my 'magic' fishing rod where all I had to do was cast it in to pull the fish in; and during the night an insidious bout of the flu had taken hold of me and laid me low. By morning my voice had gone, I was aching all over, and I felt very weak. There'd be no fishing that day.

Up until now, neither of my older brothers (Leanne and Mark were too small) had been the least bit interested in fishing, but when they learnt of my plight they cast longing eyes over my 'magic' fishing rod they'd heard so much about the night before.

"Mum, can we have a lend of it?" they implored. "We promise we'll look after it."

"No," she said, "that's Laurie's special birthday present."

"But we promise we won't hurt it," they begged. "Pleeeeeease … "

I was so sick I could barely utter a word, so they turned to me: "We really promise we'll look after it," they went on … "we won't hurt it." I was far too weak to fight them. In the end I reluctantly surrendered and trusted they'd keep their word and all would be fine.

The follow day, which was a Sunday, Brian and Darryl were up early to get the fire going to cook their porridge for they had a big day of fishing ahead of them. They even brought a bowl of porridge to my sick bed to make me feel better (which they'd never done before). Then, entrusted with the most precious thing in my life, away they went across the back lane on their fishing quest.

That evening they arrived home with no fish and my precious fishing rod snapped in two.

Brian and Darryl burst through the door, crying out, "Hey mum! Look what happened! An angry Scotsman snapped Laurie's rod over his knee because we'd cast our line over his."

"What?!" exclaimed my mother. "Do you mean he actually broke it in a temper because you did that?" My brothers sadly nodded. My mother was absolutely livid that a person could be so mean to two little boys who'd made a simple mistake. Then and there she sat down at the kitchen table and wrote a letter to *The Sun* newspaper explaining the whole sorry saga of what happened and how angry she was! But because my mother's mind was so focused on me lying sadly in my sick bed, and how much the rod meant to me, her letter clearly stated that it was me, little nine-year-old Laurie Smale, who was so rudely dealt with by that unfeeling Scotsman.

A week later I arrived home after school to find a big black car with two men in dark suits (one with a big camera) waiting for me out the front of our humble rural abode. My mum got in my ear first: "These are the men from *The Sun*, so remember that it happened to *you* and *not* your brothers."

I had no time to think, for the reporters were upon me with their questions.

"What actually happened?"

"I cast my line over his and it got tangled." My mind was racing at a million miles an hour.

"What did he look like?"

"He was old." Then I got a flash. I remembered that Scotsmen wore tartan. "He had a tartan beret on," I affirmed with confidence. They wrote all this down. They finished by taking a contrived sad photo of me holding my broken fishing rod. The big black car then drove away down dusty Wells Road to who knows where.

Two days later a headline appeared in *The Sun* on page two: "Scotsman's ill will towards young fisher". The article went on to outline the reporter's interpretation of what we'd told him. A bit like Chinese whispers, his story expanded on ours to the point of painting this Scotsman as a menace to society! This caused a furore. A flood of letters to the editor followed, lampooning the Scots for their dour outlook on life. An irate Irishman even stormed into *The Sun* head office with a brand new fishing rod "for the poor little lad". "This is typical of the Scots," he was reported to have said. I even had one fishing club send me *four* fishing rods and tackle!

The whole thing was spiralling out of control.

Living a lie

At school I was becoming a bit of a celebrity because of the story, and found it hard to live this lie that was beginning to have a life of its own. One of my classmates quizzed me: "What time were you there on Sunday?"

"I was there in the afternoon."

"I was there all afternoon and I never saw you."

"Well, I *was* there!" I adamantly replied, and quickly terminated the conversation.

That was close! I thought, and steered clear of that kid for a while.

These events had all become too much for my brothers, and, in a quieter moment, they confessed to me what really happened on that fateful day. Walking home from the beach, where in truth they didn't do a lot of fishing, they decided to amuse themselves by trying to flay butterflies in the long grass with my fishing rod. At the height of this exhilarating operation a fence post got in the way and broke my rod in two. Terrified of what now might happen to them, they concocted the 'Scotsman story' as they slowly made their way home across the back lane.

An epic journey

But this is not the end of the story: my mother thought it a good idea for me to make the long journey into Melbourne and say 'thank you' to *The Sun*. Keep in mind that I was only nine and I'd never been to Melbourne by myself before. But she assured me I'd be quite okay and I'd manage.

And manage I did. My mother got me dressed in my best clothes and a nice warm coat with a 'shiny green pound' pinned to the inside of it in case of emergency. She cut a nice lunch for me to eat when

I got hungry; then she walked me across the back lane to the station, bought me a return ticket, and put me on the train for Flinders Street Station in Melbourne.

As I got closer to Melbourne I remembered familiar landmarks I'd seen, like the MCG and the *Herald Sun* building when I'd travelled there with my mother. When I arrived there, which I did okay, I walked to the big clocks at the front of the station as instructed. Then, just as my mum had told me to do, I walked up to a friendly policeman and explained where I needed to go. I often wonder what he must have thought of this little boy; all dressed up and wandering the streets of Melbourne. But I had such clear purpose in the questions my mother had set me to ask – like, "Where is the *Herald Sun* building?" – that he couldn't help but respond in kind. The young policeman was very helpful and walked me across busy Swanston Street. "It's not far," he said, "just two blocks down on the left." He then wished me good luck and sent me on my way. Everything seemed to be going well.

When I arrived at the *Herald Sun* building, which seemed to tower miles above me, I managed to climb the formidable steps and enter the equally formidable granite foyer. *I've come this far*, I thought, *what do I do now?* Then I remembered the words of my mother: "Go up to someone in a uniform and tell them you're here to thank *The Sun* for helping you." By this time, I was beginning to believe the story myself.

I don't recall what happened next, but my next memory is being taken into a big room of reporters sitting in front of their desks and typewriters. I recall it being very noisy with lots of people coming and going. Everyone was making a big fuss over this little boy who had confidently marched into their office to say thank you.

Then a familiar face appeared; one of the men in the big black car who had driven all the way to Seaford to interview me. "Hello, young Laurie," he said. "I think we'll go for a drive to the beach to take a photo of you with one of the new rods that arrived for you." Pleased though I was with the excitement of this embarrassing revelation, things were now getting completely out of hand!

Nevertheless, to the South Melbourne Beach we went in another big black car, to do some 'fishing' and take another photo of me. On the way the reporter ducked into a fish shop and bought a big bream to put on the end of my line. I was beginning to get the hang of this newspaper game. My photo was published in *The Sun* the following day with the caption 'Fishing tale ends', followed by a positive little blurb. It shows a beaming Laurie hauling in his prize catch over the railing. The inference here was that this also happened on the Seaford pier.

I'm not sure how I made the journey all the way back home to Seaford after this dizzying experience, but the reporters must have safely put me back on the train at Flinders Street Station, and home I went. All I would have had to do was keep my eye on the stations and get off at mine. Then a brief mile walk across the back lane to the nice warm dinner that would be waiting for me and sharing how this incredible day had unfolded.

Although this new photo created a new bout of notoriety for me at school, I felt comfortable with it because it really happened to me. But that kid who had nearly brought me undone with the first photo by saying he hadn't seen me there that day made an uncomfortable comment with this photo, too: "That doesn't look like the railing of the Seaford pier?" he sneered.

"The Seaford pier is not the only place I go fishing," I hit back. I steered clear of him till things died down this time as well.

This wouldn't be the last time I told a fib and had to dig myself out of some uncomfortable hole, but my feelings of guilt and close shaves with this experience have certainly made me reflect on it. It causes me to ponder on the heavy price a compulsive liar would have to pay; always trying to cover things they've previously said and how this would affect their quality of life.

Alighting from a conveyance the man's way

Notoriety seemed to dog me in my younger years. Around the time of the 'fishing rod' incident, my younger brother Brian and I were coming back from Frankston on one of Melbourne's old 'red rattlers' (the much loved train of the time) when I got a bright idea: "Hey, as the train pulls into the station, why don't we get off *the man's way*?" Brian seemed to think this was a good idea.

Let me explain exactly what this term meant to us. Whenever we'd seen old gangster movies and the like, the cars of the time all had running boards below the doors. And invariably the characters in these movies seemed to get on and get off these vehicles *when they were still moving* by way of the running board. Brian and I referred to this as *getting off the man's way*. As our red rattler had a kind of step like a running board, and was now approaching the Seaford station, we were looking forward to putting our version of *getting off the man's way* into action.

'We' decided that Brian would go first and I would follow him. Keeping in mind what we'd seen Humphrey Bogart and company do in the movies, we quickly ran through how we were going to emulate them: we would stand sideways on the step holding onto the door handle; then, just as they do, we'd step off while the train was still moving so we'd hit the ground running. We decided our cue to embark on this adventure would be the moment the train had passed the end of the station. Before we knew it we were about to step into the movies.

We already had the door open as the end fence of the station went whizzing by. "Don't forget what to do!" I yelled over the rattler's noise. "Now … Go!" Brian stepped off the carriage and I quickly followed him.

What happened next is imprinted in my memory in slow motion. I could see Brian's legs crumple under him and then he skated face-down along the rough asphalt platform. But I could do nothing to help him because I was already airborne myself. When I hit the tarmac my legs crumpled too, and I went flying along the gravel into the cyclone fence at the back of the platform. The pain was excruciating. I was about thirty metres from Brian, lying half under the old chain fence. I then heard concerned voices: someone yelled,

"Get a stretcher!" Through my delirium I saw them carry Brian away. Nobody saw me. Somehow I managed to squeeze myself under the fence and crawl deep into the bushes beside the Kananook Creek behind the station. My head was swimming and everything was fast closing in on me ... I lay down beneath the undergrowth to feel a bit better and ease my pain.

I don't know how long I lay there; all I knew was I had to get home and tell mum about Brian. How I got myself home across the long back lane I don't know, but somehow I managed it. Delirious and covered in painful gravel rash, I finally staggered into the front yard and collapsed. Through the haze of pain I caught a glimpse of an ambulance and a strange car parked out the front. I saw a suited guy with a camera. "Here's another one!" he cried, absolutely astonished at this new casualty that had fallen at his feet. My distraught mother was quickly at my side. The surprised ambulance officers, now faced with an additional first aid emergency, sprang into action.

Now I don't know where they got the inspiration – maybe my mother put the idea into their heads – but the next day's headline in the local newspaper screamed 'Boy Jumps Out of Train to Save Brother!' I was getting used to being a newspaper celebrity, even if the stories weren't always entirely accurate.

Like the 'fishing' story, for the next few weeks I had to fend off awkward questions about how this could have happened and why Brian had fallen out. My response was simple: "I don't remember much about it."

After these experiences, I'm a bit sceptical about what's flashed across the media and taking things in the news at face value.

The great duck saga

I did mention earlier that when I enter into a project I never do it by halves.

Often I would wistfully look across Mr Proctor's dairy farm that abutted our back fence at Maxi Wiltshire's ducks his dad had in their impressive fox-proof duck enclosure. Remember, we lived right next to an extensive swamp that was teeming with wildlife, including foxes. I was impressed with the way this substantial enclosure was built: tall fences, covered in chicken wire that went down into the ground to stop wily foxes digging under it, as well as a nice strong gate with a lock on it. They had lots of fresh, clean straw to sleep on in their tin shelters and plenty of water to drink. The ducks themselves were Muscovy ducks, the ducks that stand with their bodies flat and really do waddle from side to side when they walk, whereas the yellow-billed Pekin ducks tend to walk upright like small geese. What impressed me most about Maxi Wiltshire's set up was these snow-white ducks seemed so happy living in such a lovely place where they were looked after so well. Then and there I decided that I would do the same. Here was a ready-made blueprint for my own duck farm, each simple step laid out for me to follow. Now all I had to do was duplicate it.

Someone once said a dream, coupled with enthusiasm, is a pretty powerful combination; well, I certainly had plenty of that – I couldn't wait to get started. But how was I going to make this happen? I was a very small ten-year-old; I had no building materials like fence posts, chicken wire and corrugated iron; I had no tools to speak of, bar my mum's rusty shovel, crowbar and hammer. I had no nails or wire; I had no money; and I had no ducks!

But I *did* make it happen, for when you are single-minded and focused, it's amazing how things come your way. I begged, borrowed and scrounged all sorts of bits and pieces to make my dream come true. For a start, Old Bill Menzies in the local junkyard kindly gave me a wooden box-cart with two bicycle wheels and long handles like a rickshaw to bring things home in. I must have looked a sight running around the streets loaded with 'building materials' like old sleepers; bits of usable timber and planks; chicken wire; fencing wire; scrap bits of tin and corrugated iron; in short, anything suitable I could glean from the Seaford tip and elsewhere. I didn't care what I looked like for I was a man on a mission.

Next I had to curb my enthusiasm somewhat and bring my mother into the dream, for nothing could happen without her approval. So I told her I was building a *little* duck yard down the back and I'd be able to produce lots of eggs for her. This was my selling point, and she seemed to buy it. I'm sure she was thinking of a modest lean-to with a couple of ducks in it, not the Taj Mahal of Duckdom I had in mind. With my mum's acquiescence in the bag, I set about the task of constructing this magnificent edifice with zeal.

Every weekend, my trusty box-cart and I would scour the neighbourhood for suitable material, for I had an exact picture in my mind of what was needed. For example, I estimated I needed sixteen old sleepers, which were duly wheeled home one at a time from the tip and from a heap of railway cast offs. One day I even found an old box of really handy tools at the tip, like a saw, some wire snips, and a big pair of pliers. Perfect! Things were progressing nicely. Now all I needed was a heap of nails to tie it all together, but I had no money to buy them.

No problem. With my nifty little box-cart I scoured the foreshore for lemonade bottles to cash in, and old scrap metal I could sell to Old Bill Menzies at the junkyard.

I can remember going down to the local iron monger and proudly asking him for two pounds worth of 'duck yard' nails. The iron monger smiled. "What do you need to attach?" he asked.

"Bits of wood, chicken wire, corrugated iron … "

"Well, what you need are some clout heads for the chicken wire, roofing nails for the corrugated iron, staples to secure the wire, and some bullet-nose nails for the timber." A few more questions on size and thickness and I had my package of precious fasteners to hold all my materials together. I strode home across the back lane quite pleased with myself.

Over the next few weeks I worked like a lad possessed. The first thing I had to do was set all the sleepers in place, for they were the framework to which all else was attached. The problem was they were twice the height and weight I was. I learned to upend them onto the wheel barrow, carefully manoeuvre them into position, then tip them into the holes I'd dug for each one. As I had no cement to set them in place, I packed each post in with old bricks and bits of concrete, which held them firmly. Then there were the cross ties of timber upon which all else would be attached. This would be a formidable, six-foot-high enclosure.

As this monument slowly emerged in her back yard, my mother was having second thoughts about it all, but I kept reminding her of that endless supply of eggs.

The final touch was to make sure the chicken wire was buried two feet deep all round, and the gate (an old door) would firmly shut with a steel clasp, in which an old bolt was placed for extra security. It really was something to look at – even my mum was impressed. Now we just needed the ducks.

Again, it came down to money. I did know of a big poultry farm way up the end of Seaford Road, so I walked there to see if he had any ducks. And lucky for me he did, and they were Muscovy ducks. What's more, they weren't too expensive. I figured that with my lemonade bottle collections and scrap metal scrounging I would be able to buy two ducklings at a time to build up my flock. Good, but not the ideal situation for an impatient young duck farmer who wanted to *immediately* duplicate what he could see in the Wiltshire's enclosure across the way.

When I was able to buy my first two ducklings, a boy and a girl, I soon forgot about what the Wiltshires had and concentrated on how to buy more of my own. Each day after school I worked on gathering those empty bottles and scrap metal, and before long I had about twenty young ducklings happily waddling around their enclosure. Peter Furness, the baker's son, was so impressed with my set up that he said I can have as much old bread as I wanted. Wow, that was great because they did eat a lot and a bag of pollard didn't go far. I did supplement their diet with frogs from the swamp, which they went absolutely crazy for and would swallow whole!

I took Peter up on his generous offer and made a weekly trip to the bakery with my rickshaw. By the end of that first year I was the proud owner of about twenty-five fully fledged snow-white Muscovy ducks. I just adored them, and would sit and watch them for hours. And the promise I made to my mother about lots of healthy duck eggs coming her way was more than being fulfilled.

Then something even more remarkable happened.

Someone, I can't remember who it was, left us a big Muscovy drake called Henry because they could no longer look after him. Now, let me tell you about a full-grown Muscovy drake; these are not your run-of-the-mill cute little drakes you'd expect to see on the local pond. These fellas are the size of a massive turkey, with attitude; they're fearlessly confident and throw their weight around; their eyes and bill are rimmed with red fleshy protrusions which make them look angry as they thrust their heads forward and hiss; their massive wing span and taloned feet the size of small dinner plates would cause any would-be predator to think twice about making the likes of Henry their next meal. They really are the Duckzillas of the duck world. Notwithstanding these aggressive qualities, Muscovy drakes can be extremely lovable. It didn't take long for Henry to settle in and befriend my new little brother and sister. It was nothing to see them sitting together in the duck yard, Henry in the middle and little Mark and Leanne with their arms around him. And woe betide anyone or anything that dared mess with those kids.

Henry soon became the undisputed king of his domain, and within a matter of weeks there were at least four happy, clucky ducks sitting on clutches of Henry's fertilised eggs; snug in their cosy little shelters among the nice dry grass and straw I'd gathered near the swamp for them. And what joy, a few weeks later, to be greeted by the peeping of three dozen newly hatched ducklings.

These fluffy little balls of down would need extra care. I was now busier than ever preparing their feed; catching them a frog or two from the swamp; and making sure their comfortable dry grass and straw was changed often. What a thrilling sight it was. At last I could stand back and admire my handy work. Almost single handedly, but with some kind help from others and qualified support from my mother, I'd actually duplicated the Wiltshire's duck farm just as I said I would – in my own way. That night I went to sleep with a smile on my face, for all was good with the world.

The next morning I was up bright and early, for not only did I have to light the woodfire stove to get hot enough to cook our breakfast, I had a whole community of my feathered friends to look after before school. So after my nice bowl of porridge, I headed out the back door to feed them and see they were okay.

The scene that greeted me held me spellbound. The whole back yard was covered in an early dawn snow; the grass, the trees, the outhouse, the duck yard, *everything* was covered! But there was something eerily strange about it … as my eyes became accustomed to the light, this snow was tinted with a deep crimson, and the snowflakes weren't right for they looked like feathers. Then I saw them … all my beloved ducks strewn about the yard, slaughtered. Swamped by a tsunami of grief, I desperately fought back the tears as I tried to comprehend the unthinkable; in deep shock, I whispered, "My beautiful ducks, all gone … the foxes got them." Then I noticed the wide open gate. I'd forgotten to put the long bolt in the clasp.

Then something moved in this blood-soaked battlefield; a bedraggled but very-much-alive Henry stood bewildered among his massacred family and friends. Struck numb with what I'd experienced, I staggered inside to break the awful news.

My mind recalls nothing more of that heartbreaking day. But the experience remains as a marked tragedy in my childhood. Yet life did go on …

Half a lifetime later, I'd just dropped the kids off at school in suburban Blackburn when a handsome young fox darted across the road in front of my car in broad daylight from a roadside park. There was nothing I could do to avoid it, and I hit the back part of its body. Concerned for any animal in pain, I pulled over and ran back to check how it was. The poor creature was in a bad way, so I wrapped it in a blanket from my car boot and lay it down on the front seat beside me. Without a second's thought I drove straight to the Royal Society for the Prevention of Cruelty to Animals (RSPCA) hospital in Burwood for it to be humanely put to sleep. You can imagine the looks I got as I walked straight past the line of people to emergency with a severely injured fox in my arms!

But as I approached the desk, the fox died. "I just ran over it," I said to the lady. "I couldn't leave it lying in pain ... it was alive as I walked through the door."

"We'll look after it," she said, and gently took it from me.

I then sat in the car reflecting for a while. *Isn't it funny*, I mused, *here I am caring for a dying fox when its very forebears broke my heart when they wantonly killed all my ducks*. My thoughts wandered on as I drove away ... *I don't think there will ever be a system that is 100 per cent fail-safe. It always pays to double-check ... it only takes one single bolt to be left out of the clasp ...*

My ferrets

Although completely shattered at the time, I did get over my duck tragedy and Henry the drake lived on to be part of the family. But I've never been one to dwell too long on the painful experiences of the past, and it wasn't long before I was smitten by my next exciting project: I was going to be the best ferret breeder I could possibly be! Which is interesting, for here we have another blood-thirsty animal which is part of the weasel family, and if let loose could dispatch my ducks as quickly as the foxes did. But I didn't see it that way. If they were housed and trained with loving care, they could be as faithful and as lovable as a cat. And this is exactly what I set out to do.

First, as with my duck farm, I needed a blueprint for what was required to breed and train ferrets. Then I remembered the kind farmer who sold me my ducklings had some ferrets as well. *I'll go and speak to him*, I decided. And boy was he helpful. Infected with my enthusiasm, he spent a couple of hours with me explaining everything I needed to do because ferrets were very sensitive and needed to be carefully looked after. That night, I returned home all fired up with my priceless blueprint of each step I needed to follow. But equally valuable to my formative mind was the way this generous farmer had unselfishly imparted his years of experience on me. And it had a lasting effect. ***I've never been afraid to ask someone who knows - then listen and learn. Nor have I been unwilling to share what I've learnt from life with those who need help.***

That afternoon, I walked home with a clear picture of exactly *what* to do and *how* I was going to do it. Here's a summary of what he told me: the cage doesn't have to be that big – a metre-and-a-half long and half-a-metre high will do; you need a cosy nesting box full of straw and a little entrance hole for they are very secretive and like it to be dark – if they are disturbed they could kill their young; and the other half of the cage has a wire mesh floor for their droppings to fall through. They eat and exercise in this area. If trained properly they are a very clean animal, and always go to the toilet in the same place. A quick hose once a week is enough to clean it; they will become used to your scent as their keeper and never bite or attack you. But for anyone else (or rabbits), that is another matter! Their favourite food is blood or liver, which is what they get from killing an animal in the wild; you only feed them bread and milk to keep them docile, otherwise they go crazy. A small treat of chopped liver once a week is all they need to keep them in touch with their ferret instincts; they are occasionally prone to footrot, which can be effectively treated with sulphur and lard.

So there I was with my newly acquired knowledge on everything I needed to know about ferrets, gifted to me by a kindly farmer in a couple of hours. I couldn't wait to make it all happen!

It wasn't long before I'd built a magnificent ferret cage similar to the one I'd seen on the farm, with a few minor variations. Luckily I'd found an old wooden cabinet around the right size at the tip, with detachable legs which made it easy. I managed to wheel it home on my rickshaw and modify it according to plan. And it ended up looking wonderful: its secluded nesting box with its little entrance hole where they'd feel at home and safe; the steel mesh base for them to wander about on; a securely locked service door; and that all-important tin sheeting round the sides and roof to keep the weather out. I was halfway there.

All I needed now were my ferrets. So it was off to the foreshore to collect more empty lemonade bottles and generate some cash. Old Bill Menzies at the junkyard (another father figure in my life) was always good for some advice. "We'll have a look in the *Trading Post* mate," he said, "and see who's got some ferrets for sale."

"That'd be great!" I said. We found a guy in Pearcedale who had a buck and a doe for sale within my budget … just what I needed for my breeding program. I rang him and made a time to come and get them the following Saturday. Pearcedale was only an hour or so away, so I'd hitchhike there. That's how you got around in those days.

The big day came and I made my way to the rural address in Pearcedale without much hassle. The man was impressed to see one so young making all this happen by himself. He got me to follow him into an old barn to a ferret cage against the wall. And there they were, dancing excitedly around inside, as ferrets do. My heart was racing.

"Well, there they are," he said. "The white one's the doe and the multicoloured one is the buck."

I fell in love with them straight away. "Here's the money," I said, fearful he'd change his mind.

"Have you got a box to take them home in?" he inquired, aware that I didn't.

"No." My heart sank.

"Just a moment … I think I might have a spare ferret carry-box you can have."

"But … I've got no more money."

"I said you can have it," he said, reaching to a shelf and taking down a proper ferret carry-box with a strap that goes over your shoulder. Then he reached into the cage and firmly picked each of them up by the scruff of the neck, reminding me to handle them this way till they got used to me and my scent. I looked at them in awe. The little white one had pink eyes and was gorgeous, the other one was a beige-brown with black rings around his eyes like a badger. They were now *mine* and in *my own* ferret box. I shook the man's hand and sincerely thanked him.

By the time I reached the main road I'd already named my new-found friends: they'd be Suzie and Jiggy. I turned onto the main road and hitchhiked home the way I had come. How happy I was.

When I got home the first thing I did was get Suzie and Jiggy acquainted with their new surroundings. Before going inside I double-checked the padlock on the service door and then took the key with me to hang on a nail at the end of my bed.

Suzie and Jiggy soon settled into their new home and became my friends. Not long after that, my younger brother Brian and I got the urge to take Suzie and Jiggy into the surrounding fields to catch some rabbits for mum. In those days Australia was plagued with them, and everyone ate rabbit. There's nothing like a plate of nice roast rabbit with mashed potato and peas, swimming in gravy! My kids have never tasted rabbit; how things have changed … But I digress; let's get back to the art of ferreting. And it is an art.

First, you've got to survey the burrow and make sure you have all the little escape holes covered with your ferreting nets. Then you put a ferret down the burrow and listen for the 'bolts' reverberating through the ground; ferrets are a rabbit's natural enemy, and as soon as they sense one is near they instinctively 'bolt' for it. The rabbit gets caught in the net and can be humanely dispatched, which we learned to do. If the ferret catches one, which is rare, three things can happen: it can nonchalantly walk out of the burrow when it's good and ready after a satisfying feed; it can curl up and go to sleep (in this case you have to be patient and wait a while); or you can put your ear to the ground listening for noises of a struggle, then dig a smaller hole down to the burrow below, dangle one of your dead rabbits down it head first, banging it on the sides like a struggling rabbit, then, when the ferret latches on to it, pull it out.

One way of avoiding all of the above is to put a little muzzle on the ferret, which doesn't hurt it at all. But whichever way you approach this, make sure you give your ferrets a little treat of rabbit liver after a good day's work so they know what's in store next time you put them in the ferret box. We pretty soon became experts at all of this.

Our older brother Darryl wasn't part of any of this; in his mind we were too immature and he had outgrown our company – which in many ways was true. Eighteen months is a large age difference between primary school siblings. So Brian and I didn't have a great deal to do with him, and we followed our own path of interest. But on occasion we did take little Leanne and Mark ferreting with us in the nearby fields where they didn't have to walk far. One day I let little Mark hold Jiggy, but because Jiggy wasn't familiar with Mark's scent he latched onto his eyebrow and wouldn't let go! So there was tiny Mark screaming with a ferret hanging off his face! It was only when I grabbed Jiggy by the scruff of the neck as mother ferrets do and gently coaxed him to let go that Mark was saved. Mark has never forgiven me for telling him "they're lovable things and they won't hurt you".

The long way home

One day I said to Brian, "Hey you know Vern who works in the junkyard ... He told me that the creek embankments, just on the other side of the country town of Officer, are great for ferreting because the ground is so hard that the rabbits don't dig very deep ... Why don't we go there?" This was the only information I had, but I did know that Officer was on the Princes Highway just before Pakenham. What I didn't tell Brian was Officer was fifty miles away; a hell of a way to be hitchhiking with a heavy box of smelly ferrets! Easily led, my younger brother said, "Okay."

I always made it a rule to only give my mother enough information about our comings and goings to allay her fears, so all she got this day was we were going ferreting in the fields to get her some rabbits. We packed some cheese and Strasbourg sandwiches, and loaded ourselves with our ferrets and nets – I even brought and extra carry-box to bring home a couple of live rabbits. Then, off on our epic journey around ten in the morning we went.

Vern's trusting words stayed in my mind: "You can't miss the creek; look for the telltale line of trees about a mile out of Officer." I kept up a positive line of commentary for Brian's sake that we'd have no problems getting there. To my pleasant surprise we scored our first four-mile ride to the corner of Dandenong Road the moment we raised our hands; the same thing happened for the ten-mile stretch to the Princes Highway; but we had to walk a little way before a jovial truckie stopped to help us with the final forty-mile stage of our journey to Officer. The guy couldn't believe that we'd hitchhiked all the way from Seaford, and showed a genuine interest in what we were doing. Miraculously, on the other side of Officer we found that line of trees along the creek just as Vern said we would. We thanked the friendly truckie then climbed the fence near the creek. By then it was mid-afternoon.

We couldn't get to work quickly enough, but Vern Blumfield was right: the red clay ground was hard as a rock. And as a consequence, the burrows were narrow and shallow. We decided on a smallish set of burrows to start with for there didn't appear to be the massive warrens you find in open fields. After a brief search for escape holes, we set all our nets (we had ten), then let Jiggy go in the main burrow. And wow! Did this create a ruckus! The rabbit-bolts shook the hard ground as they scurried for their lives. The next instant, rabbits were bursting forth from secret escape holes in every direction. This was going to be trickier than we thought. The root systems of the gnarled gum trees along the creek offered perfect cover for these smaller escape holes, so they were very hard to discern.

As we could only fit two rabbits in our extra carry-box, we decided that would be all we could take home with us. So we spent the next hour or so giving Suzie and Jiggy a run and let the rabbits go. If they caught one they could have it, but if they didn't we'd catch one for them as a reward. And, in fact, this is what we had to do. So with sunset upon us, we happily headed for the highway with our two live rabbits and ferrets. Well, that's what we thought, for suddenly Brian screamed out, "Suzie's gone!"

I froze.

"What do you mean, *she's gone*?"

"She's gone … she's not in her box!" Then I saw the little leather strap wasn't clipped on properly and only Jiggy was in there. Desperately I ran back over the ground we had just covered, calling out her name, hoping she'd hear me. But nothing. Not even a rustle among the gum leaves. By now it was almost dark. Then we both saw it … a small flash of white in front of us on the bank. I stopped and called her, and she pointed her little weasel head in the air. I gently pushed the ferret box near her so she could catch Jiggy's scent. She tentatively sniffed the air and moved forward to check it out. My hand moved like lightning and I grabbed her. She didn't resist as I put her safely back in the carry-box with her friend Jiggy and made sure the strap was fastened. "That was close," I said to Brian … "If she had gone down one of those burrows … "

Night was now upon us – we could barely see where we were going. The only guide we had was the car lights speeding past on the other side of the barbed wire fence. Within minutes we were standing beside the highway with our ferrets, live rabbits, and all our gear. Now we had to try our luck for the long trek home in the darkness of the night.

A car was approaching, so we put our thumbs up as was the hitchhiking custom in those days. One can only imagine what the driver thought when he saw two very young lads standing in the darkness, far from anywhere with ferret boxes on their shoulders, begging for a ride. The car pulled over about two hundred yards in front of us.

"Quick!" I yelled to Brian. "Run up and tell them I'm coming!" While Brian took off to tell them to hold on, I did my best to catch up, loaded down as I was with ferrets, nets and rabbits. I could see Brian opening the front door of the car, then he turned and yelled something in my direction but I was still too far away to make out what he said. I kept struggling forward, encumbered with all the gear, but the car didn't drive away. Brian was yelling out again, and this time I clearly heard his words: "It's Mr Jackman!"

Breathless, I staggered to the open door and uttered a relieved, "Hello, Mr Jackman."

"What have you got there young Laurie?" asked Mr Jackman, indicating the baggage loading me down.

"Ferrets and two live rabbits," I proudly replied.

"I think we'll put them safely in the boot," he said, and proceeded to do so. Brian and I sat back in the comfort of those seats, still finding it hard to believe how the day was panning out. The good thing was Mr Jackman lived in Frankston on the other side of Seaford. This meant we didn't have to hitchhike the forty miles to Dandenong Road; we didn't have to hitchhike the further ten miles to Seaford Road; and we didn't have to hitchhike the last four miles to our home from there. We could be driven straight home. And that's exactly what Mr Jackman and his wife did on that dark, lonely night for those two exhausted boys they found standing by the highway so far from home.

Sometimes the universe moves in mysterious ways. And that night it was moving in mysterious ways for those captive rabbits too. The next morning when I went to check up on them in the makeshift hutch I'd hurriedly shut them up in – they'd escaped! And I thought, "Lots of good things to you too!"

Suzie and Jiggy became a loving couple, and it wasn't long before Suzie was going to have baby ferrets. This meant I had to make another cage for Jiggy because Suzie would no longer let him into the nesting box. No problems there, for I now knew what to do; so a new cage was duly built for Jiggy. The little babies were beautiful; they weren't white like their mother Suzie, they were cute little beige-and-black badgers like their proud father Jiggy.

For the next year Brian and I ranged widely throughout the nearby paddocks and fields with our ferrets, working as a team at outwitting the rabbits. Our mother was especially pleased with the outcome because she was assured of a steady supply of rabbits for dinner to supplement her meagre pension. And we always made sure that our prized friends got their special treats of liver at the end of a working day. Our ferrets had a pretty good life.

I've already mentioned that I spent a lot of time at Old Bill Menzies's junkyard that went all the way from Wells Road right down to the railway line at the back. To me it was a veritable wonderland because you could find anything there. And as well as Vern Blumfield, there was another worker there called Joe who I got to know. He wasn't what I'd call a really close friend like Old Bill, but he was likeable enough. I'd say he was in his early thirties and had a slight Dutch accent. I'd also heard he could be a bit unreliable at times. Anyway, he got wind that I had some ferrets, and one day he appeared at our front door. "I was wondering if you could lend me your white ferret for the weekend," he boldly asked. "I'm doing a bit of ferreting down at Cape Schank."

My heart sank. My precious ferret Suzie was the most important thing in my life at the time. And I knew the burrows at Cape Schank were in the sand dunes and could be very deep, unlike the shallow ones in the hard clay at Officer. My whole being was screaming, "No!" But I said, "Yes, but look after her."

I felt I was being emotionally blackmailed because he was much older than me, because he knew my friend Bill Menzies too, and because he promised me faithfully that he'd look after her. It was with a heavy heart that I handed my dear little Suzie over to him, for I expected the worst. And sure enough, on the Monday he returned with her empty box saying simply that he'd lost her down a deep burrow.

It took me quite a while to get over that.

I genuinely consider myself a very giving person and always willing to share, but nowadays, when faced with situations like the above, I will speak my heart and say, "No, I'm sorry, I can't do that."

A last word on my ducks, my ferrets – and my extraordinary mother: it wasn't at all unusual to have a sick duck or ferret, sedated with half an aspro, wrapped in a cosy blanket and asleep on a nice warm water bottle on the end of my bed.

Kiwi

As I grew older in primary school, I was always looking for ways I could help my mum. One day I said to her, "Mum, if you buy me a bike I'll be able to do a paper round and give you some money." Now that's easier said than done, because a new bike at the time would have cost twenty-five pounds, and that's all my mother got for her two-week pension. Unbeknown to me, she must have thought on this for a while, looking for a way to wrangle her finances to make this happen.

"As it's getting near your birthday," she said to me a few weeks later, "I've bought a special present for you and it's waiting for you to ride home at Mr Jennings the ironmonger." I couldn't believe my ears: "A new bike for me! Oh, thanks mum!" I was off across the back lane.

When I got to the ironmongers there it was, my shiny, brand new bike! It was hard to believe. Boy was I going to pay my mum back!

"Before you ride it away, let's make sure the seat and handlebars are set right for you," said Mr Jennings. I was in his hands and let him lead the way. A few minutes later I was out the front of his shop riding on *my very own* new bike. Words can't describe the incredible feeling I was experiencing looking down at myself and my bike at the same time. Down the main street of Seaford I road, past my primary school, and I turned onto the back lane.

Then the worst thing I could imagine happened.

Bernard King, otherwise known as Kiwi, the notorious school bully, came up behind me and grabbed my bike seat. He was twice as tall as me, intimidating, and not to be messed with. *I'll play along with him till I'm safely across the lane*, I figured would be the best way out of this.

"Got a new bike, eh?" he said. "Sit on the cross bar and I'll give you a dink," he ordered. I had no choice but to comply. Then with his long legs straddling to the ground, and small me on the crossbar, we began to roll. The next thing I know Kiwi is pushing me and my new bike over the edge of the nine-foot drop of the back-lane into the mud and reeds below.

I picked myself up out of the mud and looked at my bike. I could see the handlebars had twisted around, which I did my best to twist back. What really made me mad was my mum had sacrificed her whole pension to give me this incredible birthday present and Bernard King had tried to wreck it in two seconds. Kiwi thought all this was funny. After dragging myself and my slightly damaged bike back up onto the lane, we continued walking along as if none of this had happened. I showed an interest in whatever he was saying as if I were an equal partner in his amusements: "Cigarette?" he offered, pulling a packet out of his pocket. My mind was ticking over fast – I was in survival mode because I simply didn't trust him.

"Yeah," I answered with a grown-up swagger, although I'd never smoked. On we walked with me puffing away on the cigarette while he bragged about his inane exploits. I took note that he was wearing a brown suede jacket with an open pocket right next to me. After a credible time had elapsed with the smoking, I casually dropped my live butt into this open pocket and thought no more about it. At least I'd done something to get even and teach him a lesson.

About a quarter of an hour later, just as we were reaching the end of the back lane, Kiwi began to madly wave his arms about and make weird noises. I was taken aback. I then saw smoke pouring from the inside of Kiwi's jacket as he desperately tried to get out of it.

I saw my chance to escape and jumped on my bike! As I glanced over my shoulder, the last thing I saw was Kiwi stomping on the glowing red lining of his jacket, trying to put it out. I sped off yelling over my shoulder, "Next time don't push young kids and their new bike over the edge of something!", leaving Kiwi to continue his desperate dance of extinguishing his smouldering jacket – as well as to think twice about bullying someone smaller than himself in the future!

My paper round

I did go on with my paper round, but as I only got ten shillings ($1.00) a week it wasn't a very lucrative enterprise, so mum ended up with hardly anything. With the wisdom of hindsight it was sheer exploitation even for those days, for I'd start my fifteen-mile round straight after school and some days not finish till eight o'clock at night! After a few months of this I began to feel depressed, watching all my friends going to the beach while I did my interminable paper run. One balmy night I decided to conclude my paper round earlier than usual and join my friends at the beach by way of an ingenious, undetectable plan: I stuffed half of the papers down a stormwater drain.

The next day half of Seaford complained that they didn't receive their newspaper, which of course I adamantly insisted I'd delivered. Unfortunately for me there was a heavy downpour that night, and dozens of these incriminating papers floated out of the drain as damning evidence of my foolproof plan. In those days what I did was pretty serious, for people counted on their deliveries; they were the main source of news about what was going on in the world around them. So I'd effectively blacked-out half the community's daily contact with the outside world. I lost my job as a result of this, and even copped it from my mother as well. But it was a small price to pay, for I soon regained my life and returned to my friends at the beach. *The exploitative aspects of this tedious and lonely undertaking for a 10-year-old lad had blinded me to what responsibility towards others really means.*

Turning grass into lawn with a Victa!

When my mother signed up for a brand new Victa motor-mower for us, not letting people down took on a whole new slant; this mammoth undertaking on my mother's part gave me an opportunity.

Decades before the days of professional lawn-mowing rounds, Brian and I started one and were able to not only pay our precious motor mower off but bring in some regular extra dollars for our needy family as well. We pushed that thing for miles around the streets of Seaford with a four-gallon tank of petrol strapped on top of it, drumming up business and establishing our bank of loyal clients. We took immense pride in our work and went beyond the norm to never let our customers down.

One time we even had to chop off the heads of a guy's chickens for him – and pluck them as well because he said: "You don't kill your mates!" This we humanely did and got a generous $5.00 for it … but he had no qualms about *roasting* his mates with nice potatoes, peas and gravy and eating them for Sunday dinner!

One little surprise we had for any unsuspecting friends we had in tow was to get them to help us check the motor of our mower for what we called 'engine concussion.' We'd gain great delight in getting them to hold the spark plug while we pulled the cord and watching them be flung backwards a metre or so by the electrical jolt they received. Great fun.

Part II
Frankston Tech and beyond

(1960 to 1976)

CHAPTER 6

Frankston Tech and my maths torments

The shift from Seaford Primary to Frankston Tech was pretty uneventful. I still had to walk across the back lane, but I then had to catch the train to Frankston. My actual stay at Frankston Tech was a very short, unhappy existence. I barely made it to the end of year seven; only thirteen years old, I ran away from this dreadful place to the sanctity of Bill Menzies's junkyard.

The dominant thing that influenced my thinking during this trying period at Frankston Tech was my growing fear of maths, which just grew worse and worse. As a result I was allocated to 1F with all the problem kids. Our maths teacher was Mr Ludge, a very tall, imposing figure and a major in the Citizen Military Forces. He used to strut into class in his full military uniform and order us around as if we were on the parade ground. "Smale!" he'd bark out, "Have you done your algebra homework?" … knowing full well I hadn't. "Well come out here!" he'd order. And he'd cruelly lash into me with his big leather strap.

This is what I had to look forward to in my maths classes, and I used to dread them. His brutal teaching methods caused my mind to completely shut down, for I hadn't the faintest idea what any of it meant. Never did he sit down with me and explain that *everything* out there had some *interesting* link to mathematics; for example, the spirals of a snail shell can be measured mathematically; as can the complex shapes of snowflake crystals; and the change I receive when I buy something, which I already had no trouble working out, is mathematics. Even this modicum of interest would have given me hope and not driven me away. I would have appreciated this, and genuinely tried to change my disruptive behaviour out of respect for the teacher's concern. But nothing like this came my way. All I got was belittlement and humiliation in front of the class; as if that was going to win my respect, expand my mind, and inspire me to want to stay on for five more years of it!

It was all about Mr Ludge dominating an unsure child and never about him truly teaching me or really trying to understand *why* I was so disruptive. Even though Mr Jackman had also failed to detect my maths problem in grade six, he had genuinely cared, effectively nurtured other aspects of my learning, and did everything he could to help.

A good deal of my time at Frankston Tech was taken up worrying about how to get out of my next maths class or how to survive it. One day I got a bright idea on how to cheat time by hurrying it along in these dreaded maths ordeals. I'd buy myself a new watch! So from my meagre savings I bought myself a brand new one from Edments The Jewellers with the specific purpose of placing it on the desk in front of me and watching the second hand whiz by. They say "a watched pot never boils"; well, I learnt that a watched watch in maths class only prolonged the agony.

I only tried it once.

Another day some mates and I were throwing old ballast stones at each other down at the rail yards during lunch time (don't ask me why, but that's what we were doing) when a rock hit me on the head, splitting my scalp. Now as you might be aware, a scalp wound bleeds profusely and can sometimes look worse than it actually is. All my friends could see was this effusive flow of blood and they panicked. With blood streaming down my face and matting my hair, they rushed me into the school grounds heading for the sick room. By the time we got there we'd created quite a commotion and gathered a large crowd.

"He looks like he could have concussion," said a concerned Mr Pinjaro. "We'd better lay him down."

I'll play along with this, and feign sleepiness I thought, for the next two periods were maths with Old Ludge. But I wasn't counting on what happened next.

Before I knew it, two ambulance officers were wheeling me out on a trolley and loading me into a waiting ambulance. Then it was off to Frankston Hospital with sirens wailing. I must say I felt a bit embarrassed about all this attention, but it was a small price to pay if it meant missing my maths lessons. They put me in a comfortable hospital bed, monitored me as required, then let me sleep for two blissful hours. Later that day, as had happened in Mr Jackman's class, I had a miraculous recovery from it all and returned to my normal self.

Menzies home for boys

I was now thirteen. Then, as if Old Ludge's torments weren't enough, something else added to my woes: my mother took ill and had to go to hospital again. And like the other times she fell sick, this time it would be the Menzies Home for Boys in Mt Eliza that would look after me for three months.

I certainly didn't expect what happened to me there – children can be very cruel to each other.

I hadn't been there long when one night in our sparse dormitory all my fellow dormitory-dwellers gathered around me and began to crowd in on me in a very intimidating way. I had no idea this was a sort of pecking-order ritual that newcomers were put through so they would know their place in the scheme of things.

"You think you're smart," they taunted, poking me on the chest. "Well, you're not!" I was roughly pushed over. Totally bewildered, I got back up, uncertain of where it was all going. Then, without warning, the leader of the pack, a dark-haired kid, punched me in the stomach, right where I'd had my 'bottle smashing' operation. White as a ghost and unable to breathe, I fell to my knees and crumpled over. They collectively took this as cowardice and turned their backs on me. They'd have no more trouble from me.

A couple of weeks later I found myself doing some chores in the laundry when the kid who had punched me came in and had a go at me for no reason. He was spoiling for a fight to reinforce his hold over me. He tipped my folded washing out on the floor and sneered, "Pick it up."

Now, because I am small of stature I've always avoided fights. My weapon has always been to adroitly talk my way out of tricky situations to get by in life; but this was not the language this belligerent kid understood. This time it was me who got in first. Filled with pent-up anger and humiliation for what he had done to me earlier, I punched him in the stomach as hard as I could, then followed with a barrage of merciless blows to his face. Johnny Truscot, who had just walked in, had to pull me off him. I now had a witness who saw me stand up for myself, and word quickly spread about what had occurred in the laundry. From that day on, the bully grudgingly left me alone and I walked those halls with a new respect. This respect followed me to Frankston Tech, for quite a few of my fellow inmates went there as well.

But it was not all gloom and doom at this secondary school – there were a few rays of hope and sunshine and people who genuinely cared. It's just that I had to live another three decades of life's trials and tribulations to understand this.

The snake and the kookaburra

At Frankston Tech they didn't have an art class as such where you did drawing and painting, they only had clay modelling. In clay modelling I was a perfect student – you wouldn't get an ounce of disruptive behaviour from me. It was here the artistic talents I'd so prominently displayed in primary school were encouraged to come to the fore. I can recall groups of teachers marvelling at my works … which came quite naturally to me. I clearly remember sculpturing a kookaburra and a snake locked in mortal combat. The snake was curled around the bird's neck, while the kookaburra had the snake firmly behind the head in its strong beak. My inference with the piece was that the kookaburra had the upper hand and would probably win. This piece of artwork caused quite a stir, both in class and among the teachers. This was all very perplexing to me; in one class I was the lowest of the low, while in another I enjoyed being the highest of the high.

And the same thing happened in my English class. One day Mr Walker set us the task of writing an adventure story of our choice, using the whole of the last two periods of the Friday. This didn't daunt me at all, for I'd always been good at writing and telling stories in Mr Jackman's classes at Seaford Primary School. So away I went.

I began with the end in mind, and asked myself, *what interesting things along the way will these people get involved in? What conflicts can I have my characters experience that lead them to this interesting end?* Then I began to write and let the story tell itself, with that end in mind and what was happening along the way. When finished, we had to hand in our work.

The following Monday we were all surprised when Mr Walker spent the first period reading out my story. But the thing that really surprised me was the way this usually restless class listened attentively while the story took them on a voyage to that lost volcano and what happened to the characters as they travelled there. I felt very pleased with myself; *a little praise, a little recognition, can plant the seeds of future fruition.*

Most teachers did care

More and more I began to get the feeling that this large, forbidding institution did harbour some feeling, that there *were* people who cared, and maybe there *was* some cleverness about me ... But the damage had been done, for my mind was already made up to leave school. I had no idea the creative potential that had fleetingly flashed through the darkness and given me some hope would have to lie dormant for more than thirty years before I found the courage to try to ignite it again.

When I reflect on things I can now clearly see, there were signs that certain teachers were becoming aware of the danger of me leaving school and squandering what they'd so far discerned as very impressive potential. And I might add, I wasn't completely blind to this potential myself. But for the moment, all I wanted was the torment of maths to go away. And the most logical way for me to do this was for *me* to *get away* from *it*! Even Mr Vincent, our history teacher, seemed to care. He pulled me aside one day and said, "One day you'll learn the appreciation of things," which I didn't understand at the time, but I'm forever grateful that he said these prophetic words to me; now I appreciate lots of wonderful things.

Like I said, all I wanted to do was get out of there. Mr McClaren, my sheet metal teacher, must have been in on this 'save Laurie Smale' thing as well, for he gave me a philosophical father-like talk too. I remember him saying, "And stop pulling faces while I'm talking to you," which I distinctly recall doing.

But the clincher that proved the teachers had been talking among themselves and really saw something special in me was the day Mr Tyrer, the Headmaster of the Frankston Technical School, personally visited me in the junkyard. He was a small, slight man with wavy silver hair and black horn-rimmed glasses. I was still only thirteen, and with three weeks to go before the end-of-year holidays, legally I should have been at school. I got the shock of my life when he walked through the front gate and spoke to me like a friend; one simply did not enter the rarefied air of talking to the Headmaster unless you were in trouble. Mr Tyrer's interest in me and concern for my future was genuine, and I'll always be grateful for that visit for it wasn't in vain; it completely supplanted the negative view Mr Ludge had instilled in me about Frankston Tech; the truth is there were other teachers there who really did care for their students.

The great race

One other important thing I learned at Frankston Tech was to be my own person and think for myself. But I didn't learn this valuable lesson in the classroom; I learnt it in the school yard.

Gary Laughton was the undisputed leader of our group at Frankston Tech. He had everything going for him: that indefinable charisma that girls loved; a magnetic personality that people were attracted to; and whatever he said was followed without question. And if Gary didn't like something or wanted to disparage it for whatever reason, all he had to do was deem it 'weak' and that was the end of it. Gary had spoken. And so it was with the school marathon towards the end of year seven – my one and only year at technical school.

I felt bad when Gary deemed the marathon 'weak', because at primary school I had been a very good runner and I was actually looking forward to it. On the day of the run I decided I would defy the earlier 'Laughton pronouncement' and take part in the race, so I brought all my running things in my school bag. Prior to the race I casually mentioned that I would be taking part in it "for a bit of fun". But really I was going to treat it very seriously and try to win it, which was actually a pretty tall order as both seniors and juniors from the entire school were participating at the same level.

Near racing time, I made sure I was in my racing gear and ready to go. There we were all lined up in the quadrangle, a thousand strong, when Mr Tyrer stepped up to the microphone and addressed us. He explained the straightforward route we would be taking: left into Cranbourne Road, then straight along to the Langwarrin Hall where we'd get our wrist stamped, then back to school the way we came, then between the big cypress trees to the finish on the oval. "There will be flags and marshals along the way, so you don't get lost," he said.

"Then there's something else," he added. "This year we have a very special guest who is going to give you a ten-minute start and pace you! Victorian under 18 cross-country champion … " I didn't catch his name because I was intently watching him dance around at the back in his white running gear and smart red sash.

"Please welcome him with a round of applause!" I heard Mr Tyrer say.

Right at that moment, one of my school mates pushed me, and a teacher yelled, "Smale, come here!"

Absolutely crestfallen, I walked over to Mr Vincent. "I didn't do anything," I pleaded. "Someone pushed me!"

"Just stand there," he said. Then there was the deafening noise of the starting pistol and the whole school moved off as one – except the Victorian under 18 cross-country champion – and *me*. For what seemed like an eternity I saw all the runners disappearing across the oval, then turn left into Cranbourne Road … and the clock ticked on. I felt really bad because it just wasn't fair. Then the starter gave the okay for the Victorian under 18 cross-country champion to go, and he too took off across the oval. Then Mr Vincent said, "Okay Smale, let's see how good you are!"

Bursting with frustration and anger I surged away like someone possessed.

I don't think I have ever run so fast in my life, and I felt good. I wasn't puffed, nor was I fighting for breath. On I surged. It wasn't long before I passed all the stragglers, including Gary Laughton, as if they were standing still. On and on I ran, for there were runners stretched out as far as the eye could see, but still I passed them. I was a man on fire. Still I ran and still I passed other runners, many of them seniors. On I ran, new found vigour with every stride. I wasn't feeling tired at all. It was as if something had thrown a switch in my mind, where I had to prove a point concerning many things about the school and my life and this was my only chance to do so.

I was now approaching the halfway mark; I got my wrist stamped, and set off in a higher gear still for the final leg. I passed another group of bunched up runners who had hit a wall, whereas I only seemed to be going faster. I knew within myself that I had already passed hundreds of runners, but there was still three miles to go. I could see a mile ahead of me and there were a few solitary runners. I still had my point to prove and kept on running. I kept on passing more solitary runners. Then I saw the giant cypress trees of the oval and pulled that bit more out of the box; in fact, I began to sprint.

I could see no more runners on the road, except those who had just turned onto the oval. I swept past the massive cypress trees and the oval came into view. And there, right in front of me – a bright red sash! I couldn't believe it! And ten yards in front of him, three more runners; the front group!

I could now see the finish line. The first three runners staggered over it, closely followed by the under 18 Victorian cross-country champion, and right on his heels was pocket-size runner Laurie Smale!

One of the officials at the finish line was Mr Vincent, and he just stood there agape: "Smale?!! What are you doing here?!" he incredulously blurted.

"Show me your wrist!" I showed him my stamp that proved I had completed the run, then collapsed on the ground totally exhausted. I still hear an incredulous Mr Vincent saying, "I can't believe it … that was the run of a champion!"

And I guess it was, for I had a lot to prove that day. *Never again have I let others negatively influence my thinking when it comes to me testing my limitless potential.*

Midnight excursions

Before we move on with our story, there is one more thing that closely relates to Frankston Technical School. Allow me to set the scene: I once did an eight-year stint as an emergency teacher at Ringwood Secondary College, where they'd ring me up every once in a while to help out. And there was one small lad (we'll call him Rodney) in year seven who had some unmistakable echoes of me; he could be a real handful, he was likeable, and he was intelligent. He trusted me enough to confide that he would often haunt the city-loop underground rail system in the middle of the night, dressed from head to toe in black playing chicken with trains. Although this shocked me, I kept my straight teacher's face, for he trusted me enough to confide in me; I listened to him, seeking to understand *why*. I didn't condemn him. When I asked him how he managed all this in the wee hours of the morning, as well as turning up for school, he told me that his parents had no idea this was going on. Through my own discreet research I later learnt his home life was pretty unstable.

Three years later I did another emergency stint in this school and a tall young teenager came up to me and said, "Hello, Mr Smale." It was Rodney. I asked how things were, and he said fine. He had a part-time job and was doing okay at school. When I broached his *secret* 'midnight excursions' he said, "I don't do that anymore."

"Good," I said, "that's sensible." He went on his way, pleased that someone he respected had taken a genuine interest in *him* and *his* world.

High adventure on the Frankston line

Right now you might be thinking, *what has this got to do with Frankston Tech*? Well, like little Rodney, it seems I had a penchant for doing crazy things with trains. This was probably my third day catching the train to school, and it was nothing out of the ordinary sitting in the compartment of one of Melbourne's quaint old 'red rattler' trains. But it was what happened next that was *extraordinary*.

To my absolute astonishment, about a mile from the Frankston station, three young boys I knew suddenly hauled themselves into the carriage through an open door from somewhere under the train! They didn't seem perturbed at all; in fact, they were enjoying themselves.

"What are you doing?" I asked them. "Where did you come from?!"

"We change compartments by holding onto the step along the side of the carriage and walking along the bar under the train ... but you've got to start just out of the Seaford station to get back in the carriage before Frankston ... Meet us in the morning at the Seaford station and we'll show you how to do it."

"Okay, I'll see you in the morning," I said.

I met the boys on the platform the next morning as planned. Fortuitously, just then a train going the other way passed by, so they were able to show me the long, slant-ended bar that we'd be using to inch our way along under the carriage. They told me it was easy. All you had to do was lower yourself down and let your feet find the bar ... then simply hold on tight to the ledge above and crab-walk along to the next doorway. Then haul yourself in. That was it. This was all the instruction I got.

It wasn't long before the next train pulled into the station and we climbed on board. Luckily we had the compartment to ourselves. There were three of them and one of me. One after the other we lowered ourselves out of the doorway down to the cross bar, and crab-walked our way along, holding onto that narrow ledge for dear life. As the doors of the old red rattlers opened outwards you had to keep your head down while edging along the bar.

When we reached the halfway mark we were right at the Overton Road level crossing. God knows what the poor motorists who were stopped at the boom gates thought when they saw four thirteen-year-old lads right in front of them crab-walking along that bar under the train carriage surrounded by grinding wheels! But they were the days before electronic communications. Nowadays the cops would be there at the station to greet us on our arrival!

Anyway, I made it in one piece. I only did this twice. It's funny how parents are sometimes not aware of what's *really* going on when they *think* they *are* … makes me think of my *train turntable* experience in Donald … and stepping off the train *the man's way* with my brother Brian …

After a lifetime of learning what not to do, I tend not to rush into a quick judgement of others' behaviour before I get a fuller picture of what's going on in their lives.

The incredible junkyard

It was inevitable that I gravitated to Old Bill Menzies and his junkyard for it was a source of income from the scrap metal I could scrounge from the tip and other people's rubbish, as well as the empty beer bottles I'd gather where I'd get a few pence per dozen; all transported in the trusty rickshaw he'd given me.

As there was a nine-year difference in our ages, around this time I'd often take my little brother and sister on excursions to the beach for a picnic lunch in the rickshaw, with them peeking over the edge of it like diminutive *Mr Foos*. Although very young, Leanne tells me she clearly remembers this. Reminds me of how my mum used to hurtle around the streets of Donald with us three kids on her bike!

Bill Menzies was a great friend and treated me with respect. I no longer needed to be disruptive or silly when threatened by maths, for here that torment was gone. Here I soaked in Bill Menzies's worldly wisdom and his years of experience in antiques and the different hallmarks of the precious metals he'd glean from the scrap metal. And I'm talking about gold and silver and all sorts of other valuable items sold to him for a pittance as 'junk'. Nowadays I can watch the *Antique Roadshow* and appreciate all they are saying, for I had three years steeped in this knowledge with this kind, worldly man.

I'd call him Bill, and he'd call me mate. I knew he had a family and his sons Johnny and Bob helped him run the business. But there was no doubt who was in charge. Of an evening, Old Bill would sit beside his open fire with his glass of red wine and Prince, his yellow dingo, sitting beside him. It was a surreal scene seeing them sitting there together, but it was true. Old Bill was a very handsome man of dark complexion, with hints of an Australian Indigenous ancestry about him. This was just my inkling, but nothing was ever said of this. I would listen enthralled for hours as he told me tales tall and true of his early exploits in outback Australia, and how he learned to discern real treasure in the trash and cast-offs of others. Old Bill Menzies might have looked rough and needy, but he was not a poor man.

Prince the majestic dingo

Where Prince the pure-bred dingo came from, no one knows. He simply walked into the junkyard one day, settled in with Old Bill and made himself at home. Someone must have brought him in from the bush, and feeling lost, he must have wandered off seeking something else; he found what he was looking for in Old Bill.

Prince really was a majestic beast. He didn't bark like domestic dogs do, he howled. And it was nothing to see him effortlessly carrying around his favourite toy in his powerful jaws: a three-kilogram cast iron trolley wheel! And woe betide anyone who went near it. During the hot summer months Prince would instinctively dig himself a deep hole in the cool earth to lie in, just like he would have done in the wild. In the daytime Prince was a lovable animal and would placidly walk around the yard saying hello to everyone, but once those gates were shut no one would dare come into that junkyard! In time I grew to love Prince the dingo, and like Old Bill, he became my mate too.

One evening when I was about fourteen, I was sitting by the fire with Old Bill and Prince and my mind drifted off into the future, and I found myself saying, "One day I'm going to wander around Australia with Prince and become known as *'The Boy and His Dog'*."

Old Bill took a puff of his ever-present clay pipe and smiled: "Mate," he gently said, "One day you're going to understand that there are more important things in life."

Six decades later I'm still pondering Old Bill's words of wisdom.

A ten-pound roll, a TV idol and looking for Jim

Another day I'd just finished sorting out a heap of scrap metal into its various drums when something caught my eye lying on the path near me, a path that various people visiting the junkyard would walk along. I thought, *Surely this can't be …* I stopped what I was doing and walked over. Sure enough, it was what I initially thought it was; a roll of ten-pound notes as thick as your wrist, a veritable fortune in those days. Now on occasion I'd seen Old Bill put his hand in his pocket and pull out a roll of notes and peel one off when he needed change, but never a whole roll of *red* ones like this!

I immediately ran inside and showed him what I'd found. Old Bill was shocked, for this money was the week's takings. He was so grateful that he gave me *two* of the red twenty-pound notes as a reward for being honest.

Karma has repaid this deed in my life; on more than one occasion my lost wallet has been returned to me with money and credit cards intact.

Another day Melbourne television idol Graham Kennedy came into the junkyard looking for things he could use in his show. I nearly died. I ran inside full of excitement and awe: "Bill," I cried, "Graham Kennedy's in the yard!" I was awestruck. All I could do was stand near him without a word. Years later – you'll learn – I would meet him again.

Another day a beautiful girl around my age rode up to the front of the yard on a big brown horse and asked me: "Have you heard of a 'Jim Kana' around here?" Eager to please such a beautiful girl, I ran into Bill's office (really a cement-sheet shack) and asked him,

"Do you know someone called Jim Kana around here? A girl is out the front on a horse and she wants to know."

Old Bill laughed. "A *gymkhana* is a horse riding event with obstacles," he said. I've always been pretty quick on the uptake, and I ran back to the girl and confidently told her where this competition was probably being held, as if I'd known all along. Funny, with girls I could confidently interact with them in general situations like this, but anything else, like trying to win them over, I would freeze. There were mountains I had yet to climb.

The Italian connection

While Old Bill Menzies's worldly wisdom was expanding my mind in the junkyard, my older brother Darryl was working in a little Italian glass factory in Frankston called Murano Mosaic Tiles. When my brother had gone to work somewhere else, I plucked up the courage to ride down and ask the Italians for a job, and they said yes. Little did I know this Italian connection would change my life … and continues to do so.

I was a bit scared for I knew nothing of their culture, their language, or their food. All I had in my head was the misguided concept of the 'dirty dago' who was not to be trusted and was best avoided. This view certainly didn't come from my mother, for she was totally against racism or disparagement of any form. But it was the accepted concept of the times and I was tainted with it. But I pretty soon changed my mind – their food was delicious and the Italians treated me so well. What's more, they sang all the time, and even though I didn't speak their language, they encouraged me to sing along with them! What I experienced quickly put paid to the lies that they weren't nice people, that they were dirty, and that they ate rats and yucky things like that.

Tosca by fire light

I grew to like them so much that for the next two years I virtually lived in the place. I used to sleep on the nice warm sand by the furnace, as a nightwatchman keeping an eye on the molten glass to see its correct heat was maintained. (One memorable night while the glass mixture was 'cooking', my Sicilian friend Pietro sang a shortened rendition of Tosca for me using the sand bin as a stage.)

I'd then work with the day shift making the glass mosaic tiles for the girls to cut in the factory. My job was to take my long paddle and gently stack the freshly pressed glass pancakes in a special kiln to cool and prevent them from cracking, not unlike leaving a freshly baked cake to cool before you handle it.

And the food they lavished on me! Each day there was something delicious. Every scrumptious Italian dish you can think of, all out of the goodness of their hearts. I even got a fresh roast chicken every Sunday for a friend of theirs owned a roast chicken shop! In the end I wanted to be like them and learn their language. I must have driven those poor Italians crazy with my incessant questions: "How do you say this in Italian?", "How do you say that?" But this is how I learnt; a new word here, a phrase there.

I went on to immerse myself in the Italian language for a whole year in the ancient Etruscan city of Perugia in the central Italian region of Umbria when I was thirty-two years old. I continued with my Italian studies at Melbourne University and proudly walked out with an Honours degree in Italian when I was forty-one years old. I can honestly say that for a full three decades after my negative Frankston Tech experience, the Italian language was my saviour, for it kept a faint glimmer of hope burning as I continued to wrestle with my demons; it kept a flicker of hope burning that I *was* clever, that I *could* learn, and those bright rays of potential that shone when I was young *weren't* flukes at all, they *really* happened and were just waiting to be rekindled.

Italian islanders

My crowning glory with my Italian experience was with a wonderful group of Australians of Italian descent who wanted me to help them discover their lost language. Their forefathers emigrated to Australia in the aftermath of WWII from the Aeolian Islands, a small group of volcanic outcrops just north of Sicily, the most famous of which is Stromboli. They arrived in Australia with not much more than the clothes on their backs and a couple of suitcases. In the wake of WWII it wasn't a good time to be Italian in Australia, because people still remembered the Italian dictator Mussolini and his association with Hitler. So it was best to keep your head down, drink cups of tea, and definitely *not* speak your own language. In fact, one of them told me, "Just to conform and survive we had a sign in the window of our fruit shop which said, 'Only English spoken here'."

The factory 'characters'

But getting back to the glass factory ... The thing that worked the magic for me all those years ago was the exuberance and generosity of the Italian people I worked with, even though their command of English was pretty limited. I taught them conversational English and they taught me conversational Italian. All of them, in their own way, served as a valuable father figure to me and boosted my confidence in some way. First there was Peter, Tony and Sammy, three dark and swarthy brothers from Sicily, who stayed on to raise their families in Australia. I ended up living with Peter and his wife Maria as a member of their Sicilian family for two years, a thing unheard of in 1964. I vividly remember the celebrations of the wine making, the bottling of the tomato puree, and the baptisms; what a privilege it was! Then there was the Venetian, Aurelio, who brought the idea of glass making with him from the legendary Island of Murano. He had the classic Italian face you'd see in a painting, Roman nose and all. He was a natural comedian and would have us laughing all day, even though we were working in front of an open furnace. The heat didn't seem to matter when you were in Aurelio's presence. What's more, he had a wonderful voice, and when he wasn't making us laugh he was serenading us.

And finally there was Lino from Genoa. Now Lino was somewhat different to the others, for he had lived in America for three years and spoke very good English. He sported a crew cut and was short and stocky like a Roman soldier. I'd say he was somewhere around thirty-five. He was rather reticent and not as outgoing as Aurelio and the Sicilians, but he did have a good sense of humour. I remember once he asked me, "Hey Laurie, what does *pupello* mean?" And I said, "*Pupello?*" I've never heard of any word like that. And he said, "Yes there is ... in America they always sing it: 'For he's a jolly *pupello*.'" I burst out laughing, and said, "It's *good fellow*!" Poor Lino laughed too; he'd wondered about *pupello* for years but never got around to clearing this perplexity up with anyone.

The factory set up was straightforward: the furnace was down the end, from which Aurelio drew the molten glass with his long steel rod; next in line was Lino, whose job it was to snip the glass paste with shears and then press it into a mosaic-tile pancake using foot power; and the last step of the process was me placing the cooling pancakes into the cooling oven to stay overnight. Each day we would make about three thousand of these pancakes, each batch a different colour.

The following day, aligned down the other side of the factory, the girl tile-cutters would cut and paste the tiles on sheets of paper ready for packing, which we would do when we finished making the glass. The Sicilian boys mainly worked at night, preparing the glass for us to start working the following morning at 6 am. Just think, every single sky-blue glass mosaic tile that adorned the sides and courtyard of Melbourne's landmark Southern Cross Hotel – the place where the Beatles stayed in 1964 – was made by *our very* hands!

Watching all the girls go by!

The Italians were far ahead of their time when it came to being socially minded and employing the disabled. I can remember mentally disabled 'Mary' quietly working with the other girls for as long as I was there, and being paid the same wage as the others.

And talking about girls, with me being an incurable romantic and finding myself in a room full of them, I'd often fall in love with one of the tile-cutters. But I never had the courage to do anything about it. I remember Aurelio once asked one particular girl I was pining for what she thought of Laurie. "I love him," she replied. I felt good when he told me this, but all I could do was be the friendly funny man within the confines of the factory. And then there was another beautiful Greek girl, Eleni, who I was madly in love with. I used to dream of living on a farm with her and collecting freshly laid eggs for breakfast for us to have together – but that's as far as it went! Oh, the pain of it all!

Incredible stories

The actual operation of drawing out the molten glass and transforming it into mosaic tiles took us from 6 am to around midday each day. At face value this could be seen as a very boring, repetitive task. And rightly so. But with Aurelio singing and being funny, and me listening to Lino talk about his travels as we worked, the time just flew.

In these quiet, reflective moments I found I was developing the skill of drawing things out of others that they wouldn't normally share. For example, in one of our deep and personal sessions, Lino told me of the time he had to ride for his life a hundred miles on his racing bike because the Germans were after him. They thought he was up to no good and working with the Italian partisans. There was no mercy for people they suspected of this, so Lino was desperate to escape the patrols who were searching for him. He took the hidden back ways where possible, and had a close call when he had to throw his bike in a ditch full of bushes and jump in after it till a German armoured car went past. He told me he could hear the guttural sounds of their voices, which sent a chill down his spine. He snuck into his isolated village in the mountains near Genoa, safe and sound in the middle of the night. These were the sort of stories my fertile mind absorbed as I got Lino to open up and tell me things he'd probably never shared before. As a result we became very close.

The legendary Coppi and Bartali

I especially liked to listen to Lino's riveting stories of the monumental battles between the legendary cyclists Fausto Coppi and Gino Bartali around the end of WWII. At the time, these two champions were godlike figures in the world of cycling. During our repetitive work in front of that blazing furnace, Lino and I would escape into the world of their amazing cycling exploits, the behind-the-scenes skulduggery, and even acts of heroism during the war.

I would listen in awe as Lino told me of how Gino Bartali would risk his life by using his wide-ranging bicycle training as a cover to rescue thousands of Italian Jews. He would use his fame to carry messages and documents to the Italian resistance while wearing a jersey emblazoned with his untouchable name. Lino told me that neither the Fascist police nor the German troops would have risked upsetting a nation by arresting him.

In my subsequent research I've learnt that Gino Bartali is a central figure in the 2014 documentary *My Italian Secret: The forgotten heroes*. He was a humble man who never boasted of his success; he'd simply say: "The good is done, but it is not said. And certain medals hang on your soul, not on your jacket."

Life on a sheep station

One day a fifteen-year-old girl started work cutting tiles in our glass factory. Her name was Fay, and she had just arrived from spending the last first few years living on a vast South Australian Outback sheep station in Copley with her family. Wow! I was fascinated and eager to know more. So I employed the drawing-out techniques with her that I'd developed while listening to Lino. And what an absorbing story it was: the sheep station was hundreds of miles wide with tens of thousands of sheep. I learned about the shearers; the boundary riders; the school of the air; and the Flying Doctor. The more I listened, the more I wanted to be part of it.

That very night I sat down and wrote a letter to the station owner asking for a job. I'd love to have a copy of that letter now to show you, for it would be fascinating to see what I actually wrote in my young, ignorant hand. I do recall telling him things along the lines of: how old I was, that I was born in the country, and I was working in a factory. I also told him I had lost my dad as a little boy and would love the chance to learn and grow on his sheep station. I told him that I could get the train to Adelaide, then make my way to his sheep station from there. Then I posted the letter and thought no more about it.

About six weeks later I received a one-line telegram from the manager of the sheep station, which I distinctly remember said: "Come when ready."

When I told Lino and Aurelio of my decision, they were shattered for they had no idea that all this was in train. And for my part I was too young to understand the effect of just upping and leaving people who really depended on me. I was so caught up in the excitement of it all, I was totally unaware of just how half-baked this venture was. But my mind was made up and I was going.

A close call

About a week before I was to depart for the complete unknown, I jumped on my bike and headed for the corner store for my usual bottle of milk and cheese biscuits for morning tea. On the way back to the factory, I stopped at the level-crossing boom gates to let a train pass. The boom went up, the end of the train went rushing by me, I jumped on my pedals – and a car horn let out a deafening blast behind me. I stopped dead. Five feet in front of my face another train hurtled past in the opposite direction from behind the first one.

I came out in a cold sweat, and will always be grateful to the driver of the car behind me who saw what I couldn't see.

Maybe this was an omen of what lay ahead.

Before I pulled away I carefully looked both ways – and have done so ever since! Down Overton Road I went, full of adrenalin, and turned into our street towards our factory. Lino happened to be out the front of the factory, and as I pulled up he made the offhand comment, "You look good on a bike, you'd make a good bike rider!"

Now, whether I was still shaken by what I'd just experienced, or whether a real fear of the unknown was beginning to take hold, I blurted out: "I'll stay if you buy me an Italian racing bike … but I'll pay you back!"

"Okay," said Lino, and that was that. Not another word was said about the sheep station. We simply continued as if this weird interlude had never happened.

There is an interesting adjunct to this story: in 1981 I found myself leading a group of outback tourists on a journey through central Australia, past the formidable Oodnadatta Track to Adelaide. About 560 kilometres north of Adelaide at the foot of the harsh Flinders Ranges we drove through a dusty abandoned settlement, with one pub still standing for those brave enough to visit it. The now abandoned Ghan railway station looked neglected and forlorn, its rusty enamel sign hanging askew in the wind. The squeaking nameplate sent a shudder right through me, for this was all chance and not part of our planned adventure. It read "Copley".

My God, I thought. *And I nearly rushed off to this godforsaken place to fulfil my dreams!*

CHAPTER 7

My cycling career

Lino kept his promise and took me to Nino Borsari's cycling shop in Carlton. If we were going to get a real Italian racing bike, this was the place to go. Nino had all the credentials: he was an Italian Olympic gold medallist and revered by millions around the world; once settled in Australia he used his fame to bring many Italian cyclists to race here. I was so excited for I was going to be riding a real racing bike exactly like them. My career in cycle racing had begun.

For the next four years I did nothing but *eat*, *drink* and *sleep* bikes! In fact, during the night I kept my precious bike in my room beside my bed. My ultimate aim was to have a room full of cycling trophies – and have girls flocking all over me. In time I became a very good bike rider, but my fervent wish about the girls never came to fruition.

My first road race

I'll never forget my first road race. It was mid winter and rather chilly, but I was eager to prove a point. Now, I certainly had the bike and the fancy clothes that go with it, and I certainly had the heart and enthusiasm to win. But I didn't have the fitness or the hard-learned strategies needed to outwit the opposition, for competitive cycling is indeed a clever game of cat and mouse – but you've got to be very fit to play it. So here I was on the starting line for a forty-mile road race at the Mornington Cycle Club. I felt really good, for I'd ridden the forty miles from Seaford to get there at a comfortable pace, so I was nice and warmed up. Aurelio and his family were there to see me off. This was going to be a cinch.

The route went down Tyabb Road, then left into Hastings Road for twenty miles, then back onto the One Chain Road to where we started. These types of road races in Australia are handicapped: that is, each rider sets off at a given time according to his state of fitness and ability. As I was an unknown quantity, the handicapper put me somewhere in the middle of the field. Maybe he thought it best to err on the side of caution with someone with such an impressive bike.

The riders depart at a set time according to the handicapper's assessment of their ability. The further back you went the more powerful the rider. Those at the end were the most intimidating and powerful of all. The idea is that if the handicapper gets it all right, everyone should approach the finish line around the same time. But bike riders are a wily lot and do their best to outwit the handicapper.

It was soon my turn to move off. I waved goodbye to Aurelio and his family and away I went.

For the first ten miles or so I felt okay, then the rider behind me caught up with me, which worried me a little. I managed to stay with him for a while, but he then drew away and I couldn't keep up, as once there is a gap between you and the bike in front there's no more slip stream to pull you along.

I struggled on, my rhythm now somewhat erratic. At this stage we must have been somewhere around the halfway mark. I was really starting to feel the pinch.

Then, without warning, a massive bunch of backmarkers whooshed past me like a massive steam train as if I were standing still. There was nothing I could do, for my legs had turned to lead. I felt humiliated as I watched them, so fit and so fast, disappear out of sight.

No one else passed me. I was running last. And there were still twenty miles to go. I'd slowed down to a crawl – that's all my tired legs would allow. It had even started to rain. On and on I struggled for what seemed like hours, till darkness was upon me. I turned the corner into Tyabb Road and realised I'd reached the finish, but no one was there. The organisers must have thought my friends had collected me or I'd chucked in the towel and ridden home. I remember trying to get my weary legs out of the toe clips and toppling over into the mud beside the road and crying.

As I lay there on that cold, wet ground I thought, *you can't just stay here in the cold … you've got to free yourself and ride home!* Somehow I managed to undo the clips and get myself upright again. I took a deep breath, switched on my bike lights, and slowly rode the 40 kilometres back to Seaford.

That night before I dropped off to sleep, I resolved that by the end of the following year I would be as big and as strong as that bunch of backmarkers who had trounced me is such a humiliating way.

So my journey of redemption began. Within days my mind and body had recovered and I was able to enjoy my training rides, for I was a man with a mission. Slowly and surely my legs and body strengthened as the weeks and months went by. This was reflected in my handicap mark. I now found myself being put further back in the field. On occasion I even managed to win a race or two. Although a tremendous boost to my confidence, it wasn't enough. I was still nowhere near the hallowed status of the best cyclists.

My mission continued.

Revenge is sweet

Finally we were nearing year's end and the Club Championships were upon us. By now I was the undisputed B-grade champion of the club – yet I still had to defend against worthy contenders like Terry Clark. What's more, the championship race was not handicapped, so riders were judged on merit and ability alone. Both the A and B grades would start together and find their own level as the race progressed.

The big day came, and how different I felt to that first day when I was nervously waiting at the start. This time I was still keyed up – that's only natural – but now I was more experienced, more sure of myself, and more in control. The starter's whistle blew and we all moved off as a group, and stayed this way for the first mile or so. Then we approached the sharp incline to Foxeys Hangout and things started to happen.

Within seconds the club's six A-graders had opened up a break on all the B-graders, of which I was one. My heart sank, for I could see the gap between the two groups getting bigger by the second. The other B-graders seemed content with their lower status and quite happy to fight for the B-grade championship among themselves, with no one willing – or capable – of giving chase. But my mind was focused, for I could see my dream slipping through my fingers. By now the group of A-grade riders was far ahead.

I knew it was now or never.

*I've outgrown B-grade and am now worthy of A-grad*e, I thought, frustratingly hemmed in and dancing in my pedals. Earlier I mentioned that there are two important ingredients in being a successful bike rider. You've got to be very fit; and you've got to be a clever strategist. Although it was an extremely tall order for me to even *try* to catch those elevated riders, there were two things in my favour. One: they had probably dropped off in speed in the firm knowledge that the gap between the two groups was now almost impossible to bridge, and they could now afford to coast along, saving their energy to fight out the A-grade championship at the finish; and two: they were probably not counting on me being an exceptional mountain climber, as good, if not better, than any of them. And I still had two miles of very steep incline to take advantage of this and catch them unawares.

And there was one more thing the complacent A-graders weren't counting on: me being possessed by that superhuman effort that had taken hold of me in the Frankston Tech marathon! This day I was no defeated rider lying in the mud. I sprang away from the B-grade riders as if they were standing still, and set off in hot pursuit of my quarry, very cognisant of one great equaliser; there is no slipstream advantage when climbing a mountain, for it's each rider battling against gravity and his own weight with no slipstream opportunities, and I was not that big.

As my window of opportunity was only two miles long, I chose not to set into a steady mountain-climbing rhythm as one would normally do; my plan was to gamble on a *sprint* up the mountain to catch them before the summit, then tack on behind them to recover in their slipstream. So all I had to focus on was a two-mile mountain sprint as against the fifty-mile road race it really was. *Catch them before the summit!* was all that was on my mind.

On I rushed in my two-mile dash, my lungs nearly ready to burst ... then I saw them about six hundred metres from the crest of the last steep incline. They had no idea I was looming behind them. *I've got to reach them before they get to the top*, I told myself. *If they get over it first I'm done, for I'll never catch them!* With one last desperate effort, because that's all I had left, I turned Nino Borsari's bike inside out and caught up with them just before the summit. Another ten metres and I wouldn't have made it.

To say these riders were surprised when I snuck in behind them would be putting it lightly. They were full of admiration, and respect. I knew I wouldn't have to worry about them ganging up on me or anything like that, for after my awesome feat, they'd nurse me all the way to the finish line safe in their slipstream.

And that's just what they did. I felt like a real winner riding with the A-graders as an equal. When we got near the finish line the atmosphere changed and things got serious. Placings had to be decided. After being effortlessly sucked along in their slipstream for most of the way and now decidedly fresher than they were, the idea flashed through my mind of sprinting past them and scooping all the glory. But it was just a flash, and that's all it remained. I stayed where I was and let them sprint it out to determine their legitimate A-grade champion. I followed closely in their wake with both hands in the air as if I'd just won the Tour de France.

Sarge Clerk

After the presentations, a tall, square-jawed, middle-aged man approached me and introduced himself as Sarge Clerk. He asked, "Have you ever thought of someone coaching you?" I told him I wasn't sure but I was willing to give it a go. The truth was I'd just done a sterling job of racing with the A-graders and felt there wasn't a great deal more I could learn. The arrogance of youth. But I kept this to myself, and agreed to meet him the following day. Before I rode home, someone whispered in my ear that Sarge Clerk knows what he is doing because he coached Murray French, the winner of the Melbourne to Warrnambool Classic; a famous road race of the time. Now that impressed me!

I was already waiting at our rendezvous when Sarge Clerk drove up in his olive-green classic Ford Pilot. He unwound himself from the front seat and walked over: "Here's what I want you to do," he said. "See those two lampposts?" I nodded. "I want you to do your best riding between them. I'll hold you up and roll you forward just this side of this first post." The simplicity of these directions just reinforced my initial scepticism. But I was willing to stay with him. So I strapped myself securely into my toe clips and Sarge rolled me forward. What really egged me on was the big stopwatch in his hand!

I put everything I had into that hundred-yard dash, then rode back pretty pleased with myself – to a serious-faced Sarge.

"That was pathetic," he said. "You started off like a slug, and it was half way before you got going … and when you did it wasn't that good!"

I was shocked. I'd honestly thought I'd just done the best I possibly could. He told me the exact time it had taken me to get from one pole to the other.

"Now," he said, "I want you to do that again, only this time I want you to turn that bike inside out! I want you to start by getting out of that saddle and lifting those pedals as well as pushing down on them! I want you to be leaning over that bike as you do this! I want to see that back wheel snake as it responds to all this! And when you near the other post, I want you to throw yourself and your bike at it to pip the other riders at the post!"

This was all new to me but it made a lot of sense. I looked at Sarge with a new respect as we moved into position. In the space of a few minutes my closed mindset had been supplanted with an open one. This time my approach would be a hundred per cent different from what I did in my first attempt: this time it was against *my unlimited potential* and Sarge's stopwatch.

I took off with a brand new purpose and followed Sarge's instructions to the letter. But this time I rode back with none of the smugness I had before ... yet I felt elated. I knew there had been a marked improvement with this attempt compared to the previous one. And this time Sarge didn't look so stern – there was even a glimmer of warmth on his face. He was looking at his stopwatch. "You beat your first attempt by four seconds," was all he said. Remarkable! ***In that one half-hour coaching session I learned that our potential has no limits, and that often it is wise to let others open our closed minds and show us the way to realise this.***

Over the next three years Sarge went on to lift me to great personal heights.

A new bike

While all this was going on I was still working in the glass factory, for bike riding was a very expensive hobby. Every penny I earned was invested back into my cycling. One day I took ownership of a brand new track bike I'd had specifically built for velodrome racing. I chose the colour of its frame on a whim, an iridescent pink. And I was just itching to try it out. So one Sunday, I decided to invite myself to the Melbourne Olympic Velodrome to do this. I must have looked a spectacular sight for the early 1960s, sitting on the train all decked out in my Italian racing gear and bright pink bike! I got a real feeling of importance from it all. Anyway, I got off at the Richmond station and walked my sensational new bike across the road to the velodrome.

I got to the main entrance and there was not a soul in sight, so I simply walked in and made my way through the tunnel into the main arena of the board track. And what a thrill it was to be actually standing there where my idol, Australia's world champion Sid Patterson, had performed his incredible cycling feats. This was hallowed ground. I walked over to the actual boards and bent down and touched them. Then, to my great dismay, I noticed there was a big boom stretching across the track with a lock on it.

What was I going to do now? I thought. *How could I get a feel for what it would be like riding around the Olympic Velodrome on my fantastic new bike? ... To hell with it! ... I'll do it anyway!*

I looked up at the steep sides of the track towering above me, which didn't daunt me at all for I'd seen pictures of famous riders racing around them with ease. All that was needed was a certain velocity to hold you tilted over as you sped around. I figured I could get a real feel for this centrifugal force if I started on one side of the boom and got myself off the track before I hit it on the way round. But I'd yet to learn that even with the flatter part of the velodrome, you've got to have a fair momentum to sufficiently tilt over to prevent your outward pedal from hitting the hard wooden boards. Ignorant of the physics of this, I mounted my bike and slowly rode dead upright from the flatter stretch of the boards into the sharp incline of the velodrome. I'd gone but a metre into the incline when my outside pedal dug into the boards and severely bent my crankshaft, tipping me over onto the concrete pavement below.

This was my inglorious – and extremely short – introduction to Melbourne's Olympic Velodrome, which I decided nobody would ever know about … until now! But being a person with a philosophical outlook on life, I simply swallowed my pride and wheeled my damaged but fixable bike back to the station and caught the train home.

Tomorrow was another day.

In time I would have some racing success on this very same track. But for now, we're still back in those early days when Sarge took me under his coaching wing.

The unforeseen

The fitter I got, the more confident in myself I became. I'd even check the progress of my leg muscles reflected in shopfront windows as I rode past. One day I was feeling on top of the world, decked out, as was my wont, in my full Italian bike-riding regalia: fancy sunglasses; white and green racing shirt with *Pellegrino* written on it; kid-skin racing gloves; black nicks and special racing shoes; and my genuine racing helmet. I couldn't help but be impressive! That's a more common sight these days, but back then it was a rarity.

The sun was shining, the birds were singing, and I was riding down the main street of Frankston enjoying it all. Then I spied two nice-looking girls walking towards me on the other side of the road. *Here's a go!* I thought, and began to dance in the pedals hoping they'd be attracted by what they could see of my rippling leg muscles.

Right at that moment my world turned upside down.

Distracted as I was between my reflection and the girls, I didn't see the back door of a van that had just swung open in front of me. I hit it full on. Up in the air my bike and I went, and we came down in a crash with the handlebars all bent and the front wheel buckled beyond recognition. I was more humiliated than hurt. My bike was a mess, and I heard the girls comment as they walked on by,

"Did you see that?!", as if it was a triviality to be dismissed because of carelessness.

Maybe, I thought as I picked myself up and surveyed my wrecked bike, *people aren't as interested in me and my bike riding as I think they are.* I had plenty of time to reflect on this as I limped the five miles home with my wounded pride and mashed bike on my shoulder.

Slippery Sam

Notwithstanding the bruising to both my pride and my bike, it wasn't long before I was back into training with the view of one day being a world beater. But it's not always our own misguided thinking that can hold us back from fulfilling our dreams; sometimes it can be the meanspirited behaviour of others. There was one cyclist who used to visit the Mornington Cycle Club who was a likeable sort of character but had a shifty air about him (I'll call him Slippery Sam). He was somewhere in his forties, with the best days of his bike-riding career behind him, so he would resort to subtle under-handed tactics to share in the winnings. Because I was young and naïve, I was unaware of this and took him at face value.

One day we were all lined up on our handicap marks about to start a five-mile sprint. I had improved markedly since Sarge had been coaching me, so I was now a back marker not far from the very best riders. Slippery Sam took it on himself to be my minder; that is, to hold me up and push me as hard as he could the second the starter's whistle blew. Little did I know he had something else in mind. On the sound of the whistle, he might have looked like he was running and thrusting me forward, but what he was really doing was holding me back and not letting me go! That day I learned a little more about the *slippery* side of human nature.

After the race I said to Sarge, "He held my seat and wouldn't let me go!" Sarge thoughtfully nodded as if he'd figured that out, and said, "We'll keep that in mind."

The Tour de Cranbourne

The crowning glory in my brief but character-building cycling career was my canny move in The Tour of Cranbourne that outwitted them all. Keep in mind that I was still only seventeen while this was happening, and was up against a formidable opposition of seasoned professionals – but I had Sarge Clerk on my side.

A bike rider has to know his strengths in order to play his cards cleverly. For instance, it would not be to my advantage to try to go toe to toe with the top sprinters at the finish, for they were much bigger and stronger than I was and I would not have been able to get past them. I did not have the brute kinetic force they could generate. But on steep climbs it was a different matter. It all came down to you being able to pull your dead weight up and over the mountain without the benefit of a slipstream. So the lighter you are the easier it is, and if you have a penchant for hill climbing all the better.

Our plan was for me to put pressure on the rest of the field about twenty miles out of Cranbourne, on a hilly stretch of road of some length, by opening up a break on the field with those who could keep up with me. We figured the main bunch would not be in a hurry to catch us as we were so far from home. They would prefer to leave us dangling way out in the unprotected front to tire – and that's just what they did. Being a much larger group than we were, they were able to keep themselves fresh with continuous slipstream changing, just as a flock of geese do when flying in V formation. They would bide their time by playing cat and mouse with us, then pounce when we were spent at the last moment. But they didn't know that crafty old Sarge and I had other cards to play.

So mile after mile the main bunch continued with their game of leaving us in the elements to weaken, aware they could be upon us at the moment of their choosing. About twenty miles from the finish, our small group of six riders approached the corner of Clyde and Thompson roads. Sarge had taught me not to free-wheel around corners as most riders do for safety reasons and to take a breather, but to do what we did between those two lampposts and sprint away to test the strength of the other riders and also tire them. Our secret command for me to do this was one nod from his expressionless face. But on this day on this corner I received *two* nods – which meant "once you have the break, keep going!"

So much by surprise did this move catch my group as they casually free-wheeled around the corner that I'd opened a fifty-yard gap before they realised I was gone. It was now me against the elements. Would I be strong enough to make it? In the meantime the game of cat-and-mouse continued, for the main bunch was blissfully unaware of Sarge's deft move on the chessboard. All they could see was that small group of riders tiring half a mile in front of them. They themselves were feeling fresh and relaxed – it was now the simple matter of when they made their crushing move on the bedraggled group before them. They decided to bide their time a little longer …

About ten miles from the finish they decided to pounce on their prey. But even then they did this in a half-hearted fashion, for catching these tired riders was a pushover. Tony Birkett, the English grass-track champion, told me what happened next. He told me that as soon as they joined our group, someone said, "Smaley got away and he's way out front!"

Tony said, "To say we were surprised is not the word for it! While we were fiddling away for an hour watching you guys … *you* were getting away from us!"

Giving chase

Then, like a well-oiled machine, twenty professional bike riders took off in hot pursuit of this cocky little upstart who had outwitted them; there was no way this could be left unchallenged, for if not addressed they'd be made to look like complete fools.

I was tiring fast. I was riding solo and doing all the work against the wind. I knew it was a case of my timing being right and me lasting the distance. My biggest worry was, *did I go too early?* My tired, aching legs powered me onto the South Gippsland Highway heading for the finish line in the town centre.

"Four more torturous miles," I whispered. "I've got to keep going!"

On surged my humiliated pursuers as if possessed. They had to catch me at all costs, and were closing in on me fast. Their reputations depended on it. They too were now hurtling along the South Gippsland Highway, less than a mile from the finish line. My legs were becoming leaden. A terrible thought went through my head: *maybe I won't make it?*

Then I saw Sarge on the side of the road, and he could see the bunch of savage riders closing in on me at a tremendous pace: he was no longer complacent and expressionless. His arms were madly waving. He was going berserk! "Keep going!" he screamed. "There's only one hundred yards to go! … You're back between those two lampposts! Now get up and go!"

And get up and go I did! A powerful strength took hold of me and momentarily rejuvenated my tired, spent legs. With my last ounce of strength I threw my exhausted body at that second 'lamppost', just as twenty desperate riders came roaring past me … But too late, for I'd crossed the finish line only inches in front of them! This was the sweetest victory of all!

The Austral Wheelrace

Equal to this bike-riding thrill was my appearance in one of the finals of the 1964 Austral Wheelrace in front of a packed Olympic Velodrome in Melbourne. And yes, it was the same Olympic track that I'd snuck into two years before and come to grief. Since then, I'd learned how to ride on a velodrome, and even dive like a swallow from the top of the steepest incline to the other riders below.

Even though I was still a bit green in velodrome experience, I confidently put my name down for this classic race. And what a thrill it was to be involved; me, Laurie Smale, actually racing on Melbourne's Olympic Park Velodrome in the finals of the Austral Wheelrace.

I remember the part I played in these finals very well. I felt so fit I was jumping out of my skin, and felt there was nothing I couldn't conquer in the whole world. Perhaps it was a combination of this cockiness and my inexperience that was my undoing. The majority of the riders in the Austral Wheelrace were hardened professionals who knew all the ropes and the way you were expected to play the game. Sarge Clerk had given me a general idea of this, but I really didn't comprehend the significance of it all. I went into that professional environment full of beans and eager to do my own thing, just as I'd always done at the Mornington bike club.

Swooping down on them

Here's what I remember of my one night in the spotlight at the Melbourne Olympic Velodrome. I don't remember how I got there or the start of this particular finals heat. I do remember feeling like an extremely fast rider and afraid of nothing as I surveyed the field below me from the top of the board track, contemplating my next move of diving down onto them. A voice over the loud speaker mentioned my name and described me as one of Victoria's up-and-coming road cyclists, which made me feel extra special in front of that large crowd. The last thing I remember is gracefully swooping down to execute my plan of tucking in behind the three leaders, when bright lights suddenly blinded me and someone was rudely shaking my shoulder. A concerned voice was saying, "You're in Prince Henry's Hospital ... You had a crash at the velodrome and we're looking after you ... you're in good hands."

From there my mind is blank.

I don't know what caused the crash but I'm told it was quite spectacular, with me and my bike tumbling from halfway up the track to the unforgiving concrete pavement below. As this occurred among the pack, no one really saw what happened. Was it due to my inexperience of racing on boards? Was it my attitude of feeling indestructible? Or ... was it foul play to bring this cocky little upstart into line? I'll never know the answer. What I do know is, I suffered a broken collar bone, a fractured skull, and numerous other cuts and bruises … I was in a bad way. But the strangest feeling of all was, all I wanted to do was get back on my bike!

Promoter Bill Long takes an interest

Two days later I got an incredible surprise when Bill Long, Australia's renowned entrepreneur of sporting heroes, paid me a visit in hospital and offered to take me home, all the way to Seaford. I couldn't believe it; Bill Long! The man I'd seen on television promoting world champions and the big events that went with them. If you were associated with Bill Long you'd either made it or you had great potential. And Bill Long was right here in hospital, visiting *me*, and wanted to drive me home! Although I'll be forever grateful for this kind gesture, Bill Long had obviously had his eye on me as a potential star in his stable of champion cyclists.

I have to get better quick! I thought, *and not let this chance slip by*. Bill kept his promise; the following day he picked me up in his flash Porsche and drove me all the way home to my astonished mother.

Two weeks later I was back on my bike, arm in plaster and all, tentatively riding the roads. But as the months went by, and try as I might, I never really regained the confidence and pinnacle of fitness I'd had before that fateful day, in effect heralding the end of my short but telling cycling career. There was, however, one unexpected outcome from this full-on sporting experience of me racing over hill and dale for three years.

An unexpected bonus!

Remember the close call I had with that broken bottle accident when I was nine years old? Well, a year after I'd decided to hang up my bike, I had to visit Dr Ready for a general check-up to see how I was going on my long-term path of recovery. You may recall that Dr Ready was the doctor who saved my life on the operating table when 'smashing bottles the Scotchie way' went awry. I recall him examining my stomach with incredulous wonder: "But there was nothing there," he said, gently feeling my stomach with the sensitivity of a blind person. "There were no muscles, no tissues to speak of … it was all gone. What have you been doing to build it up and strengthen it so well?"

"I became a racing cyclist," I said.

"Well, you've done a great job of it," he said, still shaking his head in admiration and wonder.

So a sincere "thank you" to the world of cycling; without this body-strengthening interlude, I would have gone on living my life as someone always prone to the slightest knock in the stomach.

CHAPTER 8

Stage struck

My show biz journey begins

One thing I've never been that good at is dancing, so I decided to face it head on and go to a dance school. This is where I met my mate Dario, probably the oldest friend I have. We were both in the cha-cha team, and ended up winning a category in the Victorian dancing championships at the Palais de Dance, which is something I'm proud of. It's still the only dance I can do properly. And there were plenty of girls there too, which was good for my confidence.

When I left home for greener pastures, I felt really guilty as Leanne and Mark would no longer have a father figure, a role I'd taken on myself to fill. So I left them with a year's dancing school enrolments to kick their confidence along for a good start in life. Years later, when I'd forgotten all about it, Mark told me how much it meant to them and how much they enjoyed it, which made me feel good.

It was this thrill of performing before groups that I'd always enjoyed, which brings me to my all-consuming – yet misguided – obsession of becoming the best I possibly could in show business. This obsession was to fill my thoughts for the next twenty years.

I still had a lot to learn – that there's more to life than striving for one single goal to the detriment of all else, for when you finally reach a specific goal, what then? The next day the world is still spinning and life's challenges haven't gone away. You may have won your gold cup, but it now sits *empty* on the shelf. I was near forty when I began to learn how to fill it … and in time, have it runneth over with all the small things I'd hitherto been blind to.

I don't know why I suddenly decided to try my hand at being a singer or entertainer, but that's what I did. Perhaps it was because I'd been singing non-stop for two years with Aurelio in the glass factory and genuinely thought I was pretty good; perhaps it was the gaping void left in my life with the sudden demise of my promising cycling career; or perhaps it was because of my urge to be seen as clever and talented before people, which was the only way I could be noticed and appreciated. But this turned out to be a hollow victory too, for underneath my well-rehearsed and polished performances was a shallow and lonely person who had left school when he was thirteen and couldn't even add up! So living this lie amid all the superficial glitter, with the ever-present fear of *the truth* about me being found out, was an awful burden. There did come a time when I could run no more and had to face reality and confront all this, but we will come to that later. For now my career in show business was about to begin, and I was brim-full of enthusiasm about just how easy it was going to be.

Sometime after my promising bike riding career had come to its abrupt end, I remember flippantly saying to Lino, my Italian mentor, "I'm going to be a singer." He looked at me and smiled. "It's not that easy," he said. "I knew a young lady in Italy who wanted to be an opera singer and it took her twenty-five years to get there."

"It won't be anything like that for me!" I quipped with the blindness of youth. "For me, becoming an overnight success is going to be easy!"

Lino's sage words turned out to be right.

New Faces

At the time there was a new TV talent show called *New Faces*, compered by Frank Wilson, a famous theatrical performer of the day who'd made the shift to television. It was a big deal, and people watched it for the way contestants would make fools of themselves. My mind now firmly set on rocketing to stardom, I sent off the necessary entry forms.

The number I chose to sing was probably one of the worst songs ever written: *Son Don't Go Near the Indians* by the cowboy singer Rex Allen. Mercifully, in those days they would tape over the previous show's performers to save money on recording tapes, so there is no record of this ever happening. But it was a good first-time experience on how to appear on television and work to a camera. Over the next ten years I became somewhat of a regular on the show, appearing in five Grand Finals. Granted, I didn't win any of them, but it was no mean feat to make each of these finals again and again. And I still hold the record for this.

Over time it began to dawn on me that they were using me as a convenient fill-in because I specifically chose numbers that were novel and entertaining. Never was I offered a professional part in a show, never did I get that lucky break. Maybe there was something missing? Something I was yet to discover?

Another memorable showbiz experience was my three appearances on *Showcase*, Australia's top talent show of the '60s and '70s and a precursor to *Australian Idol* and similar shows. *Showcase* was compered by the famous English actor, singer and TV personality Gordon Boyd. In its heyday, *Showcase* was an enormous success, and it was quite an achievement to get through the stringent auditions and appear in the heats – let alone win the final. I consider myself very fortunate to have appeared on this prestigious talent show on three separate occasions.

My first appearance was on *Showcase 68*. I still remember my introduction by Gordon Boyd. His words went along the lines: "In my extensive career of stage, screen, and song, one of the toughest items I've ever had to master was the patter number *Trouble in River City* from the musical *The Music Man* ... and how surprised we were when a young lad appeared before us in the auditions and did a sterling job of it!"

Things were now moving fast for Laurie Smale; I honestly thought I'd made it, and this was how things would keep rolling along in my life. But I must admit, coming from my humble beginnings, all this was kind of overwhelming and felt a bit surreal. Just think; there I was, sitting on a stool beside the renowned conductor Hector Crawford with his silver, shoulder-length wavy hair, in front of his full symphony orchestra helping me run through the number I was about to perform Australia-wide on *Showcase*! I really did have to pinch myself. But having to return to my normal life the following day brought me back to earth a bit.

The Top Hat Review

All the time this was going on I was taking serious singing lessons with Ian Fields at the Grosvenor Academy in Melbourne, to develop my voice and acting abilities. In addition to this I joined The Top Hat Review, a group of amateur and semi-professional entertainers who travelled around entertaining the sick, the elderly, and the needy. What was good about this was our audiences were never judgemental and were always appreciative. And no matter who they were, they'd get the full show, for we treated this very seriously with a full rehearsal every week. It was in this group that I made lasting friends, honed my skills, and tried out new acts. I was with them as their compere and all-round entertainer for twelve years.

What a joy it was to have a hall full of elderly citizens, folk who are often forgotten by the youth of the day, rollicking to the songs and music they used to listen to when they were young; what a joy it was to have them laughing their heads off at our sketches and the corny jokes of our stand-up comedians; and what a joy it was to see them infected with our youthful vigour and the sparkle of appreciation reflected in their eyes. I even took Leanne and Mark to see these shows and they loved them.

But heartfelt appreciation is not always so easily detected. One time we were putting on a show in the Bundoora Geriatric Centre for about fifteen elderly people in wheelchairs in various stages of dementia, Alzheimer's disease, or who were simply too old and frail to respond. Unfazed, we set ourselves up at the front of the room, with an unused hallway as a makeshift dressing room. The show was going on!

As usual we put our heart and soul into the show; we stepped out with a show-stopping opener, then into our full vaudeville review with a segment of songs from *My Fair Lady*. When the curtain finally came down, the only ones who clapped were the small handful of carers and nurses.

Later, over a cup of tea and cakes, one of the nurses shared some of the responses that were evident to them but we didn't see. She said, "They loved your show more than you may think. One lady who hasn't responded to anything for years was quietly singing to herself with a shine in her eyes we've never seen before … and the quiet old man with dementia sitting next to me gently squeezed my hand every time you sang."

After comments like that, you drive home thinking it's all worthwhile; these people were once vital and young themselves with people dear to them.

The legendary camel act

I did mention that we used The Top Hat Review to test out new acts and material, one of which was my legendary 'camel act'. Let me tell you how this unusual act came into being, and the extraordinary circumstances surrounding its last tumultuous performance.

I roped my post office workmate David Hinson into being a part of the act without giving him too many details. All he got was it would involve a camel, an English explorer, and the Sahara Desert.

I deliberately left out the fact that *he'd* be the camel and *I'd* be the English explorer. "We'll worry about who does what later," I told him. Before we go into exactly what happened, a few necessary details to help you understand what the audience experienced, followed by a brief overview to help you visualise things.

Esmerelda the camel was a lifelike puppet as tall as a man that looked like a *real* camel. The body itself was sewn together from hessian bags with uneven 'fur' from a synthetic carpet glued to it; Esmeralda's back legs were the puppeteer's; her front legs were manufactured with their own authentic-looking camel feet and knee joints. These 'knee joints' were really the operator's fists as he held the top of the 'leg bone' where the knee would normally be, as one would hold a walking stick. The operator was leaning forward to do this. The camel's head was carefully carved from polystyrene with embedded glass eyes. It was then fixed to a long balsa-wood neck, which in turn was attached to a bicycle helmet which the puppeteer strapped on tightly; there was a small, hidden slit located on the crop of the neck so the operator could see where he was going; and finally to bring Esmeralda to life the whole thing was fine-tuned with her hessian and fur covering. Esmeralda really did look and walk like a camel. We couldn't believe what we'd created!

The second part of the act was the eccentric English explorer Sir Archibald Thomas; a Terry Thomas–type character sporting a waxed moustache, pith helmet, army boots and socks, oversized army shorts and shirt, and a riding whip.

The act starts with Sir Archibald introducing himself in a loud, English Sergeant-Major accent. He stands ramrod straight and looks ridiculous. During this brief introduction, Esmeralda stands beside him: a pointed glance of understanding flags this incredible beast might have some sort of human insight. Sir Archibald then gets straight into a narration of what happened as they ventured forth one fateful day in search of some mythical tomb beyond the pyramids. Sir Archibald's narrative is all very general with no plot to speak of: they depart; encounter a marauding band of Bedouins; fight them off and escape.

The hilarious fun comes from the slapstick way Sir Archibald and Esmeralda interact as they try to fight the Bedouins off and escape, especially the way Esmeralda can forget she's a camel and become human-like for a second or two. For example, at one stage during the fray, Sir Archibald pleads in his Sergeant-Major voice to his faithful companion who is on her knees, "Get up and fight like a man!", and Esmeralda is suddenly upright on her hind legs, shadow boxing with her front legs *like a man*. The audience are in fits of laughter with this unlikely transformation, then, just as quickly, Esmeralda resorts to being a camel and the focus is once more on Sir Archibald's wild ramblings.

We're now in the midst of the fray and Sir Archibald's narrative gets more desperate and nonsensical: "There were Bedouins to the right, Bedouins to the left … the horrifying flash of the scimitar … the blighters were getting the better of us … " He raves on in his high-pitched English voice. "We had to make our escape! … So I leapt into the saddle!" Here Sir Archibald leaps onto Esmeralda's back – and she collapses in a sprawling heap … the audience is in hysterics. This looked very real because poor David never knew which direction I'd be leaping from! They make their escape with Sir Archibald precariously hanging on to Esmeralda's back while they both simulate a galloping camel; Sir Archibald's meaningless narrative is lost in the uncontrollable laughter this scene evokes.

The act finishes with Sir Archibald breathlessly stating; "In the end the blighters turned left at the pyramids while we went straight on – and lived to tell this harrowing tale … Cheerio now!" Sir Archibald stands to attention and salutes, and they both march off to the strains of Rule Britannia! Esmeralda turns and looks at the audience, waves goodbye with her front leg, and gets the last laugh.

This act began as a simple idea of little substance – but it worked in our minds and we couldn't wait to share it with a live audience.

An offer we couldn't refuse

While we were working all of this out, David's dad, who was high up in the echelons of the Masonic Lodge, asked us if we would like to be part of the entertainment for their end-of-year gala dinner in a couple of months' time.

"Something to make us laugh," he said. He went on to say there would be about three hundred guests there, plus a top-line entertainer travelling all the way down from Sydney to join us on the star-filled program. We said "yes", and that "we'd really work on something good," but later we panicked. David's parents would be there with all the big wigs from the Masonic Lodge, as well as many influential people from business, politics and society. There was no room for error.

"What are we going to do?" we asked each other. "How are we going to compete with this top-notch entertainer from Sydney?" Then I got an idea: "Why don't we do our camel act? We have plenty of time to polish it up in front of real people in the Top Hat Review."

"Why not!" David said. "Let's do it!"

As time was of the essence, the very next Friday at the Hampton Elderly Citizens' Club, Esmeralda and Sir Archibald Thomas strutted their stuff and brought the house down. The audience was doubled over with laughter.

"It really works!" we excitedly affirmed when we walked off the stage.

"Now we'll have to do it again to prove that this wasn't a fluke!" I declared.

A call for help

As luck had it, the following day I got a phone call from Bob Phillips, former producer of Graham Kennedy's top-rating television show *In Melbourne Tonight* and now running his own entertainment agency.

"I need a class act for next Friday at The Village Green Hotel," he said. "Can you help me out?" Our camel act flashed into mind:

"No problems," I said. "I've just finished polishing up a new act and it's ready to go."

Bob was fine with that for he knew me through my TV appearances over the years and gave me the gig. We were ecstatic, for this is exactly what we needed, a real acid-test performance in front of a live, unruly audience. If we could survive in that environment – and even win them over – the end-of-year gala dinner at the Masonic Lodge would be in the bag.

A different mindset

As David and I pulled into the Village Green Hotel carpark we had to remind ourselves that this was not going to be a room full of friendly old folk all primed to be entertained and enjoy themselves. But when we entered the venue we were thrown somewhat to learn that the room we would be performing in would be full of the general public who were not necessarily there for a show. In fact, most of them were unaware that there was to be some extra entertainment apart from the resident band playing a few songs. And to make matters worse, by the time we'd be stepping onto the small stage at the side, the majority of patrons would have had one too many and be a touch unruly and rowdy.

I made an important decision: "I've got to get their attention right up front or we're dead!" I said to David. "Tonight Sir Archibald is going to be much more forceful than last time; and he's going to command attention and order these people around! So Esmeralda's got to be larger than life too and respond to this!" Dave was always quick on the uptake, and I knew I could rely on him. As far as this audience was concerned we were not invited there to perform at all, so we had to take control and invite ourselves!

So that evening the explorer Sir Archibald Thomas and his friend Esmeralda the camel really did throw themselves to the wilds of humanity. Only a few people near the stage saw this oddly dressed fellow and a 'camel' step onto the stage and giggled a bit; the other three hundred in the room were unaware of our presence. Then, fully immersed in the character of Sir Archibald Thomas, I stepped up to the microphone. Everyone in that room sat up and listened when they heard the very English parade-ground voice of Sir Archibald boom out: "Good evening ladies and Gentlemen ... My name is Sir Archibald Thomas, explorer extraordinaire, and I'm here to tell you exactly what happened in my latest sorte into the Sahara desert with my faithful camel, Esmeralda."

At this point Esmeralda stepped forward and took a human-like bow by crossing her foreleg and coyly lowering her head. We got our first laugh! From this moment on we had them in the palm of our hands, and everything we did was funny. Sir Archibald kept the momentum going and Esmeralda generated the biggest laughs with her human antics. In fact, those way down the back of the room were standing on their chairs to get a better look. And their being a bit 'under the weather' made what we were doing even funnier; the contributions of the wags in the room only added to the fun! All we had to do was stay in character and stick to the simple plot, which we did. We proudly strode off that stage to cheers and a standing ovation.

We'd done it! Now all we had to do was transfer that to the more sophisticated environment of the gala dinner in the Masonic Lodge ballroom.

Unbeknown to us, the Channel 9 producer Bob Phillips had turned up and saw the act! He was so impressed he offered us a job on the spot travelling around Australia with it. And guess what? I had to refuse! I took a deep breath and told him why: "I'm travelling to Italy in three weeks to study Italian for a year ... it's a life-long dream I've had." I could see Bob was disappointed because he could see real potential here, but we shook hands and he wished us all the best.

How ironic; never before had I been offered a professional part in some show; never before did I get that lucky break. And when I finally did, I said "no". This was indeed another sliding door moment in my life. But to tell you the truth, in a way I was glad, for although I felt a million dollars when entertaining people, when I stepped out of the limelight I often returned to my lost and lonely self and a shiver went through me: *what if things didn't change even though I'm making hundreds happy? What if I still felt lost and lonely when I stepped out of the limelight as I often do? Wouldn't this simply perpetuate how I feel now?* My thoughts raced on: *maybe there was something I couldn't see … something I was yet to discover?* Reality brought me back to the present: *right now we've got a gala night to concentrate on so we better get cracking!*

The show of shows!

And boy, was this gala dinner something else! Row upon row of fancy tables peopled with folk all dressed up in their finest. As special guests, David and I were even wearing dark suits and bow ties!

After the success of our last performance, I felt very confident with our act and knew we wouldn't let his dad down. And unlike the challenges of our pub gig, in this venue we'd be easily seen for there was a proper raised stage with classy curtains, allowing our audience to join us on a journey of uproarious laughter and fantasy. I looked along the table at our dining companions to get a sense of how they were feeling. Everyone seemed to be relaxed and having a wonderful time … a good omen. *I won't have to fight for attention with this lot*, I thought. *They'll respectfully tune in from the start like the elderly citizens.*

The top act from Sydney

Opposite and slightly to the left of me was a dapper silver-haired man who was obviously the top-flight entertainer flown down from Sydney. At a guess I'd say he was in his early fifties. I introduced myself and David as the other act on the bill that night, and wished him all the best for a great night. He leaned across his dinner and pointedly said to me, "You know you're gonna die tonight."

I thought I must be hearing things or he was trying to make some sort of joke.

"I'm sorry," I said, "I didn't hear you clearly." He repeated what he had just said, "I said you're gonna die tonight." I smiled innocently, played dumb, and returned to my meal. *I can't believe what he just said!* I thought. *How can a grown person be so spiteful and hurtful … the guy doesn't even know us!* I decided then and there that tonight's performance was going to be one for the history books; then and there I resolved that this nasty, insecure piece of work sitting opposite us was not going to wreck all our efforts and ruin the promise of success David had made to his father. For the moment I made sure David was oblivious to all this.

As we were the supporting act, David and I were to go on first. We gave ourselves plenty of time to get ready so we didn't feel pressured and were in the right frame of mind. Full of nervous excitement and keen to get out there, we could feel a buzz of expectation in the air. Then we heard our introduction; and to warm applause, Sir Archibald the famous explorer, and Esmeralda the camel, strode purposefully into the limelight.

The audience gasps

The audience gasped with astonishment to see a 'real' camel walking on stage, then deliberately turn and look at them as if it understood! Everyone was laughing. From then on the laughter never stopped, with Esmeralda acting out Sir Archibald's outlandish narrative. It got to the point where people were begging us to stop for they could take no more. When we said goodbye, as with our previous performance, this audience stood cheering and applauding as we rode off into the sunset.

One thing was for sure: *we didn't die that night!* I'd go as far as to say that no artist in the whole world could have entertained that audience, at that time, and in that space, any better than David Hinson and I did for the fifteen hilarious minutes we took those people along with us. That night I was spurred on by something much more powerful than blind ambition. I was determined that in spite of that spoil-sport's mean-spirited intention, for us this night would be successful for we had earned the right for it to be so.

Bring on the top act!

After the main course it was time for the top-billed star of the evening to be introduced – our contemptible table companion. He stepped into the spotlight and began unveiling his polished magic show. Now whether these people had had their fill of entertainment with our act, or whether we had sapped all their energy, the audience was lethargic and unresponsive to this magician's wisecracks and deft sleight of hand.

When he brought out his Chinese ring trick, it all came back to me: this was the magic man I'd seen fifteen years ago in grade three at Seaford Primary School! Back then he was funny, lively, interacting and *giving* to the kids. But the self-centred meanness he'd somehow gathered along the way had brought him to be the lonely figure we saw on stage that night. Karma had paid him a visit; it wasn't David and me who *died* in their performance, it was he who bombed something terrible.

The dinosaur and Graham Kennedy

All my life I've had a boyish, naïve air about me; that I'm probably not as capable as I might think I am. This faulty idea of me not being quite up to it, which I naturally radiate, has forced me to always have to prove myself and *exceed* all expectations to get ahead. But I've learned to live with this state of affairs of me seeming a bit of a pushover, and often turn it to my advantage. With this in mind, I'll never forget the time I got the better of Graham Kennedy and upstaged him!

Now for you readers who are not familiar with Graham Kennedy, *he was the king of Melbourne television* throughout the '60s and '70s, and everyone watched him. In fact, he is still reverentially called the King. But *no one*, and I mean *no one*, ever upstaged Graham Kennedy – except me! I was about twenty-two at the time.

Ever keen to get my head on television to further my showbiz career, this particular night I was comfortably sitting on the couch watching TV when a call went out for novelty acts to be in the studio within the hour for Graham Kennedy's *In Melbourne Tonight*. "I'm off," I said to my friends Joe and Nicky, "and don't forget to watch me!" And off I raced to the Channel 9 studios in Richmond, formulating an idea as I went.

Now Graham was my idol and I adored him, but I had his measure. His schtick was to get laughs at the expense of others, and an array of people making fools of themselves with their 'novelty' acts had Graham in his element. These segments were hilarious from beginning to end. My aim was to play his game and let him get a few laughs at my expense, but *I* would have the last big laugh at *his*!

So there I was nervously waiting in line behind the scenes amid the props and scenery for my turn. The audience was in fits as Graham tore each 'act' to shreds and milked it for all the laughs he could get. To give you an idea of the 'quality' of the performances, which played right into Graham's hands, the two that preceded me were:

- The first was a lady of substantial build who said she was a chook laying an egg, and she proceeded to cluck and squawk and flap her tucked-in arms like wings. Then she lifted one of them and out fell a tin-foil egg from her armpit. That was it. That was her act. You can imagine the field day Graham had with that!
- The next was a balding old guy who walked out with a bowl of water. When asked what he was going to do with it, he said, "I'm going to impersonate an outboard motor." He pulled a straw out of his pocket and blew bubbles into the water. Graham had a lot of fun with that one too.

Then it was my turn, so out I walked into this atmosphere of 'friendly' humiliation.

It was a really exhilarating feeling to be standing right beside my idol Graham Kennedy, the crowned King of television. For a few seconds I forgot why I was there and closely looked at him while he segued from the previous act to me. He was only a little guy with bulging eyes and a funny face. He was not much different to when I stood near him in the junkyard as a wide-eyed kid twelve years prior to this; only then he was more serious as he was looking for possible props for his show. Graham's voice broke my thoughts: "And our next act is Laurie Smale," he said as he shook my hand.

"What are you going to do for us?" he enquired, searching for possible laughs.

"I'm going to impersonate a mechanical dinosaur," I confidently announced.

"A mechanical dinosaur," he repeated, pulling those special faces that were peculiar to him and drew a barrage of laughter. Unfazed by this, I explained, "But this is no ordinary dinosaur, it is one of those mechanical ones like in the original Godzilla movie that don't look real." Saying this, I immediately became one of these monsters. Kennedy responded by generating waves of laughter at my crouching stance, my slow-moving Tyrannosaurus head, and my waving claws. This was manna from heaven for Graham Kennedy. He continued generating laughs by turning his back on me and conversing with the audience as if to say, "This one's a real doozy!"

This was exactly what I wanted! The 'dinosaur' fixed its beady eyes on Graham's form, moved its head slightly to size up its prey, then opened its jaws and let out a blood-curdling scream and leaped onto Graham Kennedy's back! The audience screamed with laughter. Graham, genuinely in shock, had to steady himself by holding onto his desk. "I think I'll have to change my daks!" he quipped, milking the scene for one more laugh.

Graham warmly shook my hand as if to say, "Well done, I've met my match," and he thanked me for being on his show. Sadly, I think this priceless gem of a segment has been lost by being taped over to save money, as was the custom in the early days of television. At least *I've* never seen it replayed, nor could I find it on the internet.

CHAPTER 9

Maths, my inner demon

You'll notice that none of the things I've been involved in so far had anything to do with mathematics or algebraic questions, for my abject fear of them was now too entrenched for me to recover, so I simply steered clear of them. And the same went for all my future jobs, which were always hands-on and of a menial nature. This left my creative mind to roam freely and daydream about other things ...

But one thing is for sure, no matter what job I've done, I've always done it with pride – even digging muddy, gravelly draining trenches for a plumber. I can remember him saying to me, "One thing about you is, your trenches are always nice and clean so I don't scrape my knuckles when I lay the pipes," which made me feel good. *I've carried this philosophy with me all of my life; whatever it is that I am doing, I've got to be able to stand back and say, "That looks good ... I'm proud of that!"*

Chelsea City Council

After my mind-opening sojourn with the Italians in the mosaic-tile factory, I moved on to the Chelsea City Council as a general rouse-about, where I did everything from laying bluestone curbing to being a 'runner' beside the garbage truck. I was now eighteen. Interestingly, the garbage truck of the 1960s was vastly different to the closed-in ones with internal hydraulic ram presses we have today. Ours was an open tray tipper where we two runners had to throw each household's garbage can up to a guy standing atop the rubbish in the back of the truck, squashing it all down with his hobnail boots. The guy who did that loved this task for he had first go at the odd 'treasure' he'd find! *He can have it!* I thought; I was content keeping fit running beside the truck.

Concrete works of art

The job I coveted most was working with the concrete gang; the way they could sculpt a work of art like a beautiful driveway from a heap of inert concrete intrigued me and I wanted to apply my artistic talents to that too. But the trick was how to wheedle my way into this specialised group of artisans. I bided my time, doing the best I possibly could as I was alternated between the bluestone layers and the garbage collectors, till one day someone was away sick and I was moved in with the concrete gang. *You beauty!* I thought. *Now's my chance to figure out a way to stay in it!*

What I did was elect myself to take on the most tedious job of all: at the end of the day, without being asked, I'd go round and gather all the dirty wheelbarrows and tools and wash them all clean of sand and cement, then wheel them all back and load them on the truck.

With envious eyes, I'd painfully watch the rest of the team. They actually seemed to enjoy fashioning these works of art; a sort of therapeutic reward for the backbreaking work of shovelling the wet concrete into place. How I yearned to join them … but the weeks went by and Jock Lang, our dour Scottish foreman, never invited me to do so.

One day I simply picked up a trowel and joined them as they fashioned the complicated sloping wings of a driveway. As I was doing my best to deftly emulate the others, which came naturally to me, Jock Lang happened to be passing by. A small, wiry man of few words, he stood and watched me for a minute or so, thoughtfully mouthing his roll-your-own cigarette on his bottom lip, then he walked on. I was in! And I had Jock Lang's imprimatur!

What I really liked was there was no jealousy on the part of the others, because I'd already won their respect by taking it upon myself to look after the dirty wheelbarrows and tools for the past two months – which I continued to do.

Jock Lang must have got word back to big Harry King, the Clerk-of-Works, that I was a valuable worker and he wanted to keep me on his team. I was safe! Now the garbos and bluestoners couldn't poach me!

We'd travel the world

Now that I had been promoted to the elite artisan class of the concreters, I wore this as a badge of honour for not everyone could do it. But the best part of all was, with the heavy work done, I got to talk to Bill Hale and Sandy the Scotsman for hours as we went through the finishing-off stages together. This was something that couldn't be rushed, so we had plenty of time to travel the world with each other while we waited for the concrete to dry and then trowelled it to the next stage.

Being a good listener

And as I used to do with Lino, my Italian working companion, all I could do was *listen* as Bill and Sandy kept me enthralled for hours with their stories, for I hadn't travelled anywhere of importance and had little to contribute. Little did I know that this misconception of my own capabilities was actually helping me develop one of the most important ingredients of all when it comes to being an interesting conversationalist – knowing when to shut up and *be a good listener*! So what I was doing without knowing it was using my genuine interest in egging these guys on to talk! My questions would prompt them: "What happened then?" I'd eagerly ask as their stories unfolded, and away they'd go for another fifteen minutes with me responding with spontaneous listening comments and exclamations along the way. This made me a real part of the interaction, a real part of the conversation, but I was totally unaware of what I was doing. It was only many years later that I was able to look back and really understand what I'd learned with Lino, Bill and Sandy all those years ago: *to be an interesting conversationalist, you've got to first be interested.*

One of the constants in Bill Hale's stories as he travelled around Australia was his six-foot-eight travelling companion Jonno, who I warmed to, and I looked forward to what he'd do next. I loved it when big Jonno would unwind himself out of the front seat of their Mini Minor and nonchalantly saunter over to a smart-alec who was giving them trouble and say, "You gotta problem?", and the dude would back off fast! In fact, I got to know all the characters in his travels, so I could even take part in the stories with comments like, "What did Jonno have to say about this?"

Sandy the Scotsman was different again. He was a real enigma. Every Christmas he would go on a drinking binge and return to work a month later than he should. Everyone turned a blind eye to this and welcomed him back when he was ready to return. No one knew why he did this, nor did they know anything about his past, for he kept to himself and didn't say much. Other team members would say to me with surprise, "You and Sandy get on and seem to chat away with each other as you're trowelling off." Feeling a little embarrassed about being able to get someone to open up who usually kept to himself, I'd say, "Oh, we just talk about stuff as we're waiting for the concrete to dry."

I grew fond of old Sandy, for in many ways he reminded me of Old Bill Menzies from my junkyard days, only Sandy had a strong Scottish accent. And like Old Bill, I saw Sandy as a father figure; he was a man after my own heart, for he shared my philosophy of taking pride in your work. In his rich Scottish brogue Sandy would always tell me: "Always remember your work's gotta be pleasin' to the eye!"

Away with the birds

One particular day Sandy came to my rescue. This day I was feeling pretty tired. I'd been rehearsing in a show with The Grosvenor Academy till late in the evening, and didn't get home to Seaford till one in the morning. I was living two lives at the time, for these worlds were so different. Anyway, I did my best to concentrate on the job at hand because Jock Lang could be a pretty ruthless boss. Somehow I got through the day, which was warm and sunny and made me feel even more tired and lazy. I had just finished my usual job of cleaning up the tools and was wheeling a barrow-load of watery slurry and tools down the road. I was a million miles away, day dreaming with my eyes wide open. I was just going through the motions, for my body had done all this before and knew what it was doing – but I was away with the birds.

I turned with a running start up a driveway with the intention of tipping everything out and finishing the cleaning of the tools in a vacant lot on the other side of the footpath. But there was just one problem: I'd ploughed into the beautiful new driveway we'd spent the last three hours working on! The barrow buried itself up to its axle, tipping the slurry and all the tools out, making a real mess of our handiwork. I snapped out of my reverie and just stood there trying to take it all in. Jock's booming voice made me feel like an utter idiot: "What the fuck are you doing?" he bellowed. There wasn't a lot I could say. I was mortified.

Jock Lang was the sort of guy who could sack you on the spot without any qualms at all. But that day there were angels in the air.

Instantly, Sandy was on the spot with his trowel in hand, closely followed by every other person in the team. Within ten minutes that driveway was as good as new, and I was wide awake finishing my job of cleaning the tools – well away from it! Not a word was ever said about the event by anyone; however, I did sense that Jock Lang never forgot the episode and was more watchful of me from then on. This didn't worry me that much because he was away most of the time supervising other works. But because he respected the more mature

Bill Hale and Sandy the Scotsman so much he never interfered with the pleasant times I had with them as we put the finishing touches to our concrete works of art.

Sid the slave driver

Around the age of nineteen I found myself standing in line for a job digging sewer line trenches *by hand* in the sand belt near Chelsea and Carrum on Port Phillip Bay, for ten dollars a day. It was like the Great Depression of 1929 – Australia was under a severe credit squeeze and jobs were very scarce. The simple truth was, if you didn't have a job you couldn't pay your way, so you took what was available. I was given a job on the spot and was told to get to work immediately by big Sid the overseer.

'Overseer' was the right term for him, but 'slave driver' would have suited him better. Sid was a very tall, square-jawed man who used to stand atop our trenches with a pipe in his mouth barking commands. He reminded me a lot of Charlton Heston, the legendary actor of epics like *The Ten Commandments*. He made Jock Lang look like a kindergarten teacher. I clearly recall my first day contemplating my blood-blistered hands after swinging a sledge hammer for twenty minutes. The pain was excruciating, and I was nearly in tears.

"What are you looking at your bloody hands for?!" Sid barked at me. "Keep that hammer swinging or get out of here!"

I'd never met anyone so cruel and insensitive as this man, but because I was desperate for the money I tried to shut out my pain and anger and I kept that hammer swinging. There were a lot of hungry people lined up to take my place for that ten dollars a day, cash in hand. That night I went home and bandaged my blistered hands as best I could. I dreaded the following day, but somehow I managed to drag myself back.

The job we were expected to do digging these trenches by hand was incredible. There was a gang of about fifty of us lost souls who were expected to make it happen. Each section of trench was to be about fifty metres long, two metres wide, and well over three metres deep. A huge timber frame was laid out on the surface and you'd simply stand inside this perimeter and start digging out the soft, mobile sand.

On my first day digging in 'the frame' I got right into it as best I could, shovelling the endless sand out and over the edge, when an older man behind me said: "Hey mate, if you keep shovelling like that you'll do your back in and won't last an hour! … You've got to rest the shovel on your thigh and use the weight of your body to push the shovel forward … then using your thigh as a lever, use it to help you sling the sand on its way." I listened to what he said and it made sense, so I tried it. And by a simple change in technique, from one moment to the next I was able to shovel more sand and do it a lot more easily. I turned and thanked this considerate man for his help, but there was something familiar about him. *I know this guy from somewhere …* I thought. Then it struck me: this thoughtful guy had been our 'dunny man', the unfortunate one who in the light of the silvery moon had tumbled into our man-trap with a full can on his shoulders! I kept my mouth shut on this one and focused on getting through another day.

It is interesting how a person's station in life can dehumanise them to the point where you'd never approach the smelly 'dunny man' for a friendly chat; yet away from that unsavoury context, the same seemingly unapproachable person becomes human and helpful. I discovered that our kind and thoughtful 'dunny man' even had a name … it was Harry.

The interesting thing about this job was once you got used to it, down in those sewer trenches we were all equals. I came across doctors, lawyers, tattooed bikies, my old school mates, and even Leroy the station porter who once caught me for not having a train ticket – but we got on well in the trench. You name it and they were down there.

Communication breakdown

One day I found myself working beside a young guy around my age, and got talking to him as we shovelled that wretched sand. After a while he opened up enough to tell me he was the son of one of the top CEOs of Beecham, one of Australia's biggest companies at the time. "There's no way I'm going to tell my dad I've been reduced to this," he confided. "He doesn't understand … So I've got to get through this myself!"

Even in the most unexpected places I was beginning to notice things and question why our communications sometimes break down. I was still too inexperienced to ponder the complexities of this, but I did wonder why someone with a rich dad could end up so distressed and alone in a deep, cold hole. I can still hear his pitiful cries of anguish as he'd catch his bruised and lacerated knuckles while working. *That day I got an inkling that all the money in the world won't help if pride and stubbornness are blocking the way … someone has to reach out and make the first move.*

A lighter side

But there were lighter moments in the trenches too, for in order to survive and keep our wits about us we contrived our own ways of getting around Sid and laughing anyway. The fitter we got, the more confident we became and the more fun we had. Like the slaves of old, we composed and recited poems and songs and worked to them. I distinctly remember setting our own words to the spoken hit of the '60s, *Big Bad John*. Part of our words went: "The crack of whalers and the rush of sand, and all you could see was his tremblin' hand … "

Sid didn't seem to mind these shenanigans; as long as our shovels kept throwing that sand up and over the edge he was happy. He in turn was answerable to Bill O'Keefe, his invisible master who ran this heartless trade in human misery. Our focus was one of pure survival, and that cash at the end of the day.

I've been back to that foreshore once since then and stood on that sand where we destitute souls toiled under Sid's ever-scornful eye. I remember thinking quietly to myself: *none of what happened here would be allowed today.*

Working in other factories

Still steering clear of anything remotely associated with mathematics, for the next two years I earned my money working in a series of factories of a day, which allowed me to further my showbiz career of a night and a weekend. The first of these jobs was with the Bata Shoe Factory in Seaford. My task was to pick up shoes from a fast-moving line, two at a time, and place them in a very hot, narrow drying cabinet which had another fast-moving chain belt inside it to receive the shoes. The trick was not to burn your arms on the drying cabinet's sides while the rest of the shoes were building up behind you. It was like juggling fifty balls at once! It reminded me of a Charlie Chaplin movie I saw as a kid called *Modern Times*, where the machinery in the factory gets the better of him when he can't keep up with the nuts he has to tighten as they race past on the assembly line. In the end *he* gets caught up in the whole thing and becomes a part of the machinery.

Well, this is what almost happened to me.

One day that bloody red-hot drying cabinet was continually burning my arms; and the shoes on the conveyor belt had bunched up so badly they were spilling onto the floor; an alarm was sounding, which made me feel like a real idiot, as if I was wrecking the joint. The operation to which I was entrusted was totally out of control, and I hadn't a clue what was going on … and that bloody alarm just kept on buzzing! In the end I just stood back and looked at the jumbled mess I'd created. *This is one place*, I thought, *where I have absolutely no desire to climb through the ranks and be top dog*. Something told me: *if you want to get the best out of people you've got to support them and train them.* I picked up my jumper and just walked out of there.

The three other factories I worked in weren't much better. Flavel was a car part factory specialising in oil seals. Those days there were no computers, and car seals were all made by hydraulic press and a human operator. The idea was to put a little round metal frame in the metal mould first, then put a small cube of specially cured rubber on top of that, close the mould, then with heat-proof gloves place it gently in the press. You'd then pull the safety door down so you couldn't crush your hands, and 'cook' the seals for a prescribed time as you would a cake. During the summer months it was uncomfortably hot among all those hot moulds and presses. What's more, the place was full of acrid smoke because of the curing rubber. But the thing that sticks in my mind most was the nice guy I was working with.

It's the people you meet

He was a very dark and tall Indian Fijian with wide brown eyes and an infectious laugh. His story of being a 'Fijian Indian' fascinated me in itself and I was eager to learn more. Again, as we worked together in those trying circumstances of heat and smoke, my innocent, non-judgemental interest allowed him to open up and tell me how his ancestors came to settle in Fiji and how he came to be here in Australia. For someone who had yet to travel, this gentle man would take me away with him to strange and interesting places and I'd listen to him for hours. I found out that he was a taxi driver by night and took on this second job in the factory during the day to support his family; those who had joined him in Australia and those still living in Fiji. Sometimes we'd look at each other, helplessly standing there in that grimy smoke and stifling heat all covered in sweat, and simply burst out laughing at the unenviable situation we'd found ourselves in. Our spontaneous laughter said it all ... Then the timer would go off and we'd get back to our tedious work.

Then there was Vic Locaitus, our Lithuanian leading-hand, an imposingly tall man with a slanting scar on each cheek which he seemed to wear with pride. I wouldn't say Vic was a very talkative man, but I liked him because he always gave me the time of day.

It was his job to see that our bins were constantly topped-up with supplies and to generally supervise his section. When he did find time to pause for a quick chat, I enjoyed those few minutes of company with someone I respected. When I asked him how he got the scars on his cheeks he was a bit cagey and said a wild elephant got him when he was in Africa. I might have been young and gullible, but I didn't believe that! His wry smile gave him away anyway. In the end I did get the truth out of him (fencing badges of honour!). Over time I also gleaned a snippet here and a snippet there about his beloved country of Lithuania.

Years later I bumped into someone who'd also worked in this car part factory only to learn that Vic Locaitus had died, which saddened me. When you're young you don't think much about dying, and you believe that larger-than-life characters like Vic Locaitus would live forever.

The Jam Factory

The next factory I went to work in was the South Yarra Jam Factory, which hadn't changed much since it was built in 1858. The Jam Factory was originally established as the Victorian Brewery, but in 1876 it became the Victoria Preserving Company. I recall its red-brick structure was very big and foreboding, with hardly any interaction between its workers. Each Friday night you would pick up your pay from an expressionless pay clerk from behind a steel-mesh window as if you were just a number. It was soulless places like this that made me strive to do something better with my life.

The first job I was allocated in the Jam Factory was with old Toby, a semi-retired part timer who always dressed in overalls. He was in charge of stacking large tins of apple purée in the warehouse. When I say 'in charge', it was *me* Toby was in charge of. Because he was an older man, Toby was put on light duties. His job was to tap each large can with a little metal tool and listen to the noise it made. He knew if this sound rang true or not, for every once in a while a can would be put aside to be thrown out. Toby was a man of few words, apart from telling me where to stack the boxes. So after a couple of days working with a taciturn Toby and the monotonous tapping noises emanating from his baton bouncing around the warehouse, I began to wonder how long this would go on for.

I could see there was no way known Toby would – or could – strike up a conversation with me, so I began to tentatively ask him questions about what he did in his spare time. And boy did I strike gold! He told me he was part of a crew of volunteers on a coast-guard rescue vessel on Port Phillip Bay. And the more I asked him about it, the more he warmed to me and my questions. In time I was able to freely ask Toby how he spent his weekend, and did he go out on the boat? By making an effort to be interested in him, I was able to change the atmosphere in that dank, boring place and make life more pleasant for both of us.

Next I found myself in the canning section. Talk about occupational health and safety! This small-ish bare-boarded room was something else! I was involved in the first step of the operation; checking the empty cans. Their conveyor-track entered this first-floor room from a hole in the wall at least thirty feet high near the ceiling, then the open-ended cans snaked and rattled their way back and forth all the way down to waist level, where they were checked and sent on their way to the cannery. Imagine for a moment, hundreds of shiny, empty cans, all rattling their way down this two-hundred-metre winding raceway at the same time, their fiendish sound confined to this one small room. You couldn't hear yourself *think*, let alone speak! It was an endless cacophony of deafening noise.

During my brief stay in this hellhole I met Jacques.

Jacques was a young Frenchman on holidays in Australia. He was fairly tall with natural blonde hair and piercing blue eyes. He didn't speak a word of English, and my French consisted of "oui" and "bon". Not that this helped, for we spent the whole day yelling at each other over the deafening din of those rattling cans. But through our frustrated laughter, broken words and sounds, and our feeling of utter helplessness, we somehow managed to communicate with each other. I learned that he was on his way to New Caledonia to seek his fortune. I've often wondered how young Jacques went in his quest.

So meeting interesting people, especially people from interesting places around the world, was beginning to strike a chord with me; I'm not sure why, or where I picked this up, but for some reason I was becoming interested in international affairs. Although I'd hardly read anything in my life and had run away from school early, I clearly recall rushing to page three of *The Sun* newspaper when I was working in the glass factory to read what was going on in the world. One day I vividly remember reading about East Pakistan splitting from West Pakistan and becoming Bangladesh. Even at that age I could see that having two parts of the same country three thousand miles apart didn't make sense. In a column or so of plodding and thoughtful reading, I'd educate myself about these things – especially the awful things mankind can do to itself. And I've carried this interest with me to this day.

I always knew I was destined for bigger and better things, and these jobs I'd fallen into were nothing more than mind-expanding stepping stones as my 'career' moved forward. I met some wonderful, hard-working people in these so-called dead-end jobs who would probably spend their whole lives doing this kind of work as they struggled to manage their lives and support their families; and I learned a lot of valuable things about life from them. What I didn't realise at the time; *I was learning to relate to people from all walks of life and to never look down on anyone no matter what job they do - a life-long philosophy that's stood me in good stead as I've mingled and worked with all levels of society over the years.*

CHAPTER 10

Geoff Gion

It's interesting how I came to be a student at the prestigious Grosvenor Academy in the centre of Melbourne when I was digging sewer trenches by day twenty-five miles away in Carrum. I had just appeared on *New Faces*, Melbourne's well-known talent show of the time, as a very raw albeit 'promising' talent, singing – as I mentioned earlier – *Son Don't Go Near the Indians*, probably one of the worst songs ever written! Notwithstanding this, I befriended the winner of the evening and he saw the potential in me: "Why don't you come along to the Grosvenor Academy for some singing lessons from my teacher, Ian Field?" he said with genuine interest. I acted on this the following day.

Musical genius and heartfelt friend

It was at the Grosvenor Academy that I met Geoff Gion, the resident pianist. He was around my age, and could play anything from the classics to the Beatles and everything in between; he was a musical genius in every sense of the word. Through his unique musical prowess he could give the impression of a full orchestra and energise an entire musical. What's more, he was only twenty and already a music lecturer at Melbourne University.

Geoff and I hit it off from the moment we met. He laughed at all my jokes, appreciated my talent, and took me into his heart as a friend. He was the one who deftly arranged all my music to suit *my* voice and personality, and made me look like a star. Whenever I auditioned for a show, his arrangements would impress the musical director. Geoff and I were inseparable for the next three years – until fate dealt her cruel hand.

While all this was going on I continued with the Top Hat Review, for they were dependent on me and I couldn't let them down. To help with my performances, at the Grosvenor Academy I was learning to breath properly from the diaphragm, resonate my voice, and add polish to my performance. I took part in many musicals, such as: *The Music Man*; *Brigadoon*; *The Boy Friend*; *South Pacific*; and *My Fair Lady*. I felt I was moving in the right direction. What's more, I brought young Leanne and Mark to see me perform in *The Boy Friend*, the first live theatre show they'd ever seen; and *My Fair Lady* on the big screen. They sat there enthralled. Their young minds were learning how the arts can transport us to incredible places full of intrigue.

During my first year at the academy Geoff kept mentioning this 'Joe' friend of his. "You've got to meet my mate Joe," he'd say. Geoff had known Joe for years; they'd virtually grown up together and Joe was the singer in Geoff's band. One day I did meet the mysterious Joe; he was a bit like me in a lot of ways, for Joe was from a large family and working-class background. But unlike me, Joe was tall, blonde and handsome, whereas I was small and rather ordinary. He was a fabulous dancer, and I had two left feet. He had a wonderful 'natural' singing voice, whereas I had to work hard on my novelty musical comedy numbers which relied more on my personality than my voice. But most of all, Joe had charisma by the bucket-full. All he had to do was walk into a room and women would flock around him. And Geoff was the same; although he was a scrawny little guy who looked a bit like a combination of Bob Dylan and Woody Allen, the moment he sat down at a piano, magic happened and women would fast gather round. This was what I had to contend with, so I'd work hard on my acts to balance things up and have my own little pedestal of 'cleverness'. In spite of this, we saw ourselves as equals, and would have done anything to help each other.

All hell breaks loose

The twenty-five-mile drive all the way back to Seaford each night was beginning to take its toll on me. Once around midnight, I was driving home along a dark and isolated road with my radio and heater on, thinking of my nice warm bed, when all hell broke loose. The air was filled with crashing, wild bumping, and metallic noises … then everything was absolutely still.

I opened my eyes. A startled cow was staring at me through the window. It emitted a mournful moo and steam came out of its nostrils. Slowly I looked around, trying to take in this eerie blueish-black moonlit scene in. Then it dawned on me; I'd fallen asleep at the wheel! Shaking, I gingerly got out of my car to assess the situation. To my horror I could see that I'd careened across the road, miraculously missed any oncoming cars, and ploughed through the soft earth between two lampposts.

Gee, I thought, *that was close! I'll drive with the windows down and the heater off in future!* To the continued bewilderment of the cow, I unwrapped some barbed wire from the front fender of my damaged but still operational FB Holden, backed onto the road, and drove home to bed with the windows wide open.

Joe's new flatmate

A welcome solution to my dangerous nightly commutes came my way. At the time Joe was living in an old Edwardian share house in Kew and needed someone to flat with him to help pay the bills. I jumped at the opportunity, and made my first momentous move from the country to living in the Big Smoke! Even though this was my first experience at this, I slotted in well because of the independent way both our mothers had brought us up.

Our menu was pretty basic and I recall it clearly: chops or sausages with tinned green beans and boiled potatoes, always followed by tinned peaches and cream – but we ate well. Our washing machine shared the cooking area with us, and when it wasn't functioning as such we used it as a bench. When it was doing the washing we had a problem: it was made to be bolted to the floor but it wasn't. As a consequence, during the spin cycle we had to rush in and sit on it or it would do a thumping crab walk across the kitchen. But we took all this in our stride.

We'd practise hard, we'd play hard.

Joe and Geoff would use our all-purpose living room for band practice till the early hours of the morning, and we'd drink a lot in those days. Although I wasn't in the band, I'd join in the drinking, the banter and the fun. But deep down I didn't like the drinking.

When this wasn't going on, Geoff and I would be seriously putting in at the Grosvenor Academy. At the end of a night of lessons and rehearsals we'd always finish off skolling drinks at Hosie's Bar in Elizabeth Street. Then, well-charged, we'd race our cars back to Joe's around the Kew Boulevard at breakneck speed; it was a wonder we never ended up in the Yarra River. I shudder when I think of what we used to do.

Geoff and I had great fun with our relentless teasing of Joe for his 'Dutchiness', for he'd come to Australia when he was twelve and still had slight twangs of Dutch about him. When he didn't quite get something, which was often, we'd call him *Mr With It*. But nothing fazed Joe, and he'd give back as good as he got.

In time Joe met his ideal match in Nicky, and they got married with Geoff as their best man. While I was working for my friend Len Zenith in his electrical goods store, an expansive residence on top of the shop became available for rent, which became Joe and Nicky's home until they saved up a deposit for their own. But it was hard for Joe, Geoff and me to jettison our immature ways overnight, so Geoff and I tagged along, with me continuing the arrangement I'd had with Joe in our share house, only here it was Nicky who did the cooking. There was an old piano way down the back and we would play, drink and sing around it for hours.

During this period I introduced the likeable Dario Salpietro – my lifelong Aussie/Italian friend – to the group. Dario had progressed from working in his family's fruit shop in Frankston to being one of Channel 2's top cameramen. Born here of Sicilian extraction, Dario was the quintessential Italian-looking Aussie with a broad Australian accent, and he fitted in well.

In time, Nicky would be a modifying force on our group as Joe and she thought of raising a family; but it wasn't easy for her. Our behaviour was engrained and we thought our drinking and shenanigans would go on forever, as most people do at that age. We'd have fun with the odd seance and drinking games of 'bottles', where you had to speak in turn in 'multiples of seven' and skol a glass when you made a mistake; many was the night I never got past 'seven'.

There was a period when we'd play a friendly game of poker at least twice a week. We didn't bet much, just a few cents. One penalty we had if you lost was you had to eat a spoonful of tinned dog food. And of course it was a lot funnier when you were half sozzled. I can still see Geoff picking up the can of dog food after losing a hand and saying: "Let me read those ingredients again ... ", which was hilarious in itself for he was very funny and would milk each line for laughs.

"Come on! You've gotta eat it!" we'd chorus. But no one ever did ...

The Fishing Trip That Never Was

One night, my mind harking back to distant exploits, I talked the boys into going on an early morning fishing trip off the Mordialloc pier. I've always referred to this as 'The Fishing Trip That Never Was'.

"Wear old clothes," I told the guys. "We'll hire fishing gear and buy bait from the store when we get there."

I recall it was a Friday evening and we played cards well into the night to kill time before our early morning start. Around 2:00 am we decided to make a move. Nicky had long since gone to bed, and we were half-charged as usual.

While the others were sorting the cars out, Joe and I were skylarking around: "Ah, you're weak," I said, "you've got no hope of catching me!" Now Joe was a big, energetic guy full of pride and hated losing at anything, so I took off at speed down the middle of Malvern Road with Joe in hot pursuit. Right at that moment a cop car appeared from nowhere and screeched to a stop beside us. The cops jumped out and grabbed us.

"What the hell are you doing?!" they demanded.

"We're going fishing," I honestly replied.

"Going fishing are you?" one of them said. "Well, we've got news for you!" They bundled us into the back of the paddy wagon. Joe strongly resisted, but that only made matters worse. The back door slammed shut and away we sped to who knows where.

Bewildered criminals

It wasn't long before we pulled up at the Malvern police station behind the historic Malvern Town Hall. I wouldn't say we were blind drunk, but we'd had a few. Joe and I were unceremoniously marched round the back and thrown into a cold police cell.

"You can reflect on things and sleep it off for a while in here," said the copper, and he clanged the formidable door closed behind him. Joe's earnest protests of wanting to contact his pregnant wife fell on deaf ears. All we could do was laugh nervously, for neither of us had ever been in trouble with the police before. In the space of ten minutes we had gone from happily driving away on our fishing trip to being thrown into prison as bewildered criminals.

We spent an uncomfortable cold night in that horrible jail and were let out at 6:30 the following morning, charged with disorderly conduct. "You'll be advised on the date of your court case," the duty officer advised as he set us free. We ran the five kilometres home to get warm.

Geoff recalled later: "When we couldn't find you guys, we went back inside thinking you'd returned to get something … we couldn't understand it … you'd simply ran round the corner and disappeared into thin air!" When Joe and I finally staggered through the door like two dishevelled bums from Cannery Row, a heavily pregnant Nicky enquired of her husband: "Where the hell have you been?"

"You really don't want to know," said a contrite Joe. " … We've been in jail!"

We decide to defend ourselves

On reflection, Joe and I decided to defend ourselves in court, believing our minor misdemeanour certainly deserved a stern warning but did not warrant a criminal conviction. On the day of our court case we decided to at least look like paragons of innocence and we wore our best suits. The Justice of the Peace was an elderly fellow who had an air of fairness about him. The police prosecutor, however, looked a mean piece of work; a stern-faced, middle-aged officer.

The police prosecutor was the first called on to present his report, which he delivered in monotonous police-speak: "We first saw the two accused running down the middle of Malvern Road at 2:00 am, in hot pursuit of each other," he intoned. "'I'll get you!' yelled Kloprogge to Smale," declared the prosecutor, "and we called on them to stop." At this stage the prosecutor paused and looked at the Justice of the Peace: "On close inspection we noticed that the accused Smale had his fly open." There was a slight titter from the gallery, and the prosecutor continued with his report. When he had finished Joe and I were permitted to have our say.

I was first. I respectfully explained that we hadn't meant any harm, that we were really about to go on an early-morning fishing trip, and that I'd challenged Joe to a harmless race and that's all it was. The Justice of the Peace looked over the top of his glasses and asked: "And what about your open fly?" This time the gallery laughter was audible, and the JP had to ask for order.

"I had my old fishing pants on," I said. "The zip was broken so I had it done up with a safety pin, but that burst open too!" This time the laughter was loud and unrestrained; they were enjoying this. The JP banged his gavel. He then invited Joe to the stand. Joe came across more serious than I did, and stated the fact that we were normal law-abiding citizens who were doing nothing more than having a bit of harmless fun that didn't hurt anybody.

The Judge didn't take long with his deliberation, and dismissed the case. We'd won! Joe and I felt pretty pleased with our legalistic efforts, and walked away without any black marks to our names. But there was still one more fateful twist to all of this.

But wait, there's more!

A few days after my brush with the law, another Italian friend of mine, and a mate of Dario's, Alfonso, was pulled over for a routine check by the police right in the same area that Joe and I had been arrested. Alfonso panicked, for his licence had recently run out and he was driving *my* car – which I'd lent him for a day to get him out of trouble.

"Licence please," said the young constable, eager to impress the sergeant standing beside him.

"I'm sorry, sir," said the nervous Alfonso, "I've left it at home."

"What's your name?" asked the officer sternly.

Now here I've got to tell you this guy was of swarthy southern Italian heritage, and he looked like someone straight out of *The Godfather*; he had nothing whatsoever visually in common with the owner of the car, Laurie Smale of British lineage. With nowhere to go and a possible jail term staring him in the face, Alfonso spotted one of Geoff Gion's musical arrangements sitting in the car with the name *Laurie Smale* written on the bottom of it.

"Laurie Smale!" said Alfonso with as much confidence as he could muster; the officer wrote this down.

"Please present your licence to the Malvern police station within the next seven days," he said, and he let Alfonso off with a severe caution to always carry it with him from then on.

When Alfonso brought my car back the next day he said, "I'm sorry mate, but the cops pulled me over and I had to give them your name … you have to show your licence at the Malvern police station within the next week."

"What!" I said with horror. "If the cops who pulled you over are the same ones who grabbed me and Joe, they'll know the difference between me and you!" After my recent brush with the law I was not interested in any more trouble.

"You'll just have to do it," said Alfonso. "They could have been different cops?"

I nodded, but with great misgivings.

The next day I parked my car a good block away from the police station just in case we were noticed together. I took a deep breath and pushed open the front door of the police station, leaving Alfonso to sweat it out behind a big oak tree – we both had a tremendous stake in the outcome of this.

Once inside, the policeman who had arrested me walked out from behind a partition and said, "Can I help you?" And then he recognised me.

"Back again …" he said, expecting some sort of complication.

I jumped in before he could continue: "This is nothing to do with the other night," I said. "I was stopped for a routine check the other day and have to present my licence. And anyway …" I added with all the nonchalance I could muster, "my mate and I were larking around a bit the other night and there are no hard feelings."

"That's fair enough," the young constable said.

I handed him my licence. He completed and stamped the required paperwork and returned my licence to me. The gods were with us this day; he obviously *wasn't* the young officer who had pulled Alfonso over for the routine check.

"Hope I don't see you soon," I quipped as I made a beeline for the door.

When I came out into the fresh, free air, Alfonso was still sweating behind the tree where I'd left him … there had been a lot riding on the outcome of this meeting.

Geoff drops in one wintry night with my music

One stormy night Geoff arrived at our place above the shop with an arrangement he'd written especially for an important audition I was preparing for. All I had to do was hand this to the musical director and I'd feel at home. We retired to our old upright piano in the back room where Geoff familiarised me with what he'd done by running me through the piece a few times till I got it right. He was magic, and always made me look and sound good. After that we spent a few hours drinking round the piano, playing and singing creative nonsense, which seems a lot funnier when you're half shot. But in the light of day there was often some good stuff in there.

Around one in the morning we bid each other goodnight and Geoff drove off into the wind and rain. Back in my room I was so happy about my arrangement, for only Geoff understood me and my strengths and knew how to transcribe them into music and make me shine. I curled up in bed feeling pretty good about the world and the friends I had.

But that was the last time I was to hear my dear friend Geoff's voice; and it was the last time we would be blessed with his presence.

The following morning I was up at my usual 6:00 am about to do a bit of guitar practice when something on the radio brought me up with a start: I heard the newsreader clearly saying, "A twenty-two-year-old man, Geoffrey Gion, was killed early this morning when his car hit a tree in Mont Albert Road … " The rest was a blur, for I just sat there absolutely numb.

Then the incredible weight of it hit me. "Geoff … killed?!" I said, finding it hard to comprehend. I got up and burst into Joe and

Nicky's room. "Geoff's been killed in a car accident!" I yelled. Joe was instantly out of bed, shaking and on the verge of crying ... hoping it was just a very sick joke.

"I just heard it on the radio!" I said, to get him to see it was real and that *no one* would joke about his friend's death.

We ran across the road to the phone box, to the sound of Joe's heartwrenching sobs and him saying over and over, "It can't be ... It can't be ... not Geoff! ... ", on the slim hope I'd heard wrong. Stifling his sobs and shaking like a leaf, Joe dialled triple '0' and spoke to someone. He then went silent and hung up the phone.

"It's true," he softly said. From that instant our lives changed forever. Our beloved Geoff was no more.

Overnight I'd lost a kindred spirit, a part of my soul, and it was years before I found it again. Without Geoff to shore me up I was now living in a void and on my own again. When it came to him helping me, nothing had ever been too much trouble. It took me a long time to stand on my own two feet and feel safe about who I was once more.

One thing is for sure: in our hearts Geoff will stay forever young.

However, there is a sobering lesson in Geoff's sad and untimely passing; we did drink a lot. From that day on I've only ever had alcohol in moderation.

Joe and I are now in our seventies, still the best of friends, and often mention our forever-youthful friend Geoff. And both of us regularly travel along Mont Albert Road, which is noted for its magnificent elm trees. Recently I said to Joe, "Do you know what tree Geoff hit?"

He said, "No."

"I don't know either," I said, and we left it at that.

A victim of circumstances

I was just going about my life doing the everyday things we all do when, on three separate occasions and relating to the *same* people,

I was accused of wrongdoing. The absolute truth was, in spite of what things *looked like*, there were three different perpetrators and I was totally innocent in each case – I was determined to clear my name.

In these types of situations all we can do is walk tall and be true to ourselves, for most times the truth will come out in the end. And even if it doesn't, even if that circumstantial evidence doggedly remains, keep walking tall because you know *who* you are and *what* your true values are. ***You must stand up for your integrity and the truth as you know it to be. You must not allow other people's wrongdoings to brand you as something you're not.***

In the first instance, when I was twenty-one, I went to work for Len Zenith, a very close friend of mine, in his electrical appliance and whitegoods store. I met Len in the Top Hat Review, which was always ticking along in the background. Len enjoyed singing too, but what I admired about Len was he dragged me out of those dead-end jobs and gave me employment where I'd be wearing a suit and stepping up in life! As Len wasn't much older than me (he was thirty-five), he started off as the last father figure in my life, but soon grew into being my friend. I thought he was a wonderful person and would do anything for him.

One thing I did have a few pangs about was, because I'd be in a suit, would there be any mathematics or algebra in this job? This was my dark secret that not even Len could know about and I'd have to get around by myself. Lucky for me I'd never had a problem with counting and dealing with money, for as far as my mind was concerned, this has nothing whatsoever to do with mathematics (which of course it does). My mind had never made the arithmetical connection with the basic act of spending money to old Ludge's maths class, so handling money in Len's shop was no problem to me and I felt safe. Now I could sleep peacefully. Selling things and dealing with money would be straightforward for me. It would only be when I had to deal with percentages and fractions years down the track that I'd run into a brick wall. But I wasn't to know that. For now, all would be fine, for all I had to do was sell things as per their price, or if a deal needed to be done I could get advice. And that's what I did. As I gained more and more product knowledge, I began to combine the skills I'd been honing making friends and chatting to people in the various jobs I'd had, and it worked its magic with these folk too! I did have one bit of extra pressure though; Len's business partner Jack was ambivalent about the wisdom of employing me, so with him I had something to prove.

It certainly was a different world to what I was used to, although Old Bill Menzies had taught me to be polite and how to serve people when they came into the junkyard, so that helped. What I really liked about my new job environment was there was no Sid the slave master lording it over me; there was no incessant heat and fumes; and there was no mathematics that I could see! All I had to do was dress up nicely, be friendly to people, and help them to get what they want. This was my simple formula and I began to sell things.

One day when Len and Jack were out of the store something untoward happened that I was completely unaware of. Entrusted to be left in charge of the store as I often was, this day Grant Chandler, a regular representative and associate of Len's, called and made himself at home behind the front desk. When I'd finished with the customer I was talking to I came over and said hello. I now know that this unscrupulous individual took advantage of my trusting, boyish naïvety by saying, "How's about going to the kitchen and getting me a cup of coffee?", which I duly did; anything to please Len and Jack for entrusting me to run the store all by myself. When I reflect back on this incident, Grant Chandler didn't hang around for long after drinking his coffee and quickly went on his way.

A week later, while reconciling the week's takings, Jack said to me: "Where's the two hundred dollars that's missing from the till?" I stood there flabbergasted that he would even *think* I had anything to do with such a thing. "I don't know," I simply said. "I didn't take it."

What really hurt me was Len was sitting beside him watching all this, but I knew deep down he really believed me. My mind was racing … then I remembered Grant Chandler's sly visit.

"Hey, Grant Chandler came in when you two were out the other day and got me to make him a cup of coffee … and he was sitting behind the desk … he could have taken it!"

"Look," said Jack, "you were in charge of the store and the money's gone." Jack deliberately left that thought to linger in the air. I knew I wasn't guilty and was determined to have the last word, "Well, I didn't do it." But as it was my inexperienced word against the familiar personage of this respected representative, a black cloud of mistrust was left looming above my name.

When I thoughtfully reflect on the situation, I continued working in Len's store for another two years and I don't recall Grant Chandler ever visiting the shop again.

About three weeks later I'd been tasked with delivering a television set to a local customer. I found no one in attendance so I returned it to the store. As parking was always a challenge at the back of the store, I parked the van in the driveway and rushed inside to do the paperwork; leaving the back of the van open with the TV set still in it. I do remember seeing a couple of shifty characters out of the corner of my eye standing near a big furniture truck a couple of doors down the road. *I wonder*, I thought, *will the TV be all right sitting in the open van? … I'll race in quickly so it should be okay.* And I tore off inside and did my paperwork.

Fully aware of the tenuous situation I'd put myself into, I was back at that van in five minutes flat. But the TV set was gone. I made a quick calculation that within the time span available, it could only have been those two shady characters who were now gone from sight. I guess in hindsight I should have gone into the house and confronted them for they wouldn't have had time to hide the TV set properly, but there were two of them and one of me – and they were twice my size! Instead I rushed inside and blurted out to Jack, "Someone's just stole the TV set out of the van!"

"Yeah?" he said sarcastically, "which of your mates' houses is it sitting in now?" That Jack could distrust me for a second time wounded me terribly.

"But there were two shifty guys out there near the Bamford's furniture van and they must have stolen it!" I plaintively explained. My heartfelt protestations fell on deaf ears for Jack's mind was already made up. I was a habitual thief. Thankfully Len stood by me and believed my story. But the fact was, I now had two black marks against my name and reputation, with next to no defence that I wasn't guilty.

Now you're going to find the next part of the story hard to believe: about a year after these happenings, Len and his family decided on a sea-change, so they shut up shop and moved to Hobart in Tasmania. I was still only twenty-two and at a bit of a loose end with my life, so I decided to join them for a two-week holiday before returning to Melbourne. Being on a limited budget, the best way for me to do this was to share a room in a boarding house with a guy who had his eye on one of Len's daughters. Now I didn't know Tom that well, but he seemed friendly enough.

Towards the end of my holiday I'd almost run out of money and had to watch every cent, to the point of conserving a dollar in the pocket of my coat hanging behind the door for a homemade pie that night for dinner. So this night, after some job hunting around Hobart and very much looking forward to that pie, when I went to get that dollar note I'd carefully tucked away, it was gone.

That's funny, I thought, *I specifically remember putting that dollar in my coat pocket.* Instinctively, I opened the door and looked out into the empty corridor. The door opposite was slightly ajar, and a young man was peering out with a furtive look in his eye. The scene reminded me of those shady fellows standing near the furniture van who I strongly suspected of filching that TV set … He quickly pulled the door closed.

What to do in this case? *It's only a dollar*, I thought, *maybe I didn't put it in there and I'm getting mixed up with something else I did.* So I let the matter rest, but it was still pretty perplexing, for I went to bed without the comfort of having eaten that nice meat pie.

When Tom got home that night from his part-time job as a butcher, we were both relaxing on our beds when he said to me, "What have you done with my money?"

"What?" I said, astonished. "What do you mean … I haven't touched your money."

"There was a hundred and fifty dollars in my bankbook and it's gone! … So, what have you done with it?" he repeated. All I could do was say I hadn't touched it.

"Sure you haven't," said Tom cynically.

"I haven't," I pleaded. Then I remembered the mysterious disappearance of my precious dollar and the strange guy I'd seen peeking guiltily through his door.

"Hey, I know who's taken it," I said. "Someone pinched a dollar from my coat pocket too! I saw a suspicious guy looking through the door opposite us." But Tom was having none of it for he'd no doubt got wind of my two other supposed thieving episodes and this proved that what he'd heard was true. My heart sank, for I knew that Tom's version of events would get back to Len and there was nothing I could do about it.

Well, actually there *was* something I could do – and I *did* it. I wrote a letter to Len spelling out that on each of these three occasions I was the *innocent* bunny in the crosshairs to be taken advantage of and blamed for something I didn't do. All three scenarios pointed squarely at me as the unmistakable guilty party.

"My only defence to this overwhelming circumstantial evidence," I told Len, "is to reiterate that I am in fact the honest person you have always believed me to be … I write this letter to help you understand that *I* was the *victim* and *not* the perpetrator in all three of these events. The only common factor in all these unrelated happenings was *me*, the *innocent* victim!"

If some unfair thing like this ever happens to you, don't just leave it because it can affect your view of you and who you are in a permanent way. At least do what I try to do and never leave things undone; I always do my best to set things straight. Only then can I move on, learning more and more about who I am, my values, and what makes me tick.

Connection from the past

One remarkable interlude happened while I was working at Len Zenith's home appliance store; I was twenty-two at the time. Every other day, two young girls a bit younger than me walked past the shop and warmly smiled at me. Naturally I'd warmly smile back, and I felt a certain attraction there. This went on for quite a few months. One day I decided to check out a particular address two streets away from the store that my mother had mentioned every now and then for years. This address had meant something very personal to me but I'd never had the daring spirit to go there. So after a year or so, I plucked up the courage to venture there and I knocked on the door.

To my great surprise, the two pretty girls I'd been exchanging smiles with for six months opened the door:

"What? … You!" they exclaimed. I said, "I think you're my cousins."

"Hey, mum!" they yelled over their shoulder, "One of our cousins is here!" And my Auntie Gwenda appeared, my father's sister, a person I was looking at for the first time in my life! I did have a picture of my dad in his army uniform and she looked just like him.

And what a joyous reunion it was! Auntie Gwenda made this long-lost cousin very welcome, and introduced me to my three new first cousins, for the girls had a brother. I spent most of that summer with them at the local swimming pool. I even had the privilege of meeting my dad's mother, Grandma Ethel, for the first time before she died – that's pretty special. All linked to Ken Smale, the long-lost cousin I'd met after my much later Donald trip.

I'd heard my mum mention these people over the years but they'd meant little to me, but now I could see they're directly related to my dad. This chance, incredible interlude in my life answered many of the questions of my extended family that I'd often wondered about.

Many years later I was to discover much more about my family history and build on this.

Time passes you by

If we can fast-forward thirty-five years for a moment: I was once driving down High Street Road in Glen Iris with my eleven-year-old son when I saw an Aintree Road sign to our left.

"Just a minute Rich," I said. "I want you to meet someone."

I turned and pulled up outside the little red brick house and saw the door I'd gingerly knocked on all those years ago. I walked up the same garden path again and rang the bell. An elderly lady answered the door. I wasn't sure … "Auntie Gwen?" I tentatively enquired.

"She died twenty years ago," said the lady in a dismissive sort of way. I was stunned, for I'd expected things to have remained just as they were when I first met them all when I was twenty two. Still a bit shocked, I thanked her and got back in the car. "My father's sister used to live there," I said to Richard, who must have wondered what was going on. We drove on home as if we'd never stopped.

CHAPTER 11

Faint heart doesn't win fair lady

Apart from my painful unrequited love with Pat Merton in primary school and one or two of the girls in the glass factory, I really was a living example of the old adage, "Faint heart never won fair lady". But ever the optimist, I was always hopeful I'd find someone.

The work experience girl

One day this gorgeous fifteen-year-old girl walked into the glass factory while we were working, and I instantly fell in love. Her name was Denise. To my eyes she was petite, blonde, and made in heaven. She was going to get some work experience over the holidays.

One lunchtime I plucked up the courage to ask her out to the pictures, and to my absolute surprise she said yes. I met her at the Chelsea picture theatre the following Saturday for the midday matinee. The movie I chose to suitably impress this young damsel was *The Lone Ranger Rides Again*. After about an hour of sitting silently watching the Lone Ranger's heroic exploits against the baddies with his Native American sidekick Tonto, without warning I threw my arm uncomfortably over her shoulder and left it there like a dead branch for the rest of the movie. I then took her home on the train, and that was that.

After her stay at the glass factory, our 'relationship' just seemed to fizzle out. Maybe my incessant talk about racing bikes had something to do with it? Who knows …

The landlady's daughter

By the time I was seventeen, I had been living in a boarding house for a few weeks and had my eye on the landlady's good-looking brunette daughter Cyndy – and apparently she had her eye on me! One day, completely out of the blue, she said, "Do you want to go down the beach with me?"

"Okay," I said, feeling happy yet slightly uncomfortable. When we arrived near the water she said, "Let's go up among the dunes where it's not so windy." I nodded and we headed inland, but my habitual panic began to set in. *What am I supposed to do?* I thought.

When we'd found a nice secluded place among the dunes, she lay her beautiful body down on her towel before me. I lay down beside her. She had her eyes closed with the sun shining on her enticing face, waiting … waiting for me to whisper nice things to her, waiting for me to do something gentle, even a soft kiss on the cheek … but … nothing! Not a sweet, gentle skerrick of a thing did I do. I was totally humiliated, and we walked back home without a word.

I left that boarding house soon after, for I could not bear to face her or the shame and weakness of it all anymore. I also let this confidence-shattering experience solidify my faulty notion that my love-shyness was an innate part of who I am and how I will always be.

But nothing is going to happen unless you make it happen!

Donella the dancer

By the age of nineteen I'd moved on to the Grosvenor Academy, where I was doing advanced singing lessons and learning a higher level of stagecraft. And there were lots of nice girls there, such as Donella the dancer, who happened to live way out in the back blocks of Springvale, about half way to my distant home in Seaford. *Great*, I thought, *I'll contrive ways to give her a lift home!* So I set about devising a foolproof strategy where there could be a bit of romance as well.

One night after rehearsals at the Grosvenor Academy, the plan was I'd give Donella a lift to her place on my way home to Seaford. But I had additional things in mind. I'd heard that girls liked a new drink called 'screwdriver', so I bought six cans of it the day before. That evening I carefully laid the cans in a drink cooler and packed them with ice, so they'd remain nice and cool while we were rehearsing. My intention was to pull over somewhere on the long trek home, offer Donella an enticing drink of screwdriver, then we'd chat away together ... and, well, who knows? That was my carefully laid plan.

The night started off perfectly. We finished rehearsals and home we drove, with those screwdrivers sitting enticingly on the back seat of the car, covered with a towel and beckoning me to speak up. Donella and I chatted about this, that and the other, and the miles went by.

Before I knew it we were approaching her street. I pulled over a few houses down from her place and said: "Do you want a drink?"

"No, I'll be right," she said. She got out, thanked me for the lift, and went on her way. "No problem," I said, and headed for home ... *To hell with it*, I thought, *I'll share them with my mates.*

If you wait, wait, wait, she'll simply fade away

A year or so later there was another girl at the Grosvenor Academy who attracted my attention because she was simply a nice person who happened to be beautiful and happened to be French. Her name was Adele. All I know was, I genuinely was attracted to her as a person, for she laughed a lot around me and had a captivating smile. But I thought that she was a cut above me, and my background wouldn't match hers. All she knew of me is what she saw in my talents and personality at the Academy. She was a primary school teacher and I was digging sewers. She was highly educated and I was yet to go back to school.

I took her out for coffees and even went on a picnic with her to the beach. But the gorgeous Adele never joined us on our boozing sprees and was totally unaware they happened; I don't even think she drank. One thing I was acutely aware of: she only had eyes for me, and I was beginning to feel the same way about her, yet I was incapable of doing anything about it and our relationship remained painfully platonic … it was a case of the embarrassing 'sand dune' episode repeating itself. This unrequited relationship was also doomed to end because of my acute love-shyness and my obsession with leaving my mark on the world in compensation.

Three years later, and all decked out in my bright yellow oversized wet-weather gear, I was riding my bright red Vespa along Commercial Road South Yarra, returning from an important Australia Post delivery, when a flash new car pulled up beside me at the lights. Instinctively I turned my head – and my heart skipped a beat. There, sitting in the passenger seat not two feet from me, was Adele. Mercifully she couldn't see me because of my helmet. The man beside her was in a business suit, overweight, and looked rather stern. He seemed to be lecturing her. I wondered if she was happy.

The *big star* that I had told her I was going to be was sitting right beside her as a glorified telegram boy. I was relieved when their car pulled away.

My first steady girlfriend

Then there was Alicia, my first steady girlfriend whom I met at a party when I was twenty-four and she was seventeen. Or I should say that she met me, for Alicia was the one with the forward personality and all the confidence. When it was time to go, she was the one who threw her arms around me and gave me a kiss, which neatly circumvented my ingrained shyness and I warmly responded in kind.

The notion of me not having confidence was hard for anyone to comprehend because at the time I was both running and performing in The Top Hat Review. But because of Alicia's outward confidence she brought out a similar confidence in me, so my fears and shyness in breaking the ice with the opposite sex remained hidden. And that's how it stayed. Although we were together as a loving couple for eight years, she never got to know the anxiety-ridden Laurie who still had a lifetime of inner fears to contend with; she never got to know about my constant fear of being found out for being an uneducated fraud; and she would never know the deep depression I fell into when she was gone.

Sadly our relationship was doomed for I was incurably star-struck and dreamed only of proving myself to the world as a well-known celebrity performing to my adoring fans before the big lights. How sad. Yet Alicia understood this 'showbiz' thing about me and supported me with it. I guess she thought in time I would simply grow out of it. She was there at every show, she was there at every television performance, year after year. She was a very special person.

Although she doggedly considered herself an Australian, her parents were World War II Polish immigrants who welcomed me into their family as a son, and a future son-in-law. Twice a week I would spend the evening with her at her parents' or her sister Maria's place enjoying their warm Polish hospitality and their delicious food. And it was simply accepted that one day I would become a part of the family.

Alicia got to know all of my post-office 'family' and my Italian friends and associates, and became accepting of all this too. But I'd always said to everyone (including Alicia) that "I was never going to get married". She probably didn't believe this as a concrete declaration. The sad, misguided thing was, I was already married to my illusory dream of being a famous entertainer.

One painful day I simply walked away from Alicia and all of the above, sincerely believing I was doing the right thing for everybody. I was off to London – to be a Big Star. My justification was that a life of living in hotel rooms in exchange for footlight fame wouldn't be fair on anybody – least of all Alicia. And there's probably real truth in this, for a decade later, after years of lonely travel and shows, I finally saw the light before this destructive obsession destroyed all possibility of me ever being happy with someone.

Thankfully, a few years after this, I heard that Alicia had found lasting happiness, which lightened the heavy burden of guilt I'd had to carry for the pain I must have caused her. I will always be grateful to Alicia for her gift of opening a refreshing window of love and stability in my life. But there's one thing left to say on this: *I can't undo what's been done in the past through ignorance and misguided thinking, but I can learn valuable lessons from it. I can go onward a more insightful and aware person, for there are now others in my life I have to keep in mind and look out for. I can move forward understanding why, and forgive myself.*

CHAPTER 12

The post office

When I got back from my holiday in Tassie I was broke and desperately needed a job. I picked one up at the South Yarra Post Office delivering parcels and telegrams on a zippy red motor scooter (the one I was riding when I saw Adele). I was to feel at home there for the next seven years. I steadily progressed to telegram clerk then on to being a postman – a respected position in society in those days, and I loved it.

I was twenty-four when I started, and was much older than the fifteen-year-olds who made up the rest of the telegram boys. And it wasn't long before I was put in charge and made Telegram Clerk. Right up to the mid 1970s telegrams were the way an important message was delivered, and the boys all wore a smart uniform and rode a big red Post Master General (PMG) bicycle. Their bicycles were simply thrown into the bike shed at the end of each day and received no maintenance. So, like doing the dirty job of washing the tools in the concrete gang, I took it upon myself to reorganise the bike shed from top to bottom so finding a bicycle that worked wasn't such a haphazard affair. Not only did the Post Master appreciate having a functional bicycle shed where the bikes were maintained, the telegram boys did too.

Something interesting happened to my restricted thinking while working in the role of Telegram Clerk.

The lost boys

For most of my life, all of my focus had been on *me* and *my* fears, and how *I* was going to survive. But these young kids discerned none of this; all they saw was a confident young man in charge of them, who they looked up to and respected. A bit like Vic Locaitus was to me in that car part factory. But I soon discovered that leadership *wasn't all about me* and my problems at all, for these young kids had their own worries, their own fears, and their own concerns about how to survive. Pretty soon I learned that most of these boys came from challenging situations and broken homes, and that working at the post office in their uniforms gave them a certain feeling of importance and purpose in their lives.

In time they grew to trust me and shared things with me they'd never shared with anyone else before, and I did my best to steer them onto a different path. For example, one young lad, who ended up being a respected worker with Australia Post for more than twenty years, confided in me that he and his mates would often roll people in the park and rob them. I'm really proud of how this guy turned his life around – if he gets to read this he'll know who he is.

Bobby Edwards

Then there was Bobby Edwards. Now initially Bobby didn't work at the post office but most of his mates did. Consequently, he'd always be hanging around there, and he gravitated towards me as an older person he could talk to. One day as I was returning to the back of the post office on my nippy little Vespa, Bobby jumped from behind a tree and blurted out: "Can you get me a job?"

Now this is funny; through their own network these kids preferred to ask *me* for a job rather than using the normal channel via the Post Master. But that was fine; by then I had a warm relationship with the PM because I'd sorted out the horrible mess of the bike shed, and I somehow knew how to manage the telegram boys to be dedicated and reliable.

"I'll see what I can do," I said to Bobby. "Come and see me tomorrow."

The next day Bobby was standing patiently beside the tree, knowing I'd come out when I could. As soon as I got the nod from the PM that he was willing to give Bobby a go, I wandered out the back to find him. When I did I simply said, "You've got a job, and I've vouched for you. Come in tomorrow at eight o'clock and we'll fit you out with a uniform." The smile of relief on his face said it all.

Bobby was waiting on the doorstep bright and early the following morning, eager to get started. He turned out to be a model worker and didn't let me down. Although Bobby was always smiling and laughed readily at my jokes, I detected a sad air about him and wondered what it meant.

One day he opened up and told me what he went home to of a night – and more. His father was a drunkard and yelled at him and treated him badly. He hated living there because the house had no love in it and the place was a mess.

"Is your mother there with you?" I asked.

"No, she died in my arms of an asthma attack two years ago."

There wasn't much I could say to that … after a while I said, "What about brothers and sisters?"

"I had a sister who was very close to me," Bobby said sadly, "but last year she died of the same thing while I held her too."

It took me a while to take in the enormity of what this fifteen year old had just told me. When I did find my voice I said, "Tell me about your mum."

Bobby told me what a loving, caring person she was, and how much he missed her. He went on to tell me that his mum's favourite song was Nat King Cole's *Lazy-Hazy-Crazy Days of Summer*. I thought to myself, *it must be awful to go home to all this sadness and negativity every night; what can I do to bring a bit of sunshine into his life?*

I thought carefully, then said, "Bobby, I don't know the reasons why your dad's an alcoholic and treats you badly, but there's something *you* can do: you have to live in that place too, so why don't you surprise your dad and take it on yourself to clean up the front yard; then scrounge a few flowers from the neighbours and plant them – then see what happens."

The following Monday Bobby came up to me and said, "Hey, I did what you said to the garden and my dad was rapt! And he actually said nice things to me!"

"That's great," I said. "Make it your responsibility to look after it, for that will make you feel good too."

Not long after this I said to Bobby, "How would you like to help me out in a bit of a show I do? I need some help carrying a few things."

"Sure," he said.

"Great! It's next Friday night so keep it free!" Little did he know that it was the full-length Top Hat Review I've been telling you about. We were always in need of extras to be in skits, ensembles, and chorus work, so we'd get unsuspecting participants in by them 'helping to carry the bags' first. In time I had all the telegram boys doing something in the show. But Bobby Edwards was the first of these 'budding entertainers' to be roped in.

Bobby joins the show

David Hinson (of 'the camel act' fame) and I picked Bobby up after work and away we went to entertain the folk at the Mission for Seamen near Melbourne's docklands. Now this venue had a full-sized theatre and stage to perform on, and we'd normally play to three or four hundred seamen from all over the world, many of whom couldn't speak a word of English. But that didn't seem to matter, for we had a great variety of acts, including juggling, magic, song and dance, and visual comedy. Bobby Edwards couldn't believe his eyes – he had never been involved in anything like this before. Straight off we had him helping backstage with props and equipment, and he was beaming. So I struck while the iron was hot: "How would you like to join us in the show and be in some crowd scenes, sing in the chorus, be in some sketches … ?"

"That'd be great!" he said. And so Bobby Edwards became a valuable part of the Top Hat Review for the next four years, and I proudly watched him come out of his shell and grow; both as a person and in confidence.

A precious message

A few weeks after this I received a letter addressed to me at the post office. It was from Bobby Edwards. I have long since lost this precious hand-written message, but I clearly remember the gist of it expressing his heartfelt thanks; and I vividly remember the opening: "This is the first letter I have ever written to anyone." And the ending: "Thank you Laurie, you taught me how to smile again."

Our legendary Christmas parties

But we're not leaving the South Yarra Post Office just yet as there are still some interesting things to share. One of which was the legendary Christmas parties I helped to instigate. These Christmas extravaganzas were spurred on by the first Christmas get-together I experienced with the post office staff; a pretty modest affair at the local hotel on the next corner. It didn't amount to much; a few plates of sandwiches on a bare wooden trestle and that was it. Everyone got their own drinks and just stood around talking in their own little groups. It was truly boring. After an hour or so people just wandered off home.

Over the next few weeks an ambitious thought began to manifest in my mind: *there's a lot of space in that big room at the hotel: for the Christmas party next year how'd it be to put on a specially customised show there with skits about the post office? I could certainly drum up the talent and organise it!* My musings went on … *We could probably get that big room for nothing if I promised the publican a crowd of a hundred people.* I honestly didn't see a problem with this for we'd done it all before with the Top Hat Review. I decided to choose the right time and run the idea past Geoff Cloke, the Post Master.

When I did catch his ear he thought it was a great idea: "But who's going to organise all this?" he queried. I guess he was afraid it might all fall on him.

"Don't worry, I've already approached the publican and he's amenable to it; people would buy their own drinks and give us five dollars each to cover the cost of the finger food. I'll look after everything else."

"Done!" he said. "I'll leave it all to you. You certainly know how to make things happen!"

Sowing the seeds of success

For the rest of the year all I had to do was keep my eyes open for suitable sketch material and get those involved enthusiastic about the project, with plenty of time for rehearsals to build up their confidence. About two months out we seriously started working on it, and to generate the numbers I'd promised the publican, I sent out an enticing invitation to the four other Post Masters of our district and all their staffs. This paid off. On the night one hundred and fifty people turned up, including our two district inspectors from Head Office!

There was no turning back now, and the pressure was on for me to deliver the goods! As self-appointed 'producer' of this production, my biggest challenge was half of these guys had never done anything like this before and I had to keep shoring their confidence up. In the end, their inexperience and their mistakes made the whole thing even funnier. We even had a section on ballet dancing with all the telegram boys and a couple of the posties decked out in ballet dresses and football boots doing their version of Swan Lake, which we called

Swamp Lake, to the music *Dance of the Sugar Plum Fairy*. And the skits sending up their fellow workers and Australia Post identities were absolutely hilarious; no one was in any doubt about who the characters were meant to be. Even the cleaning lady, Mrs Hartnett, made a stunning appearance!

The verdict on the evening was unanimous: "It was absolutely wonderful and we'd do it again next year!" And that's exactly what happened. In fact, it went on for the next *four* years, ending only when it was time for me to move on in my life. I was learning that *when a group works enthusiastically together it's amazing what can be achieved.*

I become a postman

Staying with the post office, after two years of managing the telegram delivery section I moved into an entirely different world … I became a postman. As I mentioned earlier, in the 1970s a uniformed postman, like a station master or a bank manager, was a highly respected person in society. In fact, many of my customers yearned for a snippet of conversation whenever my presence was heralded by the friendly sound of my whistle. I'd talk to them about the weather, the health of their cat and any other happenings in their lives. But I had to keep my eye on the clock for my run took in four large suburban blocks with over eight hundred customers eagerly waiting for the postie to brighten their day with a letter and a bit of a chat. Some even invited me in for a cup of tea or a nice cool drink.

For many of the older folk, the friendly postie was their only link with the outside world. But all of this presented its own pitfalls, for if I stopped to have a cup of tea or fifteen-minute chat with everyone I'd never get home! So I had to devise some clever strategies for how to extricate myself from a conversation without hurting the other person, unlike listening to Lino tell his stories in the glass factory for hours, or travelling the world with Sandy the Scotsman while we were trowelling the concrete, where time wasn't that critical.

So after sincerely asking after Tiddles the cat and commenting on how nice the roses looked, I'd gently start my bike rolling and say, "Well, I best get delivering the rest of these letters! … It's been nice talking to you," and I'd give a cheerful wave and keep rolling. This simple little strategy hurt no one and worked a treat. I still use the same friendly strategy when I have to extricate myself from an enjoyable conversation because of the time or some other commitment.

A letter could mean so much

These days were long before the whiz-bang electronic communications of today; then, the letter was king. People used to sweat on the postman for that vital piece of information they were waiting on, and be expectantly hanging over the fence when they heard his approaching whistle. The vital messages he carried in his bag could mean all sorts of things to the addressee – even life and death. Everything we do today with modern technology to convey what we want to say, the humble letter had to do. So a postman took his job very seriously indeed, and did his absolute best to ensure that precious letter arrived safely at its destination. The postmen of yesteryear truly believed in the old adage 'the mail must go through'.

I thus played my part in this timeless image of the suburban postie we thought would go on forever: a friendly person who did nothing more than ride his bike around the streets putting those precious letters in the letterbox.

The truth is, being a postman was quite an onerous job. In those pre-electronic days a postman was already at his desk sorting his mail for the day's delivery around six o'clock in the morning, and wouldn't finish till two o'clock in the afternoon. This included redirecting wayward letters and doing his best to find the rightful owner of poorly addressed mail. This was crucially important, as often a single letter could mean the world to someone.

Discreet care

One day, a Christmas card from Canada, addressed to a customer in my area, was returned to my desk with the word 'Deceased' scrawled across the front of the envelope in loud red ink. Now, in those days the strict rules of the postal system required me to add *Return to Sender* and send it back to Canada. I remember sitting there unhappy about this, thinking: "There must be a more sensitive way of handling this sad news." After all, I knew this kindly man who had died. Over the years he'd become my friend for we used to enjoy a regular chat.

So I took it upon myself to cover the insensitive announcement with a white sticker and, after some discreet inquiries, put the letter in a new envelope with a note of my own: "Sadly Mr Jones is no longer with us. He died peacefully in his sleep three weeks ago. Laurie, Postman, Round 7, South Yarra Post Office, Victoria, Australia."

I popped this in the mail and thought no more about it. A couple of months later as we were sorting the mail, I received a letter from Canada addressed to: Laurie, Postman, Round 7, South Yarra Post Office, Victoria, Australia. I wondered: *who on earth would know me in Canada?* When I opened it, I discovered it was a letter of profound gratitude, thanking me for letting them know their dear friend was now at rest as they had worried about him for some time. They were particularly thankful for the thoughtful way I had conveyed the sad news of his passing.

In the midst of the friendly banter going on around me as my friends sorted their mail, I stood there reflective and deeply touched. All the money in the world could not buy the way I felt at that moment. *Some rewards simply cannot be quantified in monetary terms; they are priceless. And being sensitive to the feelings of others is one way of making them happen.*

Man's best friend ... ?

Dogs have been purported to be the bane of a postman's life since time immemorial, but not with me they weren't – that is, until this day. Now I'd seen this black-and-white Border Collie hanging around Hope Street for two years or so, and always said hello to him as he stopped and looked at me or padded by. Never was there an ounce of trouble. But I never knew where he lived. This day I had a registered letter to deliver at a particular address, which of course required the addressee's signature. After no response at the front door, I decided to try once more around the back. So I unlatched the side gate and walked through.

I was a million miles away in my thoughts when this flash of black-and-white snarling fury lunged itself at my face with long yellow fangs and rolling red eyes – that's exactly what my mind registered. I reeled back in terror, doing my desperate best to ward the ferocious beast off with the only deterrent I had; the bundle of letters I was holding. He was vicious and tore at them mercilessly. Somehow I managed to back out of the gate and lock my assailant in, but not before he'd given my finger a severe bite through the latch. From the safe side of this flimsy barrier I could see it was my Border Collie mate I'd been saying hello to for years. I guess he thought it was okay out there in the street, but *not* in his own back yard! I was still shaking when I wrote the addressee a note to collect a registered letter from the post office. That day I delivered the whole of Hope Street's mail all tattered and torn with the compliments of man's best friend and a little explaining to do on my part.

Another time I was accosted by two toy terriers in a most unlikely situation with unexpected consequences. As I explained earlier, I was on pleasant talking terms with the majority of my customers who were always eager for a friendly chat with the postie. And the middle-aged gentleman who tended the garden and the hedges in a small block of flats on Toorak Road was no exception. For years we'd stop for a minute or two of friendly small talk to pass the time, and we always had a smile and a friendly wave for each other. This particular day I had an important express delivery package for the person living on the third floor of this apartment block. I parked my bike in the front of the building, made my way up the stairs, and knocked on the addressee's door. The door flew open and I fell back as two pint-sized Australian terriers tore at me, yapping loudly to defend their territory from this unwelcome intruder.

"What do you want?" snapped a very old lady over the canine cacophony.

"I have an express delivery for you," I yelled; the ferocious little beasts actually nipping at my heels.

"Give it to me," she said, snatching the package from my hands. She gave it a cursory glance then disappeared inside, closely followed by her two sullen but still growling bodyguards. As the door slammed shut behind her, the last image I had of this event was their two small faces snarling at me with bared teeth as if to say: "You've been warned!" The whole unnerving episode was over in less than a minute.

Rather shaken, I staggered down the stairs and out into the open air again. On my way to my bike I saw my friendly gardener tending his flowers and stopped for a quick 'hello' to get a bit of normal balance back into my day.

"Who's the old bag with the two dogs on the top floor?" I asked, nowhere near recovered from my ordeal.

"That's my mother," he said. There wasn't a lot I could say in answer to that. I don't ever recall getting a smile or friendly wave from this man again.

You live and learn.

Stop thief!

But rabid dogs weren't my only worry in my distinguished career as a postman. I remember an afternoon on one of those lazy days of summer where you haven't got much energy and it would be perfect to simply lay down and have a nice nap. So in this lethargic state of mind I was working my way down Milswyn Street when I heard a faint cry in the air: someone yelling out words I couldn't quite make out. I was wide awake now and cocked my head: "Stop thief!" I heard a woman cry. "Stop thief!" she cried again.

Then I saw them running towards me: a short, middle-aged man with a small-brimmed hat on running like the clappers; and a much younger woman in hot pursuit, rapidly gaining ground. I watched, transfixed. Then something remarkable happened: the woman launched herself horizontally through the air and brought the fugitive down (I learned later that she was a gym instructor – this guy had met his match!). By this time I'd reached them and leapt upon the now hatless thief myself.

He wasn't going anywhere, and he knew it.

Citizen's arrest

"I caught him inside my house ransacking the place," she cried breathlessly. "And his pockets are full of my jewellery!"

"Don't touch a thing!" I ordered. "The fact that he has your stolen property on him is vital evidence! ... Somebody call the police!" A shopkeeper duly did this, and incredibly a car full of police screeched to a halt in what seemed like five minutes. White-faced and defeated, the dejected crook lamented to no one in particular: "I'll be getting a long time for this." And I thought, *yeah, you probably will, but you should have thought of that before you did it.* I think the thing he was really scared of was this wasn't the first time he'd faced a judge for a similar offence, and this time they'd throw the book at him.

This was my one and only citizen's arrest; and I am extremely proud that I was able to help that brave young woman make sure this brazen thief, who'd invaded the privacy of her home, didn't get away with it.

Madame Loftus

Then there was Madame Loftus, another of my customers. Madame Loftus was a very dignified French madame who spoke English with a very thick accent and always greeted me with a warm "bonjour".

I'd say she was well over eighty, and always wore the same frock and a large, light-blue hat with coloured flowers on it. She was a real character with an infectious personality. She used to wait for me to bring her letters from France, seated on her couch on her little terrace at the front of her overgrown cottage garden. When she did get close, which was difficult for her legs and ankles were swollen, I noticed she had wispy hairs on her chin, which seemed to add to her unique charm and eccentricity. Apparently she'd been living in this little terraced house for many years, long before my appearance in her life, and we became good friends.

In spite of my ongoing struggle trying to teach myself the Italian language, I decided to further expand my mind and learn French from her – a real teacher. Entering the home of Madame Loftus was like stepping back in time, as if things were left just as they were years ago and had not been touched since. To anyone else her house was full of dust-covered junk, but to her it was filled with precious memories. She pulled up two chairs at a little table and pushed enough stuff aside for us to put our books down and begin our lesson.

"We will start with a children's book and work forward from there," Madame Loftus announced in her thick French accent. Then, producing a little green-covered textbook from the distant past, we started our lesson. And what a wonderful teacher she was: measured, understanding and patient. Remember that I had been driven away from school because mathematics terrified me, which in turn wiped my mind clean of all I had learned – including English grammar and punctuation. So here I was, ten years later, sitting beside kind Madame Loftus, being encouraged to learn something interesting in a non-threatening and structured way. A great weight was being lifted off my shoulders, and I felt inspired. I couldn't wait for my next lesson. And of course no one was aware of any of this at the post office. This was purely between Madame Loftus and me.

In our second lesson, seated at the same dusty, junk-filled table, we returned to our French children's story where I was introduced to a naughty cat who gets into all sorts of trouble. During this lesson I learned a quaint little sentence that sticks with me to this day: *La merchant chat tue le pauvre petit souri* – the wicked cat killed the poor little mouse. We laughed at the wicked cat's exploits, but for me, it was much more than learning French; I was breaking down long-held learning barriers. I was really getting somewhere and eagerly looked forward to my third lesson.

Our third mind-opening lesson

As I turned into Hope Street, I clearly recall darkness had already fallen – winter had begun. I'd done all my homework for our third lesson and felt good about it. I went to open the picket gate and a young man was standing near the open front door, which struck me as strange. I entered and walked towards him.

"Are you after Madame Loftus?" he asked.

"Yes, I have a French lesson with her."

He paused a moment. "I'm her nephew," he solemnly said. "Last night she was run over and killed by a car in Greville Street Prahan." I stood there shocked, unable to speak … When I did find my voice I thanked him for letting me know and walked off into the darkness.

Poor Madame Loftus, I thought. *The wicked car killed the poor little mouse.*

But for me, Madame Loftus's legacy went far beyond mere French lessons; she had a profound effect on my future learning; she had bequeathed me real hope that in the right place, with the right teacher, learning can be fun; and with time, I could recover my lost ground.

Enter: the Italian Institute of Culture

For years as a postal worker, I'd ridden past The Italian Institute of Culture (IIC) in Domain Road South Yarra, an arm of the Italian Government, and yearned to go inside and enquire about possible Italian courses but never had the courage to do so. But thanks to

Madame Loftus, one day I found myself entering the building and confidently approaching the counter.

"Yes, we do have courses," the young lady responded to my enquiry. *If only I'd known*, I thought, *I could have saved myself a lot of bother and heartache years ago!* I immediately enrolled in the beginner class. I was now twenty-four years old and my *formal* Italian learning journey had begun.

What surprised me was the range in age, ethnicity, and vocation of the people sitting in that room with me learning Italian. And all were there for different reasons; some were going on a holiday to Italy; others were there because of some Italian link; while still others simply wanted to expand their minds by learning Italian. One of the textbooks we used in the course was *Basic Italian Grammar* by C.A. McCormick. Incredible! I'd be understanding Italian grammar *before* I understood the grammar of my own language. Through this journey of first understanding the basic building blocks of a language, conversation and writing in this language would become much easier. I was to continue with my once-a-week studies at the IIC for the next six years, until I was ready to leave for my long-awaited sojourn in Italy.

An Italian theatrical extravaganza

During this time my long-held dream of being a famous entertainer never flagged, and in my mind, being good at Italian would somehow end up being part of this. As it happened, not long after I joined the IIC, they put out a call for interested parties to take part in a theatrical extravaganza to be presented at the Alexandra Theatre in Elwood. It was called 'The Revolt of the Ciompi' – *Il Tumulto dei Ciompi*. It was about the first organised workers' strike in history by the Florentine wool workers and dyers (the Ciompi). The Italian Government would not be sparing any expense; it would be presented in both English and Italian on alternate days, with a cast of one hundred drawn from Italian theatre companies and elsewhere.

There would be a semi-trailer load of wool bales set up on the stage for scenery; there would be special effects; and a professional producer would be engaged to make it all happen! This was right up my alley and I applied immediately.

And an extravaganza it turned out to be! Period costumes and props were hired from the various opera companies, which helped create the illusion of actually being in Florence at the time. A priest was hung from the rafters high above the audience, which brought gasps of horror from the crowd. There was lots of action – with many of my telegram boys taking part in the crowd scenes – and an actual plot that took us somewhere. But there were two highlights that stand out.

A bone-chilling scene

The first was a bone-chilling scene I was involved in where I had to chop one of the Ciompi's hands off. The stage was blacked out but for one spotlight on our scene to the side. When it came time for the hand to be chopped off, my paper mache axe, hardened by special glue, would come down on the chopping block with a terrifying bang! And Geoff Marsden, one of my telegram boys, would let out a blood-curdling yell, and a rubber hand covered in blood would fall off the chopping block onto the stage. Well, that's how it went for the first three performances – but things didn't go so well on the fourth. As this was the last performance, I put a bit more power into it; my full-strength blow with the glue-hardened axe missed its marked spot on the chopping block and actually hit Geoff on the wrist, sending out a more authentic whack. That night Geoff's spine-chilling scream was more real than ever and made *everyone's* blood run cold! Lucky for him, all he suffered was a nasty bruise.

Mario the fruiterer

The second memorable moment was of a lighter nature. As I mentioned earlier, the production was bilingual with alternate performances in English and Italian. It only stands to reason that some of the amateur Italian actors were more proficient in their mother tongue than their adopted language of English. And so it was with Mario the Italian fruit shop owner.

In one scene during an English performance, Mario the fruiterer was playing the part of one of the priors, a kind of senior council official. He was facing a bevvy of stern judges lording it over him from the bench in their Florentine finery. Mario's job was to convince these haughty judges of the Ciompi's guilt. Straight after a barrage of learned legal comment from these powerful big-wigs looking down on him, Mario, in his respected role of prior, was expected to deliver a learned response in return. But English not being his native tongue, poor Mario forgot his lines and went completely blank. He just stood there desperately looking at the grim-faced judges for some sign of assistance. But they were no help; decked out as they were in their legal robes, they were well and truly into their parts.

You could cut the air with a knife ... as if some momentous decision was about to be pronounced. The audience was dead still, and the dramatic seconds kept ticking by ... After what seemed like an eternity, a defiant Mario pulled himself up to his full height with purpose and took a challenging step towards his intimidating foes ... he sized them up one last time, then boldly announced in his thick Italian accent, "I see you later!", and strode arrogantly off the stage. As one, both audience and the whole cohort of actors and crew broke into uncontrollable laughter, which lasted a good two minutes.

A memorable moment indeed!

Time to say goodbye

But the time had come when I had to say goodbye to my beloved post office, the place where I'd discovered some certainty and stability and I'd come of age. Sure, a lot of my internal baggage had yet to be dealt with, but I was now able to stand on my own two feet and move forward with confidence into the unknown. When I told my workmates that I really was leaving for Italy the following week, they simply didn't believe me for it was beyond their comprehension. In those days you stayed in a steady job like this until you retired or died, as most of my colleagues ended up doing. For me, life was a wonderful adventure into the unknown, and I wanted to be part of it. But standing up in that lunchroom bidding my farewells to my friends was like saying goodbye to my family. That day my tears flowed freely.

Part III
Italy and my overseas exploits

CHAPTER 13

Italy

The first image I recall from when I arrived in the ancient town of Perugia in central Italy is the red terracotta roofs and the 'Italianness' of it all. We were situated on a hill, and you could look away to the snow-capped mountains in the distance with the mauve-coloured villages sloping away below us. It was a brisk spring morning, and the people who were walking in the town square were immaculately attired in tailor-made coats and shoes as if this was the norm. *It's true!* I thought as I took all this in, because it was what I'd been told. But the first thing I had to do was make my way to Palazzo Gallenga, the renowned seat of learning for foreigners in this famous Etruscan city, to make myself known.

My Italian home

In the foyer I joined all the other bewildered students trying to find their way in their new surroundings, when I heard an elderly gentleman calling out, "Una camera! Una camera?" Luckily I knew that this meant 'a room' and not 'a camera'! So I jumped in before anyone else could and said, "Si". I followed this kindly man to a door in a row of tenement houses that probably went back to Michelangelo's day. I followed him up the narrow stairs, and there I met his equally charming wife, a lady in her late sixties, who fitted the stereotype of an Italian mama perfectly. After our introductions – to them I was Lorenzo – they showed me my 'camera'; a quaint but sparse room with a single bed and desk, and a beautiful view onto a sunny little courtyard. This was to be my home for the next nine months.

That afternoon, Signora Maria and her husband Anello took me on a trip to the town market to buy something for dinner, to which I was invited. I was reeling with all the new sounds, smells and images that were assailing my senses within the space of the last twenty-four hours. At the market, Signora Maria bought two plump pigeons (dead) for our dinner. And why not? We eat chicken! That night she roasted them to perfection, with potatoes flavoured with rosemary and a tasty side-dish of spinach. Absolutely delicious! What a start to my magnificent Italian adventure. I already felt at home.

The following day I went back to Palazzo Gallenga and enrolled in the highest level of Italian possible – I was going straight to the top. But this was a big mistake, for I'd sit in those elevated classes feeling lost, way out of my depth, and understanding little. I quickly ate a nice helping of humble pie and changed to something more on my level: 'il corso medio'. But even here I struggled; because my English grammar was so poor I had no solid foundation against which to compare the new Italian grammar I was learning. So I decided I'd learn the Italian grammar *first*, then learn the English grammar from that! And that's exactly what I did. To achieve this, I didn't do the three-month 'corso medio' once, as normal people do; I repeated it *three* times during the nine months I was there. If I'm nothing else in life, I am persistent.

Unforgettable Miss Viscardi

Our Professoressa for the corso medio was Miss Viscardi, a middle-aged lady who dressed immaculately and wore large designer-made dark glasses. In fact, everything she wore was designer-made. An extremely likeable person – but boy, was she a hard task master! She would peer over her glasses to tease out a response, and had a habit of readjusting them every so often. I've witnessed grown men sweating with fear because they hadn't done their homework! To add to the mix, she was an incurable anglophile and simply adored everything English.

At the end of one of the courses I did, Miss Viscardi announced that we'd be having a special social evening as a reward; a play reading in English, *The Importance of Being Ernest.* I suspect this was more for her love of English than for us; but because my entertaining career had been put on the backburner during this Italian interlude, I eagerly put my hand up to keep my main dream of becoming famous ticking along.

The play reading was outrageously funny, more because we kept losing our places and making things up as we went along than our acting prowess.

Do what the simple folk do

There were two things I learned quickly in Italy which not only helped me get by, they helped me understand these lovable, effusive people better. First, keep your ear to the ground to find out where the locals go to eat. When I first arrived in Perugia I went to a restaurant in one of the tourist hotels for a meal and quickly realised that my limited savings wouldn't hold out the nine months if I kept paying out like this. So I asked around to find out what the locals did, as I certainly didn't see them in the hotel restaurant. Then I learned of the 'mensa popolare' – *the people's table*, a no-frills eatery with chequered table cloths and simple fare. You could get a generous bowl of spaghetti, followed by a quarter of chicken with salad and freshly baked pasta dura, and a small bottle of sparking mineral water, all for ten dollars! Not only was it economical, you got to meet the locals! The university had a similar set up with their own special card. Whenever I found myself in a new Italian town or city, the following sentence came in handy: "Scusi, c'e' una mensa popolare qui vicino?" – *Excuse me, is there a people's table around here?*

Maybe it's because my mother always encouraged us to approach someone of importance if we needed to, or perhaps it's some kind of survival mechanism; whatever the reason, I've learned to never be afraid to ask.

Assisi: the town of St Francis

The second thing that helped me get by was learning what is normal and acceptable to Italians. I'd only been at the university for a couple of days when I spied a poster advertising a day trip to Assisi. *Great*, I thought, *I'll be in that!* And I carefully checked the departure times and where to catch the bus.

The following morning I was up bright and early to be at the bus stop by the fountain in Perugia's main square by 7 am. I got there at 6:40, just to be sure. People began to appear and stood waiting at the bus stop, while others were milling around. As 7 o'clock approached my heart began to speed up; I was so excited, for I'd heard so much about this legendary town linked to St Francis.

At 7:01 a large bus rolled into the square and pulled up at our stop outside the fountain. The automatic doors flew open with that decisive noise they have. As there was no queue as such, I politely stepped back to let the bulk of the people in front of me make their way inside the bus, as I'd been used to doing in Melbourne. Then something remarkable happened. All these hitherto smiling and placid people transformed into something else: they piled on board as one clamorous entity, leaving me standing open-mouthed in their wake.

The door thumped shut as quickly as it had opened, and away went the bus – with me still standing by the fountain wondering what had just happened.

I didn't get to Assisi that day.

If you can't lick 'em, join 'em!

It was some time before I figured out what was going on and understood that these people weren't being rude at all; they were simply doing what Italians had been doing for thousands of years in their markets, bazaars, and town squares; if you didn't move fast, or have the loudest voice, or spin the most convincing yarn – you missed out! In those times the concept of sedately forming a queue was beyond reason and would have made no sense at all. So, once I'd twigged to how the game was played, I started observing how clever Italians were at getting served first and began to join in this game myself. From then on it was very rare for me to 'miss the bus'; and if I did, I took it in my stride because I now understood.

Saint Mary of the Angels

When I finally did get to see the iconic little town of Assisi I loved it and explored all its historical wonders and environs extensively. One thing that caught my eye on the way there was the imposing presence of the Basilica of Saint Mary of the Angels, which loomed up from the bottom of the valley below Assisi in the town of Porziuncola and dwarfed everything around it. Even today, you can see it shrouded in the morning mist from miles away. Porziuncola's claim to fame is St Francis both studied and died there. In the early days the original church of this little town was a tiny chapel – the basilica came later.

I felt compelled to stop and take a look inside. And when I did, it took my breath away. Just the sheer size of it all … in the semi-darkness I respectfully wandered from the front to a small wooden enclave at the side of the main alter with a chest-high, small metal grid in front of it. Intrigued, I lent forward to see what was inside.

Without warning, a dark, shrouded apparition appeared in front of me: "Money for the poor!" it croaked accusingly, banging a wooden receptacle on a ledge. I jumped back and let out an involuntary gasp! It turned out to be an old dark-hooded nun who had taken it on herself to scare the hell out of questionable believers like me to change their ways. She obviously knew what she was doing and enjoyed the immense power she wielded. Without question, I found myself grabbing some small change from my pockets and dropping it into the proffered bowl. I made a mental note of the experience for future reference and went on my way.

Three months later at the end of our school term, I again found myself heading for the quaint little town of Assisi, this time with four fellow students from the university for company.

"Let's stop at the Basilica of Saint Mary of the Angels in the valley just below Assisi," I suggested to my colleagues. "There's something very interesting I want to show you."

"What is it?" one of them asked.

"It's a sort of relic that glows in the dark and no one knows why … they say it's something to do with sunbeams that shine through the steeple." I'd got their interest.

Once inside, and exactly as had happened to me, the magnificence of it all took their breath away. *I hope she's still there*, I thought to myself.

"This way," I said, "it's down here." As we neared the carved wooden alcove with the small steel grid in front of it, I lowered my voice to intensify the effect: "Mary, you and Joan go first. You've got to get your faces close to the grid and let your eyes focus … and then you'll see the icon begin to glow."

I felt a little deflated, for nothing happened at first … then two stifled screams rent that holy air! *She was there all right!* I chuckled.

The Sordellis

Then there was my Milan experience. By way of contacts and friends I'd met at the university in Perugia, I found myself living in the palatial apartment of the Sordelli family in the town centre of Milan. The deal was, in return for board and lodging I was to help Mario, the father, with his translations from Italian into English; and for Guido his son, my job was to be his hands-on assistant as he spent his days with his two rich mates hang-gliding in the Alps. The mother had died some time before, but I did learn from the maid that she was a Baroness and the Sordellis were descendants of the Beretta gun family which made them more than well off. So this was the life I lived for the whole extended eight months remaining on my study visa. The good thing was, not only did we all get on well, we were all proficient in English and Italian and could help each other with our communicating effectiveness. I especially enjoyed my time with Mario and we established a very warm relationship.

Mario Sordelli

Mario was a tall, handsome man around seventy, with light, thinning hair, a sparkle in his eye, and a great sense of humour. Mario would take on his translations from Italian into English, as well as run an English school in Milan, to keep his mind sharp and "keep dementia at bay", as he would say. He loved having me sitting at the table with him to help him with these projects. We'd verbally explore possible nuances and interpretations for hours. A project I especially remember was a pamphlet on yacht racing for those who can afford a million-dollar boat on the sparkling waters of the Emerald Coast of Sardinia. What got us in was the thrill of discussing all the different Italian sailing jargon and expressions and then translating it all into good English; all the while doing our best to be true to the original text. No mean feat! I felt comfortable with my role in this as my Italian was more of a verbal nature than a literary one, and Mario did all the writing. We both felt a real sense of achievement when a project was finished. For me personally, this was a great boost to my intellect and confidence when compared with the mind-numbing menial jobs I'd been doing most of my life.

Once I got him talking I learned more and more about Mario and his life as an officer in the Italian Army under the corrupt and violent dictatorship of Mussolini. After his march on Rome in 1922 where he seized power and took control of the country, people realised what a threat Mussolini was. But it was too late; his Blackshirts soon ruled the whole country with an iron fist. His military misadventures in Ethiopia, North Africa, Greece, and the thousands he sent to die on the frozen Russian steppes all ended in disaster. By the end of WWII he'd led Italy to being a bombed-out ruin.

Mario was swept up in this horrific maelstrom. His view of the Italian Army elite was scathing: "Che pagliacci!" – *What a bunch of clowns*, he'd say. "They'd send truckloads of white satin gloves and champagne for the officers in the desert instead of weapons, while the soldiers fighting in stifling heat were given winter greatcoats!" Little wonder tens of thousands of these long-suffering soldiers decided they weren't going to blindly sacrifice their lives for the buffoon who was leading them and his disastrous stupidity. Mussolini had bound them all to Hitler with their infamous Axis pact; when the Italians discerned the truth of being hoodwinked into this conflict, many rebelled and joined the allies. The notion that all Italians are cowards is simply ridiculous. Those images of thousands of Italian soldiers we see giving themselves up to a handful of English guards in the North African campaign had nothing to do with cowardice; they'd just had a gut-full of bumbling stupidity and watching their mates die, for what? The megalomaniacal dreams of a madman? In the end Mario felt betrayed too and crossed over to the Allies to join in the just cause of freeing his country from the cruel yoke of fascism and German occupation. And I'm with them … in their shoes, I would have done the same!

The Italian partisan

In sharp contrast, the Italian freedom fighter (who came from the same stock as those hapless draftee soldiers sent to their fate in the desert) was a formidable foe because his heart was hell bent on freeing his country from the trauma of German oppression. Just ask any German soldier if he thought the Italian partisan army were a bunch of runaway cowards and they'll tell you the truth: the Italian partisan freedom fighter remained a deadly thorn in the side of the German

Army by ceaselessly harassing and demoralising the German military machine right to the end.

Italian war prisoners in Australia

I'll conclude my thoughts on the matter with a story told to me by an Italian descendant of Italian war prisoners held in Australia who decided to remain here and raise his family as good Aussie citizens. Julio related how, after his father was released, he worked his way up to finally owning his own fruit shop in Balaclava Road Caulfield, of which he was very proud. But there was one awful flaw that put a dampener on it all and made his family feel bad and keep their heads down.

Every other weekday, a middle-aged Australian on his way to work would walk past their store on the *other side* of the road and yell out, "You dirty dago bastards; You filthy dago *cowards*!" Julio told me, "This went on week after week, month after month, for at least two years." His voice went inward as if he'd never shared this with anyone else before me: "As a little boy I used to wonder why my father never said anything and just kept his head down."

Day after humiliating day the torment continued.

One day Julio learned his father had contracted cancer in his chest and arm and was told he only had a few months to live. But work still needed to be done, and he was forced to stack the shelves with produce with his arm in plaster – in spite of the continuing abuse. One day their tormentor got bolder and crossed the road to the front of the shop, where his sick dad was tending the fruit and vegetables. "You dirty dago coward," he hurled in his father's face. "You dirty dago bastard!"

That finally did it! For the first time ever, Julio's father drew himself up to his full height and turned to face the long-time tormentor; then, with every ounce of his failing strength, he hit him hard on the side of the head with his plaster-covered arm. The habitual abuser reeled under the impact and fell cowering to the ground. "Don't hit me," he pleaded. Julio's incensed dad was now standing over him:

"Don't you ever abuse me or my family again!" he shouted in his broken English. "We are decent, hard-working Italian immigrants, *and we are also proud Australian citizens*! Now get out of here and find another way to go to work!" These last words were said with such vehemence that this obnoxious guy took off and they never saw him again.

Julio told me that not long after this incident his father passed away. "But I think he died happy because he had at last found his voice and stood up for us all and our rightful place here in Australia. That day my dad became my hero and will always remain so," said an emotional Julio. *I think I could safely add that the tremendous courage displayed by Julio's dying father - of not remaining silent when bad things were happening - makes his dad a hero to us all.*

Guido Sordelli

We now come to my remarkable experiences in the Italian Alps with Mario's son Guido. But first, a word or two on the Alps: they're big! Much bigger than anything Australia has to offer. For example, Australia's highest mountain, Mt Kosciuszko, is only 2228 metres high, whereas Italy's Mt Blanc is more than twice the height at 4810 metres! This formidable barrier that sets Italy apart from the rest of Europe, with over one hundred peaks over 4000 metres, was the rarefied environment in which Guido and his rich mates took me to be their hang-gliding 'caddy'.

Alpine seasonal magic

And what a privilege it was. My eight months with these intrepid adventurers took part in the pleasant months of spring, summer and autumn. I had the pleasure of witnessing nature's seasonal magic; early snow-drops and emerging tree buds, wondrous blossoms, scent-filled mid-summer mountain meadows full of wild grasses and flowers, and of course the ever beautiful autumn leaves. The higher you went, the smaller the plant life became, till it vanished altogether on the highest peaks. Because it was safer, we did our practising on the lower, gentler inclines of the grass-covered foothills, with a really long rope should anything go wrong. I was the one holding the rope. But it was still scary as far as I was concerned, and I was glad it was those guys testing these flimsy flying machines and not me. My job was to help the hang-gliders set things up, be their general 'go for', and take them up and down the mountain pathways in Guido's big Russian Wasa jeep (pronounced 'Vusa'). This Russian WWII relic was Guido's pride and joy; it was built like a tank, hard to drive, and indestructible.

I remember my first time high in the Alps watching these fearless adventurers launch themselves off a mountain into the wild blue yonder. Their landing target was a farmlet miles below us in a picturesque green valley. From where we were, all you could see was the nearby village the size of a postage stamp. As they got closer to their target they would be able to discern the tiny farm and the white sheet we had previously pegged out in a field.

Thorough safety check

Prior to their take-off I couldn't help but note the thoroughness of their safety-checking operation. All equipment was neatly laid out on the ground and counted off, with each of the three guys sounding off each item in turn as a triple-check. I was impressed. And they did the same again as a final check as they stood back from the precipice in their harnesses. What struck me was the painstaking detail they went through in repeating all of these checks over and over, and I commented on it. Then they told me a remarkable story.

A couple of years prior to this, one of their very experienced hang-gliding friends, we'll call him Giovanni, was doing his final check, as was their custom, near the edge of a similar Alpine drop. But then they only double-checked *their own* safety measures without the extra voices to see all was in order. This day Giovanni was the first to take-off. Satisfied that all was in order with his hang-glider and his personal equipment attaching him to it, he approached the edge, steadied his craft against the wind uplift, nodded to his flying mates and stepped into the abyss.

Something was wrong

Immediately his friends sensed something had gone terribly wrong; his hang-glider veered crazily, and he yelled something out which was lost on the wind. Giovanni's main harness clip, which attached him to the hang-glider, was not locked in properly. They saw Giovanni desperately clinging to the hand bar of his out-of-control craft for a few seconds, then lose his grip and spiral to his death two miles below.

They stood there in absolute shock. An eternity went by before they moved; the drop to the rocks thousands of metres below was sheer, and they knew there was nothing they could do to save poor Giovanni; he was gone. It took them a long time to get over it; hence their paranoia about now triple-checking every minute aspect of their safety list before taking off.

I looked at their meticulous fussing with a new respect.

My precipitous decent

Their triple-checks all done, I stayed with them until they had all taken safely to the air. But now I faced a challenge equally formidable of my own; I had to drive Guido's cumbersome Wasa back down this precipitous gravel road to the farmlet in the valley far below. Guido had said, "You'll be right, just take your time." Which was all right for him to say; I'd only driven this monster on the flat streets of Milan on two occasions – and that wasn't easy. But this was something else again; I'd be fearfully wending my way down a narrow gravel road in the Alps with bottomless drops at every turn! With nowhere to go but downwards, I climbed up into the tank, started the engine, and full of trepidation began the descent.

Sheer weight caused it to slide

Downwards I went, wrestling with that wheel for grim death to stop Guido's four-ton pride and joy from hurtling out of control either into the mountain wall or over the edge. I was covered in sweat, and my knuckles were white for I didn't dare let go of that wheel. Bend after tortuous bend I tentatively lumbered, aware of the raw power beneath that big khaki bonnet; I kept my foot off the accelerator and let gravity do most of the work. I knew I had to somehow make it down, for the boys were depending on me to be there when they arrived. Then I came out of a particularly sharp bend, and the sheer weight of the old Russian Wasa caused it to slide on the loose gravel.

I desperately tried to keep it on the narrow road with the steering wheel and the brakes, but it just kept sliding, and over the edge we went – well, almost! Half of the vehicle went over the edge, with one front wheel in mid air and the other three wheels still on firm ground. The whole thing was tilted precariously, facing a certain plunge to oblivion with me still sitting in the driver's seat. I didn't dare look down, and managed to open the door and edge my way out, back onto the road. At first glance the situation looked hopeless. There was this massive jeep stuck halfway over a sheer drop. *What am I going to do*, I thought, *poor Guido's Wasa!* But there was one positive thing; the jeep wasn't tottering on the edge, it was solidly on firm ground with three of its driving wheels still able to grip the surface. With me, hope springs eternal!

Still somewhat dazed, I was standing there pondering what to do next when another four-wheel-drive vehicle appeared on the scene, not much smaller than Guido's Wasa. A stocky farmer type got out and walked over.

My Italian came in handy: "I'm in a bit of trouble," I said, stating the obvious.

He nodded and thoughtfully surveyed the situation: "I reckon if I put a chain on your tow bar and you got back in and reversed out in your lowest gear we'd be able to lift that remaining wheel back onto the road." He obviously assumed I knew what I was doing and that the vehicle was mine.

"Okay," I said. "You go back and hook your chain on and I'll get in the jeep and gently back out in unison on a given signal." I was sweating more than ever, for I had to guess where the lowest gear was; one wrong move into a forward gear … well that didn't bear thinking about!

Lucky for me there was a simple schematic pattern on the top of the gear stick. With the other heavy vehicle now chained to mine as an added safety brake, I gingerly climbed back into the Wasa, took a deep breath and started the engine. And then, on our agreed wave and yell, I slipped the gear into what I thought was the lowest possible reverse ratio and let out the clutch. I could feel the wheels spinning and the jeep was doing something, but I didn't know if it was trying to go backwards or forwards. Now I was really panic-stricken.

Without warning, the wheel on my side took hold and gripped and bumped its way back over the edge onto the road again. By some miracle I'd not only saved myself, I'd saved Guido's jeep! What's more, only twenty-five minutes had gone by, so I was still on time. I thanked this generous man profusely and offered him some compensation, but he would have none of it. These off-roaders have an unwritten law between them to help each other out in times of need. We warmly shook hands and bid each other a safe journey.

I nursed the jeep the rest of the way down that winding road as if my life depended on it, which it did! I was more than relieved when I finally arrived at our destination in that little green valley far below the heart-stopping excitement of my descent.

For weeks after this Guido would say, "You know, there's something not quite right with the jeep … she's not responding well."

I'd just nod and say, "That's interesting … what part's not responding."

"I think it's the steering," he'd say.

It turned out that one of the shock absorbers on the driver's side was slightly bent, which perplexed Guido. "That would've taken a decent bump," he said, "and I don't recall where that could've happened." I would nod and remain thoughtfully silent. I didn't dare tell him I nearly drove his beloved jeep off a cliff with me in it.

The wonder of Italian dialects

Another interesting aspect of Italy that I found fascinating is the variety of their dialects. Now these regional dialects can be so diverse that they are only understood by the locals and are unintelligible to other Italians. Over hundreds of years, indeed thousands, the inhabitants of the Italian peninsula have been influenced by invasions and incursions by all sorts of peoples, among them: Etruscans; Latins; Phoenicians; Greeks; Arabs; Normans; French; Spanish; Germanic peoples; and on it goes. So each region of Italy has its own particular language influences seated deep in its remote past. Today's spoken Italian is relatively new because of its universal spread by way of modern technology. For example, prior to WWII, regional dialects were alive and well throughout Italy, whereas nowadays almost everybody speaks the same version of Italian. In fact, young people now shun the ancient dialects as 'old people's language'. However, there are still pockets of die-hard people who tenaciously cling to their traditional ways and communicate with each other in their customary dialect. I've experienced an extreme case of this personally.

On this occasion I again found myself with my hang-gliding colleagues high in the Alpine foothills checking out possible launch sites; this time in the mountains behind the city of Bergamo, north-east of Milan. It was a lazy summer day and the alpine meadows were full of native grasses and flowers – their distinct scents still linger in my senses. Out of this picturesque scene appeared two peasant farmers from another age, another time; they were each riding a little donkey and leading four other donkeys fully laden with freshly cut hay. They were unshaven and were wearing scruffy work clothes; on their heads they wore old felt hats which had seen many seasons and long ago lost their shape. As they filed by us, loaded as we were with the very latest in hang-gliding equipment, time stood still. These two peasant farmers were in their own little world; they did not even acknowledge us. I tried to tune in to what they were saying to each other. But although I'd spent the past year studying Italian in the renowned university of Perugia, I couldn't understand a single word these *Italians* were saying. It all sounded like sing-song Japanese to me.

"What were they saying?" I asked Guido when they had gone by.

"I don't know," he said.

"What do you mean you don't know?" I was puzzled. "They're Italians living in Italy and we're only a little way from Milan!"

"Yes, but they're Bergamascans, probably one of the hardest dialects in all of Italy to understand."

It took a while for that to sink in ... The world truly is an interesting place.

A surprising letter

Before we close on Mario and Guido Sordelli, there's an addendum to this story of these two interesting Italians who came into my life. Around about 1985, five years after I arrived back in Australia from my European exploits, I received a letter addressed to me from Alaska. *Who the devil knows me in Alaska?* I thought. When I turned the letter over I saw 'Mario Sordelli'.

Now through the magic of a common connection with our languages, Mario and I were pretty close, so I was touched that after all these years he'd take the trouble to write to me. He explained that he, Guido and his sister had moved to Alaska and that he had found a nice lady friend. He went on to proffer the idea of we two picking up where we left off with our Italian/English translations; only this time we'd do it long distance. I wrote back and told him what a wonderful surprise it was to receive his letter, and that I'd love to be a part of his translating idea. But I never heard back from Mario, and always wondered why. These were the days before social media so I didn't have that option to follow him up.

Another letter

Around ten years after that, in 1996, I received another letter from Alaska. *Mario!* I thought. But no, this time it was from Guido!

His was a long, sad letter. He shared how his dad had died of cancer a couple of years before, and as he was going through his belongings he was surprised to come across Mario's and my correspondence to each other. "I had no idea you two were corresponding," Guido wrote. He went on to tell me that his memories of the time we'd spent together in the Alps and our endless conversations were warm and comforting. He told me how his own marriage didn't work out, and that his little boy Luca had died of leukemia when he was only five.

I did write back, but the letter was returned 'unknown at this address'. Now I don't know if he'd moved house or if there was a spelling mistake with the address he'd given me, but it saddened me greatly to have his letter sent back to me.

Later I turn to the internet

We now fast-forward to me writing this book in 2020, when a pang of guilt struck me; for I now had access to social media. I interrupted my thoughts, saved my work, and typed *Guido Sordelli Alaska* into Google. My computer thought for a while, then a coloured image of a balding man with a light sandy beard appeared. My heart skipped a beat! He'd aged a bit of course, but this was unmistakably my friend Guido. I read on … this time my heart sank. The heading beneath the picture said *obituary*. Guido died in 2011. He was sixty-five.

Sometimes the simple act of living life seems to get in the way; and even though our intentions may be noble, it's so easy to leave things too late.

CHAPTER 14

A brand new adventure

With my visa almost expired, it was time for me to say goodbye to my friends in Italy and move on to some new adventure, for I'd acquired a taste for it. It presented itself by way of a chance meeting with two young guys in a pub in London. Tom, a tall, lanky Englishman with blond hair, and Bill, a stocky New Zealander. When I told them what I'd just been doing in the Italian Alps we discovered we had a lot in common. They were about to depart on a twelve-week journey with a truckload of fifteen tourists all the way from London to Johannesburg in South Africa, which included crossing the Sahara Desert! Their route was down through France and Spain, a ferry crossing to Morocco, then the Sahara, on through central Africa, then to their final destination in Jo'burg.

Wow! They had my attention: "How does one get involved in that?" I asked with genuine enthusiasm.

"You have to go through a training program," said Tom. "Why don't you meet us in Jo'burg and help with the refurbishment of the truck for the next load of tourists on the return trip? This will stand you in good stead when you fly back to London for your specialist training."

"I'll be there to meet you on your arrival," I said. "Where do I go?"

"Book into The Soper Lodge in Hillbrow on the outskirts of Jo'burg and we'll meet there."

We shook hands on this, and pledged that that's where we'd next meet.

As funds were running low, and I had a few weeks up my sleeve, I spent the next three months doing cash-in-hand labouring work on a London building site. This was an experience in itself, working with Irish itinerant workers and others from all walks of life, which brought back memories of my trench-digging days – only here they treated you well. I'd meet the likes of these guys again before my wandering days were through. But for now I had a chance in a lifetime adventure to save up for.

A quick day-trip to Vienna

During this in-between period I found myself in Vienna for a one-day visit to meet some Australian friends of mine. They were passing through Europe on a world tour, so time was limited. We spent a couple of hours catching up at a sidewalk cafe in this beautiful city, and before we knew it the time to say goodbye was upon us.

As we did, one of them reached into his backpack and pulled out one of those flimsy plastic shopping bags with something in it. "You've been away a long time," he said. "A little memento from Australia for you."

I looked at what was in the bag and smiled … then remembered I had a train to catch! We warmly embraced and went our separate ways with the promise of meeting again back in Australia.

My plan for my return trip to London was to take the train to Venice, then across the top of Italy, through France, and back by ferry across the Channel. The first leg of this journey was the four-hour train trip to Venice. I still remember the interior of the train; all polished wood with a corridor and separate compartments. My solitary travel companion was a tall, dark-haired man in his mid thirties, but it was his attire that caught my eye. He wore bright-red patent leather shoes, beige trousers, and a light green jacket to complement the ensemble. He was aimlessly looking out the window.

Why do some people have to dress like this? I thought. *What statement are they trying to make?* For a good half hour these were the kind of judgemental thoughts running through my mind while this dapperly dressed young man continued to look out the window. *How long can this go on for?* I said to myself. *There's three-and-a-half hours to go!* Someone had to break the ice.

"Where are you going?" I ventured, not knowing what nationality this gaudily-dressed fellow was.

"I'm on my way to Venice," he replied. What a relief … he spoke English! He had an American accent and an accessible demeanour. We quickly warmed to each other and fell into interesting conversation. The next time I looked at my watch hours had gone by.

I learnt that he wasn't American as his accent suggested, but was Canadian. He was a secondary school teacher in the Canadian wilderness teaching Indigenous children English in a makeshift school of shipping-containers, and was on a three-week European holiday. Absolutely fascinating! On and on he spoke and on and on I listened as he told his intriguing story. The time kept flying by. His brash attire was no longer an issue. At one point he suddenly stopped, looked at me, and excitedly pointed at the seat beside me.

"I don't believe it!" he exclaimed.

"What?" I said, puzzled.

"There," he continued in disbelief, "in that bag beside you … a jar of vegemite!"

He explained that his fellow teacher in the Canadian wilderness was an Aussie and how, on a daily basis, he'd rave about how much he missed his vegemite. "I'm not joking"" he said, "the guy seemed to be having withdrawal symptoms for the stuff. When his family finally shipped him a jar of this precious commodity I tried some and it was absolutely horrible!" (The problem with the poor yanks and Canadians is they don't know how to eat it – they spread it on like peanut butter! ... they never get to 'savour' its *inner* wonders. Even our Kiwi cousins don't get it: they often tell me, "What is it with you Australians and your bloody vegemite? You all have it in your luggage!" For Australians, Vegemite is more than just a breakfast spread – it's an institution.)

"And here I am," our Canadian friend went on, "thousands of miles away from home and the first Aussie I meet is travelling with nothing but a jar of vegemite!"

The point of all this is: *it's so easy to jump to the wrong conclusions about someone because of their external appearance before we've even got to know them!* This four-hour train journey with a complete stranger turned out to be one of the most memorable in my life because of the incredible stories he shared. Which had nothing whatsoever to do with the clothes the guy was wearing.

Winging my way to Jo'burg

And the time did come when I was winging my way to South Africa; it was 1978, right at the height of the apartheid era. I arrived in Jo'burg two weeks before Tom and Bill were due to arrive at Soper Lodge with their travel-weary adventurers, so I could acclimatise myself to my new surroundings. I was in for a shock and had some adjusting to do. Blacks and whites were kept separated in all the main aspects of their social lives; for example, benches in the park had *whites only* written on them, and blacks had to use separate gates and train carriages on the railways. In time I was to learn there were places where it was safe for them to socially mingle with discretion.

Some mental acclimatising to do

Soper Lodge was a no-frills, fully serviced boarding house, which included all meals. It was run by a young Jewish couple who treated their staff with dignity, and for the duration of my three-month stay became my friends and I'd regularly have dinner with them. Black folk did *all* the work, something that took me a while to get used to because where I come from you washed your own dishes and did your own washing. But I did get to know these amiable people on a personal level and learn a little about their lives. I even went on a guided tour of Soweto, a ramshackle city of shacks, two-room government houses, and two million black inhabitants; it's hot, dusty, and the roads are unmade. This was where the black people of Jo'burg lived, and it was a real eye-opener for me. In contrast, Johannesburg is a modern city of skyscrapers, parks and gardens, beautiful houses, boulevards and freeways; which only emphasised the difference between the two worlds. Nowadays things have changed, but in those days the demarcation line was real.

When I first arrived in South Africa I was very ignorant about the whole scene and ran many a risk of getting myself into serious trouble. For example, one day in a little market gathering of black people, I noticed a perforated kerosene tin barbecue roasting some corn cobs. As I'm a bit partial to a roasted corn cob, and I was feeling rather hungry, I headed for the source of this enticing food. What I didn't know was corncobs, in any form, were considered black man's food, and a white person wouldn't be seen dead walking around the streets of Jo'burg chewing on a corncob. So innocent me waltzes up to these bemused black guys and asks, "Are the corncobs for sale?"

"Sure!"

"Well, I'll have two of them." I duly paid and wandered off, savouring my stick of corn as I went. I could feel all eyes upon me: the blacks proud that I had the guts to do it; the whites indignant that I would lower myself enough to eat black man's food. Despite this, I was determined to finish eating them.

In the future I trod a little more softy regarding local customs, for it probably wasn't wise to play the 'one man against the oppressor' trick the moment I arrived in the place. I learned later that this foolhardy approach could have cost me my life, for guns and knives were rife in the community and it didn't need much for an innocent motive to be taken the wrong way.

Pete the street fighter

While I waited in Soper Lodge for my friends to arrive from their daunting trans-African trek, I befriended Pete the street fighter from Liverpool. When Pete wasn't drunk he was pumping weights in his room. He was a nuggety little guy with biceps as big as Popeye's. It was he who told me he was a street fighter, and what's more, he was really proud of it. He wore the scars around his face and eyes as badges of honour.

Pete was a member of some local white gang and spent most nights swaggering around the streets defending their turf. When I asked him what the difference between an ordinary fighter and a street fighter was, he said, "There are no rules, you just do what's required to defeat the other guy."

I got to know Pete a bit, and under all his bravado he wasn't a bad sort of person and had a good heart. I don't know why, but he'd sort of listen to me as some wise councillor; living the life he lived, maybe I was the first person who'd ever shown a genuine interest in him. Whatever the reason, one day he opened up and told me he really didn't like his lifestyle and he'd like to get out of it. All I could do was wish him all the best in his noble quest for something better.

Chicken and chips

Late one balmy night, with nothing better to do, Pete and I decided to walk down the road to the top end of Jo'burg and get some chicken and chips. We hadn't gone far and were standing before some well-lit shops when two white guys came up and said, "Hi, how's it going?"

In my total innocence I said, "Fine … we're going to get some chicken and chips."

"Ah, some chicken," the talkative one said, "I've got some chicken I can share with you." And, beckoning us to follow, he led the way, all the time talking to me. I noticed Pete sizing these guys up but he hadn't uttered a word. Round a corner I blindly followed them into a dimly lit lane, with this guy chatting all the while. Now I'm not a complete idiot, but sometimes it takes a while for the penny to drop. 'Mr Talker' stopped and reached into a garbage can, pulled out a chicken carcase and tauntingly smeared it over the side of my face.

"Here's your chicken," he said.

Too late I realised I was in real trouble. I knew that standing in this dark alley with *three* street fighters meant my life could depend on what I did next; life didn't mean much to them. From the corner of my eye I saw Pete's biceps quiver: I had one second to defuse the situation before he sprang into action.

"Hey mate," I said, "I'm from Australia on holiday … I've got no fight with you … in fact I'd rather be your friend and buy you a beer." This completely threw all three of them, including Pete, who was a hundred percent ready to take them both on. If this had happened I would have been caught in the fray and copped the worst of it. But now the dynamics had entirely changed; Mr Talker said, "I'm sorry … I thought you guys were spoiling for a fight … " and began to walk all four of us out of that dark alley.

I jumped in to keep the momentum going by repeating what I'd said before: "Why would I want to fight you guys … I'm only here on holiday from Australia to meet some South African friends." We were now out into the light and I sensed they no longer felt we were a threat. I took the initiative to help them save face: "Sorry there was a misunderstanding guys … come and pay us a visit sometime in Australia!"

"No worries," they said; feeling they could walk away the winners of this little joust. We shook hands then went our merry ways. I did detect a bit of tension from Pete but I'm glad he kept his mouth shut because being a Liverpudlian street fighter with their propensity for an unhealthy stoush, he would have undone all our good work.

We didn't go on to the takeaway after this – I'd lost my appetite. When I got home I cleaned the filthy chicken from my face and thanked my lucky stars I'd successfully extricated myself from a potentially life-threatening situation.

Guns 'n' more guns

Then there were the guns. When I first arrived in South Africa, I used to lie in my bed at Soper Lodge and listen to what I assumed were fireworks. "No," the maid said to me when I asked her what they were, "they're not fireworks, they're guns … and most whites have them … even some black men have them … they shoot them into the air at night just for fun." The logic behind this was hard for me to get my head around: if bullets go up, they have to come down somewhere; even if they're a lot slower in their lower trajectory I still wouldn't want to be hit by one! So each night was punctuated by these odd angry shots and in the end I got used to them.

But it's one thing to only *hear* about guns and quite another to actually *see* one. One night I was killing time in a bar getting to know the locals when I fell into conversation with this small balding guy from Portugal. He told me he wouldn't go anywhere without his gun.

"Do you mean to tell me that you have a gun on you now?" I asked, astonished.

"Sure I do," he said, pulling up the leg of his trousers and showing me a holster with a square-shaped gun in it strapped to his ankle. I just stared at it: this is the sort of thing we Aussies would only see in the movies. Intrigued, I found myself asking, "What sort of gun is it?"

"It's a machine Beretta," he said, as if describing some benign gadget he was proud of. A chill went through me; Guido's descendants, the Sordellis, were the people who had invented this deadly little weapon.

Another time I was sitting on my bed in Soper Lodge with a young man who was spending a couple of nights there and he was proudly showing me his gun; a colt 45 revolver. One thing I remember from the western movies I'd seen as a kid was a colt 45 bullet was not only strong enough to kill a man, it could knock him over! And here was a young man legally holding one of these monstrous weapons in his hand. He was equally astonished that I'd never seen a handgun before and that we didn't carry them around with us as a matter of course as they do in South Africa.

"The only people who have handguns in Australia are those of a criminal element ... the general population like me never sees them." I ventured further: "What do you do with it?"

"I use it for self-defence."

"You mean you'd shoot them in the arm or the leg?' I was now feeling uncomfortable.

"No," he said. "I'd shoot to kill first, then fire two shots in the air to cover myself because the law says you have to fire two warning shots first." He said this with the assurance of one who believed the police were on his side and he'd have nothing to worry about.

I began to navigate the society I was now living in with a wary eye.

An astonishing proposition

This new worldly-wise view of things was put to a supreme test two weeks later. This time I was sitting in a hotel having a quiet beer when a moustachioed white guy in his mid thirties joined me and struck up a conversation. He seemed harmless enough in his orange floral shirt and white flares. After some small talk about where I was from and what I was doing in South Africa, he introduced himself as a general in the Rhodesian army and proceeded to run an astonishing proposition past me – which, I must admit, I didn't, and still don't, fully understand the gist of.

"I can help you to earn at least $1500 a day with the Rhodesian army," he said. "You'd do no combat, your job would be to stand beside the dead bodies of the terrorists we kill," he said, "and this is what you'd get paid to do ... it's for verification." He was deadly earnest as he said all this, for the war in Rhodesia wasn't going too well for the white minority. A big red light was flashing in my mind to have nothing to do with this, for it would be a one-way ticket to an early grave. I politely declined and thanked the general, who I believe was on a genuine recruiting mission, and retreated to the safe confines of Soper Lodge.

Phew! What next? I thought. There were two days to go before Tom and Bill arrived from their epic trip across Africa and I couldn't wait.

And what a relief it was when Tom and Bill finally walked in, travel weary and looking forward to a real bed. We agreed to catch up once they'd had a good night's sleep. And that went for the rest of their truckload of weary travellers who now filled Soper Lodge as well; people I would get to know over the next few weeks as they relived and shared their trials and tribulations of this unforgettable adventure – especially the time the blood-thirsty Emperor Bokassa, of his Central African Empire, held their truck up for two weeks and wouldn't let them leave till it suited him. They told me how relieved they were to escape from his murderous clutches and that it was very scary.

Tokoloshe!

As leaders, Tom was a bit of a joker and enjoyed a good laugh, whereas Bill was one of those quiet types who gets things done and was more mechanically minded than Tom should the truck break down.

On their way down through Africa, Tom picked up a dried civet-cat skin with its head still on, and for some reason brought it with him to Soper Lodge. It was slightly larger than an ordinary cat and I was intrigued by it. Then I got an idea. During my short stay in Soper Lodge I'd also learned that superstitions run very deep in South Africa, and that witch doctors are frequently consulted alongside doctors of western medicine. There is one small and terrifying mythical creature Indigenous South Africans are universally scared of, and that is Tokoloshe. Everyone knows of this fearsome little creature who can creep up on you of a night – or even during the day. So I ran my 'idea' past Tom: "Why don't we tie some nylon fishing line onto your civet-cat skin, then lay it in the gutter behind the kerb with the invisible line going back across the footpath to us hiding behind the front fence."

Tom was smiling. "I'm with you," he said. "When unsuspecting Africans come strolling along one of us can shout 'Tokoloshe!', while the guy behind the wall gives the fishing line a yank to set the furry Tokoloshe scurrying across the footpath!"

We couldn't wait to put it into action.

Boy did we have fun with this for a few days. Group after unsuspecting group of African folk would come strolling by, and all they would see was a friendly guy leaning on the front fence smiling and nodding hello. When they were in the right position, just before the front gate, the smiling guy would suddenly gesticulate and shout with fear: "Tokoloshe!" Out of the gutter would leap the dreaded Tokoloshe. To a man and woman they'd scream with terror and scatter in all directions. We even tried it with two Indigenous policemen. Down the footpath they strode, full of the importance of their role; they smiled hello and I did the same. When I screamed "Tokoloshe!" and the furry creature leaped out at them, they yelled with fear and took off like frightened children. A hundred yards or so down the road they realised what had happened, and they walked back as policemen again.

"You'd better put that away," they said, smiling sheepishly. We liked the way they had appreciated the joke and we put it away. We'd had our fun.

All the while, I'd been helping Tom and Bill with their unglamorous end-of-tour and turnaround duties, among which were: the changing of huge truck tyres; checking the vehicle was mechanically A1; giving it a complete wash and clean; and restocking it with food supplies for a new crew and return journey. Equally important to me were Tom and Bill's 'people-handling strategies', and how they won people to their way of thinking without turning the trip into a nightmare. I saw the result of their leadership skills with my own eyes and sought out their stories to find out how they did it.

CHAPTER 15

Becoming a tour leader

But it was now time for me to say goodbye to my new friends in South Africa and fly to England to fulfil my quest of becoming a tour leader myself. And I felt good about this because I'd gleaned bags of practical insights from the passengers and leaders about their recent overland experience that I'd be able to draw on. Two days later I took off for the Encounter Overland workshops in the little market town of Hitchin in South East England.

Not quite what I expected

I don't know what I'd envisaged when I got there, but what I'd had in mind was me building on being a people person; managing the different personalities effectively; and making sure that everything ran smoothly to give them the trip of a lifetime! That was my very general view of things as I mulled it all over on the plane. I'd already done fourteen years apprenticeship in organising and making things happen with The Top Hat Review, so I'd learned how to manage a group of people and keep them interested. So I wasn't scared of that. But was I in for a shock when I walked into the training workshop!

They assumed that all the 'people skills' I'd been focusing on would be learned along the way by riding 'jockey' as trainee leader on the first trip; *this* training was to assess my mechanical understanding and ability to keep the vehicle on the road. To my horror, the majority of my training would be stripping ex-army Bedford MJ 4×4 trucks right down to the chassis and putting them back together again. This practical knowledge was essential because with these long-haul expeditions, if something goes wrong with the truck, *you're* the man on the spot, and *you're* the one who has to fix it! None of this had I ever done before. With a sinking heart I put my overalls on and joined the other trainees who were all mechanically minded and had spent their lives working on cars in some way. What's more, they knew all the names of the different tools and their exact application; they knew the different equipment settings; they knew how to troubleshoot and fix problems with the electrics; and over the next few weeks all their general mechanical knowledge would be easily transferable to this type of vehicle. I wasn't even close to where they were. So for the duration of the training I decided to do my very best in learning what I could, win their respect, and save face … the future would look after itself.

Again, I did all the dirty work

With this approach settled in my mind, over the next six weeks I actually enjoyed myself and got right among it. I readily did all the dirty work like degreasing engine parts, just like I used to do with the dirty tools in the concrete gang. I asked questions and learned; then had a go myself. We all knew that I would never reach the level of being able to troubleshoot and fix an intricate truck problem in this short space of time; but I was helpful to have around and did my fair share of the work. And although we all knew the truth, I'd won them over as friends and there were no hard feelings. At the end of the six weeks working with these guys, I thanked them all for broadening my mind mechanically and wished them all the best with their trips. There was no way my mechanical skills would ever allow me to take on this role.

Before leaving, I got a message from Tony Jones, the founder of Encounter Overland, that he wanted me to call into his office in London.

A entirely new view of things

Although I hadn't passed the mechanical side of things, Tony appreciated the time I put in and the help I'd been in making the training group successful. He told me, "You get on with people really well, and what you should be looking at is being a tour leader that doesn't involve fixing trucks ... like with Contiki." I instantly saw the possibility in this, and warmly thanked him for his time. Tony Jones then did something for which I'll be forever grateful: he intuitively knew that like most Aussies wandering around Europe at the time I probably didn't have much money, and he wrote me a cheque for sixty pounds which was an absolute godsend. I sincerely thanked him for his interest in me and walked out of his office knowing exactly what I had to do.

Becoming a courier

It's also important to know that at this point in time I was desperate for some security in my life; I'd arrived in London on a one-way ticket; I was living in a basic single room, funded for now by Tony Jones's generous gift; and I needed a job! All fired up by Tony's suggestion of becoming a courier, the English term for camping tour leader, I answered the first ad I came across – AAAT Eurotours – and was given an interview.

At this interview I had to get the job no matter what, and I would draw on my greatest strength to do so; my 'gift of the gab.' I told myself: "In that dark alley in South Africa I'd talked my way *out of* a tricky situation, today I'm going to talk myself *into* one!"

It was at this interview I met the Australian Operations Manager of the company, Rod Mosely. Rod was a solid, athletic guy with a few freckles on his face, and it took a lot to make him laugh. He was a no-nonsense, even ruthless kind of manager, but if you were in his good books and delivered, he'd look after you. This was the formidable person I was facing in my second ever *proper* job interview; the first was with the post office. The menial jobs I'd had, you simply asked for a job and they either said "yes" or "no". I warmly shook his hand and sat down, with him on the other side of his desk. He appeared friendly enough but his face was non-committal. *I'm going to have to radiate confidence without making it too obvious*, I thought. *Show him you don't fold under pressure.*

Rod was a cool operator and wanted to know what I knew about the company and what kind of relevant experience I'd had. Luckily I'd grabbed a brochure from a travel agent the day before and read that AAAT Eurotours specialised in camping tours around Europe for the under thirty-fives, and was able to comment on that. I was able to share that I'd been on a P&O cruise in the Pacific four years before; I was able to highlight my year-long stay in Italy, studying Italian in Perugia and hang-gliding in the Alps; and I was able to relate my turnaround and debriefing experience with Encounter Overland in Johannesburg – as well as my training experience in Hitchin. And of course I took pains to drop in the fact that Tony Jones suggested leading camping tours without the need to fix trucks "is what I'd be best suited for". The interview seemed to be going well, and I felt pretty pleased with myself. Then Rod leaned back in his chair with his hands behind his head, smiled benignly at me and said, "This all sounds good and positive, but what's an area of your life you need to work on?"

A flash of genius

Totally unprepared for this, I just sat there on the edge of my chair and could have lost it all in that moment. Then a flash of genius came to my rescue: "As I've grown older, I've found I have a lot to say, and I've had to learn to shut up and let others share their ideas too." I admitted, "It's hard, but I work on it every day. I have a secret strategy that helps me do this; I have a little man sitting on my shoulder who tells me to *be quiet!* when others are trying to get a word in. So it's all under control and no longer a problem."

Rod seemed to like this; he smiled and nodded sagely. At this point he terminated the interview: "We'll let you know how you went in a day or two." And that was that.

The following day I got a call telling me to pack my suitcase ready for a rigorous six-week training trip around Europe … the second but more important phase of the job assessment. Seventeen hopeful couriers were to start, and only nine were to finish; was I destined to be one of the nine?

The notorious training trip

'Rigorous' was not the word for this training trip. Their philosophy was one of total humiliation and belittlement to try to break you, to see if you cracked when things got tough. It was a combination of a top commando course and a stringent history program while digging sewer trenches with Sid as your taskmaster. The pressure was so intense that every three days they would fly over two fresh trainers to keep the momentum going. You had to take notes on what was being said about the itinerary and history of the area you were passing through, and be prepared to give an interesting presentation on this at the front of the bus with the microphone. If you ever had the temerity to answer back you would be forced to get off the bus then and there and find your own way back to London. I saw this happen to three people who couldn't take it anymore.

The effects of this played into our tormentors' powerful hands. If you couldn't hack the pressure of being publicly humiliated in front of your fellow trainees, if you couldn't think straight and not crack under such pressure, you probably wouldn't be able to effectively handle a coachload of young people like a true leader and deftly cope with all the things that could possibly go wrong, like lost passports, drugs, accidents, and unexpected changes regarding destinations.

One treat on the training menu was everyone had a day of buying, preparing, and cooking three meals for fellow trainees and crew;

we were given a limited budget of AUD$30 with which to achieve this. I fared pretty well with this, for from an early age my mum had us cooking. Amazingly, we saw some real creativeness with the meagre amount of money at our disposal.

After three weeks of this physical and mental trauma we looked an unshaven, bedraggled bunch of hobos suffering from severe malnutrition; but we weren't cowed; not yet anyway.

On the verge of chucking it in

There was one thing I did have in my favour that stopped me from being cowed completely; I was able to speak confidently before groups because of my show biz background; but no one knew about this. Little did my assessors know that it was really a gigantic cover up; it was the full broadside of all I had to offer, and there was nothing else underneath it. The truth was I was sitting on that coach absolutely terrified of being found out for the fake and fraud that I was. The rates of monetary exchange of the seven different countries that we were about to travel through, of which I had no understanding whatsoever, brought my ever-present paranoia of maths to the fore: *they'll find me out when I do my cooking budget in different countries!* My frustration was that I had never had any problem figuring out transactions over the counter, for no one had told me this was maths; what I'd avoided for 18 years were fractions and percentages because *they were maths*, and *they* scared the hell out of me. I was genuinely on the verge of chucking in the towel when another angel appeared by my side in the form of Pancho.

Pancho my saviour

Pancho was one of those rare human beings who can sense someone in dire need and reach out and help. We weren't allowed to choose our seating partners on the coach, but every now and again I'd find myself seated next to Pancho; a big lovable Kiwi teddy bear with a trimmed black beard and an irresistibly infectious laugh. This drew him to me because he'd throw his head back and laugh at all my attempts at humour, which nourished my battered self-esteem and gave me hope that I'd somehow survive this gloomy experience. What such a likeable guy was doing on this whirlwind 'training trip' of tortuous humiliation I'll never know; what I did glean in the fleeting opportunities we were together was he was a science teacher and on long-term leave. *A science teacher?* I thought. *Maybe he can help me understand this rates-of-exchange stuff before I'm found out and kicked off the bus!*

Then, like two prisoners in a cell who only have a minute or so to convey a secret message or plan, I momentarily forgot I was a thirty-two-year-old man, and was back to being that frightened little fourteen-year-old boy again; my eighteen years of pent-up fear of all things 'maths' flooded upon poor Pancho in whispers of desperation: "What'll I do when they grill me on it?" I implored.

"Don't worry," he said without judgement. "I'll give you something very simple I want you to memorise that will get you through so no one will ever know." He then pulled a yellow filing card out of his pocket he'd been using to take notes on and began writing on the back of it: "If you multiply a number it gets bigger," he said softly as he wrote it down. He did the same with the next idea: "If you divide it, it gets smaller. With rates of exchange, simply multiply the currency you want to change into by entering the rate-of-exchange of the new currency and press the percentage button on your calculator." Beside these simplistic explanations Pancho drew easy-to-understand examples, reinforcing in very simple terms what they meant.

To any onlooker we were simply sharing notes. I carried Pancho's precious yellow card with me for the next two years, and it helped me get through my fearful ordeal of percentages. I'm not a religious person, but I do believe in universal kindness; so with Pancho I unreservedly use the world *angel* in the sense of a genuine saviour, for that's exactly what he was!

In later years I've tried to explain this blind fear of maths that plagued me most of my life, but most people don't get how deep this burdensome fear really was. "Why didn't you simply use a calculator," they say. But when my maths fears took hold, calculators weren't around. And by the time they were, it was too late and I was scared of them too! Any paranoia is *real* to the sufferer, be it maths, heights, public speaking, or spiders. What these people need is *understanding* and professional help to nurse them through it, so in time, they can leave their debilitating burdens behind and get on with their lives. I still had a long way to go with this, but Pancho gave me *real* hope that I was okay, and in time would be able to let mine go too.

One final 'treat'

Keeping in mind our training trip was held in the depths of winter, our benefactors had another treat in store for us; we'd be subjected to a test of endurance sleeping in our flimsy tents and sleeping bags on one of Finland's frozen lakes to see how we fared. And we're talking about twenty degrees below zero! Needless to say, everything out of our suitcases was wrapped around us that night, but we still froze. Around two in the morning Rod Mosely ventured out of the cosiness of the centrally-heated cabin he and his fellow trainers were comfortably ensconced in and crunched out onto that frozen lake. We nine remaining, shivering wretches, huddled together in two of the tents for warmth, heard him call out like some Nordic god: "Grab your sleeping bags and you can come into the cabin with us." We didn't need to be invited twice!

When we got into their balmy cabin two minutes later we thought, *you bastards! … nice and warm in your cabin while we've been freezing our balls off on that fucking frozen lake!* But we said nothing, grateful for this small gesture of humanity offered to us. We slept peacefully for the rest of that night as if in heaven.

And so our 'training' with AAAT Eurotours had come to an end, and what a scruffy, unshaven, forlorn bunch we must have looked; but inside we were elated – for we nine had made it! But none of us had the energy to celebrate. On the trip back to London, gone was the pressure, gone was the constant humiliation, and gone was the belittlement. We were now free to be our true selves again; and according to our trainers, we were now equipped to lead our own camping trips where we would be in complete charge of the welfare, hopes, and dreams of up to forty-five young people. We had plenty of time to contemplate this as we made the long trek back to London. Totally exhausted, most of us slept.

Back in London: the old tenement house

When we got back to London, those who had no home to go to were allowed to stay in the company apartment, an old tenement house in South Kensington, which was great, for most of us Aussies and Kiwis were homeless and trying to eke out a living on what meagre savings we had left. As it would be a few weeks before the camping tour season started, we had plenty of time to brush up on what we'd learned and to plan for our first trip. We had manuals, guides and recipe books to refer to, but no help other than that. We were on our own. All we were given prior to each trip were the necessary documents for the different border crossings, as well as a great wad of traveller's cheques to fund the trip – sometimes in excess of 20,000 pounds! And boy did we sweat it out over the next few weeks.

Mark Short

Another guy I'd befriended on the training trip was Mark Short (another Kiwi), who stayed on with me in the South Kensington apartment to bide our time while we anxiously waited for the tourist season to begin. Poor Mark. He'd left his native New Zealand to see the world without the blessing of his university professor father; "You'll come crawling back for support," his estranged father told him, "just you wait and see!" And Mark told me, "There is no way I'm going to ask him for help and give him the satisfaction of rubbing it in." Because this sad situation left such an indelible impression on me, I've always told my kids that no matter what, never be ashamed to ask their dad for help.

When Mark first arrived in the British Isles, his first port of call was to make himself known to an elderly, long-lost relative living in a forbidding bluestone building in Scotland. He told me he was made to feel very unwelcome, and was stuck in an upstairs room in the middle of winter, and it was freezing! He said, "Every night, all I could hear was this old guy walking around downstairs continuously coughing out loud and saying over and over in his broad Scottish accent: 'Why should I be burdened with it! … Why should I be burdened with it! … '" After three days of this cold torment Mark simply slipped away in the dead of night with his one suitcase and headed for London. So Mark and I were kindred spirits: lost, broke and lonely with nothing but our fear-filled camping tours before us … yet we both harboured a glimmer of hope that good would come out of it all.

To say Mark and I were full of trepidation is nowhere near the story; we were terrified, and both of us knew it. In the lead up to being thrown to the wolves, Mark and I would rehearse our opening spiels to each other over and over. And to lighten it up we would always finish with, "I caaan't do it!" in a broad American accent, then fall to our knees sobbing hysterically. This would always make us laugh and was a great stress release.

Another thing we did was befriend, and pick the brains of, the seasoned couriers who happened to be staying in the apartment between trips. We'd listen carefully to their stories and strategies and what they did when things went wrong; we listened carefully to their clever one-liners and the gems of stories they themselves had gleaned from those who'd come before them. When they'd gone, Mark and I would write it all down and incorporate these priceless tried-and-proven strategies into our own notes, which in turn would later morph into our own thinking. When we'd added all this to the mountain of practical ideas and inspirations we'd gathered on the training trip, we were as ready as we could possibly be. Specific aspects of each trip would be dealt with in detail in the pre-trip briefing. Other than this, all we could do was wait.

CHAPTER 16

The first trip

When it happened, things moved fast. My first trip was to be a two-week 'Midnight Sun Holiday Beyond the Arctic Circle'. Which was interesting because in our winter training trip the various governments forbade us to go anywhere near the Arctic Circle, for it was completely snowed under. So for that part of the trip I would be relying on secondhand notes dictated to me by the instructors. *I'll worry about that when I get there*, I thought. But for the most part I had my own notes from being there and seeing things with my own eyes.

Our itinerary was as follows: leave London for Dover; take ferry across to Calais in France; head north through France into Belgium; cross over into Holland; then into Germany; up into Denmark; across the straits into Sweden; up the east coast of Sweden into Finland; westward into Norway; north beyond the Arctic Circle to Narvik; return south through Norway; visit East Berlin through Checkpoint Charlie; London via Calais France. All pretty straight forward. No problems.

I was careful to carry myself as a confident leader in my pre-trip briefing with Rod Mosely, for I couldn't risk displaying the slightest hint of doubt in my ability. He in turn seemed to have a genuine trust in me to deliver; which was a real boost to my confidence. He discussed various important border documents with me; like the French *carnet*, a declaration of all camping equipment you are bringing into France which you *must* have verified with a special stamp when you first cross the French border. This stamped *carnet* allows you to take this same certified camping equipment with you when you cross any border *out* of France ... I made particular note of this because without this special clearance stamp I'd be personally liable to pay for a coachload of illegal camping gear! Then came the most important thing of all: Rod Mosely handed over 25,000 pounds in traveller's cheques to 'flexibly' manage everything from start to finish as per our contract. This lifeline for the trip went straight into my bag around my wrist and stayed there. That afternoon I went to Half Case bulk food store to purchase all my supplies for the trip so they could be stacked into the food bay in the coach for me. This was my first action as leader of the trip. My second action was to be at the start point at 7:30 sharp the following morning, ready to take these young people on the trip of a lifetime!

My head was spinning. As I made my way back to the apartment I went through everything one more time and found it hard to find fault. The coach would be filled with fuel and thoroughly checked ready for me to go; we'd be leaving nice and early, which would get us to our Belgian camping site early evening, affording me ample time to give them a quick tutorial on how to erect their tents, pack them up in the morning, and set up the camp kitchen. This first night's three-course dinner would be simple; cream of chicken soup with lots of buttered bread; ham steaks and pineapple with mashed potato and green beans; followed by tinned fruit and custard for sweets; then tea and coffee. I would set up the daily cooking squads on the long drive to our Belgian campsite, explaining the generous budget they would have for the 'surprise' dinner of their choice and how easy all this would be; and likewise for the dish-washing and hand-washing arrangements. But even the best laid plans can come to grief. And it was this factor of the *unexpected* that was to prove the biggest challenge for me and my driver, Dave Watson, on that first, fateful day.

I was already there at 7:10 when Rod Mosely strode up to me.

"All ready to go?" he said, shaking my hand.

"As ready as I'll ever be," I truthfully replied, although my heart was racing out of control. I felt a bit like a condemned man climbing the scaffold. The coach pulled into the kerb packed with my forty young adventurers, my driver came out and introduced himself, Rod Mosely stepped aboard and introduced himself as the company Operations Manager; he then introduced me as the leader of this particular trip – and one of the organisation's more experienced couriers! With that, he stepped off the coach and left me to it.

I was all on my own.

To hide the real fear I felt inside I pretended I was the confident Master of Ceremonies I used to be in The Top Hat Review and went straight into my introductory spiel about all the different countries I'd just visited with the latest European 'trip' I was involved in … and how much I was looking forward to being part of their exciting holiday of a life-time. I introduced our Driver Dave as "the man who was going to get us safely to each day's destination – as well as join in the fun!" Dave was a short, stocky guy with a number two crew-cut and a strong Northern English accent, which to me sounded very Scottish. And he had a liking for energy-giving Mars bars, which became a running joke. Finally I went through the boring list of safety – and legal – do's and don'ts so everyone clearly knew what was permitted, and what was not. I finished by saying, "Our first destination is Dover where we're due to catch the ferry across to Calais in France at 11:00 am … and in a little while I'll be coming around to each of you to introduce myself and show you exactly where we'll be going for the rest of the day on the map." I then sat down in my courier's seat behind Dave and breathed a sigh of relief.

And guess what? I didn't die! Everyone just sat there, wide-eyed and expectant, listening to my every word as if I was behaving just as a leader should with his opening remarks.

If only things had stayed this way

Once we'd made our way out of London and entered the pleasant countryside towards Kent, I kept my promise of saying hello to everyone individually with my daily map. This, I discovered, did two things: it took much of the pressure off me; and it warmed them to me for they felt involved.

"Hi," I'd say as I came to each seat of two people. "Just call me Laurie … would you like to see where we're heading today on the map?" I'd then run my finger along where we were at the time and where we were going to. They really seemed to appreciate this, so I made a mental note to do this every morning. I also had a copy of a previous Day Book with me, a light-hearted daily journal they could all contribute to, and a nice memoir they'd all receive a copy of at the end of the trip.

I'd just finished talking to the people in the last seat when disaster struck. The coach ran out of fuel! We were only an hour and a half out of London.

"How can this be?" I quietly said to Dave. "It was supposed to be refuelled by the garage team!" A pang of panic swept over me.

"Don't worry," Dave said, "I'll grab a jerry can from under the coach and go and get some fuel; you look after the passengers." I stuffed some cash in his hand and said, "Grab me a receipt." With that, Dave disappeared.

I took a breath and picked up the microphone: *Here goes*, I thought. "Friends, the coach has unexpectedly run out of fuel, so while we're sorting this out I'd like you all to get off the coach and make yourselves comfortable in that little meadow of grass and flowers beside the road while we're getting some diesel … And could I have three volunteers to help me set up a little gas cooker and the makings of a cup of tea and coffee for everyone while this is happening."

This got them all involved, and they seemed to be enjoying this unexpected distraction in the Kent countryside. While all this was going on, Burnie, a young Irishman away from his garage workshop on his first ever holiday, pulled me aside and whispered something in my ear: "I'm a diesel mechanic and this coach runs on diesel. Unlike a petrol engine, the whole fuel system has to be bled before you can refill it."

"So … what needs to be done?" I asked, fearing the worst.

"It's a job for a qualified diesel mechanic," said Burnie. "Have you got any tools?"

"Yeah, there is a toolkit there in the back bay." And with that Burnie rolled up his sleeves and got to work under the bonnet (another of the angels I talk about). Just think about it – the guy goes on this holiday to get away from years of being up to his elbows in grease and dirt, and an hour into it he's rolling up his sleeves again! Words can't express how grateful I was. Right then another angel appeared with a jerry can of diesel, and between them Dave and Burnie had the coach on the road again within half an hour. We were now two hours behind time, and it was touch and go whether we'd make the ferry across The Channel or not. I kept this to myself and we continued on our way through the picturesque Kent countryside.

We arrived at the port of Dover just in time to see the tail end of our ferry disappearing in the distance.

"Don't worry," I reassured them, "the next one won't be long." I spied a hot dog stand over to the side. "And because you've been so patient, while we're waiting I'll shout you all a hot dog." This placated them somewhat while we awaited the next ferry, which was an hour and a half away. Not a good start at all.

When it finally did arrive and we were safely on board, their spirits lifted for their trip was back on track and we were on our way again. But we were now three hours behind and wouldn't arrive at the campsite before 11:00 pm. My plans were now all over the place and I was scrambling to adjust. *My tent erecting demo will have to be done by torchlight and the camp kitchen set up will have to wait till the morning*, I surmised. And a well-prepared dinner? … Well I'd figure that out when we got closer to Brussels.

Safely aboard I breathe a sigh of relief

The Channel crossing was uneventful, and on we drove north through the greenness of Normandy. Things were beginning to go our way. But about two hours' drive from Calais in the rolling vineyards of Normandy, you're not going to believe what happened. The coach ran out of diesel again. The passengers were totally unaware of this because it was the furthest thing from their minds, for how could that possibly be? So they didn't see me go white, they didn't see me freeze, and they didn't see me begin to tremble. But Dave did: he reached out and grabbed my upper arm with force and looked me straight in the eye: "You're the leader of all the people here," he said with a conviction I responded to. "Do what you did before and I'll go and get some diesel … looks like the fuel gauge is the problem … from now on we'll work off the mileage counter."

I thrust a bag of francs at Dave and he quietly melted into the vineyards without a word of French to help him. I looked around at my by now puzzled charges and picked up the microphone.

I figured my best approach was to be straight up and honest with them by sharing what we'd just discovered: "We have a faulty fuel gauge. Dave is off getting fuel again, and from now on we'll be filling up based on the mileage counter." I sensed a few murmurings so I appealed to a nobler understanding that it was not our personal fault and we were doing our utmost to fix it. "All going well," I said, trusting in the universe to somehow help us, "we should be on our way within half an hour. This done, we'll be able to focus on tomorrow as a whole new day for there are a lot of wonderful things ahead of us."

No sooner had I finished saying this than we heard the *put, put, put* of a tractor pulling up beside us with a French farmer at the wheel, beret and all, and Dave with his by now familiar jerry can of diesel perched firmly in his lap. Spontaneously everyone applauded his genius of being able to ferret out diesel from nowhere; I thanked the farmer with a heartfelt handshake and compensated him for the fuel. The ever reliable Burnie was already at the engine doing his thing.

Miraculously the universe had answered my call; within the half hour we were on our way for the third time. Once settled down, I publicly thanked Dave and Burnie for their roles in getting us moving again, and everyone endorsed this with warm applause. I was fast learning what it's like to be a leader.

Disaster strikes again

By the time we reached the Belgian border darkness was upon us, which made it hard to find our way for most of my notes were based on prominent landmarks which by now were near impossible to discern. Then something a million times worse came into my head: "Oh my God!" I whispered to Dave, "I forgot to get the *carnet* stamped in Calais! And I'll be personally liable for all the camping gear!"

"Just explain what happened on the way to the ferry from London and that you forgot about it because it's your first trip," said a hopeful Dave.

"Okay," I said … but after the day's onslaught of demoralising events I fully expected the worst, and reluctantly walked into the French customs office next to the border gate clutching my *unstamped carnet.*

Boom! Boom!

Behind the desk was a middle-aged Frenchman wearing a dark-blue peaked General de Gaul hat. He was grim-faced and had a no-nonsense look about him, as if he'd had a bad day. I greeted him with a "bon soir", which had no effect on his sullen countenance. Then, for some weird reason, maybe because I'd known some Austrian friends for a long time back in Australia and learnt a bit of German, I broke into a mashed-up German with this haughty, stressed-out Frenchman. Now this was probably the worst thing I could have done with someone of his age and their animosity towards the Germans because of the war. "Ich forgessen der stampen," I said in my stupid German, brandishing my unstamped *carnet* before this by now very angry border official. He simply glared at my uncompleted clearance document as if it was a piece of rubbish and totally unacceptable. To make matters worse my troubled mind stayed with my broken German … but with an added communicating touch. Instead of *der stampen* (my Anglicised German word for stamped), and to help this confused official better understand my predicament, I instinctively used my upright fist with up-and-down stamping motions, causing my desperate plea to now become: "Ich forgessen der *Boom! Boom!*" I kid you not … they're the exact words that came out of my mouth! This exasperated Frenchman stared at me, sarcastically repeating my, *"Boom! Boom!"*

Then, because he'd simply had enough of idiots like me giving him a hard time, or he just wanted to get home, he disdainfully authorised our *carnet* with an exit stamp and waved me away with a dismissive "sors d'ici!", which we later learnt from our Belgian hosts at the campsite meant "get out of here!"

Into Belgium

Surely that's all the bad luck we can have, I thought to myself as we finally crossed the border into Belgium. By now it was pitch black, but with the help of luminous freeway signs we found our way to the main square in Brussels with its famous statue of the little boy doing wee … and low and behold, a Maccas! "We're not far from the campsite," I told them. "And the tents are pretty easy to put up … and I'll give you a quick demo how to do it when we get there … but as a reward for your patience today I'm going to shout you all a Big Mac, chips, and a drink."

Everyone cheered and rushed into Maccas. How ironic! They come on this trip for a very different experience from the norm and the first night they eat out – I take them to McDonald's. This, along with the day's events, ended up in the Day Book … but not in a negative way.

As we pulled into our long sought-after campsite, while I had them all seated I ran through our plan of camp set up: they would all come round to the side of the coach where they would be given a tent and a self-inflating mattress and their luggage. I would then give them a quick demo on how to put their tents up and where the two lines of them would be. I also showed them how to pack them up again for effective storage the following morning. I then 'deputised' four people, two girls and two boys to keep the balance right, to help me with the cook tent once their tents were erected. "This done," I told them, "the rest of the night is yours. As it's still very warm; the adventurous ones among you might want to go for a midnight swim in the camp lake, even a midnight skinny dip! Or you might want to just hit the sack after such a big day! ... Whatever you decide, set your alarms and be up ready for breakfast at 7:00 am."

So that's what we did, and it didn't take them long to learn how to do all this. Within two days, ten minutes was all they needed, cook tent and all. We could set our little tent village up and have a delicious three-course meal ready in half an hour flat! But they were yet to know that. Right now I had a bag of French and Belgian currencies and their formidable rates of exchange to work out, as well as all my receipts and dockets. I bid them goodnight and retired to my tent.

It all catches up with me

I opened my suitcase, laid out my sleeping bag, tipped an intimidating heap of different currencies and receipts out onto it, and stared at it for quite a while. The combination of the horrific things that had happened that day, coupled with the terrifying mystery of rates of exchange, tipped the scales of my sanity over into a total mental breakdown where I completely lost my mind. This was nothing like the severe panic attacks I'd suffered before; in this frightening state of mind anything could have happened to me, and it scares me to reflect on how vulnerable I was. After all these years of running from my maths paranoia it had finally caught up with me; this day's cumulative chain of events brought it all to an explosive head and was crushing me down. I was a broken man, kneeling and shivering in a cold sweat all alone in my tent, taunted by a mountain of different currencies and their unintelligible exchange rates scattered on the floor before me. Even though it was a balmy summer night I felt ice cold with sweat pouring out of me. I stayed very still, on my knees staring at the tent wall for what seemed like hours. At one stage I vividly recall all I wanted to do was run away into the surrounding wheat fields to curl up, hide and be safe.

Then something extraordinary happened …

Pancho's precious yellow card

The carefree laughter of young people coming back from their midnight adventure skinny dipping broke into my tortured mind. Their bubbling voices snapped me out of the very dark place I was drowning in: "I can't let them down," I whispered to myself. "They are depending on me keeping my promise to give them the holiday of a lifetime – and that's exactly what I'm going to do!"

Then I remembered Pancho's precious yellow card in my parka pocket. Between my stifled sobs, I lay his priceless guide before me alongside that heap of intimidating money and dockets. Over the next hour or so, I carefully made little stacks of the different currencies and their denominations; and in a very rudimentary way, following Pancho's simple scheme, I figured out their rates of exchange well enough to get me out of trouble. I then crawled into my sleeping bag and I slept deep and peacefully until awakened by my 5:00 am alarm. A new day was about to dawn.

I sprang into action, for I had a breakfast to organise and a promise to fulfil; life was worth living, and a great weight had been lifted from my shoulders. I'd made a few resolutions: my monetary reckonings may not be completely up to scratch when I submit my final trip report, but my outstanding leadership would more than compensate for this; I made a resolution that I would nip any disquiet in the bud before it manifested itself into a trip-wrecking conspiracy; I made a resolution that I would turn potential troublemakers into loyal deputies by making them *feel important*; and I made a resolution that I would strive, no matter what happened, to never have a complaint lodged with head office about my leadership. A tall order, yes. But it had to be this way to far outweigh my formidable accounting shortcomings.

No one has ever heard a single word about my horrific night of mental breakdown ... until now. But from experiencing how paralysing it can be myself, I've become a more insightful and understanding person. Nowadays, whenever I hear of someone who has had a mental breakdown, I don't think *stop carrying on and get over it!* I know it's an awful, debilitating experience, and not something to be glibly scoffed at. Instead, I try to reach out to them with an empathetic and understanding hand.

A new day dawns

The following morning was indeed a whole new chapter for everyone, especially me. My *Pax* (as we couriers called the passengers) were up bright and early, and to their absolute astonishment were greeted to a full-on breakfast, all laid out on table-clothed trestles for all to see. There were even hand-washing and dish-washing facilities on another table to the side. And how inviting it all looked: cereals and milk, toast and jam (vegemite for the Aussies), bacon, sausages and scrambled eggs on toast, tea and coffee. They were impressed!

"Grab your plates off the stack and cutlery from the container and come this way," I heard the cooking crew say, just as I'd taught them the night before. Things were looking good.

Packing up camp went very smoothly as everyone got into the swing of things very quickly. Dave and I did all the stacking in the loading bays till I'd trained others to take turns in doing it. *The more you get people involved, the more they feel a part of it.*

Back in control and on our way

As we drove along that morning heading for the Dutch border, this time with Dave's eye keenly on the mileage meter, I asked them: "Did you all enjoy breakfast?"

"It was great!" they chorused.

"Well, guess what?" I rhetorically asked, "From now on *you'll all* be doing that; and lunch and dinner too!"

A collective protest filled the bus: "What? ... We can't cook!"

"Our star breakfast cookers from today felt the same way with the same protests and look what they ended up doing! And you'll be able to do the same!" I thoughtfully looked at them: "Let me ask you this: Who here has ever cooked for four people? Can I see your hands?" Everyone put their hand up.

"Well, all we're going to do is multiply our ingredients by ten and use bigger pots! There will be ten groups of four people, and I've written up rosters and will post them on the back of the front seats. Breakfast will stay the same, as will our lunch; rolls filled with ham, sausage, cheese, tomato, salad and so on. But dinner will always be different because it will be *your* choice and *you'll* be cooking it. I have some great recipe books for you to choose from with simple but hearty recipes. Each team will be given the money to cover the costs of ingredients. And don't worry ... you'll have lots of support from me, and I guarantee you'll surprise yourselves!"

Despite the protests, no team cooked a bad meal on the whole trip, and some were quite outstanding. For some of the *Pax* this was the first time they had ever worked as part of a team on anything, and it was a wonderful growth experience for them. It was amazing to see the confidence and power these cooking teams wielded once they got inside that cooking tent. If you wanted a generous serving of their food you had to treat them right!

Getting to the coach on time

One thing we had to do was keep our eye on the time, for we always had a new destination to get to. So if I set the passengers off to visit something of interest for an hour or so, or to go on some added excursion and told to be back on the coach ready to go at say 2:00 pm, they had to be back on the bus ready to go at 2:00 pm. If I were to be slack on this and just let them do their own thing and wander back when it suited them, we'd have a lot of people off side and never finish the trip! Dave and I devised a little scenario to emphasise the importance of getting back to the coach on time.

On the third day out I got up in front of them and made a big deal about the importance of getting back to the coach at the appointed time after an excursion, a toilet stop or a shopping spree. While I was raving on and labouring the point, Dave chipped in to back me up: "I'll simply drive away without you because it's not fair on everyone else," he said with conviction. This all came across as pretty real and logical, if a bit harsh.

Later that day, as we stopped for a twenty-minute toilet break I announced "I'd be ducking into a supermarket for some supplies". I deliberately got back to the bus eight minutes late ... just in time to see Dave preparing to drive away. I ran up and banged on the door, "Hey! What are you doing?" I yelled. "Open the door and let me in!"

"I told you I'd leave if you weren't back on time," he yelled back, "and that applies to you too!"

"Ah, come on ... let me in ... I was just getting some supplies!"

"Well, this time okay, but we can't play favourites and make exceptions." Dave grumbled and sullenly opened the door. You could see he wasn't happy.

Somewhat flustered and out of breath, I leaped up the stairs and sat in my chair looking a bit embarrassed for breaking my own rules. Doing his best to keep a straight face, and without another word, Dave pulled out of the car park and drove away.

From this point on there was never any problem with people being late back to the coach.

Turning a troublemaker into a respected 'tent stacker'

One thing I was told to watch out for was opinionated people who thought they could run the show better than you, or always had something to say in conflict with your ideas. If they weren't dealt with quickly and adroitly you could end up losing control and the respect of the whole group.

On this first of my trips, one such person was Bill, who was fast rubbing everyone up the wrong way. He was a burly red-headed guy, an ex-footballer, and he was used to throwing his weight around on the football field. I had to act fast, not only to undo any damage already done, but cleverly win Bill over to become a positive influence on the holiday instead of a negative one. So here's what I did: in a quieter moment when no one else was around, I sidled up to him and said, "Hey, Bill, I wonder if you could do me a favour?"

This got his attention, for we all like to feel important.

"I have a special job I want to allocate to someone but I don't want to give it to just anyone and be stuffed around!" Bill stood up straighter, threw his chest out, and listened some more.

"You know when they stack the tents in the morning and it becomes one big messy heap?"

He nodded.

"Well, I want someone who can take charge of it all and keep the stack neat … then see that they're stacked economically in the loading bay … and that goes for the cook tent too … Do you think you could do that for me?"

"I think I could."

"Fantastic! You'll be in charge of all that from now on and I'll let everyone know."

That day, as we were driving along I announced that Bill was now in charge of all loading in the bays, and all you had to do was stack your tents neatly beside him of a morning and hand him your suitcase when it was ready for stacking. Everyone thought this a great idea, namely because someone else was doing it instead of them! I noticed Bill was now sitting quite proud of the fact that he was now a respected deputy in the whole concern. Remarkably, his prickly 'digging' at everything stopped and he became quite helpful in many ways, and people were appreciative of the energetic work he'd taken on each morning with their tents and valuable belongings. Collectively we'd transformed Bill from a potential trip-wrecker into a wonderful asset who we now respected and who took a positive part in everything.

I was able to utilise the likes of Bill in other ways as well, for my eyes couldn't be everywhere at once. Now that Bill and I were on the same page, one day I quietly said to him, "If ever you hear someone say they don't like something, just secretly tell me and I'll do my best to rectify it."

One day he did: "A couple of people complained they're not getting enough sausage and cheese in the lunch rolls," he confided.

"No worries," I said, "I'll see there's more put in 'em." And I did! If I hadn't, he would not have helped me anymore. It was little strategies like these that nipped any disquiet in the bud so that all complaints were dealt with on the road and never went any further.

The art historian

I enjoyed all this play acting, for it was assuaging my burning desire to be a world-renowned entertainer, which had taken a back seat while all this tour guiding thing was going on but it never really went away.

I was to use my illusory acting talent in other ways to get me out of trouble, especially on this first eventful trip. One particular instance occurred in Holland's Rijksmuseum in Amsterdam, which houses precious Dutch art and artefacts from the Middle Ages to the present day. The piece of art in question was Rembrandt's 1642 iconic painting *The Night Watch*. Now I had never set eyes on this painting as famous as the *Mona Lisa*; nor had I ever set foot in this legendary museum! Yet here we were, an hour away from these priceless wonders and all I had were some secondhand notes about them, handed to me by another courier the night before we left. But I had made sure I read them through, and thought about them.

As we pulled up in front of the Rijksmuseum I said something along the lines of: "One work of art to watch out for is Rembrandt's 1642 painting *The Night Watch* … It's noted for its colossal size and the dramatic use of light and shadow … I want you to look out for the guy with the red sash over his shoulder standing in the front with his left hand stretched out … I want you to take note of how Rembrandt has the light shine off the man's white sleeve and casts a shadow of this hand over the white tunic of the officer standing next to him … It's almost as if the hand is reaching out of the picture." I then gave them a time to be back at the bus and I disappeared down the coach steps into the crowd.

Well … not really. Straight up the main stairs I rushed, through the main entrance to the information desk: "Could you tell me where *The Night Watch* is?" I asked the attendant.

"Round to your right sir," she said.

"Thank you." And back I raced out the main doorway; I stopped; then casually descended the stairs meeting my charges on the way up, "*The Night Watch* is through the doors and round to your right," I nonchalantly informed them … "We'll see you back at the coach."

Later I asked them: "Did you get a chance to see *The Night Watch*? … Did you see how Rembrandt deftly used the light and shade on that outstretched arm?"

"Oh yes," they said. "Quiet impressive!"

The Little Mermaid

For a blissfully uneventful stretch, ever-northward we travelled through wonderful Germany, then we crossed into Denmark; the first of our Scandinavian countries. One thing they all wanted to know about was *The Little Mermaid*, the mythical sea creature from their childhood memories. The truth is her statue is pretty small and sits on a bunch of tawdry rocks on the edge of a modern industrial harbour; a setting that is not very mythical or romantic. So I had to beat it up a bit. This is where a touch of drama and the art of storytelling (which I'd also been working on) came to my aid.

To get to the statue of *The Little Mermaid* you've got to first walk through one of Copenhagen's beautiful botanical gardens. But the *Pax*, distracted by the beauty around them, were totally unaware that the object of their affection was so close by. So just before we rounded a bend in this lovely garden path, I stopped my eager charges and asked them to gather round. I was learning fast that grown ups are just kids in big bodies and that everyone loves a story!

"*The Little Mermaid*," I told them, "was born of a fairy tale by Danish author Hans Christian Andersen ... *The Little Mermaid* wanted to gain the soul of a human to win the heart of a handsome prince who lived on the land, but he was shipwrecked and perished at sea ... the statue incarnation you're about to see still sits wistfully looking over the water longing for her lost prince ..."

When they took those few more steps to the other side of a screen of trees and garden beds, *The Little Mermaid* awaited them a mere twenty metres away, and the whole thing became magical and real to them. They caught their breath at her beauty, and took lots of 'selfies' and group photos with her.

Without the story to stimulate their childhood imaginations, there would have been no magic, no fairy tale enchantment. I was beginning to see that my show biz experience could be transferred to other settings too.

Another thing I had a lot of fun with in Denmark was the statue *The Lure Players*, a twenty-metre-high monument in Copenhagen's City Hall Square. It is very impressive, with its two figures playing a Bronze Age, horn-like instrument called a lure. Dave and I tested this out on our first trip. It was decided that Dave would drive slowly beneath this imposing monument while I got them all to look at it while saying: "Legend has it that the lure players should blow their horns whenever a virgin passed them." Dave continued to pass it by.

When the coach had completely passed it I commented, "I didn't hear anything ..."

Disaster on the scenic railway

But there was one thing that happened one evening in Copenhagen's famous Tivoli Gardens amusement park that wasn't funny at all and nearly brought the whole trip to an abrupt end. It occurred on the Mountain Coaster scenic railway, one of the world's oldest wooden roller-coasters that is still operating today. As part of our training we were urged to show an interest in what our camping tour clients were doing, and when possible, join in the fun. And this was one such case. I'd just highlighted the fact that Denmark's Tivoli Gardens opened in August 1843 and was the second oldest operating amusement park in the world, and that went for its wooden roller-coaster ride as well. So, all excited, in we went to spend a couple of hours there. I was especially interested in this ancient wooden roller-coaster that was still operating, so I decided to first try it by myself and that's what I headed for.

I recall it was a well-lit, balmy summer night with pockets of pitch-black darkness where the myriad bright carnival lights didn't reach. I soon found the quaint wooden ticket box, exactly as it would have been in 1843, and bought my ticket. And it was thrilling; round the curves the coaster flew, up and down the inclines it raced at break-neck speed.

Towards the end of the ride we were flying around a particularly tight curve when the centrifugal force of the vehicle ripped my irreplaceable money bag from my wrist – containing the trip's 25,000 pounds in traveller's cheques – and flung it away into the darkness! To say I panicked would not do my feelings justice ... I was having an out-of-body experience of superhuman determination *to get that bag back!* ... blind with fear, over and over I was saying to myself, "I've gotta get it back ... I've gotta get it back ... I-have-to-get-that-bag-back!"

The roller-coaster finally clanked to a stop. My mind was a blur, and like a beast possessed I clambered out of the vehicle and pushed past those in line at the ticket box.

"Hey, where are you going?" the guy in the box said.

"I've just got to get something," I said, and disappeared into the darkness under the white trestle work. The pitch blackness away from the lights was on my side as I began to blindly climb the triangular supports like a blabbering idiot: *This was that last curve before the end*, my troubled mind was saying, *this was where I saw it fly out into the blackness*.

Then, still clinging to the trestle with the roller-coaster crashing past above me, for some reason I was drawn to look at the leaves of an adjacent elm tree silhouetted against the night sky; and there, among the dark leaves was another shape with a straighter outline standing out against the starlit background. *Could it possibly be?* My heart leaped out of my chest. I narrowed my focus to the dark outline I was trying to make out, when something moved! And there, swaying gently in the breeze, was the unmistakable handle of my bag!

I scrambled down that trestle work in three seconds and rushed to the trunk of that blessed elm tree. Its smooth, high trunk towered above me with not a branch or imperfection of any kind for me to grab hold of. Now I've seen documentaries where macaque monkeys and Indigenous climbers effortlessly shimmy up one-hundred-foot palm trees to get coconuts; well I don't know what got into me that night, but I did the same!

With a superhuman effort my knees locked around that trunk and up I went. Then out onto the branch I crawled and stretched, finally reaching out and … the bag toppled off! But that wasn't so bad because this time I knew where it was. I back-tracked along the branch and more *free fell* than shimmied my way back down to safety. In that pitch-black darkness it wasn't easy to find my matching black bag, but I did it on my hands and knees by feel, like a blind cave-dwelling insect would find its prey; then I felt it … and latched on to it so it couldn't get away! With my bag now safely attached to my wrist, I casually walked out of the darkness from beneath the roller-coaster trestles, gave a friendly nod in response to the ticket attendant's quizzical look, and went happily on my way.

The whole episode had taken less than twenty minutes.

What more can happen? I asked myself. *None of this was part of my training!*

I hadn't walked far when I bumped into a group of my passengers. They took one look at me and said, "What happened to you?!" Realising I must have looked a bit unkempt, I said, "I fell over in the dirt near the roller-coaster." They seemed to accept this as just more quirky behaviour from their likeable but bumbling leader who, in spite of his unusual attributes, miraculously solves problems and gets things done.

When we did get back to camp around midnight, and still recovering from my extraordinary ordeal, I made my way to the shower block to wash it all away with a nice warm shower. The apparition I saw in the mirror startled me: my hair was dishevelled; I was covered in dirt, grime, and grease; my shirt was torn in places; and a pocket of my trousers was hanging loose. I had to agree with my *Pax*; this was a lot of *unusual* damage for a light fall!

With this accumulation of *not-so-ordinary* happenings, they couldn't help but have an interesting perspective of me. All I could do was play along with it, for these *interesting* things just kept happening! But there was no way known anyone was going to know the truth of this last one.

From Denmark to Sweden

It was now time to move on from Denmark to our next Scandinavian country, Sweden. Nowadays one can drive the twelve kilometres across the Kattegat Strait from Denmark to Sweden by way of the breathtaking Oresund Bridge and the Drogden Tunnel. But when I was there in 1979 the only choice was the ferry from Frederikshavn in Denmark to Gothenburg in Sweden. I had learned from other couriers that this was the ferry where you could supplement the meagre 20 pounds a day we got from AAAT Eurotours by buying whisky in the ship's supermarket at a third of the price you could sell it for in Sweden because of their higher tax regime. At the time I'd made a mental note of this; but this first time round I had enough on my plate to worry about than risk a bit of grog running as well!

Renowned for forethinking and innovation

Apart from being a beautiful country, Sweden is renowned for being innovative and punching well above its size industrially; we have all heard of companies like Volvo, Scania and Saab. As we drove along I informed the group, "They're ahead of the world in other ways too; for example, in 1977 the safety-conscious Swedes were the first country to require widespread use of driving with your car head-lights on ... and if you all look out the window you'll see this!" ... and they did. "In fact," I added, "all modern Swedish-sold cars have the lights turned on automatically." I found that these little snippets of information made the journey interesting for them.

Another interesting aspect of the forethinking Swedes is their unique concept of the *freedom to roam*: 'Everyman's Right' is a freedom granted by the Constitution of Sweden, and gives a person the right to access, walk, cycle, ride, ski and camp on any land – with the exception of private gardens, the immediate vicinity of a dwelling house, and land under cultivation. I'd only gleaned a bare outline of this intriguing concept from a brochure I'd picked up at the last minute in London, so I knew none of the intricate details. So when I told them about it I had to use my own interpretation by inferring that you could pretty well go anywhere as long as you respected the other person's property.

One day we were driving up the east coast of Sweden in the middle of nowhere and we stopped for a break to stretch our legs and admire the view. Below us among the pine trees was a fairy tale meadow as green as green and very inviting. I invoked the Swedish

'Everyman's Right' and said they could wander down there as long as they treated it with respect.

"Let's take a couple of frisbees to toss around," someone suggested, and away they happily went. Dave and I remained behind to catch up with some admin stuff in the bus.

Barely ten minutes later I heard a commotion as they all came rushing back and staggered breathlessly onto the coach.

"What happened?" I asked.

"An old guy came screaming out of the forest with a shotgun and chased us away!"

"Oh," I sheepishly said, "there must be bits of that 'Everyman's Right' that I don't know about." We settled back into the coach and drove on without much more said about it. Laurie's version of 'Everyman's Right' did get an ironic mention in the Day Book.

As the old saying goes, "When in Rome ... " Well, the same concept applies in Sweden. And the Swedes love their nude swimming, so "for those courageous enough to give it a try", I ventured, in a very low-key way, "there is this option in a special swimming pool; for those who want to stick to what they're used to, there's a normal pool too."

My big mouth meant I had to at least try it once, and quite a few of the passengers did take up the nude swimming option as we travelled through Sweden, including the quietly spoken Burnie – our legendary diesel mechanic – who thought it was great. This all stopped when we crossed into Finland. The Fins, apparently, aren't as uninhibited as the Swedes.

Locked out

Part of our training was to always ring ahead to confirm venues and camping sites are open and ready to receive us as planned. But this day there was no phone handy to do this, so I just assumed all would be fine. But when we arrived at our destination in the northern town of Harappa, tired and worn out after a long day's drive and sightseeing, we were greeted by a padlocked gate to the campsite entrance. By now used to automatically setting up their little tent village in ten minutes, then relaxing and making themselves at home, my coachload of tired passengers began to panic: "What are we going to do?" they wailed. "Where are we going to stay?"

"Don't worry," I said, with more confidence than I actually felt, "we'll sort something out." We pulled into a side street takeaway place to give me some frantic thinking time. In the takeaway a well-meaning young passenger, Jimmie, took it on himself to solve the problem: "We've got to find somewhere to stay," he declared. "Give me that phone book!" He started flipping through the pages with all its unintelligible Swedish writing and images. While this was going on I desperately rushed out onto the main road and flagged down a passing police car. And what a sight! Really stereotypical Swedish police they were, smart uniforms, blue eyes, and blonde hair down to their shoulders – and they spoke English!

"I'm the leader of a coachload of stranded tourists," I blurted out. "Our campsite is closed and we're desperate to find somewhere to spend the night!"

"Just a minute," they said, and conferred with each other in Swedish, then made a phone call … I waited for what seemed like an eternity; then they looked at me with their non-committal Nordic faces: "We've organised a chalet for you in the nearby hills," they said, and gave me the address.

I reached through the car window and shook their hands warmly. "Thank you so much!" I fervently said, then rushed back to my dejected passengers. "I've just organised a Swedish chalet in the nearby hills with the local police for us to spend the night!" I announced. "Grab your things and let's go!"

On the way to the chalet, I took special care to thank Jimmie for his genuine efforts to help, so he wouldn't feel overshadowed by what I'd done, for I was as astonished as anyone. "Between us," I pointedly said to Jimmie, "*our* collective endeavours solved the problem."

A veritable Switzerland

And what a fabulous place the chalet turned out to be, nestled among tall pines overlooking a very green valley. I didn't ask why it was available at the height of the tourist season or why we got it so cheaply; whatever the reason, we were so grateful it fell into our lap! Each couple had their own warm cabin; we could dine in a magnificent dining room with a thirty-five-seat oaken table; and our 'chefs' of the day had use of a professional kitchen in which to weave their culinary wonders.

And what a memorable night it was. I threw down a challenge: using only the contents of their suitcases they had to draw on their creative talents to dress 'formally'; there would be waiters and drink waiters, also appropriately attired from their suitcases; and there would be a fashion parade for the best 'formal' outfit, with the winner announced by proclamation. Dave, the Chief Judge, would present the award of a block of chocolate, and I was to be the master of ceremonies of this gala event. This spontaneous evening turned out to be one of the highlights of the whole trip. *Isn't it amazing; even when things are going really bad, good things can suddenly turn up.*

CHAPTER 17

Into Finland

The town of Muonio

The following day we crossed over the border into Finland, the next Scandinavian country on our agenda. Our destination was the isolated town of Muonio, located in far northern Finland above the Arctic Circle on the country's western border. In fact, it is the last significant stop before Norway, and we drove a few hundred kilometres across the Finnish wilds to get there. We weren't too perturbed about arriving late, for we were now well and truly in the land of the midnight sun where, for six months of the year, the sun never goes down. And even though we were now beyond the Arctic Circle, at this latitude, and at this time of year, we weren't covered in ice and snow; just the opposite, for although the summers are short it was quite warm. We pulled into the Muonio campsite around 11 pm and it was broad daylight. As was our habit, we immediately set about erecting our miniature tent city, but there was one thing we weren't counting on: the Muonio mozzies!

These were the biggest mosquitoes I've ever come across; they were monsters, attacked in swarms, and boy did they bite! I learned later that they drive the reindeer mad, and the only way they can get relief is to bury their noses in the snow. These merciless monsters hit us the moment we stepped off the coach, and pretty soon caused everyone to give up on their tents and retreat to the safety of the coach. The situation was untenable, so I braved their dive-bombing all the way to the campsite office to get some cans of repellent to make life bearable. I gave myself a good dose for the journey back, and it worked a treat for my antagonists backed off completely. I've been around a bit in my life and I've seen a few mozzies, but *never* anything like the mosquitoes in Muonio beyond the Arctic Circle in Finland.

Pigging out on pancakes

This unexpected problem out of the way, we quickly fell back into the pattern of life we were now used to and returned to the tent set up. It was nudging one o'clock in the morning and still broad daylight; far from being tired, everyone was wide awake and eager to do things. Our internal clocks were finding it hard to work out why it wasn't dark. Julie, an American, suggested, "Why don't we pig-out on pancakes?"

"Why not?" I said. "If the cook team tonight doesn't mind putting off the dinner we were going to have till tomorrow … we've got plenty of eggs, flour, milk, butter and jam … so let's do it!"

"Yay!" they all cried.

"Julie," I said, looking at her with encouraging enthusiasm, "do you reckon you could lead the cook team tonight and show us how Americans cook a decent pancake?"

"Sure!" she said. And for the next two hours, under a warm and bright midnight sun far beyond the Arctic Circle in Finland, that's exactly what we did; pigged out on delicious homemade American pancakes! It was around three in the morning when we hit the sack.

Throughout the trip, for most of these party nights I drank my own watered-down wine from a pre-prepared bottle which had barely any alcohol content at all, just enough to give me a 'happy edge' and allow me to keep up with the youthful vigour of the group. After all, I was the one who had to be up at 5 am each morning, bright-eyed and bushy-tailed to iron out the unexpected and ensure things ran smoothly.

To finish off our midnight sun experience in Finland, we thought it a good idea to join the locals for a dip in Muonio's local indoor swimming pool. So after breakfast when everything was packed up, Dave and I sent them all off down the main street (for that's all there was) to the swimming pool, where we'd pick them up after we'd settled things with the campsite office.

This done, we parked the coach in front of the pool and made our way inside. And it was packed! The whole town of Muonio must have been there. There were people of all ages enjoying themselves in the pool, including all our passengers and especially that lover of water, the mild-mannered Burnie.

I'd just come out of the dressing room having changed into my bathers when I found Dave doubled over with laughter.

"What's the matter?" I asked him.

"It's Burnie," he managed to get out. "He still thinks he's in Sweden and I just saw him dive off the high diving board with nothing on!" Now I was laughing! But we quickly snapped out of it because poor Burnie was blissfully unaware of this, splashing happily about as he was with the local inhabitants of Muonio. Dave rushed over to him. "Burnie!" he yelled, "we're in Finland and you've got to have your bathing costume on here!"

Well, the look on poor Burnie's face was one of sheer shock. He was out of that pool like a rocket, grabbed his towel and wrapped it around himself, and disappeared into the dressing room to get his clothes back on. Poor Burnie. He never went back in the water but quietly stayed on the bench fully dressed. Back on the coach we didn't make a big deal about it, but this entertaining episode did find its way into the Day Book under the heading *Burnie the flasher*.

Norway: our last Scandinavian country

The next day we crossed the border into Norway, our last Scandinavian country we were to visit. Our main purpose in visiting Norway, the highlight of the trip in fact, was to witness the summer solstice on 22 June within the Arctic Circle, because as we discovered in Muonio, the sun behaves differently above the Arctic Circle. Below it, the summer days are longer, but north of the Arctic Circle, for six months of the year the sun shines 24 hours a day. So the northern city of Narvik, deep inside the Arctic Circle, was the perfect place to observe this and that's where we headed.

While driving north in Finland we'd missed the marker for crossing into the Arctic Circle, but it was quite prominent in Norway so we all got out to enjoy the experience. It was a very eerie feeling, for although you couldn't hear a sound, it was as if you strangely could, just like the song says: *the sounds of silence*. It certainly felt a lot colder. Perhaps it was because we were higher up in the mountains than Finland. We wandered into the small general store there, had our photos taken by the Arctic Circle sign, and were soon on our way again.

Stave churches

Another thing Norway is noted for is its stave churches. If I can just put my tour guide's hat on for a moment; a 'stave' is a vertical wooden post or plank in a building, and stave churches are considered the most important examples of wooden medieval architecture in Europe. The Viking stave churches are directly descended from these palisade constructions; logs split in half then rammed into the earth and given a roof. This simple but very strong construction could last for centuries. "We'll be seeing a wonderful example of one of these surviving Viking stave churches," I promised them, "on our way back home through Norway."

The mighty Rombak Bridge

And further north we drove. As I mentioned earlier, our training trip never went anywhere near this northern part of our journey because it was in the depths of winter and all snowed under. Hence

I'd been running on somebody else's notes once we'd passed halfway up the Swedish coast. So when the time came for me to speak about the massive Norwegian Rombak Bridge as we approached it from the south, all I had to go on was what had been dictated to me by Rod Mosely.

I clearly remember Rod saying, "Don't start your spiel till you are rounding the headland with the two big rocky outcrops on it, so that as soon as you are on the other side the massive bridge will be looming up in front of you."

"Got it," I said, and made a note of that.

As we slowly made our way along a mountain road flanking the Rombaken fjord, we came to a headland with two big rocky outcrops jutting out from it. I was relieved for that's what I'd been looking for, and I gently slid into my spiel of how the suspension bridge linked to the important town of Narvik, the massive 765-metre length and its 41 metres clearance to the fjord below. I was on a roll, and continued to wax lyrical about its wonderful attributes: "For a bridge built in 1964, there were few like it at the time," I enthused. Then, using Rod Mosely's own words, I said: "As we round the bend, get ready – the massive bridge will be looming up right in front of you."

Everyone was on the edge of their seats and craning forwards; you could hear a pin drop as the coach began its turn.

Everyone gasped – with laughter and bewilderment, for there, a good ten miles away, was a postage-stamp size Romak Bridge stuck on the horizon! Dave could barely control the coach he was laughing so much.

Wrong bend and wrong rocky outcrop!

"You'll see the real size of it when we get a bit closer," I said, as if all was well. They weren't to know I'd never been there; they weren't to know I'd never seen it; to them it was just more of my quirky bumbling they'd experienced all along that warmed them to me, which didn't really matter for things seemed to fall into place. I twigged to this and played along with it.

When we did get to the Rombak Bridge twenty minutes later everything I'd said rang true.

Narvik and the summer solstice

We were to find that the town of Narvik is rich in its own history and an interesting place. The ice-free port of Narvik proved to be strategically valuable in the early years of World War II, and the town became a focal point of the Norwegian campaign, in particular the battles of Narvik, fought from 9 April to 8 June 1940 as a naval battle in the Ofotfjord, and a land battle in the mountains surrounding Narvik. But here we were in quieter days, and the only evidence of these former life-and-death battles was in the adjacent War Museum.

The following day we set ourselves up with our cameras and a picnic lunch on some smooth granite rocks to witness the spectacle of the summer solstice above the Arctic Circle. The weather was perfect.

And what a show it was! We settled ourselves down on our cosy rocks around 3:00 pm so as not to miss anything. The picture of it all is still etched in my mind. The sun seemed larger than usual, intensely yellow with an orangy-red corona, and shining brightly. The sky was a rich cerulean blue, forming a fitting backdrop for the main protagonist, the sun … and became lighter towards the horizon. The surrounding grey-mauve granite mountains framed all of this to complete the picture; which in turn was all reflected faithfully on the still surface of the fjord. This breathtaking spectacle alone was worth travelling halfway around the world to see. But now the real show was about to begin.

Keep in mind that we were beyond the Arctic Circle, so the sun behaves differently. We watched in awe as the sun went down as far as four o'clock in the afternoon, which of course was still broad daylight. It seemed to hover there for a minute or two, then started going back up again! We couldn't believe it!

With this incredible memory safely locked away, it was now time to turn south and continue our journey home through Norway.

The magnificent Svartisen Glacier

A few kilometres south of Narvik and travelling through Nordland County someone caught my attention by brandishing one of AAAT Eurotours brochures and saying, "Why can't we go see the Svartisen Glacier, as it says in the brochure?" This was the first I'd heard about it.

"Can I see that?" I said. He handed it to me. It read: " … and the possibility of seeing the Svartisen Glacier." I pointed the wording out to him … that it was just a *possibility*.

"Well, why did they put it in there?" he said. He had a point. Then I did something really stupid that I regret to this day.

"Okay," I said, "we'll go and have a quick look." I *now* know that to see any glacier, anywhere, there'd be a number of hours involved. But I'd fallen for the same trap of making a momentous decision by superficially looking at a brochure as I'd done with the Everyman's Right debacle. I got Dave to turn down an unmade road with a small white sign on a post saying 'Svartisen Glacier', not knowing what to expect but with a growing sense of foreboding.

These feelings weren't unfounded. We hadn't gone but ten kilometres when the road gave way. Yes, you read right, the road simply gave way. The coach violently lurched forward as the right front wheel thumped into a big two-foot hole that had opened up beneath it. Everyone was thrown forward over their seats and the coach was tilted on a perilous angle. People were screaming and beside themselves with shock. Dave was just sitting there, head against the windscreen gripping the wheel. I opened the side door and helped everyone out; thankfully no one seemed injured. By this time some people were hysterical and no one was in control …

"Phone a tow truck!" someone demanded.

"There are no tow trucks around here," I said. "We're in the middle of nowhere … but we'll get the coach out of this." I could see I'd have to assert myself in a forceful way. I got Dave and a few people to unload some of the luggage onto the side of the road to make the bus lighter; for what reason I had no idea but it looked like I knew what I was doing. Then in the distance I spied a farmer on a big tractor working in a field. I ran over to him and in sign language explained our predicament. Everyone's heart lifted when I returned on the tractor with the farmer, and he attached a big tow rope to the back of the bus. He gently put this powerful machine into a low gear and began moving forward till the rope was taught. But try as he might, the coach wouldn't budge for the wheel was stuck fast deep in that hole. In the end, the farmer had to give up and drive away; and along with him went our hopes and we were left sitting despondent on the side of the road.

A ray of hope

Then a car load of tourists pulled up behind us, and a middle-aged Norwegian man walked over to me and Dave and sized up the situation – thankfully he spoke English! "Down the road a bit there was a big bulldozer doing some roadwork," he said. "I could go back and ask him to pull you out?"

"Would you mind doing that? We'd be forever grateful."

"Sure," he said, and the family drove off the way they'd come. None of the group heard this conversation – it looked like I was just explaining the situation to some tourists. I walked over to the group and said, "I've just organised for a bulldozer to come and pull us out from some nearby roadworks." They heard what I said, but they were beyond placating.

About fifteen minutes later our ears pricked up, for we all heard a faint chugging on the breeze. *Could it possibly be?* I thought ... *did that kind man really make it happen?* And sure enough, right on cue, this gigantic front-end-loader with rubber wheels much taller than a man came chugging down the road. The front scoop alone was twice the width of the bus. The operator clambered down from his cabin and assessed the situation. He then positioned his machine in front of our stricken coach and gently dug his enormous scoop down under both our front wheels. He got down again to check that all was where he wanted it to be, then climbed back up into his cabin. Then ever so gently he lifted our precious coach out of that hole and onto firm land as if it were a toy.

I was disciplined enough not to cry because I was the one who had to be strong and show leadership. I reached into my bag to give this angel of a man some compensation for what he'd done, but he would have none of it. After flattening out the road again he waved us all a friendly goodbye and chugged off from whence he'd come.

Unbelievably, our coach was none the worse for wear, and we reloaded our belongings as quickly as we could and scuttled back to the safety of the main road while it was still daylight.

As we drove along you could cut the air with a knife. Something needed to be said for this was *someone's* fault; when the road gave way poor Dave had been at the wheel, but under *my* instructions. I picked up the microphone and took a deep breath: "As the leader of this trip I take full responsibility for what just happened, for I gave the instructions to go there. What I am grateful for is that no one was hurt and we can all now safely continue our adventure together."

Relieved, Dave looked at me and said, "Thanks mate." But still the bus was silent. Then … slowly at first, but increasing as it went, a wave of emotional applause filled the coach. I guess it was a tension-releasing applause for us all, for we'd all got through this momentous ordeal together.

Interesting, not a single word was said about this to Head Office. Even more wondrous was the Day Book ended up with a double-paged artist's impression of the whole event. Needless to say Head Office never got a copy of this either!

Rearrangement of plans

Because of what had just occurred, I had to hurriedly rearrange our plans for the day. An hour or so down the road, I casually mentioned,

"I've had to re-jig our plans a bit after what happened ... so I'm sorry, we won't be able to visit the stave church that was near here."

"But you promised," they protested. "We were really looking forward to it!"

"Well, there is the famous Gol Stave Church at the Norwegian Museum of Cultural History in Oslo ... we'll visit that instead," I tentatively suggested, which we ended up doing. But in their eyes, the Gol Stave Church wasn't the same as the first one I'd promised. We made up for this disappointment with a visit to the Oslo Viking Ship Museum. The museum is most famous for the completely whole Oseberg Ship, excavated from the largest known ship burial in the world.

From then on I went a bit easy on my build-ups and always left the door open for the unforeseen. And I always had a plan B up my sleeve, and even a *plan C. Never make promises you can't keep.*

An en*light*ened leader ...

From Olso we continued our way down to the border with Sweden to catch the ferry from Gothenberg back to Denmark on our way home. While driving along the freeway in Sweden I noticed something *extraordinary* that really caught my eye: "Hey!" I exclaimed. "Look at that!... All the cars have got their lights on... it must be an important funeral or something... it could even be the King and Queen of Sweden in convoy!" Everyone looked at me blankly, for they thought I was joking; after all, it was I who had given them such a detailed description of how advanced the Swedes were with their road safety measures. When they saw I really was serious they let out a collective groan. Then I remembered: *Oh yeah, the lights... they drive with them on.* By then they'd gotten used to me... it goes without saying that this found its way into the Day Book under the heading, 'Someone turned Laurie's lights on!'

CHAPTER 18

West Berlin and Checkpoint Charlie

The final highlight of our adventure, because by now this is what our holiday had become, was a visit to the famous Checkpoint Charlie in West Berlin; the only place those visiting Berlin could cross from West Berlin to *communist* East Berlin and back again. (Remember, this was before the Berlin Wall came down.) At this time all of Berlin was still deep inside the Soviet sphere. So West Berlin could only be accessed by the infamous hundred-kilometre Berlin *Corridor* from West Germany. This precarious life line is best described as a narrow, fear-filled conduit constantly patrolled by fanatical East German border police. Not a reassuring place to be traversing with a coach full of apprehensive passengers.

The infamous Corridor

I saw little difference between these border police and Hitler's callous and violent SS. I remember seeing them strutting about in their smart uniforms and sunglasses, checking everything out with their binoculars. As we drove by, run-down houses and buildings stood forlornly on either side of this enclosed highway, looking like they hadn't been touched since the war. We even saw a group of road workers with East German border guards watching over them with machine guns. All this was a taste of what living in East Germany must have been like. We felt totally at their mercy and couldn't wait to reach the relative freedom of West Berlin.

When we got to the end of The *Corridor* we were still not out of the woods, for boom gates and a formidable border check awaited us. An East German police officer arrogantly walked up and down the coach in his shiny boots and Nazi-style uniform, checking each of our passports in an intimidating way. He would open each passport and look at it for a few seconds; then back to the terrified person his impenetrable sunglasses would go; then back to the passport again – all this devoid of any expression. He'd then dramatically snap the passport shut and unceremoniously hand it back to its fearful owner … then on he'd go to taunt his next victim.

It was an unmitigated show of brute force and intimidation and won no hearts from our side. He played on the fact that we were vulnerable and felt completely powerless under his control. We were glad to finally see those boom gates go up and deliver us from this uncertain darkness to the safe haven of West Berlin.

What a difference it was to find ourselves in this 'Island of freedom', this enclave of more than two million free people. West Berlin was heavily subsidised by West Germany as a 'showcase of the West'. The infamous Berlin Wall had split Berlin right down the middle into East Berlin and West Berlin, and tripwires that set off deadly shotguns ensured nobody could get near it to escape to the West. The only way to get to the East and safely back into the West was through Checkpoint Charlie. This fear-filled venture into communist *East* Berlin was to be the last heart-racing experience of our trip.

We venture into the unknown

If all that had happened so far on our adventure was sent to test me, you could multiply it all by a hundred when considering my fear of losing someone in communist East Germany; they would be on their own, and there would be nothing I could do for them. So I made sure everybody had their passports secured safely in their flat belly-bags; I implored people to stay together as a group and in no circumstances wander off to check something out. We were going to experience a local suburban train and travel on it to East Berlin, the capital of communist East Germany; we were going to visit Alexanderplatz, East Berlin's main square, and visit a few shops to get a feel for how the people lived and felt. We would then follow our original footsteps and take the same suburban train back to Checkpoint Charlie. "If for any reason anyone does get lost," I reiterated, "make your way back to the same station we got off at and catch the same train back to where we started." I got them to write these stations down and store this information safely with their passports. This done, we were ready to go.

And filled with much trepidation, we ventured forth to Checkpoint Charlie.

The border guards were no less intimidating than they had been in The Corridor but we all got through without a hitch; but getting safely *back to the West* was the thing most on our minds.

The overall impression for us was that everything was somewhat drab and plain when compared to the modern liveliness and sense of freedom within reach on the other side of Checkpoint Charlie. Even the buildings had a feeling of this same drabness about them. But most of all the East Berliners seemed rather sad, living as they were in the control of such an oppressive regime.

To round off our experience we all had a coffee or drink in an outside cafe in Alexanderplatz, where we found the waiters a bit offhand and uncaring. I guess they didn't have a lot of incentive to put their hearts into it. I did a quick roll call, for it was now time to make our way back to the station and catch the train back to the safety of Checkpoint Charlie.

Where's Ben?

And what a relief it was to find ourselves approaching the narrow walkway to the final turnstile of Checkpoint Charlie. But then, someone cried out, "Where's Ben?" We all froze. Fearing the worst, I did a quick survey and confirmed that Ben definitely *wasn't* with us. By now other people eager to get back to the safety of the West had bunched up behind us and were pushing us forward. We were all worried, for anything could have happened!

"Did anyone see him get on the train?" I asked. No one could really confirm this. As with all the other crises we'd had, and in spite of my own rampant uncertainty, I took control. I decided it was important to get everybody else through the checkpoint first and then worry about Ben: "We'll go through the checkpoint and wait for him on the other side," I said. "He's got the addresses of the stations and will find his way back ... we've got to be patient and wait for him. The important thing is we're waiting here for him when he walks through."

What we all went through as we waited for Ben on the safe side of Checkpoint Charlie is hard to describe, for we suffered his fear and the panic that must have taken hold of him.

An agonising hour had gone by when I decided we could wait no longer; I'd have to report Ben as a missing person to the East German authorities – this was not a pleasant prospect. But then, Ben suddenly walked through the turnstile, white as a ghost. We all rushed over to comfort and reassure him that he was now safe, but it was all too much and he broke down and cried. Once he'd composed himself a little he was able to explain that he'd gotten talking to a couple of locals who spoke English and missed the train ... "then I caught the *wrong* train and went the *wrong* way!" he said, reliving the terrifying experience. "In the end, a kind lady found me traumatised all by myself and brought me back to Checkpoint Charlie."

Wow! What a way to wind up the trip! By the time we arrived back in London Ben had fully recovered from his ordeal, for he'd found comfort with his adopted family.

Leadership by default

Now I don't know how I really fared on this, my first trip, for I was just a lost and lonely guy trying to find my way in life (perhaps even find myself) when I landed this out-of-the-ordinary job in London; and what a job it was! The truth is I expended my whole time fending off these testing trials that relentlessly kept coming at me; I was simply trying to survive.

But one person saw things differently and wrote in the Day Book:

> **Laurie Smale, Our Intrepid Leader**
>
> Don't be fooled! Behind this bumbling clown who always seemed to be putting his foot in it was a very polished professional who knew precisely what he was doing: he was always the last to retire; yet he was *always* up at dawn working tirelessly behind the scenes to ensure each day ran smoothly. He led from behind by empowering us to believe that *we* were running the show! And when things didn't work as planned he'd always pull something out of his hat that was even better! Thank you Laurie for a fantastic trip!

This little note in the Day Book meant a lot to me, for it was *their* collective voice of gratitude and it said it all. From this astute summary I was able to understand that *true, effective leadership is not being up front all the time and doing everything yourself; it is empowering others to be a part of this leadership too. And I've used this tried-and-proven leadership template ever since.*

Developing my own speaking style

One valuable thing I'd been doing without realising it was getting used to 'chatting' before groups as the imperfect person I am, as against trying to speak in a formal public-speaking style and get everything 'right'. This warmed my listeners to me and made me more accessible to them. And I never forgot the panic-free approach that worked so well for me. Years later I was to formulate this unique approach into a panic-free coaching program so others could effortlessly connect with their listeners as the natural person they are too.

What others had to say …

An interesting note on others' views of my efforts as a courier: one day I was talking to my friend Mark Short, one of the survivors of our infamous training trip, who had just returned from helping set up some permanent campsites in Spain when our boss, Rod Mosely, paid them a visit, and my name happened to be brought into the conversation. Word must have spread around from the accountant at Head Office about the appalling state of the monetary side of Laurie Smale's trip reports. At the mention of my name, one of Mark's mates chuckled as if to say, "Oh yeah, we all know about *him* … ", and Mark readily admitted that he joined in. But Mark went on to tell me that in response to this disparaging behaviour, Rod Mosely said: "Laurie Smale is one of our best couriers."

Mark did not have to share this piece of personal information with me – but he did. And I'll be forever grateful to him for doing so. Mark and I had been through a lot together and he was a true friend. He knew that having Rod Mosely's imprimatur meant a lot to me.

That night as I was unpacking my suitcase in my hotel room, my head started spinning from extreme mental and physical exhaustion, and the magnitude of the last two weeks simply overcame me. I sank to the floor and slept soundly where I fell for the next three hours, then crawled into bed and continued this restful sleep till twelve the following day.

Brunswick and grog running

Before we close on my European tour escapades, there are two more episodes worthy of mention that happened on two other trips: one was the 'Brunswick incident'; the other returns to the prospect of me supplementing my flimsy 20 pounds a day courier allowance with a dabble in grog running.

First the 'Brunswick incident'.

Now, I don't know whether it was the older vehicle they gave me or whether I had a propensity to attract bus trouble, but it seemed to come my way with disturbing regularity. Brunswick is a city in north-central Germany, which we'd normally bypass as we traversed through Germany to Scandinavia on our midnight-sun tours. But this day we found ourselves in this quintessential German medieval town by accident. We were sailing along the freeway without a care when the back of our bus began to make weird noises, then thump and wobble, and finally we screeched to a grinding halt on the side of the road.

Dave and I looked at each other with a sinking feeling: *not again* … we nervously thought. Fortunately we'd stopped right near a service station. We got out to see what had happened. To our horror, one of the back wheels had locked up completely, and was so hot that some of the wheel's metal had melted. This coach was now a beached whale and wasn't going anywhere.

Used to such scenarios by now, Dave and I sprang into action: "Unload all the passengers and their luggage to that grassy field," I said to him, "while I phone London from the service station."

A blonde, blue-eyed German, I'd say in his early twenties, served me. His English was bordering on zero but he did know one or two words. "Phone? Bus caput!" I said, indicating our disabled coach and the bunch of forlorn passengers sitting on their luggage.

"Ya, ya," he said, and indicated the phone. After several nerve-racking attempts I got through to London.

"Hello," said Rod Moseley. I knew his voice. "It's Laurie Smale here … one of the coach's back wheels has seized up with metal melted on the road, and the coach is undriveable: what can we do?"

"You're the person on the spot, you've got to solve it … sort out a local camping ground or something, then ring us with the address … we'll have a new bus to you in two days … now get moving!" And with that he hung up. I looked out the service station window at the demoralised passengers. Then I remembered what I'd done in Sweden when I'd desperately run out into the street and flagged down a police car to find us emergency accommodation. So, I tried to enlist the help of the service station assistant. In a combination of English and rudimentary German, I said, "I need camping for *schlaf* ... ", here I made sleeping signs, " ... I have money. You have friends with cars? I have money for *benzine* ... ", and I pointed to the petrol bowser.

"One moment," he said, and made a phone call ... and then he made another call. His assistant went on serving the customers while he made a few more calls. After a while he said, "Mein friends coming mit five cars to Braunchweig camping ... 20 minutes," he said, pointing to his watch. I could not believe it! We were going to be ferried to the beautiful German city of Brunswick by a group of young German locals ... wow!

When I informed the despondent passengers of this their spirits lifted. I agreed on a fair price for petrol and time for each trip, and sure enough, one by one the cars arrived and our shuttling mission of mercy to the campsite began. When we and our gear, including our camp kitchen and supplies, had been safely ferried to our campsite, we thanked our German saviours profusely with a spontaneous round of applause. Three of them came back that night to join us for a drink and a bowl of spaghetti bolognese.

And what a wonderful find it was. A tranquil little campsite set in a pristine park full of wildlife and waterbirds. It was a very warm night, so once we'd set up camp we wandered across the verdant fields to admire the ducks and waterbirds in the little brook that meandered its way through the park.

Unbelievable as it may sound, I was to learn that more often than not Brunswick was overlooked by tourists and was not on the lists of popular towns to visit. I doubt whether this local camping ground had ever had an intake of forty campers at once, because they seemed so overwhelmed by it all. They had a small building like a club house with a little bar, but that was all. Heinz, the young man running the site, was a real character who had learned his quirky English from

American soldiers stationed in Germany. We had a lot of fun with him.

That night we danced and listened to '60s and '70s music from an old jukebox and enjoyed a drink or two at the bar served by our amiable campsite host Heinz.

Later I found myself talking to a fellow Aussie passenger at the bar about what we could do tomorrow, as we had one more day to fill before our replacement coach arrived. But our choices were limited, for we'd already been down to the brook three times to admire the waterbirds.

"I guess we could wander down to the brook again and have another look at those bloody ducks," my companion slung off in that ironic humour peculiar to Australians.

"Fuck the ducks … we've seen enough of 'em," I replied in like vein.

Poor Heinz, who'd had an ear cocked to all this, exclaimed, "You fuck zee ducks?!"

"Noo! What I mean is, they're not important!"

"Why?" Now he was genuinely confused. "Because you don't fuck zem?"

"No! Forget the ducks! … We've already seen them three times. Is there anything interesting in the town to see?" I put this to him in a slow, methodical way to avoid further misunderstanding.

"Oh, yes," he said, "Many things … tomorrow I show you all Brunswick." Tomorrow Heinz was going to show us around: great!

Before we said goodnight we arranged to meet in the bar at 9:30 am, ready for Heinz's guided walking tour of the Brunswick town centre. At this stage all I knew of Brunswick was that it basked in culture, it was full of pristine nature which we'd already had a taste of, it boasted distinctive Middle Age architecture, and it had a glorious history. Now, thanks to Heinz, we were about to see an interesting portion of all this up close. So across our magnificent wildlife park we walked again, into Brunswick's breathtaking town centre.

Feeling pretty chuffed that we had our own personal guide, we followed Heinz into Brunswick's main square, the *Burgplatz* – a sight I'll never forget. The whole thing was like a fairy tale, with its red, brown, grey, black and white colours. And all so dollhouse neat and in place. The square's hand-crafted cobblestone pavement was a pleasure to walk on, surrounded as it was by a magnificent church and picturesque buildings, and its central fountain standing proudly in the middle of it all. None of which had changed much since the Middle Ages. Heinz then took us to the Dankwarderode Castle, which housed priceless art from the Middle Ages.

Having wandered through this castle for half an hour or so, we then moved over to the other side of the square to the front of the imposing Brunswick Cathedral, where we admired the statue of the Brunswick Lion, erected by Henry The Lion, The Duke of Saxony in his own honour. Heinz told us that because Henry had marriage links to the British and Scottish royal families, his Brunswick Lion still appears on their flags and royal regalia.

We topped off this magnificent morning with an authentic Brunswick schnitzel lunch in a traditional Brunswick restaurant, in compensation for the hardship endured as a result of this unscheduled stopover – compliments of the company, of course!

At 3 o'clock that afternoon our replacement coach turned up, we struck camp, loaded everything on board, said goodbye to our friend Heinz and to Brunswick, and continued on from where we had unexpectedly left off.

Grog running with Johnny Walker

On another of my midnight-sun trips to Scandinavia, John, a different English driver on his first trip, and I decided to 'revisit' the idea of supplementing our meagre 20 pounds a day wages by buying Johnny Walker Red whisky while on the duty-free ferry midway between Denmark and Sweden, with the purpose of discreetly reselling it for a profit in the heavily taxed Sweden, then splurging our extra

Swedish kroner on our passengers with extra treats while we were still in Sweden. From the very start we were extremely uneasy about this covert operation, but the other couriers kept telling us it was easy as pie and they had been doing it without hassle for years. So with great trepidation, John and I embarked on our one and only venture into grog running.

With no experience in this whatsoever, all we could do was follow the instructions of those who had gone before us. Once on board the ferry in the Danish port of Frederikshavn, I told the *Pax* to stay on the top floors and not to go down to the bus in the car park till we arrived in Gothenburg, Sweden an hour later. In the meantime John and I worked up a feverish sweat surreptitiously loading *36 dozen*, I repeat, 36 dozen boxes of Johnny Walker Red into the rear loading bay of the coach. We'd taken a random stab at this number because we figured that when spread among a coachload of forty-five passengers and two crew, we could get away with this amount if push came to shove. Anyway, we justified all this skulduggery because we'd be able to fund a lot of extra fun evenings for the passengers with our extra ill-gotten gains.

Unexpected reception

Our cache of Johnny Walker now safely stashed out of sight, the Frederikshavn ferry stately sailed into the Swedish port of Gothenburg for what we expected to be the routine wave through customs, as had always happened. When everyone was safely aboard the coach and accounted for, we rolled off the ship looking forward to the Swedish stage of our trip.

But the scene that greeted John and me chilled us to the bone; instead of the usual friendly customs officers there to welcome us to Sweden, there were two lines of Swedish soldiers armed to the teeth. *Great!* we thought, *how are we going to get out of this!* John opened the door for the inspection, for he saw no way out. A Swedish officer said, "We're about to do a routine customs check, could you assist us please?"

"Certainly," I said … and, followed by a very nervous John, whose face was as white as a sheet, we climbed down the stairs of the coach. On the last step I turned and nonchalantly called out to the *Pax*, "Just a routine customs check. It won't take long … just amuse yourselves as we go through this." But John had already accepted his fate and whispered in my ear, "We're done for!"

My mind and heart were both racing at a million miles an hour; to use up precious seconds I stood at the first loading bay at the front of the coach, hoping that by some miracle by the time we sauntered to the offending *rear* bay, all the Johnny Walker would have magically disappeared.

"Open the cargo door please," asked the Swedish officer in his lilting English, and he and a bunch of his soldiers had a cursory rummage through the tents and luggage. We left this door open and moved on to the next cargo bay … there were three of them.

"Open the cargo door please," he asked again, and he and his soldiers repeated their cursory inspection. My heart was now thumping. *This is it*, I thought, *What I say next will make or break the whole trip for these innocent people and stuff up John's and my lives forever …*

"Open this cargo door please," I heard the officer say, pointing to the rear door. I reached down, turned the handle, then I lifted the door. And there in front of us was a wall of striding Johnny Walkers, all pointing an incriminating finger at John and me!

"What are these?" asked the officer rhetorically.

"Oh … those," I said in a matter-of-fact way … "they're for our parties."

"Oh, ya, ya, *parties*," he sarcastically repeated in his lilting Swedish. "You will all have to wait here please while we assess the situation." And off he went with his soldiers to decide our fate.

The wait was interminable while they crunched the numbers. How ironic that the *maths* regarding the ratio of bottles-to-person that I'd summarily worked out in my head would either make or break us! We had absolutely no idea which way this would go – our very future was in the hands of the Swedish army and my random computation. Despite my friendly chatter to the passengers, John and I began to sweat; and the clock kept slowly ticking. Unable to bare the tension any longer, I grabbed my map and began sharing the day's travels with each couple ... Then the unmistakable clank of the coach door opening jolted me back to reality. The stern-faced officer climbed to the top step and beckoned me forward.

"You are free to go," he said to me. He then turned to the wide-eyed tourists, smiled and said, "Have a nice holiday ... and enjoy your parties!", words the passengers warmly reacted to, but didn't really get the true meaning of ... Only a relieved John and I knew what they really meant.

Without a word, John rolled the coach through the boom gate and towards the relative safety of the streets of Gothenburg. "Keep driving," I softly said out of the side of my mouth to a still white-faced John. "Don't look sideways and keep driving straight!" All we had to do *now* was get rid of this coachload of incriminating whisky!

Now, I don't know what the legal ratio of bottles per head officially was, or what they decided to do when they divided our 47 heads into 36 dozen bottles of Johnny Walker Red; maybe they disregarded the intricacies of all this and just wanted to be lenient with a busload of money-spending tourists for political reasons ... whatever the reason, we just wanted to get out of there and into some fresh, free air!

That night, in the wee hours of the morning, John and I, like two shady smugglers of old, shuttled back and forth carrying boxes of Johnny Walker Red to the home of the Swedish campsite owner, who thought all his Christmases had come at once. We gave each bottle to him for 2.00 kroner more than we paid for it, and he took the lot. Phew! It was off our hands and we still made 864 kroner profit! To assuage our guilt, we were able to splurge on champagne nights, steak nights, and quite a few other local culinary treats, all to the delight of the *Pax*. However, I'd learnt my lesson; and I never ventured into the dubious world of smuggling again!

It's a small world

Here's something that's really amazing – it really is a small world: after my first driver Dave Watson and I finished our camping-tour stint together, he continued being a driver around Europe for a couple more years. On one of these camping tours he met an Australian girl and ended up marrying her and moving to Australia. And that girl happened to be Mr Boyd's daughter … my unforgettable Legatee.

Complete paradigm shift

In between trips, and sometimes this could be weeks, I'd find myself back in London living in the company apartment in West Kensington near Shepherds Bush, or some other cheap dive. I was now thirty-two years old. I had no money, no savings, and had to somehow eke out a living. This was a very strange existence, for as courier on my trips I was absolute king, respected by all, and wanting for nothing; whereas when I got back to London I'd return to the reality of being an unknown pauper not knowing when my next meal would be, or where I'd sleep that night. And to add to this precarious existence, I only had seven months left on my English visa and no ticket home.

One night while lying in a warm bath in a seedy West Kensington boarding house, a life-changing realisation flooded my mind: *I didn't want to be in show business anymore*. I have to tease this out a little to emphasise the enormous gravity of what this realisation actually meant to me and the rest of my life. Just think; for the previous fifteen years, not a day had gone by without me thinking about my role in show business in some form or other, with me visualising myself as one day being a *big star*. And this was a genuine, concrete expectation that I'd striven towards every single day of my life since I was seventeen. And yet, this complete shift in thinking had me saying out loud to myself: "I don't want to be in show business anymore." This was nothing short of a *complete* paradigm shift.

As I lay there, it dawned on me *why* and *where* these life-changing words had stemmed from. Thankfully, although I didn't know it at the time, becoming a courier was to save me years of future heartache. I now clearly understood that I'd reached the pinnacle of being a *big superstar* in my role as courier on the coach. I was the star of the show who had the ability to make others feel the star of the show too. On *this* stage, I was not shy of girls at all, for each day I was in the spotlight and entertaining my *audience* with my one-liners and bag of well-rehearsed tricks. So that's all these people ever saw; this *external*, likeable performer; the proverbial sad clown, and never the real, deep-down Laurie. Trip after challenging trip I'd bring my passengers back to London absolutely delighted with their adventures. Yet in spite of these outstanding successes, Laurie Smale remained lost and alone, for I'd become very clever at helping others have a wonderful time, but not too clever at helping the *inner me* do the same.

As I lay in that therapeutic bath I thought, *if this is what being the big star is like in a smaller situation like a camping tour, I shudder to think what my loneliness would be if it was magnified worldwide!* Like a zombie who's just realised he has the ability to get out of his morbid existence, I just lay there repeating, "I don't want to be in show business anymore." I clearly understood that this significant decision was final, but I had absolutely no idea what I was going to replace it with. I simply stretched out, relaxed, and let the warm water flow over me; for a great weight had been lifted from my shoulders.

This mind-shifting decision, of me giving up on my long-held obsession to become a famous entertainer, also flagged the end of my short but character-building career as a camping trip courier, for in many ways they were one and the same thing. *Yet little did I realise that I'd been learning something much more important, for all of this had been a crash course in the art of handling people, an absolutely vital human quality that helps us deal with all sorts of situations as we wade through life meeting, and having to get along with, all types of different personalities.* But for now

I needed to get a job and establish somewhere to live. So I wasted no time in making enquiries.

Renovating heritage houses in London

From the first person I asked, I got a job clearing out building rubbish from renovated heritage houses in London. From there I progressed to general rouse-about driving a small pick-up to the various sites and helping with the final touch-ups. I remember one job I had to do was repair a small crack in the ceiling of a newly renovated apartment under the watchful eye of the owner. Having never done this before in a professional capacity I said to Barry, my boss: "How will I get the colour right?" As always, I was genuinely concerned about doing a good job.

"You'll be right," said Barry, who by now had seen that I could be trusted to help the other tradesmen. "Just fill it with Polyfilla, then slap a bit of magnolia on it and all will be fine." I might add that in London, everything was painted in various shades of magnolia!

Dressed in my overalls, I introduced myself to the owner as "the man to repair the ceiling", and duly went about filling the offending crack with Polyfilla. "We'll let that set a bit while I go out to the van and prepare the paint," I told the gentleman, who had been watching me with a keen eye. So out I go to get the half-used tin of 'mag', as we called it, and gave it a good stir, hoping this would somehow ensure the colour would be a close enough match for my observer's discerning eye.

Back inside, I prepared everything on a ground sheet to protect his carpet. Then I opened the can and got a real shock ... compared to what I could see on the ceiling, the shade that was staring back at me from the can was darker, perhaps a little bit too mauve. If this was so, it would stand out like a sore thumb! I felt rather nervous, and fiddled around a bit more stirring it, hoping he'd go away to let me solve the problem by myself. But the man wasn't going anywhere, and was looking at me with great expectations; and I had the brush in my hand and looked like I knew what I was doing. With nowhere to go, I climbed my ladder and tentatively filled my brush from my 'lucky dip' of magnolia … and applied its dubious contents to the ceiling.

And wonder of wonders, it was a perfect match! The man shook his head in admiration: I smiled wanly in utter relief.

"It must take years of experience to come in cold like you did and get the colour just right!" said he, extremely happy with the result.

"Well," I said, "you learn things along the way … ", a nice universal statement which covers anything in life. As I drove away in the van I thought: *good ol' mag … I got away with that!*

The night watchman

It was my *thinking on my feet* miracles like this that Barry appreciated, and we got on well … I even had Christmas dinner with his family. And working for him solved my accommodation problem as well, for I would sleep at Barry's unfinished building sites as resident night watchman to scare off robbers coveting his building materials, which saved me a lot of rent money and gave me stability. Most important, it gave me time to reflect on where to from here in my life. It gave me time to ask: *what is it that's really missing and making me feel empty when outwardly I'm everybody's friend?* At this stage I was nowhere near the answer to this complex question, but I'd passed an important milestone by casting off my all-consuming show-business obsession, and I felt good about it. Remnants of this obsession would hang around for years in other guises, but in the end would find their balanced, rightful place in my personality. But this journey was still being travelled …

As I lay in my sleeping bag of a night, I had plenty of time to philosophise about my journey in life so far, and further realisations began to fill my mind: like that most of what I'd learnt from my worldwide wanderings was superficial and had no real depth to it; all of what I'd had a tempting taste of in school had been wiped from my mind because my fear of maths was associated with it; my polished entertainment acts were great for three minutes of television, but beyond these well-rehearsed segments I was uneducated and had little to say; I was beginning to understand that being *the two-minute performer* all the time was a bit shallow and there had to be more to life; I was able to reflect on the thrill of my continuous learning of the Italian language, but even here it was a hotchpotch of learning – I'd done it all myself, and did my best to build on this when I was in Italy without a solid foundation of my own language to compare it with; it further dawned on me that my shameful lack of a real education, hidden from view for so long by my fraudulent superficiality, created a hollow show; and that maybe this was why I was always on the move, never standing still long enough for anyone to see through it all ... Yet these realisations were doing me good, for I'd never said anything like this to myself before. *But where do I start with all this now that my decades-old dream of being a renowned entertainer has been discarded?*

This was the overwhelming question that now confronted me.

A new inspiration

One day I was reading the newspaper when the headline of a small ad caught my eye: **New Course in Practical English**. *This looks interesting*, I thought, and I sent away for it. In the meantime I went and bought myself some English books to help me with my studies, for apart from a *full stop*, my knowledge of the workings of the English language was virtually non-existent. For example, I had no idea of why a *sentence* was a *sentence*, or what purpose a *paragraph* served. I had no idea of what a *colon* or a *semi-colon* was or what they did; I was a clean slate in all of this.

So with the blissful enthusiasm of the ignorant, off I went to the bookshop. I still have the four precious books I bought that day, which are: *You Have a Point There: A guide to punctuation and its allies*, by Eric Partridge; the *Hamlyn Encyclopedic World Dictionary*;

The Nuttall Dictionary of English Synonyms and Antonyms; and to broaden my knowledge of the peoples of the world, *Men and Nations* by Louis J. Halle. Over the years these four books have become *my friends*, and I regularly consult them for ideas and inspirations.

One fine day my *New Course in Practical English* arrived from Career Institute, Inc., to complete my first, life-changing library. And this comprehensive self-help course was exactly what I needed; not only did it far exceed my expectations, it helped me get a *practical* understanding of the basic building blocks of competent writing, fluent speaking, and efficient reading. Only this time it wasn't just another stepping stone towards those illusive Hollywood footlights; this time it was an uncomplicated opening of my mind to the education I'd somehow lost along the way.

So while I strived to do my best as a general rouse-about and builder's labourer for Barry by day, I'd spend my evenings working through the easy-to-follow steps of my exciting *New Course in Practical English* by night. For the remaining six months of my visa, my sparse, bare-boarded rooms of these half-finished buildings became fonts of learning, where I learned to read and write and not be scared of the intricacies of grammar. Now I could also compare the building blocks of Italian grammar I'd been learning with the English ones I'd been so afraid of. And each night I would wander for hours in the hallowed footsteps of *Men and Nations*, and how civilizations had risen and fallen.

Sadly, when my visa expired, the time had come for me to end my European escapades, bid farewell to my English friends, and wing my way back to the land of my birth, Australia.

PART IV
Back in Australia

(1981 to ... ?)

CHAPTER 19

Home again

The first thing I did when I returned to Australia was pay my mum a visit in country Victoria, and of course she was overjoyed to see her long-lost son. When I asked her, "Did you receive my postcards?" she said she did and she had put them in albums. More out of guilt than anything for not writing longer letters, I'd been sending her dozens of these over the years; the sanitised postcard version of my travels, for I didn't want to unduly worry her. She certainly knew nothing of the trials and tribulations you're reading in this book. But she liked her postcards and eagerly sweated on the postman for the next instalment.

When I saw the hours and hours she must have put into arranging each card in order of countries and places, with her own interpretation neatly written under each of them, I realised how much they meant to her. My mother had never been to *exotic places* in her life – she'd unselfishly sacrificed to bring us kids up as best she could. So by way of these magic postcards of faraway places – Buckingham Palace; Africa; castles and European farmlands; vast multicoloured fields of tulips and windmills; The Colosseum and The Vatican – my mum had travelled with me. I never really appreciated the impact these simple cards had on her. But my brother Mark told me that they had incredible impact. "Whenever we visited her," he said, "she would pull out all your postcards and, beaming with pride, take us through all the places that you had been!" Of course I now know that *exotic* places are no different to your own back yard, for loneliness and sadness can follow you there too! The amazing thing I discovered is, for the people who live in these *exotic places*, this is *their* back yard and *they* are susceptible to the same human frailties and suffering as we are. *So travelling to exotic places can be fun and pleasurable, but it doesn't solve our inner problems and misguided thinking; only we can do that.* Just think: although I was surrounded by London's beautiful parks, gardens and historic wonders that people travel the world to see, it was in a dingy little boarding room that could have been anywhere in the world that I threw off my all-consuming shackles of show business and set myself free.

Catching up with Mark

After I'd visited my mum I decided to catch up with my 'little' brother Mark, who was now one of the head designers at The Bata Shoe Factory – the place I walked out of when all the shoes were falling off the conveyer belt and piling onto the floor when I was eighteen. I was now thirty-four, and it was a good six years since I'd seen him.

As I approached this vast complex in my car I thought, *where do I start?* But in one of those quirks of the universe, I met him in the driveway on the way in as he was on the way out. We both pulled over, and after a warm embrace we had a heartfelt discussion in the carpark for fifteen minutes as he was due for a meeting. This time the tables were turned and it was my little brother giving me the sage advice. Happily married with a family himself, the gist of what he said was: "It's about time you found someone to share your life with and settled down." Mark was sincere and meant well, yet the reasons I had been roaming the world trying to sort myself out were still unknown to him. When I met Jan, my wife-to-be a year later, Mark was pleased because his words probably played a hand in this.

After years of helping other corporations like Warner Bros and McDonald's grow their businesses, Mark now runs his own consulting business, Marketus, specialising in helping companies identify unrealised potential in film, TV, music, brands, trade secrets, patents and data and how to commercialise them.

One last stint of camping trips

But what to do here in Australia? I was now at a loose end again. So as a stop-gap, I decided to do what I was already familiar with and take a couple of camping trips through the deserts and remote outposts of outback Australia. Notwithstanding Mark's comforting words, I was still in the shaky mindset of having to be 'on the move' and running away from something that was yet to be resolved …

Lindy Chamberlain

I ended up taking three four-week adventure trips. It was on the first trip that I gained knowledge of the wildlife, Aboriginal culture, and the desert environs to impart to others. One thing I'll never forget was the early morning we pulled into the Ayers Rock (more commonly called Uluru these days) camping ground to be greeted by an atmosphere of shock and utter disbelief; it was the very morning the dingo had taken Lindy Chamberlain's baby. I actually read her entry in the tourist kiosk guestbook with my own eyes.

I have always believed her innocent, for I've seen what dingoes could do in pinching heavy stuff from our cook tent, or the way Prince the dingo used to carry that three-kilogram cast-iron trolley wheel around in his mouth. And this was verified years later when dingoes on Fraser Island attacked a nine-year-old boy; and even more telling, one dragged off a small toddler in its mouth just like happened to little Azaria all those years ago, but this time the baby lived.

One of these trips, you may recall, was when by chance we passed by the forgotten outpost of *Copley*, near the treacherous Oodnadatta

Track in remote outback South Australia; the place I nearly went to work on a sheep station as a fifteen-year-old boy but for a throw-away comment from Lino, my Italian boss! Talk about a sliding-door moment!

With tour guiding out of my system, I now found myself living in Sydney looking for a job when I read an advertisement in the paper: **Engravers wanted, training given**.

I'm artistic, I thought, *I could handle that*, and made an appointment with a Mr Alan Cook for an interview.

Mr Minit

Alan Cook, the Operations Manager of a worldwide shoe repair and engraving organisation, was an extremely sharp operator who knew the kind of person he was after who had the potential to effectively operate a shoe repair and engraving stand in a major shopping centre.

"What have you been doing with yourself this last year or so?" he asked, fishing for stability and potential. When I told him he didn't seem to believe me, for that boyish corona that had dogged me all my life cast doubt on what I said.

"Do you have your passport on you?" he asked, suspecting I didn't.

"Sure." I gave it to him; I'd been in the habit of carrying it with me for the last few years. He flipped the pages carefully and verified all the border stamps from the different countries and the dates.

"The phone will be running hot today," he said, "and I'll give you a call tomorrow with the result." With that, we shook hands and departed.

The following day I got a call from Alan Cook confirming I'd got the job. A slight shiver of panic went through me, for now I had to learn how to mend people's shoes and engrave precious items! The intense two-week course was extremely rigorous and held in a simulated training centre. It reminded me of the pressure I'd gone through to be a camping tour guide. Over and over and over we repeated our exercises with someone looking over our shoulder, till we got them right and they were ticked off. Not only did our work have to be A1 quality, it had to be done quickly while the person was waiting; the company's respected brand name had to be lived up to! One thing I liked about the company was if you made a mistake, either with shoes or engraving, you simply apologised and said: "Our supervisor will be in contact with you within 24 hours to arrange a replacement," and they *always* kept their word!

I'll never forget my first day of being let loose on the public. It was in Grace Bros. Sydney department store. Now, I was fine with a couple of classy pairs of shoes I had to repair; all went exactly as had happened in training. Then a lady approached the stand with an, expensive pen to be engraved for her son's 21st birthday celebration. "I've searched far and wide for this particular pen," she confided, leaning forward to share this with me – I was now a part of formulating this present too. She went on: "I plan to give it to him with all his friends in the room so he can unwrap it in front of them."

"What's the message you want me to engrave on it?" I asked, with a pang of nervousness.

"I have it written down," she said and handed me a piece of paper. At this point I must tell you that an engraver uses a dentist drill to inscribe a message, which whizzes around at an incredible speed to get through the hardened enamel of our teeth. So it takes a bit of hanging on to.

With great care the lady handed me the precious pen, and I gently positioned it on the engraver's cushion before me. I switched the lamp on and the lady leant forward to watch the magic happen. I steadied the pen firmly with my left hand and turned on the spinning engraver. Her son's first name was David, and she watched with wonder as I crafted the first three letters with astute care ... but with the *i* I'd just finished the stem and was about to apply ever-so-gentle pressure to put the dot on it when I overdid it and the drill went right through the pen and came out the other side.

"Oh dear," I said, as if it wasn't that major, "the drill has gone right through." The poor lady just looked at the ruined pen in shock; the joy of giving she had just shared with me had been brutally drilled away. I jumped in with the emergency sentence we'd been trained to say: "Our supervisor will be in contact with you within 24 hours to arrange a replacement. Could you write your phone number down for me." I then added my own little bit: "I promise your son will have his pen in time for his birthday on Saturday, for it will be ready for you to pick up fully engraved this Thursday."

As I had a couple of days up my sleeve, I practised my 'eye dotting' on a couple of old pens and re-engraved the lady's message a few times till I felt comfortable with it. When the replacement pen arrived on the Wednesday I was ready to calmly and competently engrave her message along its side. When the lady came to collect it on the Thursday, I unveiled it to her with genuine pride and she was thrilled with the outcome.

Regional supervisor promotion

Impressed with my leadership qualities as a Stand Chief and trainer, Alan Cook soon promoted me to the position of Regional Supervisor. However, there was one thing they didn't know; I absolutely dreaded having to work out percentages. They were always having special offers with 'so much' percentage off, which terrified me because I had no way of working it out. I'd even get it wrong with a calculator. So here I was, Regional Supervisor of Sydney, having to 'guess' what a percentage might be for a given pair of shoes or boots by remembering what other operators had charged for the same discounted item – and I got away with it!

How could I share such a childlike flaw with my fellow supervisors, when they'd been told how efficient and professional I was? For a start, they wouldn't have believed me; and second, they'd probably think I'd lost the plot and was putting it on. Yet *my* reality was having to live with the constant fear of being found out!

Love knocks on the door again

In spite of this, when at my stand I was always playing the role of a confident Mr Minit Stand Chief, handling people with ease, and keeping everyone happy. I was on stage and in my element. One day while in full flight at my stand, a nice looking lady around my age from the nearby florist walked over and said hello. As she'd made all the moves, one thing led to another and after a couple of weeks I plucked up the courage to ask her out. This soon led to a deep and meaningful relationship, but after eight weeks I got cold feet that this could be permanent; that she'd soon discover this Mr Minit showman was really a shallow man of no substance. She had no idea of the deep-seated fears I harboured and that had yet to be dealt with. Our goodbye was painful, for although I tried to tell her it wasn't her fault, she was deeply hurt and was left wondering why … As a result, I felt extremely guilty and lost.

In spite of all this, in nine months I'd gone from rookie trainee to Statewide Supervisor. In fact, I turned one stand from an average $400 a week into one that consistently generated $1,400 for the same period of time – all because of the people skills I'd learnt along the way. So pleased were my bosses with my progress, they were about to expand my new promotion to incorporate all of the Canberra shopping centres as well.

But now I really did panic! Those scary percentage calculations would now be multiplied a hundredfold! My fraudulent cover was about to be blown wide open …

Suddenly everything changes

Then one fine day this debilitating fear suddenly vanished.

I had a head-on collision with a turning car while riding my Honda 250cc motorbike home from work. It was a very nasty accident – I went flying over the car's bonnet and ended up with my leg broken in two places and my right foot severely lacerated.

I remember the distraught lady saying, "I didn't see him!", and she was probably right for I was tucked in behind the car in front of me.

I was to spend the next fourteen months convalescing and learning how to walk again. Yet despite all my pain and suffering, I felt serenely peaceful knowing I would never have to go back to that position again to live under constant shame and fear. But on another level this caused me pain, because Alan Cook had put his neck on the line in giving me a chance; but what was I to do if he didn't know the truth about how insecure I really felt?

Besides my physiotherapy treatment, one of the things I had to do as part of my rehabilitation program was to hobble around the streets near my home as best I could for an hour or so each day. One day I was shuffling along the footpath of a little back street past a big red-brick building that happened to be an old primary school. It was a warm summer's day and one of the windows was open. Not only could I hear the kids animated voices, I could see what the teacher was doing on the blackboard. The teacher had drawn a huge white outline of a cell on the board with its nucleus and its other internal workings. I stopped to ponder it and couldn't take my eyes off this rudimentary outline of a cell.

The children's animated interactions with the teacher wafted out the window to cruelly mock me: so here I was, a thirty-four-year-old man who didn't have a clue about what was on the board or what these young kids were so excited about. I can still feel the bolt of shame that went through my body from head to toe, and how cold I felt: "These little children know a lot more about scientific things than I do," I whispered to myself as the enormity of this belittling realisation dawned on me … "and I'm going to miss out on it and remain ignorant!"

Then and there I decided to take advantage of my long road to recovery and turn a negative into a positive and do a massive catch-up. I wasn't sure how, but my resolve was unshakable. I found the answer the following day in the form of a Time-Life book on evolution at the bottom of a stack of books piled in a corner of the share house where I lived.

A classroom's inspiration

Inspired by the enthusiasm of a schoolroom of primary children to learn as much about the world I lived in and beyond, I was hungry to learn from any source I could. So I opened that book on evolution and began to read. What happened was amazing. I just kept reading for hours, for the easy-to-follow format of pictures and stories made my learning fun! I was well and truly taken in.

The following day I ordered a complete twenty-five-book set of these wonderful fonts of knowledge, covering pretty well everything there was to learn about when it came to the Earth, human beings and the universe. There was even a book on the history of mathematics and the interesting human stories behind it all. But I wasn't afraid of this, for the friendly format was always the same. Funny how I read this particular book without a hint of fear because of the non-threatening way it was presented and the stories of human curiosity behind every mathematical discovery; from Archimedes's invention of the spiral water pump to Ernest Rutherford's splitting of the atom. These were all stories of human endeavour I could relate to – and I loved it! Pity old Ludge hadn't taken this kind of accessible approach with me all those years ago.

So hungry was I for all this knowledge, for I genuinely thought I'd hit on the answer to all my problems, I retreated to my small cockroach-infested room overlooking Sydney Harbour. I sprayed a barrier of insecticide around my mattress on the floor, which kept the cockroaches at bay and we learned to live together. I also followed the pattern of learning I'd started in my building-site rooms in London, of reading out loud as well as normal reading. I thought it wise to inform my housemates I'd be doing this during the day so they didn't think I was losing it. Fortunately, my room, a closed-in porch, was away to the side and out of earshot. But my housemates were great and didn't think anything of it and it all turned out fine.

The one thing I did do differently to how I went about my learnings in those half-built premises in London was to record everything I read out on cassettes – the whole twenty-five volumes. My learning pattern was to read out loud with feeling as I tried to capture the true, *in the moment*, meaning of what was written; I'd then do another two hours of *listening* to what I'd recorded while *reading* the text again to set it in mind. For more than a year my mind soaked in fascinating topics like *the science of sound* and *the food we eat*, along with the broad spectrum of knowledge embodied in the other twenty-three wonderful books of the set. As for the cassettes, at the end of my year-long recovery period I ended up with a large box of 300 of them!

Many years later I found an old carton box stashed way under the house in Melbourne and wondered what was in it. I tore the side of it and something fell out. "My cassettes!" I softly said ... since that time I'd never listened to any of them.

The reality about all this was the gaining of knowledge for knowledge's sake is a noble thing, but the gaining of wisdom from life's experiences is something else again. So even though I'd now become a lot more proficient at Trivial Pursuit and game shows, I was forced to come to another painful realisation: knowledge alone was *not* the answer to my fears and uncertainties. But something else was, and the answer was now crystal clear to me; what I'd missed out on in life was a proper, structured, step-by-sequential-step education, taught in a genuine learning institution.

But where am I going to find that as a mature-aged person? I wondered. I began making enquiries.

CHAPTER 20

Back to school

As it was time for a change of scenery, I decided to move back to my home town of Melbourne for this challenging educational experience, so I phoned the Collingwood TAFE College in Victoria. It took a lot of courage to make this call, for I had a lifetime of pent-up shame and guilt about all the deep-down dumbness I genuinely felt I harboured. When I tentatively gave the man who answered the phone a superficial outline of my situation and asked him what he thought of my prospects for a year 12 Higher School Certificate (HSC), I fully expected him to laugh and say "sorry". But he didn't. He listened respectfully to my hopes and desires, suggesting their Tertiary Orientation Program (TOP), and wished me all the best.

At this stage my wildest dreams amounted to me obtaining a year 12 Certificate and becoming a Park Ranger, because wildlife and the great outdoors had been an integral part of my life as a camping tour leader. This was as far as my educational vision could go, which, to my mind, was a near impossibility. In any case, I was going back to school!

A calming influence

I was taken aback when I first met my classmates in the Collingwood TAFE College, for I was nearly twice their age and felt the odd man out. The majority of them were of Greek descent, and didn't really want to be there. They were the 'also rans' and 'drop outs' from other schools. Little did they know that I was one of them! The sad thing was that most of them weren't going to make it, for this TOP course was very intense and rather advanced.

My tour-guiding experience came in handy as a subtle calming effect on this potentially unruly group of kids, most of whom had few clues on how to study or what it all meant. Margaret, our middle-aged Australian teacher, later confided in me that she was so grateful I was in her class for this was her *first year* as a mature-age teacher. "I was absolutely terrified," she told me, "and you were such a calming influence on them; they seemed to follow your behaviour and really try."

"Glad to be of help," I said.

Mahmoud

But there was one young man quietly standing by himself, away from all the others. I walked over, reached out my hand and introduced myself. He was a very gentle, softly spoken person and he introduced himself as Mahmoud. He was a Palestinian refugee. We hit it off immediately, for we both felt lost and lonely and both needed each other's expertise; he was good at maths and I could help him with his English. He even invited me to meet his family in their housing commission home.

It was a little overwhelming, like stepping into a desert tent full of Arabic hospitality where the food never stopped coming. And they did this more than once, for I was this *Australian* who had befriended their son and was helping him. Although they knew Mahmoud helped me too, they were not aware just how one-sided our mutual arrangement was, for I leaned on him more than he did me. In time I became more enlightened about the Palestinian cause and got to know his family. This all helped in my understanding of the peoples of the world.

What I especially liked about Mahmoud was he totally *respected* and *accepted* me for who I am. He never looked down on my mathematical deficiencies for he felt the same way about his shortcomings in English, so we were an *equal* pair of helpers. No one else in the class knew about our special arrangement. We would work together during lunchtime in the cafeteria or in the local park. Here there was no need to hide or feel ashamed; we just helped each other and got on with our work.

When buying my stationery for my studies I made one monumental mistake that only added to my mental pain and suffering. When I went to buy a calculator to help me with my maths, I bought a top-of-the-range scientific one – you'd need to be Einstein to figure out how to use it! It could do everything from square roots to trigonometry, all stuff I would never use in a million years. I was not to know that a simple calculator was all I needed. Hence, my scientific one only reinforced my ingrained notion that mathematically I was innately dumb for I couldn't even use a calculator.

I struggled with this monster of a thing for the whole first term, then I met Alan Jones at the Carlton share house where I was staying; a young Englishman on a twelve-month tourist-visa holiday in Australia.

Alan

Alan was one of those rare human beings you meet every once in a while as you travel life's journey who you just click with and you become soulmates. He was an average-size guy with receding blond hair and an infectious personality. He had charisma by the bucket load and the girls loved him. And Alan thought that I was hilarious – he'd laugh at all my attempts at humour and I'd laugh at his. Age-wise I'd say that Alan was in his late twenties, and was a highly qualified engineer who'd spent a lot of time building things in Saudi Arabia. What's more, he was a whiz at mathematics. In contrast, I was thirty-four and returning to school for the first time since I'd fearfully run from it when I was thirteen. Alan didn't bat an eye about all this, for he had immediately assessed my worth from the other things I'd done in my life and what he saw in front of him. And apart from the inevitable party life and trips to the historic gold town of Sovereign Hill, Puffing Billy, The Great Ocean Road, and other iconic sights, this wonderful man found time to regularly sit down with me and help me with my dreaded maths homework from the College – as did my other mate in the house, Paul Denton the Kiwi. There was no judgement, no questions of *why*; he just did it as a caring friend would.

Alan told me I reminded him of a builder he used to work for in London who could effectively manage a site of fifty-plus people. "He'd often call on me – or even his accountant wife – to help him calculate different things and quantities," Alan told me, "because he couldn't do it himself ... But boy could he handle people and get the job done! And you remind me of him." I've never forgotten this example of how it's okay to solicit the help of others in areas you're not that strong in; nor have I forgotten Alan's kind and encouraging words.

Muggers meet their match

One night in my room, this likeable man showed another type of caring for someone in need. This night, there was Alan, me, and our housemate, Paul the Kiwi, having a late night chat when we heard a groaning and heart-rending plea right outside my window.

"Help me, I've been mugged," a feeble voice cried out. It sounded like Tom, another of our roommates. Without hesitation Alan said, "Come on guys!" and rushed out the front door and round the side into the park. He helped a bloody and groggy Tom get to his feet and said, "Where are they?"

"They ran off down Johnston Street," Tom managed from an already swollen face.

"Come on guys!" waved Alan, and he fearlessly took off after them apace, with a very nervous Paul and me close behind. We found them, and we chased those cowardly assailants for a good three miles and finally cornered them in a narrow alley. It was very gloomy in there, with its cobblestone base and high brick walls – not the best place for a confrontation. Alan picked up a steel hub cap from against a wall and we cautiously advanced into the gloom.

Two of these thugs were smaller than Alan and one was very tall and lanky. They were sizing us up and ready to fight their way out. It reminded me a bit of my South African experience in that dark alley with the rotting chicken. Alan, steaming with controlled rage, formed the pointy end of our phalanx. He stood there like some ancient god with his steel hub cap gripped tightly in his fist; Paul the Kiwi, who was even taller than the tall assailant partly hidden in the shadows, looked very intimidating; and then there was me, an unknown quantity, but I made up the all-important numbers. I guess they were hedging their bets about what to do. All sorts of things must have been running through their minds, like, *these guys must be strong and fearless or they wouldn't have given chase*. These unsettling thoughts caused them to hesitate …

Alan seized the moment. With his steel hub cap still clasped firmly in his hand, he defiantly took a step forward and said: "*You can't win*, now take that wallet out of your pocket and throw it over here … then get going!" They nervously looked at each other, ready to call our bluff … then thought better of it, for we hadn't moved. Then ever-so-slowly the tall ringleader pulled out a wallet from his pocket and disdainfully chucked it in Alan's direction. They then turned and fled.

We quickly walked back into the relative safety of the street lights, Alan still holding his hub cap just in case. On the way home Paul and I didn't have much to say because all we had done was nervously run along behind the fearless Alan to give him numbers – and back him up if it came to the crunch. But Alan didn't see it that way; he made us feel like heroes, and thanked us for courageously joining him in the chase. "We couldn't let those bastards get away with what they did," he said, and we continued on our way back to see how Tom was getting on, feeling good about what we'd done.

Deep in our hearts, Paul and I knew that Alan was the *real* hero.

Tapping from the room above

One day an unusual tap tap tapping noise from the room above me – Alan's room – caught my attention. And I'd heard it often before. This time it was a bit louder than normal. When I next saw him I said, "Hey, what's that tapping noise I often hear coming from your room?"

"Oh, that's my typewriter," he said.

"Your typewriter? Do you type?" *Is there nothing this guy can't do?* I thought. "How did you learn that?" I asked, genuinely intrigued.

"I taught myself," he said, matter of factly. I made a mental note of this and vowed to myself, *if Alan can do it, so can I*. But it had to wait a while.

A postscript on Alan: the last I heard his wandering days are over and he is now a renowned engineer in England and settled down with a family.

A lesson I won't forget!

My lessons in Practical English that I had started in London really came in handy for my Australian History and English Clear Thinking subjects that formed part of my Tertiary Orientation Program. I remember one particular 500-word essay of which I was extremely proud. I'd spent hours gathering all the necessary facts and information to effectively back up what I wanted to say. I took special care in laying out where I'd be taking the reader, I made sure I proved my leading hypothesis in the body of the work one way or the other, and finally I took exceptional care that I tied it all together in a crisp, clear, deliberate way. It was a wonderful feeling to be able to hand it in on time knowing that I'd do well. And hand it in on time I duly did.

A week later Margaret invited me into her office for a chat, and full of confidence, I looked forward to the discussion. It wasn't an *arrogant* or *conceited* confidence I harboured, but a simple, well-earned feeling that my English was progressing very well indeed. I felt very comfortable attending this interview, for I knew that it could only be a case of whether I'd be getting an 'A' or a 'B' for my latest essay.

"First of all," Margaret said, "I'd like to congratulate you on a well-structured essay that took us to somewhere of interest and made a salient point." I began to relax. All my hard work was paying off. "But," Margaret went on, "there is just one thing wrong; you didn't address the question!"

"I didn't address the question!?" I echoed, completely baffled. "What does *that* mean?"

"It means that unfortunately I have to give you zero."

I just sat there with my mouth open, totally devastated.

"Let me show you exactly what this means," Margaret kindly said, and walked me through *precisely* what the question was; then she pointed out *precisely* what my unrelated essay had addressed.

It was like being hit by a ton of bricks ... and I got it! I was focused more on *how* I did it and *how* I presented it rather than *what* I had to say in response to *this* particular question. A painful but valuable lesson on how to study and *what* to watch out for. *From that day onwards I've always read the question of any given task a few times over to make sure I clearly understand it before I even begin.*

Knowing when to stop

But there were lighter moments in these classes too, for at times those kids could be real wags. But I had to keep in mind that I was twice their age and knew when to stop, whereas they didn't. Therefore, as their barometer of how far they could go I had to be careful not to egg them on. Anyway, one day in Australian History, 'Capo', our teacher, a likeable ex-army Captain on the verge of retirement, was explaining how hard it was for those on the First Fleet to establish a new settlement in such an inhospitable land and their desperate search for a reliable source of sustainable food. So when he tossed out the question: "What does *the search for a staple* mean?" Vince, a likeable Italian kid in the back row who was more interested in his soccer than Australian History, called out: "A bent nail in a post!"

The class erupted into laughter, and so did I for it was funny. But like I said, at times I had to check myself, for it didn't take much for these 'problem' kids to become unruly and hard to manage. And as I'd won their respect as a person who could have a bit of fun too, they followed my lead in respecting the teacher's efforts in return. Being *a subtle calming influence* on the class was in my interest too, for this was my last chance of a formal education; my last desperate throw of the dice. So each night I'd keep beavering away with the task at hand, for the assignments just kept coming …

Computer terror

One subject I was particularly vulnerable in was computers. In my very first lesson I was scared out of my wits and just sat their sweating and looking at the thing. The year was 1984, and computers were pretty new and still somewhat of a novelty. What I was up against was my generation had missed out on them, so many of us had to catch up with the modern world as mature-age people, whereas the young people of today are born with them. And not only that, to operate them you had to be proficient in mathematics – there were no fancy coloured 'desktops' with easy click-on icons in those days; it was all black-and-white MS-DOS (MS stands for 'Microsoft' and DOS stands for 'disk operating system'). For me it was nothing short of terrifying, enigmatic figures and symbols. I used to absolutely dread each computer class and would do my best to try to fathom it all with Mahmoud's patient help; which at least gave me a cumulative bank of positive marks to get me somewhere near a pass. There was no doubt about it; computers were my Achilles heel, and if I didn't pass this subject the whole edifice would come crashing down. This was an awful prospect to live with. I was always worried about how I'd cope in those critical final exams when I'd be sitting there in front of the computer all by myself.

Judgment day

Before I knew it, that apocalyptic day was upon me and I thought, *this is it, this is where it all ends!* I mean I had to face reality; try though I might, I didn't get it and I couldn't understand any of it. The morning of this dreaded exam I was sitting in the cafeteria mulling over my inevitable failure when I spied a tiny piece of scrunched up paper on the floor beneath my table. I picked it up and tried to decipher it, but the jumble of figures and info didn't make any sense to me; but for some reason I stuffed it in my pocket as time was ticking away.

I had one more coffee to try to settle me down, then with an awful foreboding I dragged myself to the computer room where each person sat at their own computer. I was all alone, with no possibility of guidance or help whatsoever. When I heard the supervisor solemnly announce, "You may turn over your sheets and begin," a shiver went through me and cold sweat began running down my neck. With shaking hands I turned on the computer and logged on.

Now, I don't remember the exact words of the examination, but they went something like this: "You go into a hardware store and ask for a kilo of nails and hand over a $20 note. The nails cost $11.75 per kilo. How much will you receive in change? Formulate a program in your computer that depicts all of this."

I freaked out when I read this. I didn't have the slightest clue of where to start, let alone enter the relevant information. I just sat there for a good ten minutes, staring at the intimidating cursor which taunted me to begin … but I couldn't move, no matter how many times I re-read the instructions.

That scrunched-up note

Then, for some strange reason, I remembered that tiny scrunched up piece of paper I'd found under the cafeteria table, and surreptitiously seeking it out, I slipped it under my thumb with my notes. *I wonder what would happen*, I wildly surmised, *if I were to enter this stuff into the computer?*

I held my breath and gingerly entered everything into the computer exactly as it was on that piece of paper. Instantly the computer came to life and started doing things. Then behind me the main printer started whirling and spat out a printed sheet of A4 paper. I sat there staring at it for a few seconds, wondering if it had anything to do with me.

When no one else had moved to the printer, I furtively walked over, picked it up and read it. I had a lump in my throat and almost cried, for there were all my details announcing that this part of my computer assessment had been successfully completed!

Now, call this what you will, but that day someone in the universe was looking out for me and saved my neck; my future was now able to move forward, where I could do good for society … and get help with computers down the track.

On the way out I left the little piece of screwed up paper under the table in the cafeteria.

University?

When my final TOP score came through I couldn't believe it, for it far exceeded my wildest expectations; 289, which was pretty high, and it gave me a big advantage in choosing my tertiary study. As a joke, I put Melbourne University Bachelor of Arts at the top of my list … and to my great astonishment I was accepted! This sent me into an absolute tailspin, as I was totally unprepared. After all, my aim was to get my Higher School Certificate, which I'd proudly achieved, and become a humble Park Ranger. But Melbourne University?! It had all happened so quickly, and I felt completely run over by it all. But there was no way out, for my place was set and I'd been invited to orientation day in two weeks' time.

When I walked into the grounds of Melbourne University, a pang of panic went through me for it was like a city within a city and I wondered whether my time at lowly Collingwood TAFE had adequately prepared me for this. It was with a sinking heart that I took my place in that massive auditorium, and the Vice Chancellor stepped out onto the podium.

I cannot begin to explain my relief when he strongly advised us to consider taking a gap year off to experience a bit of life, as well as to prepare ourselves better in areas we're now not too sure of. "I genuinely recommend you consider this," I heard him say, "and don't worry about your place, for it will be here waiting for you when you return next year."

This was music to my ears. I got up and discreetly left the hall.

Gap year

Now that I'd finished with the Collingwood College of TAFE, and all my friends had left the house I was sharing in Carlton, as I now had a gap year I decided to find a new place of living. One day I was visiting my long-time friends Joe and Nicky and their two young boys Trevor and Geoff in Box Hill, when Joe said, "Why don't you house-sit here and look after the boys while Nicky and I are on holiday in Fiji for four weeks?"

"No problems," I said. This was fine with me because I'd known the boys all their lives and they called me Uncle Laurie. So that's what happened, and I went straight into my tour-guide mode. Each day I'd have to make sure they were up and ready for school, give them breakfast, and make their lunches – and make their dinner for them when they got home. One thing the boys and all their mates did like was my legendary pots of soup. I'd always have one on the go for them to help themselves whenever they liked. And we went on many a trip to favourite places of theirs and some of mine, so the whole thing was like a holiday for them as well.

As Joe and Nicky were working, when they got back they liked the routine we'd fallen into and invited me to stay till it was time for me to move on. And that's what I did. I lived with them as a family member for a year, helping Nicky out by doing the household shopping and taking the boys to their karate and stuff.

One evening I found eleven-year-old Geoff despondently sitting in the corner of his room, almost in tears.

"What's the matter?" I asked.

"I hate books!" he said, "and they're gonna make me read!" On the floor was a book he was supposed to read that he'd thrown against the wall, titled *Hitler Stole Pink Rabbit.*

"I'll tell you what I'll do," I told this distraught little boy. "You get up half an hour earlier each morning and we'll read it together … and I'll show you how easy it is." As Geoff felt he was in safe hands with his 'Uncle Laurie', he nodded his agreement that we would start the very next morning after breakfast.

The first thing I did was read the reviews and blurb on the back of the book to give him an idea of what the story was all about. We discussed who Hitler was and what he stood for; we discussed what it must have been like as a little Jewish girl living in such an unwelcome environment; and we discussed what it must have been like to have to flee their home in Germany and leave everything behind – including her beloved *Pink Rabbit.*

The story now all set in Geoff's mind, we moved on to travelling this challenging journey to France with this frightened little girl. I'd first read a chapter to Geoff, explaining things as I went, then I'd get him to read it back to me. And to help with his writing, I got him to write the same passage he'd just read neatly into a special exercise book.

For the next six months, Geoff and I would get up at 7:30 am, have a bowl of cereal, then retire to the dining room to do our reading. By the end of three months Geoff was no longer afraid of books and had become a proficient reader. In time, he became a bank manager.

Preparing for university

While all this was going on I was taking advantage of the Vice Chancellor's wise advice and doing what I could to prepare myself for *university*; a word that still didn't sit comfortably with me. The first thing I did was fulfil the promise I'd made to myself when I learned Alan Jones could type – I enrolled in a touch-typing class at the Box Hill College of TAFE. The good thing with this was there was no real pressure on me for there were no exams; all I had to do was learn it in a mechanical, repetitious way, which in time I've managed to do and is a skill I'm very proud of.

I wish the computer course I enrolled in had been as easy! The course was heavily laced with MS-DOS mathematical configurations that I had to work through and try to understand – it was heavy going. At that time it was all very primitive, for we were using floppy discs. But it must have done some good, for I could at least sit down in front of a computer without panicking, log on, and write and save an essay using WordStar. At that stage I couldn't copy or paste or do anything as fancy as that; throughout my university career all those kind of things were done by hand and photocopied.

Maths still bugged me!

But I have to do something about my fear of maths! I kept saying to myself. *What if they hit me with a barrage of that at uni?* The mere thought of this was enough to make me feel ill … Then I got an idea. I'd go to the toy department in Myer and see if they had some sort of arithmetic plaything that could teach kids the fundamentals of mathematics. *They're bound to have something like that*, I figured, and headed for town.

A little nervous, but with a hopeful heart, I approached the young attendant in Myer's expansive toy department. "I have a young teenage friend of mine," I said to this attentive young man, "who is having a lot of trouble learning maths … do you have some sort of plaything, perhaps a board game that teaches this?"

He was shaking his head: "No, I'm sorry, I can't think of anything of that nature."

"Oh well, thanks very much anyway." And I walked out. Nowadays there are any amount of things available that could have helped me with this, but not then, not in 1984.

Christmas Eve

My luckless vist to Myer in my desperate search for help with my maths was the day before Christmas; so as a pick-me-up I made my way to my sister's in the sleepy country town of Creswick to celebrate the festive season with her young family. I remember walking round the corner of their house only to interrupt a nativity scene her kids and the neighbourhood children were enacting. The whole cast was dressed in white, including 'Spud' the Kelpie who was being transported uncomfortably in the wheelbarrow, draped in his white nativity wrappings, his long snout and watchful eyes very visible from under his garment.

My sudden appearance shattered the magic of their imaginary world: Spud saw his chance and leapt out of the wheelbarrow, his nativity clothes still tied to his collar and sailing behind him.

"Quick! Jesus is getting away!" little Nicole cried out. I just stood there and laughed, for it lifted my spirits.

On Christmas Eve I was standing near the Christmas tree with my sister's little girls at my feet. They were chatting away and helping each other with their homework. I looked down and saw that it was arithmetic, and these young children seemed to know what they were doing. A shiver of shame went through me … it was like me looking at that blackboard through the window again. I felt really bad. I decided to enlist the help of a maths tutor as soon as I could.

The maths tutor didn't turn out to be as helpful as I'd expected. He was a school teacher in his mid thirties and seemed a little jaded from his experience. He seemed more interested in the money than taking me back to the very start – like my patient friend Pancho did on the training trip or the kind Madame Loftus with her French lessons – and building me up from there. Instead, he persisted with more advanced concepts which I struggled with. I got the distinct feeling that because of my age, he was judging me as a lost cause with regards to maths; quite beyond help. It took me a good three months to figure all this out and terminate our arrangement. From then on I decided to seek help from others in a reciprocal way whenever possible. But one thing I never lost was *hope*.

"I'm a freelance journalist"

I continued making the most of my fortuitous gap year by enrolling in a six-week journalism coarse delivered by renowned *Age* journalist John Pinkney. I found his insightful and practical program very useful in my preparation. He covered everything from how to craft an interesting article to how to get your name in print. My first published article was with the local newspaper. It was interesting how I made it happen, for I was becoming attuned to the possibility of stories all around me.

One day I was wandering through a bird show in the Nunawading council rooms when I fell into conversation with one of the budgerigar owners whose birds were on display. "What got you started in this?" I casually asked.

"Ah, same old story," he said. "My boy started off with the birds and then got sick of them … and guess who had to look after them after that!" We both laughed at this familiar story. I saw an opportunity here for that week's journalistic task of writing a small article for the local newspaper.

"I'm a freelance journalist," I boldly said. "I can see an interesting story here for the local paper … would it be okay if I come to your place and take a few photos and write something up?"

"No problems at all," he said. So we made a date and time, I thanked him, and I wandered on.

On the arranged date and time I went to the man's place and duly took some photos of him smiling proudly holding his prize-winning birds. I then went home and wrote the article, which embodied the age-old story of kids leaving their tedious pets for their parents to care for – after badgering them for permission to have these pets in the first place! And more often than not the parents end up loving them as their own.

My article and photo of the smiling, prize-winning bird fancier were both accepted and published in the local Leader newspaper, with the following caption: **Father Left Holding the Budgie!** I was beginning to discover it wasn't all about maths and my fears attached to it, for *I'd* made it that way for years; I was now developing other strengths, wholly independent of this, which could confidently speak for themselves.

The Rostrum Public Speaking Club

While I was living in Sydney just prior to coming down to Melbourne to study at the Collingwood TAFE, I'd attended a session in a Rostrum Public Speaking Club and found it very interesting. I wondered if they had such a thing down here in Melbourne. It would surely help me with meetings and presenting in tutorials and that type of thing.

I didn't have to look far for there was a club right near Joe's house at the Box Hill Library! I made a phone call and arranged to go along as a guest the following Monday.

This one little act was destined to change my life.

The set-up was pretty much the same as I'd experienced in Sydney, about twenty people sitting around a big table; a different chairperson each week and elected secretary each month; and set public speaking tasks for members to perform in front of the group. The overall purpose was to help people overcome their public speaking fears and learn to speak effectively before groups.

The good thing about it was you were evaluated at the end of the meeting by one of the more experienced speakers, who had gone through a rigorous training program to do so, the objective being to give people practical advice on how to be more successful with their next talk. I myself ended up being one of these key accredited trainers, but at the start I was wide-eyed and eager to learn everything.

Jan

At this first meeting I was very impressed with what I experienced, for there was a lot of laughter and fun. But that was not all that impressed me that night. I was taken in by a lovely girl around my age, by the intriguing name of *Jan Ribaux*. I didn't know it at the time but she was to become my wife and the loving mother of my three wonderful children. Anyway, from the moment I saw her my objective was not only to work on my public speaking effectiveness but to win Jan Ribaux's heart! Little did I know that she thought the same way about me!

I had my chance to make an impression the following meeting, for I was chosen to do a reading to the group. Keep in mind that one of my greatest fears was my shyness in chatting up a girl. I was okay with frivolous, funny talk among a crowd to impress in a superficial way, but go beyond this and try to say what I *really* wanted to and I'd freeze up. So I had to be the clever showman like I used to be on my camping trips and elsewhere for any magic to happen, otherwise I'd just run away. So I'd be doing my very best with this solitary three-minute window of opportunity to impress her.

The book from which I would do my reading was *The Covenant*, James A. Michener's classic historical novel on The Great Trek of South Africa's intrepid Voortrekkers; the Dutch-speaking settlers who travelled by wagon train from Cape Colony into the interior of modern-day South Africa from 1836. Now I didn't choose this book to impress Jan with my wide-ranging historic prowess – it just happened to be the first book I grabbed from my very limited bookshelf. The mystique in my haphazard choice lay in the fact that James A. Michener is a well-known author; and my hardback copy of this famous novel was very large and cumbersome. I circled a paragraph that caught my interest, went through it a few times, and that was my reading task done.

I think my choice of book did the trick, for later Jan said to me: "The thing that impressed me was the *thickness* of the book you carried with you as you stepped forward to speak; I thought, 'anyone who can read a book that big must be clever!" I might add that I did get around to reading this classic novel even though it took me three months, and I got a lot out of it. But it stays on my bookshelf for other reasons.

Jan was Club Secretary for the month when I first joined, so it was her job to issue me with my enrolment papers. Instead of waiting to see me at next week's meeting, she decided to bring them around to me personally at my friend Joe's house where I was temporarily lodging. When I answered the door and she was unexpectedly standing there with her captivating dimples and pretty face, I was totally stuck for words – all I could get out was a meek, "Oh, hi … "

She wasn't much better: "I thought I'd bring your enrolment papers around so you could get them quickly," she said a little hurriedly, trying to justify why such an unimportant task had to be done personally by the Club Secretary.

I did my uncomfortable best to put her at ease: "Thanks, I appreciate this … I'll fill them in and bring them with me next week."

That was it; not another word! Not even an invitation to join me for dinner sometime, or see a movie … nothing! I felt really bad for this was the sad, recurring story of my life.

Fifi the feral cat

The following week Jan gave a captivating talk on *Fifi*, her feral cat who she had enticed in from the bush on the rural property where she used to live. Fifi was so undomesticated that she would only eat rabbit, like the wild ones she used to catch in the fields. So Jan had to go out of her way to buy fresh rabbit for her.

In time, she won Fifi's confidence and she became her lifelong friend. When Jan moved to Box Hill her beloved and more docile Fifi came with her. As I sat fascinated with this story, I got an idea: I'd use the same line I did with the 'budgie guy' and tell her I was a freelance journalist and ask, "Could I come round and see you to take some photos, ask a few questions about Fifi and submit a story for the local paper?" And just as it had worked with the 'budgie guy', Jan said, "Yes!" And the following Saturday, in the guise of a roving reporter, I was invited into the home of the lovely Jan Ribaux and conducted a *lengthy* interview with her about her wild cat. But unlike the budgie story, Fifi's story never really went anywhere ... but I did!

However, as far as Jan was concerned publishing the Fifi saga was still in the pipeline – I must have sounded convincing. But my course in journalism had come to an end, so the pressure was off me in that regard. But right now there were more pressing matters to attend to. Jan said she had a big branch from her cotoneaster tree banging on her roof – could I help her cut the branch off? Could I help her?! I couldn't get around there fast enough, for this was a *doing thing* – the only way I could show my magnificent peacock feathers.

Then, with her help, one thing led to another ... and we did have dinners together, and we did see movies, and we did go on picnics. And I learnt a lot about her. She was born in Preston, but she grew up in the Roesbud/Dromana area on the Mornington Peninsula, where she went to school and got her first job at the local cake shop. From there she went on to the local telephone exchange. When I met her she had climbed her way up through the ranks to be a manager in Melbourne's central telephone exchange. I was impressed.

Jan meets my mother

During all these goings on and before I got stuck into study, I decided to pay my mum a visit in the country and do a few renovations on her house before university started. So I spent three weeks working from dawn to dusk painting her house inside and out. The final task was the corrugated iron roof. This particular day it was a sizzling 45 degrees and I was hanging precariously off the apex of the roof on a flimsy ladder trying to reach some hard places with a paintbrush taped to a broomstick. Sweat was pouring off me and I was just about roasting, but as there was only a little more to go I persevered in the stifling heat. Then the phone rang. It was Jan.

"Hello," said my mother in a tentative tone.

"Hello," replied an equally tentative Jan. "Can I speak to Laurie?" she politely asked.

"That bastard won't get down off the roof and help me," was my mother's reply. "I'll yell out and get him down!" This was Jan's unforgettable introduction to my mum.

We were one

Three months later I moved in with Jan as if I'd known her all my life. Just think, every situation I'd ever found myself in was always a temporary stepping stone, for in my mind it was always a case of *moving on* to something bigger and better, yet this nebulous *something* was always in the far-off future … always out of reach. Now for the first time in my life I didn't have this unsettling feeling, this *urge* to prove myself to the world and *move on* anymore. "What I've been doing all my life has *not* been *moving on*, but *running away* … and I'm not going to do it anymore because wherever I go my fears of being *found out* as uneducated and ignorant keep dogging me … I've now got Jan, and with her help, I'm going on to university and to shake them all off!" I declared out loud.

Giving up smoking

"One thing I'd really like to do," Jan confided in me one day, "is give up smoking." Now I didn't even know that she smoked – she'd been sneaking down the back to do it when I wasn't there. When Jan was growing up everyone smoked as if it was the most natural thing in the world, and it was promoted as being healthy. But one of the main reasons young people took this dangerous habit up was because it made you *feel cool* and fit in socially. Somehow I managed not to succumb to this temptation and have never smoked.

"Don't worry, I'll help you give it up," I said. "We'll go on a holiday together in the Snowy Mountains for ten days and we'll leave your smokes behind." I could see that even the thought of this made her fret a bit and she needed some reassurance. "It'll be fine," I said, "you won't have time to think about them, because we'll be doing lots of wonderful things." I said this more to allay her fears without actual knowledge of just how difficult it is to overcome a nicotine addiction. What's more, I had never been to the Snowy Mountains. But I wasn't too worried about this, for it was her health and wellbeing I was concerned about, and I had lots of hands-on experience of how to set up camp and interact with nature. So we set a departure date for the middle of summer and worked towards it.

Our life-changing holiday

The big day for our life-changing holiday finally arrived.

"Can I take a packet of cigarettes with me and leave them in the glovebox ... I promise I won't touch them!" Jan pleaded.

"No, we can't take them with us," I gently said. "This is the whole point of us going ... Take one of your Refrain tablets now and you won't even think about them." With great trepidation and a lot of courage, this she did. We then set off in our little Morris 1100 loaded to the gunnels with our camping gear and two weeks' food supply; there were no shops where we were going.

After a few hours travel we stopped at Bairnsdale for a full-on English breakfast before we said goodbye to suburbia and began the long trek into the wilderness of the Kosciuszko National Park on the Snowy River. For hours we wound our way along unmade mountain roads till we came across an idyllic little place to set up camp called Willis, on the Barry Way, an old cattle track that runs beside the lower reaches of the Snowy River. When I say little *place*, the only thing that defined it as such was a nondescript sign on a weather-beaten post. Yet before federation, a customs house stood here for the Victorian Government to collect taxes on cattle crossing the border on the way to the markets in Bairnsdale.

The river itself was about ten metres below us with large, crystal-clear rockpools and waterfalls as it cut its way through its ancient bed of greyish rock on its way to the distant sea. There was no mud on the edge of this river. It had its own enclosed beaches of pristine white sand with a suggestion of yellow. This beautiful beach sand also covered the site we'd selected above the river but it was packed tighter, ideal for securing our tent pegs. In contrast, the cliffs and rocky outfalls of the region reflected the usual orangey red colours common to the harsh Australian outback. And to complete the picture, the stately Australian gum trees with their downward-hanging leaves went for miles up and down the mountains in all directions as far as the eye could see. We really were in the middle of nowhere and had this wonderland all to ourselves.

What really surprised us was the weather. Unlike the *cold* the word *Snowy* implies, Willis finds itself nestling in a *weather shadow* of the Snowy Mountains where the weather pattern is completely different to elsewhere in this vast mountain range. In fact, for the summer we were there, every day was around 30 degrees, and some days nudged 40! It was incredible. Each day we'd go swimming in our own secluded mountain rockpool, then stretch out on the beach. We certainly didn't have this sort of holiday in mind when we left for the *Snowy* Mountains!

Each morning I would entertain Jan with my tried-and-proven camping routine of making the Aussie damper in the camp oven and swinging the billy tea round and round in a full circle to add flavour and settle the tea leaves. This would all complement the tasty breakfast I'd just cooked over the open campfire for us to enjoy. In the middle of all of this, and without any fuss, I'd make sure Jan took her daily Refrain tablet. Then we'd have to walk and swim all of this wonderful breakfast off – as well as keep Jan's mind off those insidious cigarettes. And there were so many things to do; so many things to see.

Jack's Lookout

One of these wondrous things to enjoy was Jack's Lookout, only fifteen minutes' walk from our camp. As we were already elevated above the river, all we had to do was continue along the old Barry Way to reach it. The first time we stood near its edge, the impressive views of the river and valley beyond took our breath away and held us spellbound. During our stay in this enchanting hideaway, we would visit Jack's Lookout at different times of the day, like early dawn or sunset, for a different touch of nature's magic each time. I learned later that Jack's Lookout was named in honour of a local park worker.

Birdwatching

In my quest to keep Jan *busy*, we had great fun in guessing what a given species of bird might be, for we had plenty of time to observe and take in what was happening around us. And the birds weren't in a hurry to get away. They took us as a couple of other harmless inhabitants, which gave us the time to observe them. For example, there was one bird which was behaving like a woodpecker to attract grubs on the side of a tree trunk with its pecking sounds. We quickly rushed to our bird bible *What Bird is That? A guide to the birds of Australia* by Neville W. Cayley, and discovered it was the Brown Creeper, which in the absence of a real woodpecker behaved as they do to get grubs from under the bark. We had a lot of fun doing this, and on occasion we picked the right bird! These interesting activities all helped to keep Jan's mind off her cigarettes.

Insect watching

Insects were other things that figured in this quest and captured hours of intense interest. For example, there was a little black burrowing wasp which seemed to spend all of its time throwing heaps of sand out of its burrow with its tiny back legs. Fascinated, we would sit and watch these little creatures for many minutes on end. We never saw them bringing anything back to their burrows, we only saw them landing near their burrows then digging them out some more … interesting! In contrast, we'd often see another very large Australian native wasp with big orange hind legs that dangle downwards when they're in flight. Apparently they like to hunt and capture huntsman spiders, many times their size, then take them half paralysed into their burrows and lay their eggs in them so their larvae can live on the spider when they are first hatched. We never saw them come back with a huntsman but we saw many of these magnificent insects in flight. All this made our trip special and gave another reason for being there.

Each day, wherever we went we'd stop and observe all of these wonders. One day two beautiful beetles alighted on a bush; one was a stunning iridescent green and the other was a shiny pitch black. We watched what they were doing for a few minutes, then they took off again only to land on another bush. To our great surprise, a few days later while we were walking along our favourite track down to the river, there, standing out from the background of the stark white sand, were the vivid, intact shells of these two magnificent beetles. Well, they probably weren't the exact two beetles we had seen the previous day, but they were certainly their cousins. Jan rushed back to the tent to get some tissues and we gently picked them up and stored them with great care in a matchbox so we could take a memory of this wonderful place back with us. When we got home we carefully arranged them in a small black-velvet jewellery container on a bed of cottonwool, and there they sat in pride of place on our mantle piece for years. To anyone else they were just a couple of dead beetles in a box; but to us they were a tangible reminder of the two weeks we spent surrounded by nature on our unforgettable Snowy River retreat.

Don't ask me why, but Jan's cat Fifi also had a predilection for these beetles and it wasn't a passing fancy, for she'd visit them often and move them around with her nose. We didn't mind that too much for we'd simply rearrange them. But it was when she actually bit them that the real damage was done, for – fragile as they were – they ended up as tiny little shards.

Oh well, we philosophically thought, *Fifi has now entered another chapter of our story.*

Skinny dipping in the wilderness

As we hadn't seen a soul for days, one day I decided to be really brave and go for a skinny dip in our favourite rockpool, which was in effect part of the river.

"What if someone comes?" said Jan.

"No one is gonna come," I said. "This is wilderness." And with that I plunged starkers into the waters of the Snowy River.

I would not have been in there fifteen minutes when I heard a kind of dull thumping being transported by the gentle breeze. *I wonder what that noise is?* I thought. And then I heard it again … but this time there were voices with it! I began to panic. *I better get out of here*, I decided. But it was too late. Twenty canoeists had been wrestling and thumping their boats down the shallow rapids, and were now all back in the deep water and virtually upon me. And I was in my birthday suit! There were both men and women in each canoe, a mere ten feet from me as they passed me by waving joyfully – and the water was very clear.

Backing into the shadows of a rocky ledge, I did my best to hide myself and joyfully waved back. *So much for the wilderness*, I thought. The moment they disappeared around the bend I made a run for it. All Jan could do was laugh. She had been enjoying the whole scenario and warmly waving to the canoeists from above.

Interlopers

This idyllic existence went on day after day for a whole week, then one day two interlopers pulled up in a van on the other side of some trees on the sand that led down to the river not far from us. *Oh, no!* we thought, *this is our special spot.*

Not long after this, a pleasant man in his late thirties came over and thoughtfully said, "Would you mind if we were to set up camp on the other side of those trees ... we understand that you get used to having an isolated place all to yourself."

"Not at all," I replied, "you're most welcome." They turned out to be two secondary school teachers from Warrnambool; a husband and wife team on a quick two-week getaway over the school holidays. We'll call them Mary and Rob.

"Why don't you guys share a glass of wine with us round the campfire tonight after dinner?" I suggested.

"We'd love to," said Rob, and went on his way to discreetly set up *their* own special hideaway. Rather than being an imposition on the special magic we'd created, for the next three days they added a touch of their own magic to our holiday.

Strange creatures

That night our new friends wandered over and joined us under a starry sky by the warm red glow of our campfire. Perhaps it was the relaxing circumstances away from it all, or the wonderful night sounds all around us, for we immediately fell into conversation as if we had know each other for years. The fact that all four of us had ventured into this wilderness proved that we had lots of common interests, and we spent hours talking about our surroundings and things we'd experienced in our lives. But all of a sudden swarms of what appeared to be smallish bats began flapping all around us. Wondering what was going on, we covered our heads with our hands to protect ourselves.

Then I remembered the Australian camping trips I'd recently been involved in and the things I'd learned. I happened to look up and see one of these little creatures outlined against the stars, and could clearly see its big fat abdomen like a flying witchetty grub: "Don't worry!" I exclaimed. "They're only Bogong moths and they won't hurt you … they're attracted by the light of the fire."

So with these harmless creatures now flying all around us as a living backdrop, we fell into a very interesting discussion about these icons of Australian wildlife and what they meant to the Indigenous Australians of the area. And as we sipped our wines in this unbelievable setting, we spoke of the historical role our airborne companions played as a nourishing food source for the local people. If we were that way inclined, we could have easily reached up, grabbed one of these tasty morsels and thrown it on the fire to roast.

What a night! We couldn't have staged a more incredible setting to fit the content of that evening's entertainment no matter how hard we tried.

Mountain trout

The following day Rob invited Jan and me to join him for a spot of trout fishing. When his wife declined with a firm, "No thanks, I'll stay behind and read my book," this should have been a red light that she knew something we didn't know about *mountain* trout fishing, for she'd willingly participated in everything else we'd done together. But as they say, ignorance is bliss, and Jan and I thought it a good idea to join Rob in his quest to catch us a tasty dinner.

"Don't worry about fishing gear," he said. "I've got an extra rod for you two … and wear your sneakers." We met after lunch, wished Mary well with her book, and set off on a rather warm summer's day in quest of our elusive quarry. Strangely though, we headed *away* from the river into the rugged hills.

For the next hour we lugged our fishing gear, and ourselves, up a dusty, gravelly mountain track, causing me to think, *where the hell are we going to catch trout up here?* But Rob kept up an enthusiastic banter: "We've got to climb to a stream's upper reaches first, then follow its course back down," he explained to an already weary Jan and me. Mercifully we didn't have to struggle uphill much further in the blazing sun, for Rob veered off towards a line of scrubby trees.

"Here we are," he cheerfully said, as if we'd just had a stroll in the park. And he plunged into the scrub and stood in a metre-wide stream, which didn't look too promising to me. For a start, how would you effectively cast your line with all these low-hanging trees and scrub? All this didn't seem to bother Rob, for away we went on a two-mile downhill obstacle course over slippery rocks, submerged branches, and at times almost impenetrable scrub, casting our lines when we could.

We never got so much as a nibble.

We finally emerged from our watery, thicket-strewn path onto Barry Way, very tired and somewhat worse for wear. We staggered back to camp, and Mary was there to greet us. "Did you catch anything?" she cheerfully asked, knowing full well that we probably hadn't. "No, not today," Rob said, inferring that at other times he was more successful.

All this was wonderful for Jan, for it kept her mind off her cigarettes.

The night before Mary and Rob moved on to the next leg of their journey, I delighted them with my usual Aussie damper and billy tea show, which till then they hadn't seen. After breakfast the following morning, we bid our delightful teachers from Warrnambool farewell and wished them a safe journey home. And to think that if we'd had our own way when Mary and Rob initially pulled into our personal space, we could have quite easily shunned them and kept to ourselves in our own little cocoon. But look at the fun and companionship we would have missed out on! *Sometimes it's easy to make misguided judgements about others from a distance only to find out later how wrong you were.*

A threatening bushfire

The following day a Park Ranger pulled his pick-up in beside us and walked over. He was covered in ash and his eyes were red. "There's a big bushfire coming this way," he solemnly said, "and it could be sweeping through here as early as tomorrow night. I strongly advise that you pack up and leave today."

We thanked him for his timely warning, and even then sensed the smell of burning gum leaves in the air. How ironic. We'd spent the last ten days sitting by the comforting glow of our campfire of an evening, but now the glow of *this* fire would be terrifying. A sense of urgency took hold of us and we decided to throw everything into the car then and there and get the hell out of there.

After about three hours of driving through the forests we stopped for a quick lunch, Jan's Refrain tablet, and a five-minute stretch of our legs. Then it was back into the car, for we still had a long way to go before we could rest easy and know we were safely out of the forest.

Three days later, when were safely back home, bushfires ravaged the same areas through which we had made our escape. I think it was a good thing we acted decisively, kept our cool and didn't panic.

And although Jan still had the odd pang of residual nicotine craving, which got less and less as time went on, our unforgettable adventure to the Snowy Mountains played its role in helping her to give up her debilitating habit of smoking.

All walks of life

One important thing I'd been doing all my life, yet not really being aware of it, is learning to feel comfortable with people from all walks of life. For example, my approach with Guido and Mario Sordelli was completely different to my workmates on an Australian building site, yet I didn't fundamentally change. I was still Laurie Smale through and through and you'd recognise this. Granted, as my journey in life continued I was losing a few of my rough edges, but this was because I was developing different approaches to different situations, and some people can't do this. I've come across people educated and uneducated, rich and poor who spend their whole lives in their own narrow niche and never get to know other types of people – let alone feel comfortable with them. I was learning that the rough-and-ready familiarity of a building site would not be appropriate in other social circles, and how I had to adapt but still be me. In the course of any day we could find ourselves needing to communicate effectively with different people no matter who they are or what their situation in life is. And I was training myself to be at home with this. The next step in this regard was the rarefied air of Melbourne University.

CHAPTER 21

Melbourne University

Once back in Melbourne, my time at Melbourne University was looming ominously. This time on orientation day there was no offer of a gap year, and I had to stay and face it.

The core topics I chose to major in and that appear on my degree were Italian and Australian History. One of my supporting first-year subjects was called *The Earth and Man*; I specifically chose this because I wrongly assumed it would be about people and places, something I felt completely at home with. To my horror I found it was all about topography: physics; map interpretation; water conservation and storage; and all aspects of the environment – all of which required some kind of mathematical interpretation. What's more, at Collingwood TAFE I'd only been used to 500-word essays, whereas at Melbourne University the requirement was 3000 words!

Like the fear I experienced on my first trip, I felt totally overwhelmed and just sat there shell-shocked, wondering how on earth I was going to survive. There was no being spoon fed here. In the massive lecture theatres where the lecturer did all the talking, it was up to you to take down what you thought relevant, which was hard for me as I'd never taken notes of this kind before.

A horrible feeling swept over me that this whole university scenario would require a lot of learning skills I didn't have. What was also unnerving for me was I'd developed the people skills to be in total control of an ever-changing situation when in charge of a group of people; but here in this soulless place, I felt at the mercy of *everything.*

Then I met my four wonderful friends: John, David, Monica, and Alison.

The magnificent four

Remember that I was twice their age, but for some reason we immediately hit it off and gravitated towards each other. Our relationship was mutually helpful; they'd help me with anything mathematical and study strategies they'd picked up over years of study; in return I'd help them with snippets of life's wisdom and advice on how to cope from what I'd learnt in my travels. They also used me as a sounding board for personal problems, for they trusted me and knew that's where things would stay. In this role of confidant I was almost a father figure with them; at other times I became a person of *their age* for over the years I'd learnt how to relate to young people too. But at the start I needed them 1000 times more than they needed me – I was up to my neck in perilous quicksand and sinking fast!

We were once looking at a map through a lens and had to formulate some sort of calculation of what was happening, when I whispered to one of my 'team' that I wasn't too quick on the uptake with maths because I'd been away from school for a while and could she help me; like Pancho, there was no judgement, no questioning why, just straight out help.

This went on for all of the first year for I desperately needed this conditioning. Their youthful perceptions could see that I was no fool and this boyish 'thing' was never a part of their assessment of me. They instantly saw that I had a brain and was clever. Anyway, I was able to more than repay them with my historical and archaeological knowledge I'd gathered along the way; my precious book *Men and Nations* came in especially handy and we all drew from that. I even organised lunchtime study sessions where we cooperatively completed our assignments. This took a great weight off our shoulders and taught these young folk not to leave things to be crammed on the last day as young people are wont to do.

Feeling welcome

After surviving my very first session of The Earth and Man with the help of the Magnificent Four, John said to me as if I was one of them, "Why don't we meet near the library for a drink in the pub opposite in Royal Parade at lunchtime?"

"Okay," I said, not really thinking it would happen. After all, I'd lived a lifetime of trials and tribulations that these young kids knew nothing about; they were wet behind the ears, and they were on a different wavelength to me. So I resolved to kill time sitting in the sun outside the library till my next lecture in two hours time. I hadn't been there long when, to my pleasant surprise, John walked over and said, "Oh, there you are … I've been looking for you everywhere, the others are waiting for us over at the pub." We walked over and all had a beer together, but we didn't make a habit of going to the pub every day. But I was touched for they kept their promise. I was already a valued mate of theirs.

Mutually helpful

Funny how we always tend to focus on ourselves and our own immediate problems. The fact was *everyone* was trying to adjust to this new way of university life. A few days after we four had met, I noticed that John didn't seem his exuberant self – something wasn't quite right. So I said, "Are you okay?"

"Not really," he said. "I spent most of the night trying to avoid the army and the police in the bush of the Watsonia Army Barracks after we'd climbed the fence and couldn't find our way out!" I didn't bother asking the obvious of why on earth he'd be doing that in the middle of the night – I just said, "And what happened?"

"They caught us in the end and have given us a warning that next time we'd be in real trouble. But that's not all," he confided in me, "I got notice that the university is not happy with certain things about me and I've got to justify why I should be allowed to continue."

I was astonished when I heard this, for this was certainly not the decent person I'd come to know in this first little while. Hey, we've all made stupid mistakes when we were young, yet we all still have potential to get back on track and do something fulfilling with our lives.

"What's next?" I asked.

"I've written a letter to the Vice Chancellor, and wonder if you'd look at it for me?" Which I did: I remember him writing that he was a little fish in a big pond, he really appreciated the opportunity to study at Melbourne University, and he desperately wanted to continue his studies there if given the chance to prove himself. I suggested a couple of minor changes, but left the gist of his heartfelt plea as it was.

The letter was duly delivered and was followed by a do-or-die interview with the Vice Chancellor where he had to plead his case, which we also workshopped in the cafeteria. In the end he was allowed to stay and did indeed go on to better things.

Little did I know it, but I was shortly to run a series of similar gauntlets myself.

First submission

My first ever submission at Melbourne University was in response to a question posed in The Earth and Man. To have to respond in the form of a 3000-word essay brought on a severe mental block about where to start and how to go about it. I simply was not ready to submit one of these lengthy essays. Instead I began thinking of a clever three-sentence, wisdom-packed package that said it all! I put a lot of thought into my succinct response, written in biro on a sheet of exercise paper.

A few days later my insightful 'submission' was returned with a note scrawled across the top in red ink: "This response is nowhere near worthy of university consideration!" I had years to go with my studies for my degree and this was my first *official* result after a few days – not a good start! Although this hurt, I had to come to terms with the daunting reality of getting my head around writing 3000-word essays!

I began to think about how I might go about tackling this overwhelming task: *I can already write a 500-word essay*, I reasoned, *so why can't I join six of them together to make a 3000-word essay?* This reasoning helped me realise that I used to do a similar thing with my talks on my camping tours where I had three or four ideas to cover with a main point embracing them all; I could draw on this experience, for here I would have an overall point to make with a beginning that clearly flags where I'd be taking my reader; a body that illustrates my contention with vivid, compelling examples; and an ending that summarises not only where we've been, but where to from here.

Well, in theory this was how I was going to approach it, which at least cleared my head and gave me some direction.

3000 words on prehistoric man

I didn't have to wait long for my first chance to test this theory, for a 3000-word essay on the evolution of prehistoric man came my way – a nice light topic to start with! The first thing I did was gather all the required reading, then photocopy all the relevant images I could cut and paste to back up what I wanted to say. This done, I scurried back to Jan for support in the safety of my home. Jan recalled that when I walked in the door I was as white as a sheet and began walking round in circles in the kitchen saying over and over, "What am I going to do? … What am I going to do?" She could see that this wasn't the confident Laurie she'd been used to over the last three years, and was astonished to see me on the verge of breaking down before her eyes.

She took control of the situation: "Sit down, and I'll pour you a nice glass of wine to settle you down and you can tell me how we can sort this out." I did what I was told, and the combination of the soothing shiraz and her genuine concern and support transformed my blind fear into something more bearable. Jan cleverly got me thinking and talking through my dilemma. I was able to repeat the approach of tackling a 3000-word essay I had earlier worked out in my head, drawing on the old adage of "tell them what you want to say; tell them; then tell them what you said!" Then within this overall concept, I would join six of my 500-word essays together.

"What a great idea!" Jan exclaimed. "Let's lay all the stuff you photocopied out on the lounge room floor so you can see in what order you might use it." This made a lot of sense, so that's exactly what we did. With all of these evolutionary images now laid out in sequence in front of me I was forced to ask myself, *what is it that I want to say about all of this?*

Then, recalling the valuable lesson I'd learnt at Collingwood TAFE of *always addressing the question*, I twigged that clear *directions to the answer* could be found in the question itself. So I quickly re-read exactly what the lecturer's 'directions' (the question) spelt out. And, determined not to make the same mistake a second time, I read this question over a few times and thought carefully about it. Finally I wrote the question down in large print on a piece of paper to keep in front of me as I studied the required reading.

I did glean an overall idea of what I *might* be saying simply by contemplating the expanse of sequential images laid out before me. I wrote this *working idea* down in a *working focus sentence* to give me some initial direction. Now as I perused my required reading, I could write relevant ideas and page numbers down that related to this *working idea*. With my reading and research all finished, all I had to do now was go back to my *working focus sentence* and finetune it into a clear, single-sentence statement of what I intended to say in my essay. My *final focus sentence* was now a crisp, clear *destination* of where I'd be taking my readers, and now was I ready to lay out a sequential, sign-posted plan of how I was going to take them there.

In spite of the persistent fears I still harboured, this detailed preparation enabled me to take my time and steadily plug away at this project over the next few weeks. As a result of this, and it was hard to believe that I actually did it, I was able to hand in my first 3000-word essay *before its due date*.

The first exam debacle

Then came the shock of my first exam at Melbourne University. Now, I'd sat for one or two exams in Italy with my Italian, and I'd had my Great Computer Exam Escape, but they were nothing compared to what I went through on this fateful day. And you guessed it, it was a wide-ranging series of questions from my all-encompassing subject The Earth and Man.

The exam setting was pretty standard: lines of single tables policed by roving supervisors. I walked in and sat down at one of the tables and placed my pen down. I noticed that David, one of our group, was just across the way. Then a robotic voice said, "You may turn your papers over and begin." I did so and began reading the first question … and had no idea what it meant … I began to panic. *I'd better move on to the next question*, I thought, but this was no better.

Now I was really panicking and beginning to lose it. On and on I desperately flipped and read, but I could make neither hide nor hair of any of it. In the end I simply gave up and sat there staring at my blank paper, nothing on it but my name and student number. I felt like I was in that tent in Belgium again on the verge of another mental breakdown, and I was shivering in a cold sweat. Mercifully a voice then said, "Time has elapsed, please put your pens down." Totally defeated, I slunk out of that room and headed for the open air, knowing I had failed miserably.

I hadn't gone far when David caught up with me: "I could see you were in a lot of trouble," he said. "Do you know anything about downloading?" (This was before today's understanding of the word.)

"No, what's that?" I said, still feeling empty after my ordeal. David then went on to explain that 'downloading' is one of the essential things you need do before an exam; fill your mind with possible answers that you can 'download' and tweak to suit a particular question. Try to pre-empt what the lecturer might ask about this, that or the other. Go through all your lecture notes and their handouts and try to encapsulate the essence of what they were saying and boil it down to an idea you can 'download' if necessary.

"Do the same with relevant books you have to read," he said. "Then brainstorm what general questions they might ask about characters, themes, or plots; and how would you answer them? Above all, don't sweat over these things trying to memorise them all by heart. Just spend some time mulling over it and reflecting on it all, knowing it will automatically be stored in your subconscious mind. Then when you're confronted with a certain question in an exam situation, unexpected solutions will pop into your *conscious* mind, simply because you've sown them there." This was all very clear and made a lot of sense to me. Look at the heavy price I'd paid when I'd done none of this. I was going to make doubly sure my results for the next exam for The Earth and Man would be vastly different from the first.

I wasted no time

I was very keen to get David's life-saving strategy of exam *downloading* under way and decided to take advantage of my daily 40-minute train trip to do so. First I bought myself one hundred palm-size, lined filing cards and spent days filling them with meticulous schematic and factual information on the world we live in. I grabbed every book I could from my tours on geography and the environment – even the weather – and condensed the key ideas of each chapter down to a card, and I ended up with the 100 of them all filled with info to be sown for future *downloading*.

How it worked was as soon as I got on the train for my one-way 20-minute ride, I'd find a seat and start flipping through my precious cards. Each card would be silently read through and thought about for a few seconds, then onto the bottom of the pack it would go, and I'd move on to the next one. This was all done very subtly and without fanfare. One lady sitting opposite me, and awake to what I was doing, went out of her way to say, "Good luck." I smiled at her insightful understanding and said, "Thank you."

When the time came for my next The Earth and Man exam, what a difference in me there was! This time I strode into that room with confidence, prepared and primed for efficient downloading. I paid careful attention to each of my pre-brainstormed questions and made sure I answered them as best I could with the appropriate download. Images of the cards I'd been looking at during my short train journeys flashed into my mind, stimulated by a particular question. Thus, I was able to do a quick but relevant sketch of the idea under consideration.

In this exam I was able to draw things like globes of the world with longitude and latitude clearly depicted, all with their accompanying explanations. And these ideas and inspirations happened with just about every question I faced; all flooding into my conscious mind just like David said they would.

When the results came in I was pleasantly surprised; I received an 'A H'; that is, an 'A' with 'Honours'! This was against the demoralising 'P ?' I had received with my first effort, which could be interpreted as meaning: 'This student is way out of his depth and there is a big question mark of why on earth he is here.' I carried David's downloading strategies with me throughout my whole university experience and used them in all my exams. As a result I received an 'A+' or an 'A H' for all of them.

How does one measure intelligence?

This poses the serious question about how to truly measure intelligence and self-worth. It would have been so easy to brand me dumb, hopeless and an abject failure if all one had to measure my intellectual capabilities was my first pathetic exam result, whereas with my second effort I'm now recognised as being *in the top 1 per cent* of intelligent society! Try to work that out! That's certainly not fair, for I didn't change; all I did was shift my thinking and do things differently.

Closely related to this, and one thing I'm pretty wary of, is personality tests. All they do is take a snapshot of how a person thinks and behaves at a certain stage in their life, and fail to consider that this same person can grow and learn to think differently. Twenty years later, a person doing the same test could get a very different result! *So, be true to yourself with the knowledge that our minds are always expanding, for we never stop learning to be better and more insightful human beings.*

Returning to Melbourne University, the pressure was on me to learn many other things my young colleagues had been learning for years as a matter of course. Like the effective use of footnotes and lots of other scary stuff that the average person in the street doesn't have to worry about. The secret here, I learnt, was to be consistent. If you pick a style of footnoting, stick to it and don't mix 'n' match, for this can be confusing.

And this brings us to plagiarism; that is, stealing someone else's work and putting it forward as your own. I was once struggling with one of my 3000-word essays on colonial power in the Industrial Revolution and I needed some information on how the British used their overpowering industrial might to invade and sweep aside the hapless Ethiopians in the 1860s. After a search, I stumbled across a long-forgotten book in the bowels of the Melbourne University Library which had the exact content I was looking for. *I'll use this paragraph,* I thought, *no one will know about it in such an old, forgotten book.* And that's what I did. I carefully crafted the stilted words of the past to match my modern style of writing, and I made sure the whole thing was a seamless and logical part of my essay. I then submitted it as usual. Although I felt guilty about doing this, I justified it by the clever way I'd made it look like my own work; in my mind I hadn't plagiarised at all. As it happened I got another A+ and heard nothing more about it. Not my proudest moment.

As time went on my sneaky misdoings of that day in the dark dungeons of the Melbourne University Library became a distant memory for I was growing more and more confident with my own writing voice, a voice which now embodied and reflected who I *really* was. Nowadays whenever I use someone else's words or ideas to add support to what I am saying, I simply acknowledge them.

Not having an academic background to draw on, my approach to university life tended to be somewhat unconventional, although I did my best to conform and not rock the boat. One day I was sitting with my friends among 200 other students passively listening to the lecturer talk about the Tasmanian bushrangers and the things they got up to. As he was talking I was thinking of the infamous Australian bushrangers, like Ned Kelly, Captain Moonlite and Ben Hall, who all rode sturdy steeds and ranged far and wide. But to my mind, something didn't add up: *how come the Tasmanian bushrangers didn't range for hundreds of miles like the mainland ones did … they stuck to a much smaller area?* The fact that he hadn't addressed this aspect bothered me.

Now nobody, but *nobody* ever asks a question during a lecture at Melbourne University. But this gnawing question needed to be answered. The next time he paused to look down at his notes I put my hand up and called out: "Did the Tasmanian bushrangers ride horses?" Everyone sat there stunned that someone would have the brazen effrontery to ask a question during a lecture. The lecturer himself was taken aback by this unusual behaviour and seemed quite lost for words. After a few seconds of gathering himself, he said, "That's a good question … as a matter of fact not as a rule … no, they didn't … They spent most of their time hiding in the mountainous forests on foot." I nodded an appreciative "thank you" for his enlightening response and felt my courageous question had been justified.

Now I'm not advocating that we yell something out every chance we get for no one likes an undiplomatic loudmouth. What I am saying is, *every so often we can be faced with a situation where it's probably a good thing to speak up and share what we really feel instead of remaining silent.*

Coming to terms with computers

As I've mentioned throughout this saga, computers – along with maths – have been a bugbear of mine for years, but I've tried to keep up with them, albeit in a basic way. For example, I'm now at home using a calculator for my basic accounting needs so maths is no longer a problem; I don't have to bother myself with algebra and fancy stuff like that, which I'll leave to the boffins. Computers, on the other hand, are something else again. For the duration of my university years, I struggled with a rudimentary computer that worked on MS-DOS and I used solely as a word processor. Compared with what I'm using today it was stone-age. Even so, it enabled me to edit as I progressed without all the reworking and scratchy notes with the old way of handwriting it. But one thing I did, because there was no hard copy constantly in my hands, was regularly save my work.

But it wasn't always that way.

One particular day I was putting the finishing touches to a 4000-word essay on prehistoric man that I'd been working on for six weeks or more, when Jan threw the switch on the electric kettle in the kitchen to make me a cup of coffee. My screen suddenly went black, and my computer whirred to a stop.

I froze.

"Please," I said to God or anyone else who'd listen, "*please* let my work be saved!"

I heard Jan yell out, "Hey, the power's gone off!"

"I know ...", I said, " ... I ... hope I haven't lost my work!" I began to panic – I feared the worst. I didn't dare touch the computer in case I somehow interfered with its memory and wrecked any chance I had of saving the situation. Instead, I went for a walk in the back yard on the slim hope this would ensure my essay would be waiting for me when I turned the computer back on.

When I finally did have the courage to do this, search though I might, my essay had gone without a trace. Poor Jan. I gave her a big hug and told her it wasn't her fault, which was true for our house had been built in the 1950s and couldn't draw too much power at one time. I sat down with her to recover, ponder on what I'd just lost forever, and contemplate what I could do about it.

Then I made a decision: I'd sit down in front of the computer immediately while the overall picture was still fresh in my mind and start typing. It was an awful feeling to have to do this but I had no choice. Three weeks later I put the finishing touches to it and was able to get it out of my hands.

Notwithstanding this unwanted trauma, I got an 'A' for the revamped version of my essay and was very happy with that. From that moment on I've been paranoid about saving my work, and will regularly do so in at least three different locations.

Switching behaviour to suit the occasion

Earlier I mentioned how easy it was to unintentionally egg on the younger people I went to school with. A person in their mid thirties has learnt a bit of self-control whereas an eighteen-year-old person can be still learning the importance of switching behaviours on and off to suit the occasion. One day my friends and I were standing in a courtyard chatting and admiring the scenery when an Italian lecturer friend of mine began crossing the open space where we were. Now we Aussies enjoy a bit of harmless slinging-off when out of earshot of someone so no harm is done. Yet two minutes later they can find themselves in friendly conversation with the very same person they'd just slighted from afar. This was the tricky situation I now found myself in.

Now this middle-aged lecturer was a very nice person and a warm associate of mine even though I was a student and he was a teacher. Jan and I had even shared a dinner with him and his wife. But this particular day the wind had caught his long wispy hair and he looked like Einstein on steroids, so I shot a harmless quip out the side of my mouth – "Look at the hair on that!" – which of course really set my young friends off, for they laughed at anything I said.

The problem was Mario spied me and was on his way over for a chat. But my friends were still switched on to his wild and woolly hair do! By this time I'd completely gotten past the 'hair comment' and greeted my friend. Still trying to contain their barely suppressed mirth, my friends had to walk away and watch in wonder as Mario and I engaged in a friendly, mature conversation about the weather, what was going on in the Italian department, and so forth …

When we bid each other farewell a minute or two later, John came back and said, "How do you do that?!" And I said, "They're skills you learn along the way; we've got to know when to turn off and change our tack." They still looked at me in wonder, for I could relate to *them* on *their* level with a bit of fun, then instantly switch to relating to *the lecturer* on *his* level, sincerely talking about stuff *he* was interested in. This is why we all got on so well, for we continued to learn from each other.

Diploma in Education

At the end of the three mind-opening years of my Arts degree, it was time to say goodbye to my four incredible friends and move on to my final year with my Diploma in Education. I had no burning desire to be a school teacher, but I thought the skills and qualifications would come in handy whatever I ended up doing. Although very taxing, I'd only be working with subjects I was familiar with: Italian and Australian History. And the core of it all required the confidence to put together an interesting learning program and deliver it in an engaging and inspiring way, skills I'd already had a lot of experience in developing; what with those years of entertaining in The Top Hat Review, and having to keep a coachload of young campers engaged for two weeks with my stories and planned activities. But I still carried a tangible inner fear of being stricken with pangs of panic if confronted with the unknown.

But I could see I was getting better with this and had undoubtedly travelled far. As I'd learned to do with my camping trips, my strategy to keep these debilitating pangs of panic at bay was to thoroughly plan for all contingencies, then review what I'd prepared over and over to make sure all bases had been covered. Time and energy consuming though this was, it was my means of surviving each assessment ordeal. Oh, and like my previous three years, I quickly established a platonic relationship with two young Aussie/Italian women and very soon we were as thick as thieves in helping one another, just like the others. We would discuss each others' teaching programs and workshop them together, playing the roles of both student and teacher. And we drew inspiration from my precious book *Men and Nations* – which had travelled the world with me – to help us formulate our teaching programs. And because I'd learnt to *think* like an Italian, which they found especially touching, I became an intimate friend where they didn't feel threatened and could share things with me they wouldn't dare share with their parents!

We had a lot of fun working together, and because of our friendship our Dip. Ed. Experience at uni wasn't scary at all. But away from the comfort of this supportive 'togetherness', our eight-week teaching stints out in the real world were something else again.

Baptism of feral fire

My first student-teacher posting was out west of Melbourne at the Deer Park Secondary College, purported to be one of Melbourne's toughest. Ignorant of this, I was totally unprepared for what I was about to experience. Sure, we'd had some entertaining lectures on handling an unruly class, but that was all theory and nothing like being in the actual firing line.

Hadn't I successfully organised and effectively managed coachloads of young people time and time again? I confidently reasoned, *so a room full of year 7 kids would be a piece of cake*. Brim full of confidence, I fronted up at the Deer Park Secondary College ready to wow these year 7s with my well-rehearsed strategies and programs.

As I approached the classroom I could hear the din my class was making. *This sounds like they could be a handful!* I thought. I opened the door and walked into utter bedlam. Kids of every nationality you could think of were on, under or beside their desks, totally out of control. One kid was getting back in through the window. They were screaming, firing spitballs at each other, and throwing schoolbags around. The place was full of *ferals* in the true sense of the word. I had planned a polite "Good morning," then an introduction of myself; instead I found myself screaming at the top of my voice: "Be quiet and sit down!" Which made little difference, so I had to do it again, this time even louder! This at least got them into their seats.

Now somewhat tentative, for they hadn't yet got my measure, they sat there sizing me up. "My name is Mr Smale," I ventured …

"Mr *Snail*?!," the class clown jeered, and the room went into uproar. I'd now lost all control and they could smell blood. I spent the next hour and a half – yes, it was a double period! – putting out fires and screaming for attention. When I did attempt to teach them something, everything I said was hilarious and it lost all meaning.

I honestly don't know how I got through, but when that bell went I at least stood in the doorway and took control – I thought. I drew myself up to my full height (which admittedly is not that high) and ordered, "Get back in your seats! You've all been extremely rude to your new teacher so you can sit here for a few minutes to think about it!"

"Oh, sir … we've got to get our lunch."

"You should have thought of that when you were being so rude," I retorted, still blocking the door. Then, before I could do anything, the clown of the class had grabbed a chair and climbed on it and out the window.

"Come back here!" I yelled, but he was gone. I couldn't be in two places at once and now others were clambering out after him. I'd lost the battle. Feeling pretty bad about it all, I opened the door and the mob rushed past.

I staggered back into the staffroom as white as a ghost, and slumped into a chair a defeated man. Incensed, one kind teacher realised what had happened and yelled at everyone in the staffroom: "Who the hell gave this student-teacher 7F?!" So they all knew about it but sent me there anyway. Somehow I survived this arduous eight-week teaching round, and I was more than relieved when it was over.

On reflection, I can't be too hard on these kids for I used to be one of these terrors myself. There was more than one time, as a result of my own ignorance and fears, that I'd let my unruly behaviour disrupt the class and nearly drove our poor student-teacher, Mr Wilson, crazy.

Ingenious duck hunting

The next school I was sent to was Genazzano, a noted private girls' school in Kew. Granted the older grades were rather discerning with my content and the way I teach, but I was learning more and more about strategies and techniques on how to effectively engage students and make things interesting. One pleasant memory that stays with me is the day I took the year 7s on an imaginary excursion to do some duck hunting with the Indigenous Australians.

I first explained how the original inhabitants who lived along the Murray River were very clever at harvesting the various natural foods available to them from their surroundings. One effective strategy they had was netting wild ducks. To do this, one group would stretch huge nets made from natural fibres high up in trees across a chosen waterway, while another group would wait downstream till this was done. Then, on a given signal, they would scare the ducks into flight, who would instinctively follow the path of the river and get caught in the nets. The group who set the nets would then let them drop so the ducks couldn't get away and they could easily harvest them. Now the whole class was ready to be involved in the hunt.

"Shall we have some fun?" I asked them.

"Yes!" they said enthusiastically, which was what I wanted to hear. Now it was easy for me to get three groups of volunteers to complete the *duck-hunting* scenario; we needed a group of *net-setters*; a group of *duck-scarers*; and a group of *ducks*. And like a conductor of an orchestra I lifted my teacher's baton and the whole thing came to life.

"Right," I said, "you *net-setters* get to work erecting your nets across the river, tying them to those two big gum trees!"

"And you *duck-scarers*," I pointed to the other side of the room, "walk over there, down by the river and wait for the call to scare the ducks."

"And you *Australian wild ducks*," I nodded towards the last group, "go down to the river till it's time for you to fly away quacking in fright."

"Are the nets all set?" I asked the first group, "and will you be ready to harvest them?" They were.

"Well," I turned to the *duck-scarers*, "let's see you scare those ducks into the air! And *ducks*, let's see you fly away quacking with fear and get caught in those nets!" It was fabulous; the whole scene came to life with much sound and movement as each group sprang into action. The kids loved it; the teachers loved it; and I loved it. And best of all the children *learnt* something.

The amazing thing was my first teaching experience at Deer Park might have been a dismal failure but my next one, a few short weeks after that, was an outright success. *It's so easy to let a really awful experience define who we are and what we stand for, when a more worthy definition of who we really are could be closer than we think.*

So why an education?

So there I was, somehow managing to get through a tortuous path of what turned out to be my biggest fear: obtaining a recognised education. But did the achievement of my B.A. Dip. Ed. really change me as the person I am, or is it just a fancy piece of paper?

Someone once asked me: "Why did you go on to university? What did it do for you? … They just sit around talking."

And I said, "I'll tell you what it did for me; it taught me how *to think*." I went on to say that prior to this, if I heard something on the news I'd believe it as true; prior to this I didn't read with a questioning eye, for I took most of what was in print at face value; and prior to this my simple mind wasn't geared to pick up on a metaphor or suggestion of something more meaningful.

At university we would read a set book then discuss why the characters thought and behaved the way they did; which is another way of exploring why *we* think and act the way *we* do. It didn't matter whether the book was fact or fiction, for the human predicament would be in there somewhere. The fact is sometimes an author can spend years researching and studying human behaviour to create their characters; this is why a book can end up being a font of human wisdom that we can learn from and reflect on. Through the behaviour of these different characters, real or fictional, we can even get insights for ourselves into *what* and what *not* to do. At university we used to indulge in mind-stretching discussions like this for hours, thus training our minds to think clearly and continually question and further our understanding of the human condition.

It makes me shudder to think that there are still many grown-ups who walk the streets with the narrow, one-way vision I used to have. It makes me shudder to think that these tunnel-vision people with closed minds cast a vote. I'm an example that ignorant narrow-mindedness can be dramatically shifted through education, for I am now a better member of society because of it. Now when I vote, I question and try to think clearly. *As a consequence of what*

I've experienced, I'm a great advocate for a free and universal education for everyone.

Graduation day

Then, after all my hard work, came the momentous day of my graduation. When I heard my name announced, I took a deep breath and stepped onto the hallowed stage of a packed Wilson Hall at Melbourne University. Following the recipients before me, I too made my way in front of all those learned dignitaries in their colourful capes and gowns to have my *Bachelor of Arts (Hons)* degree, with my *Diploma of Education* degree, conferred by the Chancellor himself. Wow!

Against all the odds I'd somehow achieved the impossible; my initial goal had been to somehow scrape through with a year 12 certificate. Yet here I was, proudly draped in fancy garb myself, receiving recognition for something I'd well-and-truly earned; the exhilarating culmination of a very long and tortuous journey. But I didn't share this honour alone. My real backstop was the person I went home to for emotional and homely support after each tense and stressful day; the best thing about that memorable occasion was to see my Jan proudly sitting in the third row to witness what we'd achieved together. *The other momentous thing that dawned on me as I stepped down and joined her was I knew that I didn't have to move on anymore and I could stop running away.*

Being proud of your achievements

One last word on a BA (Hons), Dip.Ed. degree. I've often heard people devalue their achievements and unintentionally denigrate themselves when asked about their education: "Oh, I only got a BA," as if it's some sort of lowly affair. This really rankles with me because I know how much pain, sweat and tears I had to go through to get mine. I feel like saying, "Was it easy?", and I'll bet they'd vigorously reply, "Oh, no!", as if my question was ridiculous. And yet they'd already unwittingly put themselves down because it's not a highly esteemed PhD or something like that. What raises my hackles even more is when I hear someone say, "Oh, it's *just* a BA." I feel like saying to them, "You try writing 3000-word essays and consistently getting an A or A+ for them over a four-year period … along with all the other studies that go with it … and see how you go!"

We humans have a tendency to put ourselves down with regard to our achievements, when what we should be doing is lifting ourselves up, cutting out the negative self-talk, and quietly feeling proud of what we've done.

Although on paper I was now a qualified teacher specialising in Italian and Australian History, I certainly wasn't confident to head helter-skelter into the blackboard jungle! I'd already had my baptism of fire as a student-teacher of how tough teaching can be. I was in no hurry to throw myself at the mercy of those kids again where I'd return home stressed and exhausted every night. I'd look for other kinds of work and keep my teaching option tucked away as a last-ditch emergency. The thing I was happy about now was *I felt educated*, which was an incredible milestone for me, and I could move forward from there.

CHAPTER 22

Then we were three

Then one day I received some news that left me speechless. In fact, everything else that had happened in my life prior to this paled into insignificance when compared with this one piece of news. Jan walked me into the kitchen, sat me down and said, "We're going to have a baby."

It took me a while to find my voice; I was now going to be a forty-two-year-old father! An incurable optimist, I simply ran with it and said, "Oh, well, from this point on our lives have changed." And indeed they had.

After all the trauma of the past few years, this new 'miracle of life' that had been gifted to us was a wonderful blessing and confirmation of our family unit. After all, Jan and I had been living together for four years, so this 'family' idea sat well with us. Everything was moving fast for there would soon be three of us! And the logical sequence to this was to get married. In those days a mother still copped flak from the banks, institutions and society if she wasn't married. (None of this worried me, for I was a new-age guy who would share the load of running a home and bringing up kids.)

So get married we did; Jan with a lovely white dress and lily-of-the-valley flowers in her hair; and me and my best man Joe in a light-grey top-hat and tails.

All we could do now was wait for little Felicity to arrive.

In the meantime ... a surprise guest!

While all this was going on, one day Jan and I returned home to find the fifteen-year-old daughter of a country friend of ours sitting on a suitcase in our sitting room. Her step father didn't treat her well, her mother couldn't cope, and she had nowhere to stay. She told us that she was about to travel around Australia with two young ex-army guys, and we immediately thought, "This doesn't add up!" We offered to give her somewhere to sleep for a couple of nights while we sorted something out, and she gratefully accepted.

Samantha ended up staying with us for two years, went back to school, and finally got herself a job in an office. Every day I'd make her super-size sandwiches to take to work and we made our spare room nice and *girly* for her. Very soon she became a part of the family, as if she were our daughter. She obviously knew of Jan's pregnancy and was following that with great eagerness too; as a result they became very close to each other.

One evening we were all chatting away preparing a tasty dinner of nice juicy steaks, mixed green salad, and homemade chips for us to enjoy together. It looked absolutely mouth-watering and we couldn't wait to sit down and eat it! We'd just finished cooking and had it all dished up, so I said: "Let's grab our plates and sit at the table," and everyone eagerly did so. But poor Jan dropped hers face-down on the kitchen floor.

Midway through her pregnancy, and emotionally sensitive as she was, Jan burst into tears and ran to the bedroom. It all happened so quickly that Samantha and I were left standing there wide-eyed and looking at each other. Then, as a tension release, we couldn't help but let out some subdued laughter, for there is a funny side to everything. We then sprang into action!

"I'll re-fry Jan's serving *for me*, to kill the bugs ... and it'll be fine," I said. "You two can have the two good ones." Samantha was a real hands-on person – she grew up on a farm and was right in her element; she took control and calmed Jan down and brought her back to the table. Ten minutes later we were all sitting down enjoying our side-tracked but nevertheless lovely dinner. It was little experiences like this that warmed Samantha to our hearts as part of our family.

But Jan and I knew that Samantha's stay with us was transitory and that all she needed at that unstable time in her life was a safe place to sort herself out and stand on her own two feet. One sad day, the time for Samantha to move on to greener pastures came.

I'm not sure where she is now, but the last I heard she is happily married and lives in Queensland with three kids. What I do know is, if ever I had the pleasure to bump into her, she would warmly embrace me for the part Jan and I played in her life when she needed it most. Goodness me, how many times have I been helped in my life! It's just nice to be able to give a little of it back.

Our first-born arrives

Then it was time for little Felicity to make her entrance into the world. As we already knew it was going to be a girl, we decided to call her Felicity, which means *happiness* in Italian. But her birth wasn't easy. It took hours, and she finally had to be delivered by caesarean section.

As I held this tiny newborn baby in my arms I realised that from now on my motivations for success would no longer be for glory, self-recognition or proving myself to the world. How shallow all that now was! Now my successes, whatever they may be, would have one purpose and one purpose only: to provide and care for my family.

A taste for mature-age teaching

While all these things were going on, Jan and I were still attending our Rostrum Public Speaking Club, for we got so much out of it. Communicating with confidence is a great skill to have. And with me now a Rostrum accredited trainer in public speaking, I was getting a taste for mature-age teaching as against school kids, half of whom would rather not be there. Nurturing the minds of our youth is a noble vocation; it's just that I feel more at home helping adults shed their fears and shift their thinking.

One day Warren Block, one of Rostrum's top trainers, phoned me and said, "Box Hill College of TAFE are looking for someone to run a public speaking short course and your name came up … would you be interested?"

I said, "Yes," and took down the details. But then my habitual fears swamped me, for this was a *big deal.* I thought, *what am I going to say over this eight-week course? And how am I going to keep them engaged week after week? And most important, how am I going to give them the confidence to be effective public speakers?* Then, as had occurred with every new venture I'd ever tackled, I began to panic. But then I remembered what I'd always done to rectify this; I'd thoroughly prepared myself and learnt every single thing I could about whatever it was I was facing.

The first thing I did was calmly remind myself I'd done ten years performing before groups with the good old Top Hat Review; I'd done three years entertaining and informing groups on my camping tours, which, whatever way you look at it, was public speaking; and I'd reached accredited-trainer level with our public speaking club. So I'd certainly *earned the right* to be there.

This sorted things out in my mind. I made an appointment to meet the respected guy who had been running the course for years to get a few tips from him about how he went about ensuring the program was successful. I got the distinct impression he saw me just as a fill-in and fully expected to take up his position again when he returned from his six-week holiday.

I sensed that his initial impression of me was, *this boyish, rather nervous young fellow has no way of coming up to expectations, but I'll humour him and give him the time of day to help him hold the fort till I get back.* But I think he had second thoughts about my capabilities from the gentle way I wheedled a step-by-step blueprint out of him for the whole eight-week course! I quietly picked his brains with questions like:

- How do you break the ice and start off the first lesson?
- What do you do to break down their inhibitions and get them up speaking?
- And how do you end the lesson so they'll want to come back the following week?

On and on I went, writing all of this down.

Now, I don't know whether it was because of my sincere appreciation for his time in helping me, or whether it was my infectious enthusiasm which got him to open up and give me every intricate detail of how he informed, engaged and enthused his charges to be more confident speakers over this extensive eight-week period, but I walked out of his office nearly an hour later feeling a lot more hopeful than I'd felt when I walked in. Clutched safely in my arms was a cardboard box of his personal notes with step-by-step strategies for each lesson, a video to reinforce public speaking concepts, and a heart full of confidence that I could carry this daunting project off! I thanked John Holland profoundly and walked out with my precious box of proven strategies he had so unselfishly given me.

An entirely new approach

My first course went really well, but I sensed there was something missing. As the weeks went by I discovered what it was; I was teaching from a box of other people's ideas, other people's videos, and other people's concepts of what effective public speaking really is.

I was mostly teaching external things like pace, pitch, modulation, gesture, where to walk, how to stand, and how to formulate your talk.

Now planning your talk can be boiled down to 'tell them what you want to say; tell them; then tell them what you said,' but all these other peripheral things we do naturally in everyday conversation without giving them a second thought. *This was all I'd do on my camping tours*, my mind started to comprehend, *I'd just stand as the proud leader I was and speak naturally as I do everywhere else … I was never concerned what my hands were doing or what I might look or sound like, for I was involved in the story and how my listeners were reacting to it.*

I looked at my box of other people's ideas and thought, *I wonder if I can buck the outdated notion of the silver-tongued orator and teach a whole new way of authentic public speaking, a freer way of natural expression where there are no hard-and-fast rules to focus on and get wrong; a freer way to look your listeners in the eye and connect with them on a human level; and a freer way of accepting who you are and the things you stand for. Not so you strive to be the world's greatest speaker, but to simply help you be accepted as the warm, imperfect human being you are; exactly as I instinctively used to do, day after day on those coaches to warm acclaim. I wonder if I can bottle this natural conversational magic and teach it to others?* Fired with this vision, I set about imparting *this* panic-free concept to my unsuspecting students the very next week.

Magic can happen

Pretty soon magic started to happen. People were concentrating more on *what* they were saying than *how* they were saying it. One talk that will live with me forever was delivered by a young lady we'll call Marie. I'll paraphrase it for you as I recall it:

Marie was just like any thirteen-year-old teenager experiencing the normal joy and pain of growing up. This particular night she had exchanged especially harsh words with her mother over the trivial observation her mum had made about the untidiness of her room.

This heated exchange culminated with Marie storming off to her bedroom screaming, "I really *hate* you!"

That night while Marie slept, her mother passed away.

Days later, a grief-stricken Marie found a letter addressed to her in the drawer of her mother's bedside table. It read:

> Dearest Marie,
>
> Mummy has been sick for a long time now. I've tried to keep it from you in the hope that I'd get better. Please forgive some of the things I've said and done over these past two years as I've never meant to hurt you.
>
> I love you very much and will forever.
>
> Your loving mother.

This letter remains one of Marie's most cherished possessions.

Painfully Marie reflected, "If only I could turn the clock back I'd make sure the last words I'd shared with my mother were words of *love* rather than words of hate."

We sat there in shocked silence.

That simple yet unforgettable talk deeply affected all of us and got us thinking. This is what I call *authentic* public speaking, where people sit up and listen! I didn't know it at the time, but freeing people to feel comfortable in their own skin and speak authentically was part of helping me discover who I really am too. But I'm not saying that to be authentic, every talk you ever give has to be emotionally-charged like Marie's; what I *am* saying is whenever you get up to speak, always focus on *the heart of the matter* and less on the mechanics of how you're saying it.

Going the extra mile

Thirty-four years later I was still running my one step to *panic-free* public speaking evening course at the Box Hill College! "How come it lasted so long?" you may well ask. Because word of my simple, *panic-free* approach spread, and as a result, my classes were always fully enrolled. What's more, most short courses are notoriously prone to drop offs as the course progresses, whereas my programs remained full to the end with almost no one dropping out.

So what was *my* secret that the others didn't have? Simple: I used to personally phone each student between classes to shore them up and give them some tips with their talks, so they *always* spoke successfully and were *never* a failure. The powers-that-be never knew about this extra strategy of mine, and I left it that way for them to think what they might. ***Sometimes doing that little bit extra can pay dividends for everyone.***

This is not to say that I didn't, and still don't, *enjoy* public speaking as a *performer*, because I do. Only now I treat it as an *extended conversation* where my listeners are included in what I am saying, for I've always been an entertainer at heart. The key difference now is, it's no longer all about me and how clever I am; whatever I say nowadays is geared to bring the best out of others and shine the spotlight on *them* and *their* cleverness.

My *panic-free* public speaking programs have now morphed into *panic-free* coaching through my personal sessions and self-help publications. What's more, that cardboard box of instructions I started out with all those years ago is now full of my own ideas and *panic-free* strategies, for I've developed my *own unique voice* and my very own way of helping fear-filled people to comfortably speak with confidence! As well as this, I now have something to say on the subject.

Then we were four

After little Linda appeared on the scene when Felicity was thirteen months old, we decided we'd all go on a whirlwind trip of outback Victoria in our little Mazda 323 hatchback. And that's what we did. We had the comfort of air conditioning and so didn't have to worry about the heat. I'm not sure why we chose to go to the outback town of Pinnaroo in the isolated north western corner of Victoria, but that's where we went. Jan and I hadn't been on a holiday since our Snowy River trip, so it was very exciting for us too.

Disaster strikes twice!

One morning, about a hundred miles from Pinaroo, disaster struck! We'd left Felicity's cherished yellow blanket behind in the motel. The moment we got to a phone many miles down the road, I phoned the lady in the motel and explained our dilemma.

"Oh, I understand," she said. "I'm a grandmother and know how important these things are! I'll package it up and post it off today and it'll be waiting for her when she gets home." I thanked her profusely and offered to pay for the postage but she declined. There's something about country folk that seems to get lost in the hustle and bustle of a city. Although she's now grown out of it, the yellow blanket sits folded at the end of Felicity's bed to this day, and will probably be handed down to her own little girl.

One of our stops on the way home was in the little town of Birchip in the Wimmera. The following morning after breakfast in our motel, little Linda was sitting on the floor and I got the fright of my life: sitting on her head was an enormous black spider rearing on its hind legs, its long front legs testing the air, and its ugly fangs ready to strike. For a split second my heart stopped; then I swiped at the back of her head to get that frightening thing off her! Linda screamed from the shock, and I finished the spider off with my shoe.

Next morning as I paid the bill I told the motel owner what had happened. He casually turned and said to his wife, "Didn't I tell you, there *was* another one o' them!"

We were glad we weren't staying there another night.

CHAPTER 23

The next few years

Home improvements

At one stage while Felicity and Linda were still toddlers I got a job as a salesman with a respected building company that has been around for decades. And yet again, my boyish enthusiasm for life and the way I approach things flagged a sort of immature incompetence which was simply not true. For example, from day one my sales colleagues took one look at me and immediately assumed I was inexperienced and hadn't done much with my life. It was as if they already knew that I didn't have what it takes and I wouldn't make it. It was obvious they genuinely doubted I had the capability of achieving things. I knew this by the patronising and disdainful way they treated me and the scornful things they were saying behind my back. In fact one shifty, older salesman, who was upset with me because I wouldn't join a dodgy pyramid selling scheme he was involved with, sneered to my face: "Do you want to go on being a loser all your life!?" But none of this worried me, for I had achieved things the likes of him only dream about – and in tougher places than this!

I hadn't been there long when an opportunity arose to sell some kitchens. The company announced they would be revamping the whole kitchen showroom and all five of its modern kitchens were going for half price – which was a saving of thousands for prospective buyers. *Here's a chance!* I thought. *I'll move on this!* Over the next few days I rang up every client of mine who had shown an interest in a new kitchen but couldn't afford it at the time, and I invited them into the showroom to check the half-price kitchens out. Every third day or so I'd escort another family through and sell another one.

I happened to hear one of the salesmen who had been putting me down saying, "Yeah, he fluked another one ..." I was on a roll and had caught them all flat-footed. On and on I went till I'd sold all five of them in two weeks ... Some fluke!

Jan pops in

My wife Jan knew about the bad way I'd been treated and paid me a visit in the showroom with our two little toddlers. "I hear Laurie has been selling a few kitchens," she chirped to the now chastened sales team. I just loved it! As for what I had to say, I let the results do the talking. But the real bonus of all this was not only could we make that month's mortgage payment (not easy to do with interest rates at 18 per cent!), I was able to buy the latest video camera to make recordings of what our kids were like as little ones. This was a real luxury item we would never have been able to afford without this extra money. Even today our friends marvel that we have many hours of video memories of our young family when people in the late 1980s hadn't twigged to the idea and most people only have the usual photos of the time as precious memories.

Decent people too

I have one more story of success to share from my short but eventful home-improvements career, for I don't mean to tar everyone in that company with the same negative brush; there were some decent people there too. One of them was Peter Corlino. Now Peter may have been a bit of a used-car salesman type, but unlike the others he wasn't ruthless and hurtful and he had a good heart.

I liked Peter, and he had time for me. One day he came up to me and said, "I've just been given the boot and I'm about to sign a deal for $86,000 and I'm determined not to give it to one of these cut-throat bastards ... but I like you, you're a decent person and not like them and I'd rather give it to you."

"But," I protested, "I'll accept only on the condition that I pay you a fair percentage of the commission." He only relented when I insisted – he was determined that no one else was going to get it. Peter secretly gave me all the paperwork; now it was up to me to close the deal and collect the commission. I detected that Peter never expected any sort of payment for this – in this shady world of home-improvement selling, people keep their cards close to their chest.

True to his word, Peter had done all the work and set the whole thing up. I just had to get it over the line. I walked into the man's office, introduced myself on behalf of Peter, and the man said, "Let's do the paperwork and get this thing done!"

I couldn't believe my ears! It happened just as Peter said it would. My commission for the deal ended up being $4500, less $1500 for Peter's agreed share. When I handed his substantial cheque over in a local coffee shop, he simply stared at it lost for words. Peter was still out of work and needed a bit of an uplift.

Professional speaking

I quickly came to the conclusion that selling home improvements and kitchens wasn't for me. As a result of my years of involvement with Rostrum and my panic-free public speaking evening courses at Box Hill College of TAFE, which were really only part time, I got to thinking, *is there any way of doing that for a living?* I made some enquiries, and soon found there was a body of professional speakers: the National Speakers Association of Australia (the NSAA – now Professional Speakers Australia; PSA). So I went along to check them out.

I soon discovered you don't join the National Speakers Association of Australia to get rid of your public speaking fears, for you're already supposed to be good at that. You join the PSA to learn from other professionals how to polish your delivery and effectively market yourself. But I'd find many worthy people among the attendees at these meetings who were overwhelmed by it all and indeed harboured secret public speaking fears. These were the people I began to help.

Initially I felt a bit out of my depth myself, rubbing shoulders with all these professional speakers of note, but I soon established my own respect as editor of the NSAA newsletter. This was yet another job I'd never done before; I fell back on my tried-and-proven strategy from doing my apprenticeship of *washing the tools first* … then picking the brains of those who had gone before me and using their work as a template from which to evolve. Thus, slowly but surely for the next seven years I rose through the ranks to become someone who could now stand on his own two feet among those he used to be in awe of.

Not cutting the mustard

One of these people was the professional speaker Graham Alford, who specialised in 'mental toughness'.

I'd always said hello to Graham at our meetings and he'd always given me the time of day, which I really appreciated. Graham happened to be in the audience the night I gave my introductory talk. On reflection, it wasn't that crash hot, as most first attempts tend to be. It was about the rise and fall of my childhood duck empire, which made the point that 'setbacks' happen and we've got to move on and learn from them. It was certainly above average, and full of raw, infectious enthusiasm, but it had no *wow* factor, no professional polish.

As Graham sat there listening to me, influenced by my boyish enthusiasm and the lightweight content of my talk, he thought, *young Laurie is likeable enough, but I don't think he quite cuts the mustard as a professional speaker*. And on this, my first attempt in front of an awesome, discerning audience such as this, he was probably right

– but that night Graham had not factored in my *growth potential.* Three years later Graham Alford was again among the audience in the grand ballroom of Melbourne's prestigious Hyatt Hotel when this time I was one of the *listed* speakers.

That evening I told the following story I'd heard in one of my public speaking workshops to illustrate the point that our accumulated baggage from the past can sometimes hold us back for years, until we deal with it:

> As a young lad in his native Holland, Johan Devries was a passionate ice skater. One crisp winter evening as he was skating home along a frozen waterway he got the shock of his life. He remembers thinking of the nice warm fire and hearty meal that awaited him … then he rounded a bend. Suddenly he received a hefty thump on the chest as he crashed into a workman's barrier. Everything went black. Within seconds he found himself sinking to the bottom of an icy canal. *I've got to get out of this*, he thought. *I don't want to die!* By now his skates were sticking in the mud and his air was almost gone. With a superhuman effort he surged to the surface, only to hit his head on the underside of the ice.
>
> Panic stricken, he began clawing his way along the slippery bank beneath the ice, desperately trying to find the hole he had fallen through. But nothing! Just more ice! Gasping for breath from a tiny bit of space between the ice and the water's surface, and strength almost gone, he began to choke. Just as he was about to succumb to the icy fingers that beckoned him down to a watery grave, his head bobbed through the hole and an unseen hand pulled him to safety.
>
> Years later, as a young man in his twenties living in Australia, Johan found himself at the beach at Lakes Entrance with his mates. Although wearing a bathing costume, it was a pretence, for he had never been in the water since that fateful day. "Come on Johan!" one of his friends called out. "Let's swim

> back to camp instead of walking back across the bridge." Everyone thought this a great idea and headed for the water. Johan froze.
>
> Suddenly he was again under that icy water fighting for his life. The terrible fear that had haunted him for years was dragging him down again. He found it hard to breathe and began to tremble all over. Johan had two choices: either walk back across the bridge and live with his fears for the rest of his life or follow his friends into the water. Weeping openly, Johan raced across the beach and plunged in.
>
> He recalls feeling a cold, clammy sweat pouring off him even under water. On he powered, oblivious to what was happening around him, each stroke leaving a little more of his long-held fears behind. When he reached the shore he leapt out of the water like a swimmer at the Olympics. "I felt like a million dollars," he told me later. Purged of the fear that had hounded him for years he has enjoyed the water ever since.

"And so it is with our accumulated fears," I told that audience. "It's only when we have the courage to plunge into those fearful waters and swim, instead of taking the easy way out across the bridge, that we can leave our fears behind and start walking a whole new path of confidence of who we are and what we stand for."

Later Graham Alford came over and said, "I have a confession to make; three years ago I heard you give your first talk and I honestly didn't think you had what it takes. Tonight you've proven me wrong! Never again will I make a rash judgement on where someone might be in the future based on what I see of them on a particular day. Never again will I be so presumptuous as to intervene in someone's potential and how they might grow." He looked me straight in the eye, shook my hand and said, "Thanks mate, I've learnt a valuable lesson tonight."

And who hasn't done that?

My mentor Winston Marsh

There was one legendary speaker who, right from the start, knew what I was capable of, and that is business guru Winston Marsh. When I was completely unknown, Winston went out of his way to introduce me on my first audio programs for he'd had an eye on my efforts as editor of the speakers' newsletter and my personal investment with top comedy coach Pete Crofts to help with the comedy side of my presentations, and he believed in my potential. Having the imprimatur of Winston Marsh meant a lot to me and helped me to walk tall. Over the years Winston sold hundreds of my books, *How to take the Panic out of Public Speaking* and *How to be a Conversational Success!*

Confidently participating in meetings

At the start, and as editor of the newsletter, whenever I went to a meeting with the decision makers of the NSAA I felt somewhat out of my depth because they were so witty with the right turn of phrase and riposte. How was I to compete with a table full of clever people like that?

Pretty soon I learned that I didn't have to. The trick was that all I had to do was make *one* contribution to the meeting that was relative to the topic under discussion. That's it. Just one. But I'd make sure it was a good one that would get the talkers going – and *I'd* get the accolades for stimulating this aspect of the discussion. And if you can't get a word in edgeways, just wait for them to pause for they've got to take a breath sometime – then jump in with your idea! I actually half raise my hand as I do this to help grab attention and make my contribution. Once you've done this you've contributed; you've played a successful part in the meeting. Now you can relax and join in without the pressure.

Hang back then follow

This corporate world I now found myself in – this land of suits and ties and pecking orders and big business – was different again to the academic world. But it was still a game, and I had to learn how to play it. Over the years I'd developed the knack of helping others to believe in themselves simply by being *interested* in them – without them knowing what I was actually doing! It was easy for me to transfer this skill to helping people communicate with confidence with my one-to-one coaching. So in these settings I kept my eyes and ears open for people with this need.

The first time I found myself sitting at a fancy corporate dinner, I wondered at the opulence and pretence of it all. So I hung back and followed the crowd. Although everything was laid out before us and I was starving, no one made a move and we kept talking among ourselves. I noted that the salad on the table was full of exotic multicoloured flowers and wondered if these people ate like this at home. I suspected they didn't. *Are these edible or just for decoration?* I thought. Anyway, it was a game, so all I could do was wait till someone made a move.

When they did, one of the managers moved first, picking up his cutlery from the outside. I deftly followed suit, and never missed a beat from then on. *My strategy to fit in when attending these types of settings was simple: hang back and follow.* This way I could avoid making mistakes. I must admit that I was always relieved to get home to my family in suburbia in *my* real world. But I was learning to step in and out of these game-like scenarios with ease yet always remain true to myself, where I've come from, and what I stand for.

Unintentional bumbler

As used to happen on my camping tours, I was always an unintentional bumbler. And I learnt that there was nothing much I could do about it, for this was just part of who I was. So I had no choice but accept the inevitable and laugh along with it, knowing that things would still get done. And so it was with me as a speaker.

On one occasion I was under the critical eye of my peers as Master of Ceremonies for the National Speakers Association of Australia's

Annual General Meeting in the Grand Ballroom at the Hyatt in Melbourne. It was a most prestigious affair, with row upon row of influential people smiling back at me. After inviting our treasurer to come forward and present her report, I politely stepped back … and disappeared off the back of the stage! To make matters worse, on the way down I caught my foot in the hem of the backdrop curtain and brought that down with me.

When I stood up, arms flapping all over the place, I looked like an Egyptian mummy trying to break loose. By the time I'd disentangled my dishevelled self and crawled back on stage, the audience was out of control. People were howling with laughter. I was told later that "a treasurer's report has never been so much fun!"

Years later I came across Andrew Gardner, a training colleague of mine who happened to have been there on the night and witnessed my fateful tumble. We warmly shook hands, then for no reason at all he said, "Remember the time you fell off the stage?"

I smiled and nodded: "I sure do!" Like I said, *we've got to be able to laugh at ourselves and not take life too seriously.*

Then we were five!

One day I was sitting on the bed and Jan came in and showed me a small white gismo. She just stood there holding it. "Look," she said, and tilted it for me to see better, but all I could see was a plus sign. *Why is she showing me this?* I thought.

"It's positive," she said.

I was still lost.

"I'm *pregnant,*" she said finally.

She told me later I just sat there stunned for a while.

"Oh, well," I finally said, "that makes five of us." Richard was soon to join the family.

At his birth, Richard seemed a lot smaller than Felicity and Linda, so tiny was he. And, as I did with the others, I gently handed this new addition to our family to his loving mother.

Who would have thought this defenceless teeny baby would grow into a formidable six-foot-six basketball player who towers way above his dad. He must have inherited this height from my father, who was also six-foot-six.

So I now had a serious family to look after, and I had to fight for every piece of work I could get. But my speaking career continued apace, with me watching and learning this craft from those who had gone before me. The difference between speaking and show business, I'd learnt, was here I could be the real me with my own voice without having to emulate other people. It was this uniqueness that I continued to develop. Yet things were never easy. And as if this wasn't enough, bank interest rates had jumped to a crippling 19 percent! So before anything else, we had to find $1500 each month just for our mortgage payment – and most of this went off the interest, making little difference to the principal.

Jan and I battled on, but the pressure of this uncertainty was taking its toll on our relationship.

Christmas comes early

One Christmas Eve we were wondering what to do – the bills had heaped up and we'd run out of money. We'd just walked in the door and there, sitting in the middle of the kitchen table, was something that took our breath away; a massive Christmas hamper overflowing with food and goodies. Jan and I stood there stunned: we both burst into tears and hugged each other. What a marvellous Christmas present! Santa had come early this year. Our kids were so excited, and started going through everything – there were even things for a Christmas dinner!

We never did find out who the kind angel responsible for this gift was. But I'll never forget the day a Christmas hamper magically appeared on our kitchen table and brought joy to a family who were at the end of their tether and who really needed it.

CHAPTER 24

Getting paid to speak

Travelling

Ever the optimist, I had to get some work!

I got wind of a guy who was looking for presenters to travel around Victorian and New South Wales country towns spreading the gospel about internet banking for a large bank. I got in touch with him and arranged a meeting. When he learned of the association of professional speakers I was connected with and that I'd published a book on the subject, he got cold feet: "I could never afford the type of fees you guys charge he said."

But he didn't know the truth, that most of the members weren't making thousands in fees at all; most members were ordinary trainers and coaches like me, trying to make a living with a job here and there.

"Tell me about the deal and what it entails and I'll give it serious consideration," I said. It was certainly interesting. They paid all expenses to get to and from each destination. The deal was local community groups would fill the hall and get one dollar per head for their efforts. My job was to fly to a central point, then drive hundreds of miles in a hire car to the destination, set all the electronic gear up, then deliver an interesting presentation with the objective of persuading my listeners to take up internet banking. On the face of it, you'd be battling to find a more boring topic than 'internet banking', so he would expect me to deliver this information in an entertaining and persuasive way.

"And your fee for each 45-minute presentation is $400," he said. "Most days there would be one presentation, some days there would be two."

I felt that this was a fair deal and I accepted. I had never been away from my family, and as this would take up three days of every week I knew I would miss them terribly.

One thing I was more than pleased about was my training would be intensive in all aspects of this computer-driven presentation on a big screen. I was more than pleased for two reasons: I was, and always had been, terrified of computers from the moment they came on the scene; and I'd never done an once of computer banking in my life ... both of which I never said a word about to my boss Brendan.

A professional trainer himself, Brendan was wonderful and patiently took me through every step over and over again for two solid weeks, until I could do it in my sleep. At the end of this intensive fast-track training I was no top-notch computer whiz, but I did know what buttons to press for this specific presentation to ensure it all went seamlessly, like a true professional. Only once did I have to ring Brendan prior to my show for technical help, and we discovered that I hadn't put a plug in!

A country greeting from local wildlife

As I mentioned earlier, I was learning that to get on in life one had to feel comfortable communicating with people from all walks of life. And the folk in these outback towns were another class again; very laidback and straight shooting, and with a great sense of humour.

On one occasion I'd just parked my car next to a community hall in outback NSW, way out in the middle of nowhere, and I was greeted by the collective screeching of thousands of galahs and cockatoos in the surrounding gum trees. *How refreshing*, I thought, *to be among so much raw nature.*

When I walked into the hall, it seemed like half the town was waiting for me – people had come from far and wide to see the 'show'. I guess it was something different for them; anyway, they made a couple of hundred dollars for their club so it was all good.

By now I was pretty slick with my set up, and I was ready to go quickly. I thought I'd break the ice with something we had in common: an appreciation for nature. "I've just come from Melbourne," I said, "and how refreshing it was to have all those birds greet me when I stepped out of the car." A wag yelled out from the back of the room: "Why don't you take the bastards home with you!" Well, the place broke into uproar, and from then on we had a lot of fun with our sorte into the realm of internet banking, for the wags didn't let up. *Sometimes you've just got to go with the flow and get the job done.*

Almost out of petrol on the Hay Plains

Then there was the time I nearly ran out of petrol on the hot, sparse and endless Hay Plains of New South Wales, purported to be among the flattest places on earth.

I had two presentations to deliver in the harsh west of New South Wales: one in the community centre in Jerilderie, famous for the Kelly Gang's audacious raid on the town in 1879, where they robbed the bank, held more than thirty residents hostage, and locked the police in their own cell. The other was in the town of Hay, situated in the Western Riverina region about two hundred kilometres from Jerilderie. My plan was to enlighten the folk of Jerilderie first, then leave at 6 am the following morning and duck across the Hay Plains to Hay for my stint with the Hay Secondary School's year 11 and year 12 students at 9 am.

The first phase of this plan went extremely well, but I had no idea just how vast, hot and flat the Hay Plains really were – they went on forever. I had a pang of misgiving as I turned onto an unmade road for my short dash to Hay. After driving for an hour or so I began to panic. My petrol was already half gone and the dead straight gravel road continued as far as I could see. A terrible thought ran through my head: *If I turned back, what was left of my petrol mightn't get me there; and if I went on I mightn't make that either.* I was mulling over this dilemma when a large dust cloud appeared on the horizon. *Someone's coming*, I thought – up to then I hadn't seen a soul. It turned out to be a massive road train full of sheep. I jumped out and waved him down.

"What are you doing way out here?" the driver asked, "and where are you going?"

"Hay," I said, "and I've got to be at the secondary school at 9 o'clock!"

"You're a fair bit out of your way," he said, "but keep going for a hundred kilometres till you hit the Cobb Highway, then turn left."

With that he waved goodbye and left me standing in a plume of Hay Plains dust to ponder my predicament … *do I go back to Jerilderie or keep going and risk running out of petrol?* I got in and kept driving.

On and on I went for another 120 kilometres along the same featureless dirt road without a single sign of human habitation. The fuel needle was now on empty and I was visibly shaking. A terrible thought went through my head: *I'm going to be stuck out here with no water and forty degree heat!* Then I saw it … a small white flash among the distant scrub, and it was moving!

"The Cobb Highway," I said out loud, relieved beyond measure. But now there was a more urgent problem: I desperately needed some petrol!

Ten minutes later I hit the highway, but I hesitated in chancing my luck at finding petrol by turning left to Hay like the truckie had told me when there could be an option for fuel nearer by. Then something caught my eye: a bewhiskered character from another age, floppy hat, swag and all, sitting in the shade of a big gum tree with his dog.

By now I was quite distraught, for nothing was going right and I had half a school of restless teenagers waiting for me! I stopped near the swaggie and climbed out of the car.

"G'day," I said. "You've got a nice shady spot here with your mate."

"We're doin' fine here in the shade," he cheerfully agreed. I told him what I'd just been through and that I desperately needed petrol.

"You're in luck," he said. "There's an old pub half a mile down that side road and they'll sell you some petrol."

I almost burst into tears ... "You don't know what this means mate," I said, "thanks a million!" And I headed for the pub as fast as I could.

A padlocked petrol bowser

And sure enough, to my massive relief, a kilometre or so further down this dusty road was an isolated, run-down pub from long ago with a 1940s petrol bowser in front of it – with a padlocked rusty chain around it. My heart sank. I immediately thought, *this is too old ... who would come here in the middle of such a nowhere place?*

I stopped the car and got out to investigate. I tentatively pushed the creaky front door open and walked into a gloomy room. Adjusting my eyes to the dimness I could see an old guy drinking a beer at the bar. The unshaven middle-aged man behind the bar was in no great hurry and barely acknowledged me. After a while of fiddling around with a cloth, he said, "What can we do for you?"

"I need some petrol," I said, fully expecting him to say the bowser hasn't worked for years.

"No worries," he said, "I'll just get the keys." This took another five minutes or so before he sauntered out to the precious bowser as if we had all day. Then he went through the complicated ritual of unlocking it and unwinding the chain. Yet when he finally got to filling my tank I never thought the sound of petrol going into a car could be so wonderful.

"Where are you off to?" he asked. When I told him that I'd tried a *short cut* from Jerilderie to Hay across the Hay Plains, he was astonished and said, "You're about a hundred miles out of your way! ... And what are you doing in Hay?"

"I've got the daunting task of presenting the exciting aspects of internet banking to a gymnasium full of two hundred secondary school kids!"

"Good luck with that!" he said in his slow Aussie drawl. I was about to turn and go ... when I had a thought: "You don't happen to have a cold beer in a bottle do you?"

"No problems there," he said, and wandered back inside. A few minutes later I thanked him, and with a friendly wave drove away: but instead of driving straight on to Hay, I pulled over to the left and stopped the car.

Grabbing the nice cold bottle of Victoria Bitter I walked over to my swaggie mate and his dog, who were still sitting under their tree, and said, "Here, have this on me ... you were a real lifesaver." For a moment he just sat there looking at me trying to comprehend ... then he reached out, gently took the bottle, and nodded his gratitude.

Thoughtful actions like this can take the edge off a rough day and make it all worthwhile. It was now 8:30 am and my audience of young minds awaited me.

Miraculously I made it

How I did it I don't know, but I drove through that school gate at 8:55 am; and like a well-oiled machine I went into my familiar routine of setting things up, and in this case, getting into the right *teenage* mindset. Which was a lot easier than trying to convince older folk of the merits of internet banking who were already extremely wary of computers. We explored what internet banking meant to *their* world and *their* part-time jobs and had a lot of fun along the way.

While sharing my morning's horror run with one of the teachers, he said to me: "You're lucky you weren't caught in a rain storm on the Hay Plains because the red mud of the area is notoriously boggy and would have had you stranded till the sun dried it out again!"

As it happened, the following day it *did* rain quite heavily as I left Hay for Swan Hill on the Murray River. After a few kilometres I had to pull over to the side of the sealed road to adjust my load on the back seat. As I walked round the car to open the back door my shoes sank deep into the sticky Hay Plains mud the teacher had told me about. I shuddered when I realised the fate I had just dodged: what would I have done, bogged fast in this sticky red mud and out of petrol miles from anywhere on the endless Hay Plains?

Life is full of these what ifs and they all add to our bank of wisdom.

The heavy price of success

Week after week, for six long months, I did all of this, playing the role of 'notable speaker' and being feted. Yet each night I'd go back to my lonely motel room and sit by myself pining for the company of my wife and young family. Then, as happened with my show business and camping tour-guide experience, when I'd tested it out I began to think of what the loneliness of *speaking success* really means. I'd already heard the heavy price the really big speaking stars pay with their family lives; and once again *the painful truth* behind the facade of fame stared me in the face – and I didn't want to be part of it no matter how much money I could make.

"I want to be near my kids and family," I said to myself. "It's time to go back home, and I'll make do somehow." That last plane trip home to everything dear to me was the sweetest flight of all.

CHAPTER 25

Emergency teaching

Blast from the past

Another answer to my inner call of 'making do somehow' came totally by chance, one more of those *sliding door* moments! I'd just started a new evening public speaking short course when who should walk in the door but Alison, one of the four *angels* who had been my saviours at Melbourne University. Now a thirty-eight-year-old woman, she had enrolled in my course with a colleague to support her friend in dealing with her public speaking fear.

We were thrilled to see each other again, and I was pleased to learn she was now a senior teacher at a leading secondary college. What is remarkable is nineteen years had flown by since we last saw each other and the only teaching I'd had the courage to face was here in this short public speaking course with grown-ups, whereas Alison was now a tried and proven veteran at it!

"Have you ever thought of doing emergency teaching?" she suggested.

"It had crossed my mind, but I wouldn't know where to start," I replied with honesty.

"Don't worry," she said. "I pull a bit of weight in my school and I'll get you a job … come and see me and I'll give you some tips on how to go about it." Not wanting this opportunity of a job to slip by – I had bills to pay and a family to support – we agreed on a time to pay her a visit in the staffroom, and soon I had the job.

Just like the old days, it was her turn to help me again. She gave me a detailed blueprint of how the system of emergency teaching worked, from the moment I received the emergency phone call to the last bell of the day. She went out of her way to photocopy valuable ideas and stimulating things for me to do with restless kids should the need arise. She gave me advice on how to handle them as a teacher, rather than a friend, for there is a distinct difference between teaching teenagers and adult students.

"Give teenagers an inch and they'll want a mile!" she warned. "You can be friendly, but *not their friend*." She left me with this final thought: "Whenever you're at school, walk tall as an experienced teacher, be friendly sure, but don't hesitate to pull rank if kids are out of line." I thanked her for all her help, then I was on my own. I was on emergency call from the following Monday.

Theory one thing, reality another

And boy, did it hit me like a ten-ton weight! When I turned up at a given classroom the first thing the kids would say was, "Yay! A subbie!" Pretty quickly I had to develop a strategy to segue from their faulty expectation of 'not doing any work' to a mutual deal of finishing the teacher's set work, then, if they'd been good, we might play a game. But *survival* was the name of *my* game. When, for whatever reason, the absent teacher had either forgotten to put instructions in the emergency teaching pigeon hole or simply wasn't able to, I had to take control and think on my own two feet just as I'd done in my camping-tour emergencies. For example, if I were left with no instructions I would often say, "Right, we'll be going for a walk to your lockers and I want you to get something to work on;

I don't care what it is, as long as it's real work! And I'll be checking on each of you to see what you've got. So let's go!" They always loved this because it was a novel break and it kept them busy rather than getting into trouble. It also taught them the value of doing good with their time.

When I was an emergency teacher in a maths or science class, I'd cover myself with something like: "I'm actually an English, Italian, and History teacher and don't specialise in maths, so during this lesson it's okay to walk around and help each other with your work." They loved this approach, and it took all the pressure off me!

As you know, I was never that crash hot with computers so with the really tricky stuff I'd get a nerdy kid to perform a particular computer function: "Bill, could you access that for me and bring it up on the screen ... ", as if I could have easily done it myself but was giving a teaching instruction to help a student grow as a leader. I was learning fast that my own adolescent kids, now bordering on adulthood, weren't any different to other inquisitive kids of the same age; and I now had rooms full of them to contend with on a daily basis.

Unruly spitball shooters

Sometimes I did things for sheer survival, like the day no work was left for an unruly year 11 maths class and all the six or so troublemakers were doing was firing spitballs of chewed-up tissue through straws at each other and disrupting everyone else from doing their work. These guys were arrogant, defiant, and towered over me. I began to panic, for only five minutes had gone by out of a lengthy double period. While I was desperately wondering what I was going to do with these troublesome guys, one of them said to me, "Sir, can we [referring to his fellow spitball shooters] go and work in the garden?"

Suddenly I saw a solution. "Where's the garden?" I asked.

"Just out there," they said, pointing out the window. I saw a small garden plot.

"Okay, you can spend the first period there ... and if I see that you've kept your word of working in the garden you can stay there for the whole two periods."

"Oh, that's what we'll do!" they said, and were gone. Every now and then I'd look out the window and there they were, carefully carrying little containers of strawberry and cabbage plants and planting them in the neat furrows they'd just prepared. And they were lost in that garden as model students for the whole two periods. I was quite pleased with the outcome. *There's good in everybody if they're given the freedom to have a go*, I thought.

A change of tack saves the day

But I didn't always get off the hook as easily as this – it was many a time that I would pull into the driveway after a rough day and put my head in my hands and just sit there saying, "How am I going to survive this?!"

With these taxing experiences I soon discovered that I couldn't change the world by holding the fort for one or two periods as an emergency teacher. So I decided to take another tack: I'd try to weave some of the human *values* I'd learnt from my personal journey into their set work.

One day I walked into a class of year 9 students for a double period and said, "Take out the novels you are reading and turn to chapter 7," as per the teacher's instructions – and was greeted by a collective groan. Sullenly they all rummaged around for their books. It was obvious they weren't too keen on reading and this was going to be tough going. So, I said, "Okay, today we're going to do something different, so we'll leave your books aside for a moment."

I pulled over a stool and sat before them: "Let me tell you a story," I said. And I began telling them of a young lad who hated reading because it was boring and he always did his best to get out of it. As far as he was concerned, he got nothing from it and only did it because the teachers said he had to.

"Can anyone relate to this young lad?" I asked the class … "Anyone here feel a bit like this?" Lots of tentative hands went up.

"Well," I said, "this young lad was *me* … But when I was twenty-two something extraordinary happened … I picked up a book from a friend's coffee table and the next time I looked at my watch two hours had gone by … I couldn't put it down! So what happened to change my mind from *books are boring* to *I'm really enjoying this book*? … Let's explore this a little."

We then had an interactive open forum discussing questions like:

- Where might an author get all their information from?
- How long might it take to write a novel?
- Where might they get inspiration for their characters and their settings?
- Where might they get inspiration for a storyline?
- What is the blurb on the back of the book telling us?

And boy was this a lively discussion on the various human values needed to create a credible story to engage the reader. Before we knew it the first period had gone by. In this one session they'd learnt more about the essence of books and the reasons for reading them than from all their previous classes put together. They learned that a book is full of other human beings thinking and behaving just like them as they face life's challenges and do their best to get by in whatever endeavour they're involved in. They learned that they can actually gain insights from the way characters behave in different situations and the conflicts they have to face … just as happens in their own lives. And while all this insightful learning is going on they can travel the world to exotic and faraway places they wouldn't ordinarily get to see.

For the next period they went back to their novels with what we'd just explored in mind, but now my students weren't sullen and uncooperative; they were eager to see what else they could discover about the characters in their story, and what they could learn from their novel. We only read three paragraphs, for we were now primed to discuss what the author was trying to do, how these young people interpreted it, and what it meant to them.

By the end of this second period, these previously reluctant readers were eager to finish the teacher's reading homework by themselves. Now their reading had a whole new purpose and understanding … and I used this value-based approach often.

My banana box

It wasn't only student behaviour I had to contend with, it was other permanent teachers who could report me for not teaching properly or being a fraud – this unwarranted negative view of myself was something I was yet to shake.

I only ever went to two schools where students and staff got to know me as a familiar face and a *real* teacher. So to keep up this pretence, I'd carry around a sturdy banana box I got from a fruit shop and filled it with all my teaching bits and pieces. It looked very intimidating indeed, for staff and students alike. It made me look very experienced, and gave the impression I knew what I was doing. The truth is I rarely used anything in it. It was all for show; my safety net. It was my *yellow blanket*.

I carried that banana box around with me for eight long years.

My subterfuge with my banana box was so effective that one day our emergency teacher coordinator, Don Motley, approached me and said, "We need a replacement teacher for a six-week stint for a year 11 class on ancient Greek history … you're a history teacher, can you help us out?"

I said, "Yeah, sure." But when I learnt we'd be studying the ancient Greek poet Homer and his epic poem *The Iliad*, I panicked. I knew nothing about Homer or *The Iliad*, so I rushed out and bought myself a copy … if nothing else, I was going to be ten paces ahead of my students.

First I read an overview of what the poem was all about: the Trojan prince Paris has abducted Helen of Sparta and spirits her off to the massive walled city of Troy; and to avenge this slight against the Greeks, the King of Mycenae, Agamemnon, leads a mighty Greek army to get her back again. The main themes of this epic poem are fate and free will, love and friendship, and honour. These themes follow all the main characters of the poem, including Achilles, who meets his fate when that proverbial arrow strikes him in his unprotected heel.

"Wow!" I thought, "this is a dramatic story and I'll package it as such."

A performance they could relate to

I had to think of something pretty novel that would involve them, for Homer wrote his poem 3000 years ago so the words and ideas are a bit archaic – and it contains 15,693 verses. My challenge was to make it relevant to these year 11 students without boring them to death.

The prospect of facing a double period of unruly adolescents for six consecutive weeks wasn't a pleasant one! I decided I'd tease the poem out in dramatic instalments to keep them hanging on. Drawing on my Aboriginal duck-netting lesson for the year 7s, I decided I'd act this epic poem out with a few props to bring the characters and their human qualities to life; this would not only entertain the students, it would help them relate the central themes of the poem to their modern world, a bit like how Mr Jackman used to read to us in grade 6 and whet our appetites for what was coming.

I'm a great believer in the old adage that learning should be fun. In the end it all worked out well, for I made this ancient poem *accessible* so it meant something to them. They loved it. But I heaved a sigh of relief when it was over. I'd survived yet another challenge life had thrown at me.

So successful was our sojourn into Homer's ancient Trojan War where we discovered people contending with the same human conditions that we all face today, our emergency coordinator Don Motley ambushed me with another of his propositions: "I've got a proposal to run past you," he tentatively said, knowing full well the enormity of what he was asking: "One of our year 12 teachers is taking leave for the next term and we need a fill-in teacher for his class in Classical Greek History … could you help us out?"

Before I knew it I was saying, "Yes."

That done, Don continued on his merry way.

The temperature's rising!

It didn't take long before the magnitude of what I'd just agreed to hit me. This would be no ordinary class, for it was a full term of Classical Greek History for heaven's sake! Learned academics spend a lifetime trying to get their heads around this complex subject … so how was I going to cope with it? What's more, these year 12 students would be switched-on young adults who were attending these classes *by choice.* And they'd expect their teacher to be well versed in the subject he would be teaching for their final examination. An incredible pressure began to crush in on me. *How was I going to manage all this?* My head was reeling. Without a moment to lose I scurried off to said history teacher for help before he went on holidays.

Lucky for me I was in the hands of a true professional. Not only did this experienced teacher leave me with an invaluable step-by-step layout of each lesson with photos and schematic drawings on his laptop, he spent his whole lunchtime explaining the workings of his laptop, the sequential order of things, and how to go about it, for which I'll be forever grateful. After this generous help I felt a million times better about my prospects of success with these demanding year 12 students. All I had to do now was thoroughly familiarise myself with each lesson before I delivered it. *One* interesting lesson at a time was the way I was going to approach this daunting task. And interesting lessons they were: from the building of the awe-inspiring Parthenon to romping through classic Greek religion and myth with Dionysus the god of the grape-harvest, wine-making and wine, fertility, ritual madness, and religious ecstasy – as well as everything else that was going on in Classical Greece at the time!

One thing that really concerned me was how was I going to seamlessly get my laptop to 'talk' to the big screen in front of the class as if I knew what I was doing! I knew that once I'd seen it done I'd be okay doing it myself, but I was loath to call on the school technicians to help for word would quickly spread of how technically incompetent I was. I employed my old trick of getting the kids to set my laptop up for me by saying: "This is a new room I haven't worked in before … could you give me a hand to get things going?" I took careful note of what buttons they pressed and what cables they plugged in so I could smoothly do it myself from then on. This potential stumbling block out of the way, I was now free to *focus on my students* and how I was going to help them through the stress of this final-year term we'd be spending together.

With their assessments I emphasised the importance of always *addressing the question* by telling them the story of what happened to me when I failed to do this at Collingwood TAFE – and the heavy price I paid for it. I told them I would not play clever tricks on them and only ever set them work that related to what we had covered; I told them that what I wanted to know is what *they* thought about things, and how *they* interpreted the situation under discussion.

The wonders of ancient Greece live on

The whole thing turned out to be a fascinating experience for both teacher and students alike, especially learning about the clever way The Parthenon was built. To the naked eye The Parthenon looks symmetrical and straight, but actually it's full of *purposefully* integrated curves which create the *illusion* of perfect symmetry and straightness. But look closely at the Parthenon's Doric columns and you'll notice they have a slight bulge in the middle; yet when this magnificent building is viewed in its entirety they seem perfectly straight. Likewise with the Parthenon's base; this too is imperceptibly curved downwards from the middle to its outer edges, which again gives the illusion of straightness. The architects, Ictinus and Callicrates, ensured The Parthenon's *deliberate* curves are hidden, almost invisible to the naked eye, so the viewer only sees what the designers of ancient Greek temples meant them to be – perfectly straight symmetry – a quality of perfection worthy of the gods.

The Elgin Marbles

A word on the Elgin Marbles, the marble sculptures that adorned The Parthenon till they were 'acquired' and shipped to England by Lord Elgin sometime between 1801 and 1805. When we say 'acquired,' Lord Elgin maintains he took these priceless friezes "to rescue them and improve the aesthetic tastes of England". They depict a battle between centaurs, those mythical creatures of half man/half horse, and a legendary people known as the *Lapith*. It is believed they were meant to be shown off in his own private home, but because he was strapped for cash he sold them to the British Government in 1816. They are now on permanent display in the British Museum. Try though the Greeks might, the Elgin Marbles will probably never be returned to their rightful place adorning the godly structure of The Parthenon ... the place of their birth.

Towards the end of this stressful yet mind-expanding term, I was hit with another staggering broadside: I had to write all of my student's school reports! To my great relief the school had templates to help me formulate what I had to say about each of my pupils. Although thoughtfully writing these reports was very time-consuming and would mean a lot to them, especially rewarding to me was everyone received an *above* average pass so I was free to keep my comments positive and encouraging. The fact is, I'd come to know these young people as they travelled this journey back in time with me, discovering how the classic Greeks lived and went about their lives, so I enjoyed singing their well-earned praises truthfully to send them confidently on their way ...

These twelve weeks turned out to be some of the most challenging times in my life, for I felt compelled to delve ever deeper into Classic Greek History in order to stay ahead of my astute and eager students. The saying goes that *chance favours those who are prepared*; well the truth was by the time I stood in front of that year 12 class I *was* prepared. Sure, I had to put on my running shoes to seek help and learn fast. But there was other *preparation* I'd been doing for years that had me ready for this incredible challenge: like half a lifetime of studying the peoples of the world and my fervent love for history; three years travelling among the Vikings and their history; and my infectious enthusiasm for learning and imparting knowledge to others.

And all the while, my unconscious journey of *finding me* kept chugging along from one incredible thing to another without me even being aware of it.

Italian takes its rightful place

As if an impromptu three-month bout of teaching Classical Greek history wasn't enough, around this time the Box Hill College of TAFE informed me that in order to keep running my evening public speaking short courses, my qualifications needed to be updated to a Certificate IV in workplace Safety and Assessment Training, which I dutifully underwent within the college itself. Another of the participants was Debbie Sirkel, the person in charge of the foreign language short courses in the college at the time. This piqued my interest. When I told her that I not only spoke Italian but I was also a qualified Italian teacher, her ears pricked up.

"I'm in need of an Italian teacher for my next Saturday morning short course," she said. "Would you like to do it?" I went into my usual panic mode when hit without notice or preparation.

"But … it's been sixteen years since my degree," I said, suddenly regretting that I'd said anything.

"You'll be all right," she calmly said. "You've been successfully teaching public speaking here for years, and anyway it's for beginners and very basic – you'll be teaching from a well-laid-out textbook."

I desperately clutched at one more straw: "I can't this Saturday," I declared triumphantly, "we're having a garage sale!"

"Get one of your kids to look after it till you get back," she firmly said. "I'll have everything in your room for you and introduce you. And you can sit in on my Thursday night program to see how easy it is." She then wandered off. It seems I didn't have a choice!

My God, I thought, *how did that happen?*

The kids did look after that garage sale, and I did muster the courage to turn up for my first lesson. I'd been studying Italian for years and knew far more about all things Italian than the students did. Using all my public speaking strategies, I confidently took them back to the very basics, and away we went on a wonderful five-week journey to the enchanting world of the Italian language and culture.

Since those first tentative steps, twenty-five years have gone by and I'm still teaching my beloved Italian! If you've put a lot into something, don't fearfully hang back for decades like I've tended to do … waiting … and waiting … for that chance to have a go. You can't always bank on meeting a pushy Debbie Sirkel to discern *what you are really worth* through your protests, then drag you kicking and screaming to that first lesson. You may never come across the likes of her. ***You've got to make it happen and courageously put your hand up and walk there yourself.***

CHAPTER 26

Home life, tough times and memorable moments

A hothouse

Jan continued for as long as she could with her job, but in the end she missed the kids so much she decided to be a stay-at-home mum. When they were really little, Jan would always be busy with them and have the kids doing all sorts of things like *Mini-Movers*, *Chat 'n' Play* and gymnastics. We'd work well as a team, for I'd help around the house and do the nappies while Jan loved cooking. One thing we all looked forward to was having our three-course dinner round the table together of an evening. This was where they learnt manners and table etiquette. I usually did the washing up, and if outside, ran the barbecue.

With interest rates still at 18 per cent, things were so tough that we even did a spate of taking on other people's ironing to help pay the bills. I bought a secondhand steam press to make things easier, and for the best part of a year we spent most of our time ironing and delivering other people's clothes. Our front room was a veritable hothouse, full of steam and clothes hanging everywhere. In the end we realised the time and effort we put in wasn't worth it and gave it up. Instead, Jan took on some child minding for friends, who brought their kids to our place, which was a lot easier for her than our laborious ironing stint.

Help with public speaking panic

After my lonely sojourns into Australia's isolated countryside to earn money as a professional presenter with the bank, I was always thinking of other ways to make money with what I do yet still be near my wife and kids. In 1998 I decided to write a book on what I know best; how to take the *panic* out of public speaking! In fact, that became its title. But the only way I could write it was in the quiet wee hours of the morning when everyone was asleep. So I'd sneak up at 4 o'clock each morning and nibble away at this project for most of that year.

Then, when the manuscript was finished, I needed someone else's money to help me publish it. So I wrote the ABC a letter, telling the producer of Jon Faine's program that I'd be an interesting interviewee on the subject of public speaking paranoia. I was indeed invited onto the show, and as luck had it, a publisher, Wrightbooks, was listening. They liked what they heard, and contacted me. They published my book, which sold six thousand copies. This not only gave me extra credibility as a *published* author, it reinforced my belief that *you have nothing to lose by asking.*

Early childhood is but fleeting

One thing I'll say about the early years of children, say from when they are born to the end of primary school, is cherish it; this magic period of them believing in everything you say and you teaching them right from wrong is all over in the blink of an eye. So make the most of this fleeting time for it doesn't last. What follows is a young person growing up and now thinking for themselves, while you as the parent have some serious adjusting to do as well. Then, in what seems like a very short space of time, they've become adults and now communicate on an entirely different level. The fact is, for young and old alike, as we grow our perspectives change too and we continue to become more insightful.

Getting back to those earlier years, it was the insignificant everyday things we used to do that weaved the magic. And it's only by looking back that you realise how precious these transitory times were, for each one is a priceless moment in time that can never return. For example, one of our favourites was to have a family picnic in the natural grounds surrounding the Diamond Valley miniature railway.

The tiny steam engines were real working models that puffed out real steam and smoke. The kids loved them, an extensive expanse of tracks through hill and dale then back to the station. We'd always go for two rides; one with dad on board and mum waving from the sidelines, then another with mum on board and dad doing the yelling and waving from the fence.

Another thing that gave us great joy was – you guessed it – feeding the ducks at Westerfolds Park. We'd dress the kids up in their duck-feeding clothes, and they'd love the magic of how they could attract and control a flock of their feathered friends from the wooden jetty with their enticing bags of bread. The other thing they loved doing in this magnificent park by the Yarra River was walking around the nature trail with its secret nooks and crannies and enchanting bridges to cross. They'd excitedly run ahead calling out the different animals and insects they discovered. This was a regular part of their lives, until they grew out of it … memories as important to me as the *big* things I've done in my life.

Our swimming pool

When Jan bought our house it already had a large swimming pool, so we had to live with it and its inherent joys – and dangers. Initially our pool didn't have a fence around it, for it wasn't compulsory in those days and there were no children to worry about. But when they came along we wouldn't let them through the side gate into the back yard. Notwithstanding the potential hazard, and always under our watchful eye, our kids grew up having hours and hours of fun in our swimming pool.

But one day I arrived home and Jan was visibly shaking … "What's wrong?" I asked. What she told me made my blood run cold … all she could manage was a whisper: "We nearly lost Linda today."

It was a cold winter's day and Jan had rugged the girls up in lots of woollen jackets and beanies. They had been with her in the laundry at the side of the house thirty seconds before when little three-year-old Felicity came rushing in and said, "Mummy, Linda in the pool!"

Hysterical, Jan rushed round the back fearing the worst … and there she was, on her back, her thick, air-filled winter clothes keeping her afloat; she was blowing tiny spurts of water out of her mouth like a baby whale. With only seconds to spare before the waterlogged clothing dragged Linda beneath the surface, Jan leapt into the freezing water and lifted her baby girl to safety.

On hearing the frightening details of this close shave, I sprang into action. Within three days I had a five-foot-high safety barrier with a childproof gate erected around our pool.

But even with the best laid plans you've got to be ever vigilant with children near a pool. One day I was doing some gardening at the far end of the pool with my now extended family of *three* kids playing on the grass beside me. Intent on making sure a plant was nice and snug in the ground, I hadn't noticed little Richard had snuck round to the other end of the pool and climbed up onto the tiled edge.

I'd already made up my mind to dive in boots and all if necessary: "Stay there and daddy will come and show you the nice flowers," I implored with outstretched hands and edging towards him. He stopped and looked at me … then slipped and fell headlong into the pool. I was already airborne, but the image I saw in that instant remains etched in my mind: Richard's little face seemed to be at peace and full of wonder; his cheeks were puffed out and his eyes were wide open; with his arms stretched wide he simply sank straight to the bottom.

It was then that I reached him, and I sprang off the bottom of the pool and surged with him to the surface. Richard took a deep breath and seemed none the worse for wear. But it was close. And this is all it takes; ten to twenty seconds for a little child to drown. After this all our kids had regular swimming lessons, and in next to no time became proficient swimmers.

Toddlers ... it only takes a moment

The following example is frighteningly like the above story of Richard falling into the pool. So scary and so surreal was it that Jan and I could never speak of it again. It was as if it never happened. But it *did* happen, and at the time it was *very* real. Too scary to even contemplate ...

Jan and I had made a pact that close families should do things together, so when the kids were small, and not long after the above pool incident, we took our little girls on another trip; this time around rural New South Wales to get a further feel for travelling with their new baby brother. This particular day we stopped for a rest break in the central NSW town of Gundagai, where the legendary dog of pioneer days sits on his 'tuckerbox'. We pulled into a pleasant park down by the river for a picnic, when we spied a sign explaining the history of the now dilapidated wooden bridge that spanned the formidable Murrumbidgee River. So Jan and I decided we'd wander down with the kids and take a look.

Although no longer used, the mile-long bridge with its warped planks and railings was still quite a sight spanning the expanse of the mighty Murrumbidgee. We were relieved to see that the end of the bridge closest to us was blocked by a three-metre-high cyclone fence. And just as well, for on the other side of the fence was a sheer ten-metre drop to the swirling dark waters of the Murrumbidgee, which, from way up where we were, gave us goose bumps! But safely behind the strong mesh fence little four-year-old Linda and five-year-old Felicity felt secure as they tentatively peeked down at the 'scariness' of it all … or so we thought.

Just out of reach

Before I could stop him, little two-year-old Richard had found a hole big enough for him to squeeze through and he was suddenly standing on a crumbling ledge on the *river side* of the fence where I couldn't get him! He was holding on to the mesh and laughing, eager to play the next part of this exciting game with his dad.

I spoke to him very softly. My heart slowed, for I knew one wrong move would be the end of it. If I startled him or yelled at him he would have turned and slipped, disappearing over the edge into the murky waters below. I'd already made up my mind to leap over the barrier and follow him down if that happened … I kept on speaking to him very softly, mindful of the precarious state we were in. His little feet dislodged pebbles and clods of dirt which disappeared over the precipice. The only thing that prevented him from falling was his firm grip on the mesh, pent up as he was for what would happen next. Then out of sheer desperation, Jan said something that changed the situation completely.

"If you're very quiet Richard, mummy's got a nice lollypop for you in her bag!" He intently looked her way, his attention now on what his mum was doing; Jan began rummaging around in her handbag frantically looking for something to give him. She was doing all this right up close to the wire with her handbag tantalisingly in his face.

Lightning speed

I moved with lightning speed. Before he could realise what had happened my hand was through that small opening and latched onto his arm like a vice. Startled, he let go and his little legs slipped over the edge … This time the sturdy fence came to my rescue and gave me support and leverage; there was no way I was going to relinquish my grip and let my little boy go. With him kicking and screaming, I managed to drag him through that hole to safety.

Though both of us were scratched, bruised and shaking all over, I bundled everyone into the car and we got away from that place as fast as we could!

The interesting thing is that now our kids are much older, Richard and the girls have no recollection of this incident at all – but I certainly do! If there's a life-saving message here it's this: toddlers move fast and are into everything. Never let them out of your sight or assume everything is completely safe and secure. Remember they see things differently from grown-ups and will probably find an 'opening' somewhere that you weren't aware of. A final word: Jan's quick thinking of 'looking for a lollypop in her handbag' undoubtedly saved her little boy's life. That day Richard's mum was the *real* hero.

The joy of giving

One thing I did get great joy from was bringing the kids little surprises, like a nice piece of refreshing fruit when I picked them up from school on a hot summer's day. But one fine day, while they were still very young, I brought home a surprise of a very different kind. On the way back from a consulting job way out in the countryside, and still decked out in my suit, a sign beside the road caught my eye; *Ducklings for Sale*. A spur-of-the-moment thought struck me: *I'll get one for the girls (Richard wasn't on the scene yet) to care for and watch grow up … they gave me so much joy when I was little!*

I'll never forget the look on their faces when I walked in carrying a box and said, "I've got a little present for you." The lively peeping emanating from it told them there was something alive in there!

"What do you think it is?" I teased, and they all suggested a tiny bird.

"Well, you're sort of right," I said, "it's a baby duck! … Would you like to see it?" This was greeted with cries of delight. Jan was used to me and my 'surprises' by now and went along with it.

Tiny yellow Pecka was a great hit … but we had to make him a home. I had to make its home secure so that a fox wouldn't get to it. Luckily we had an old kitchen cabinet that I modified with strong netting – the door panels were for him to look out, but would still be lockable of a night. Pecka could wander around the back yard during the day hunting for snails and slugs in the garden, but we'd lock him up every evening.

For now he was only a little baby and needed extra care and a nice warm bed to sleep in, so we all set about gathering lots of dry grass and cotton wool to ensure he was nice and snug. We'd acquired a new family member.

They grew up together

For the next two years Pecka gave the kids great joy, for they all grew up together. They would cuddle each other and even swim in the pool together. Pecka would dive in and shoot around under water; you could actually feel his excitement in doing this, and when he surfaced he almost seemed to smile. When Richard came along, Pecka was already a 'teenager' so he only remembers him as a big white Pekin duck.

There wasn't a snail left in the garden, for Pecka loved them, and, as I was to learn later, so did Felicity; whatever Pecka did was good enough for her! Years later she told me she liked eating them too because they were 'crunchy'. And Pekin ducks have a special type of quack that's not a defined 'quack' as such, but a repetitive "wa wa … wa wa … wa wa". One day Bertie, our eighty-year-old neighbour across the road, said, "What's that funny noise I often hear?"

"Oh, that's Pecka, my kids' Pekin duck," I said. Bertie nodded thoughtfully and seemed relieved that he hadn't been imagining things; the mystery that had been bugging him for so long was solved.

One day I was cleaning out Pecka's little home, and nestled in the straw was a nice big *egg* … Pecka was a girl! This was yet another wonderful surprise for the kids. And for the next year we received a daily gift of an egg from her, which Jan and the kids used to make yummy cakes and scrambled eggs.

Sensed something wasn't right

One morning I was doing my usual routine check on Pecka and let her out in the yard for her daily wander when I sensed something wasn't quite right. Her friendly *Pekin quack* was missing and she wasn't waiting for me at the door to be let out. I quickened my pace with a racing heart. *Maybe she's sick in the corner?* I thought; then I stood stock still and stared.

Strewn around the thicker grass near her house were lots of blood-stained white feathers ... My heart sank. "Oh, no," I whispered in disbelief ... "A fox has got her ... he's figured out a way to dig under the hutch and come up through the floor! ... Not again," I said, now resigned to the fact Pecka was gone. She was such a good duck and the kids loved her.

The deep sorrow from the last time I had witnessed this carnage swept over me; but then I thought of the kids and pulled myself together: "How am I going to tell them?" I thought out loud ... but quickly decided I wouldn't, for it would break their hearts. I immediately cleaned everything up and buried the bloody feathers. I then formulated a story of the door not being shut properly and Pecka flying away to be with her friends in a pond. The kids seemed to accept this, but certainly wanted to know *why* such a sudden departure, and *why* did she leave them?

A few weeks later we were visiting their Nanna Jean (my mother) in Maryborough, and decided to go for a walk along the lake. Lo and behold, a group of wild ducks appeared out of the reeds with a magnificent white Pekin duck swimming happily in the middle of them.

"There's Pecka with her friends," little Linda cried out.

"Yes," I agreed. "That's her, and she looks very happy." Sometimes the truth is best left unsaid until a safer, more understanding time presents itself …

More precious treasures

Before I move on to my children's later years, there are a couple more precious memories of their early years I'd like to share, for these experiences are a vital part of my evolution from a lost and lonely entity to someone who now feels fulfilled and belongs somewhere. These small observations helped me *appreciate* things that really matter and reinforced my *new* purpose in life: being a dedicated family man. The following are a series of what I consider the *true* treasures of life I could have missed in my head-long quest for greatness, for an obsessed man on a mission has no time to stop and notice them.

Unique smile

When my second daughter Linda was born, she was handed to me first because Jan was too exhausted to hold her right away. She was a little cutie just like her big sister. Holding her was another life-changing experience, for here was a helpless creature who was part of me and needed caring for. There was no room for *all about me* here; I was a father again.

"Here's your baby girl," I said to Jan, and gently placed tiny, fragile Linda in her mother's arms.

Right from the start Linda captivated everyone's heart with her unique little smile. As the years have gone by it has remained just as enchanting.

When she was really small, the right side of her body wasn't as strong as the other so she developed a unique way of crawling; she'd power along by throwing her strong little arm up and over like an over-arm swimmer and scuttle around the house as effectively as any of the others. In time it all went away and she gained her normal strength. All this helped build a single-minded little character.

Another memorable thing that touches me with little children is the way they express themselves by using their *own* pronunciation of words they've heard from their parents, just like me sounding like Elmer Fudd with my 'Ws' for 'Rs' when I was five. My kids had their own specialities, for example, little Richard would confidently ask for a *mammich* – a sandwich; Linda would refer to the *thloor* for the floor; and Felicity's word for Ronald McDonald was *Rondot*.

One day Felicity's five-year-old friend Nickie was with her in our back yard and Felicity was telling her, "Tomorrow we're having a barcaboo here."

"You mean a *barbecue*," corrected little Nickie.

"No, no, a *barcaboo* with sausages!"

"It's *barbecue*!" Nickie insisted. At this stage I stepped in; "Nickie is right," I said, "It's *barbecue*." And I guiltily walked away, for it was I who had taught this nonsense word to her. I never heard it again.

Family gatherings we never had

Among the small things that really matter to me now were our family gatherings on both sides of our family. Jan and I had missed out on them as kids and were determined our children would not experience this void as well. This could have been one of the reasons why I'd always felt alone. Anyway, each Christmas all of Jan's side of the family would gather at the Ribaux country home in Maryknoll for a combined get-together where swarms of kids and us parents and grandparents would exchange presents and have lots of fun around a banquet table.

This went on for years and became somewhat of a tradition. And likewise at Jan's sister Yvonne's place in Mooroolbark, where we'd all meet regularly to do the same. Auntie Yvonne's sumptuous dinners were legendary, supplemented by Uncle Henry's Aussie barbecues.

On my side of the family it was just as fulfilling for the kids to get to know their roots and their relations as it was for us. We'd have equally memorable family get-togethers at my sister Leanne and

Tony's place in Creswick and my brother Mark and his wife Leonie's place in Endeavour Hills for New Year's Day, and later at Quaker's Hill in NSW. The kids especially loved visiting their quirky Nanna Jean in Maryborough, whose little country home was a veritable kid-wonderland with her secret garden, dress ups, and multicoloured rooms painted with leftover paints from the op-shop. Being there to watch the stunning Highland bands marching down the main street of Maryborough became a New Year's Day tradition for us and something we all looked forward to. It was family bonding and togetherness I'd never really had before.

Wonderland of childhood fantasy

Jan and I have always been great believers in allowing children to wander through the land of childhood imagination, like believing in Father Christmas, the Tooth Fairy, and the Easter Bunny. I mean, it's not only harmless, it nurtures their imaginations! Anyway, the reality of the *real* world is going to hit them soon enough – as Jan and I knew only too well. So why deprive them of this magic, this imaginary world, this worry-free existence that lasts but a fleeting moment?

But sometimes it can be our eager enthusiasm that nearly destroys this wonderland of childhood imagination! One day Linda lost one of her milk teeth and Jan said, "Well, it looks like *the Tooth Fairy* is going to come to you tonight! We better put that tooth in a glass of salty water to keep it nice and clean for her." That night Linda went to bed really excited because the Tooth Fairy always left some money under the glass. To her it wasn't the money that she was so excited about, but the *magic* of it being there when she woke up.

The following morning Linda was heartbroken because the Tooth Fairy forgot to come. You can imagine how I felt! "We'll leave it out again tonight," I said to her, and should have left it at that. But no, the Tooth Fairy had to write her a letter saying she had been very busy … it was signed *Stella*. And guess what? Linda recognised my handwriting! So that was the end of that – and the end of the Tooth Fairy.

And it wasn't easy for Father Christmas either. One Christmas Eve I'd been waiting for hours for them to go to sleep, and around 1:30 am I figured it would be safe to put the pillow-slips of toys, as was our tradition, at the ends of their beds. Little did I know that Felicity was still awake! However, as far as she was concerned I was really Father Christmas. She told me later: "I just lay there with my eyes tightly shut and shivering with fear in case you went away without leaving me any toys!"

I guess we enjoyed these imaginative games of *giving* as much as they did. By this stage I'd experienced my share of the real world's harshness and *believing in these things* was a nice escape for me too.

It wasn't easy for Richard growing up in the feminine world of his two sisters. While he was all about his Power Rangers, Robot Men and the like, they were into their dolls and *girly* things. "I want my Power Rangers to join in!" I'd hear him say. "No you can't!" they'd say, and they'd always work out some compromise where poor Richard was on the losing side. It was tough, but he did have an outlet of playing with neighbours Calum and Zak, which gave him some gender balance. At other times we'd see them spend hours in their *secret* Veronica bush garden absorbed in their imaginary 'family' games where each played their part.

Just being there

One thing Jan and I really enjoyed doing was attending school concerts and sporting events to support the kids, things our parents rarely did for us for times were different then. Seeing Felicity in the annual school concert all painted silver and acting out the part of a robot made her mum and dad proud; another magic moment was Linda playing her violin in her mum's modified wedding dress at the Twilight Fair; and at another school concert little Richard stepping forward on his own initiative to the microphone after playing a small percussion piece and stating with authority: "And I'm only seven!" The concert hall erupted into spontaneous laughter and appreciative applause; they thought he was wonderful. And so did we.

I even went on Richard's grade 5 camp as one of the parent helpers. Two of the activities I was involved in were being the 'rope retriever' of the flying fox and 'assistant helper' with the archery. Now the kids did not know that I had never done archery before, but I listened very carefully to the instructions before we began and was able to repeat them back to my young charges when they asked questions, to the point where they really thought I was an expert on it all, although the instructor still kept a watchful eye on proceedings. I let them have as many shots as they wanted and helped them to lower their trajectory so they'd hit the target.

There were two really rewarding things for me on that camp: the kids were asked to make a big poster thanking Mr Smale for his help on the camp; most of them said, "Thank you for helping me get a bull's eye in the archery! I never thought I'd be able to do it!", which was heart-warming for we all like sincere appreciation. The other thing that pleased me was, I sensed Richard felt quietly proud to have his dad there, yet I'd treated him like any other student without making a fuss about him.

The truth was, I'd travelled the world; I'd made my way atop mountains; I'd looked out on magnificent fjords; yet I'd waited half a lifetime to witness and do these things with my kids.

CHAPTER 27

Those precarious teenage years

The blissful innocence of children when they believe everything you say and allow you to watch over them moves on all too quickly – the challenging shift into their precarious teenage years is a whole new ball game. They're growing up; their hormones are running riot; they're noticing the opposite sex; and they no longer willingly listen to what you've got to say. To all intents and purposes, they are now on their own. Sure we're still there, still in the house as we've always been, but in today's world of social media and addictive, life-destroying temptations, it's not easy for parents to keep track of their children, always know what's going on, or be aware of what they're actually thinking.

As parents during these trying years, all we can do is keep the lines of communication open and trust that we've done our best in teaching them right from wrong; and when it comes to the crunch they'll think and make the right choices. If they make a mistake, as human beings are wont to do, we're here to listen and help them as best we can.

All of this rapid change was upon our family before we knew it, and Jan and I were left grappling to keep up with it all while at the same time giving them space to learn for themselves.

Expanding their learning experience

One thing Jan and I never had as kids was a true appreciation of music, and we were determined that our children would have their chance at musical enrichment. So we chose Blackburn High for two reasons: it was a public coeducation secondary school – we thought it best they grew up feeling comfortable with the opposite sex as a part of their lives. Secondly, neither of us had ever studied music or an instrument and Blackburn High was renowned statewide for its outstanding music department. So to give them an appreciation of music and its nuances, all three of them took up an instrument: Felicity learned clarinet; Linda continued with her violin; and Richard played the trombone. Attending the school concerts and watching their minds and confidence grow as they got better and better gave us great joy. Even though none of them went on to be professional musicians, the few years they were immersed in this creative world was a valuable part of their learning experience.

And part of the parenting deal was to be an in-house taxi service on a share basis with other parents, shuttling kids back and forth to basketball and other school and social activities until they were old enough to use public transport or get their own cars. A convenience we never had as kids. Even at a young age, if you had to go somewhere you found your own way there!

You can't put an old head on young shoulders

As someone who has spent years of my life nurturing the growth and confidence in other adults, when it came time to do the same with my own children as young adults it was not that straight forward. In their eyes I'm nowhere near the all-knowing guru as I'm perceived by those I coach; I am simply their everyday father. So watching our adolescent kids apply for their first job *by themselves* was painful in the sense of not being able to reach out and help them as I can with others; they had yet to understand the value of a father's wisdom. But this was a two-way thing, for it was all part of me letting go too – they were growing up fast and wanted to learn things for themselves. All I could do when they were going for their first job was wait in the car as support while they went in and faced the music themselves – without any pre-interview help from me.

Walking on their own two feet

There's no doubt that this fronting up to your first part-time job can be a daunting experience, and Felicity was first cab off the rank. Her friend Nickie had been working for the local bakery for a year and mentioned to her boss that she had a friend who needed a job.

"Tell her to come and see me," her boss told her. I clearly remember the day I drove her there and parked the car a couple of shops down from the bakery. She knew Nickie was working there that day but still nervously sat with me a little while … she then took a deep breath, and said, "I'm going in now dad," and strode off towards the bread shop. Funny how milestone moments for your once little child stick in your mind.

Ten minutes later she walked out with a big smile on her face. "I got the job," she said, "and I start on Saturday."

Felicity, being a natural people person, took to it all like a duck to water. However, like her dad she had always been very poor at maths and was having trouble adding items together and working out the change. It was really getting to her and she began to panic. So I told her to write down a little chart with the prices and some simple additions and subtractions on it for her to refer to (a bit like Pancho had done for me all those years ago).

"Just take your time and peek at your chart," I told Felicity, "and it won't be long before you won't have to look at it anymore." And that's exactly what happened. Over the next three years she grew in confidence as she honed her people skills and learned the basics of running a store. And just as important, her fear of maths had become a distant memory – she now handled money and the cash register with ease.

Nowadays she specialises in working in upmarket coffee shops and restaurants, and can reconcile the whole day's takings without batting an eyelid. She is now very competent in the art of handling people, and can effectively manage all aspects of a high-end establishment if called on to do so.

Linda came next. Always very shy and one to hang back and let others take the limelight, Linda was more like her mother, and the exact opposite of Felicity. As with her sister, her working career also started off in the local bakery. And like her sister, she sat in the car for a minute or two before she could pluck up the courage to walk into the store all by herself and try to get the job.

Dealing with customers and working with others really helped Linda come out of her shy shell, for to a certain extent she lived in her sister's shadow. After two years she was firmly standing on her own two feet and able to communicate effectively with complete strangers, which she would always shy away from prior to her bakery experience. Linda never had any issues with money or the cash register. She had been playing 'office games' with pretend money all her life and this was just an extension of that.

She went on to work full time in the Baker's Delight franchise and ended up being a supervisor in two of their stores. After seven years of this personal growth, it was time for Linda to seek a change of scenery, fully aware that the customer service and teamwork skills she'd learnt were transferable to other situations.

I figured she'd be seeking a job in a related industry. How wrong I was. Unbeknown to me she had her mind set on becoming a dental nurse and began seeking out possible employers. In other words *she* was doing the recruiting! She knew exactly what she had to offer and what her potential was, so she was after someone who could see this too and was prepared *to pay* for her training. In return they would have a loyal long-term employee. Linda found such a person and has been there for four years as I write this. She is now a fully qualified dental nurse and dental radiographer.

Richard, always a couple of years behind his big sisters, was last to get his first job while at school. And no, he didn't go to the bakery! His mate Calum, a year older than Richard, got him a job with the fast-food outlet Red Rooster. There are a lot of negative things said about working in fast-food stores, but they do teach kids a lot of good things, like reliability; multi-tasking; customer service; and the all-important self-confidence.

Richard worked in this store for four years, and although the work tended to be boring and repetitive, his income gave him some cash to be independent, and the standardised training equipped him with fundamental skills and values to move forward in his life. I personally feel these fast-food chains play a positive role in introducing young people to the workforce, even though the food mightn't be the healthiest available.

On leaving school Richard went on to do a course in movie making at Deakin University to satisfy a long-held yearning. This course included editing, colour grading and sound recording. But after a year of it he decided it wasn't quite what he was after and he began to focus on sound recording alone. Since then he has been working with semi-professional groups on various projects like short films and ads. To help finance his intense interest in the creative world of movie making, which is a continuous learning curve, at the moment he does part-time work specialising in swimming pool maintenance.

I'm very proud of all three of my children for drawing on the values they'd been taught by Jan and I to help them somehow survive the drug-riddled teenage years of today; values they'll be able to pass on to their own children to help *them* survive in such challenging times.

Expanding their horizons

As we started having our kids later than usual, Jan was 35 and I was 42, we'd already travelled extensively and experienced many things in life. We encouraged our children to travel too, first with their annual school camps, then to more expansive horizons.

Linda was the first (financed by herself) to venture forth into the big wide world beyond Australia, a memorable trip to Japan where she stayed with a kind Japanese family as if she were their daughter. A couple of years later Richard and his schoolmate Tim followed in Linda's footsteps and stayed with the same wonderful family who had so kindly looked after her; and while at university we sent Richard on a four-week humanitarian trip to Ecuador where he lived among the locals and helped build toilets for them. He told me later he'd seen cockroaches six inches long with huge feelers like TV antennas and monster bugs like you wouldn't believe! Finally, I sent Felicity on a Contiki tour through France, Italy and the Greek Islands to give her a taste of overseas travel too, so much so that two years later she ended up living in London on a working holiday where she met the man in her life. Although tough financially, Jan and I considered these experiences priceless, mind-opening investments in our children.

CHAPTER 28

No more negative self-talk

Setting myself free

Another aspect that's interesting about this *unplanned* journey of self-discovery is I still go on finding things about myself that could easily have a negative effect on me … if I were to let them! But I'm learning not to self-talk things into something they're not. For example, even though I was only five when I discovered I couldn't pronounce my 'Rs' and I sounded like the Warner Brothers cartoon character Elmer Fudd, in my own infantile way I nipped this impediment in the bud before it took hold … but the story doesn't end there. Decades later, by pure chance I was to stumble across another potential speaking impediment that lurked within me …

I was talking to a successful businessman when he surprised me by saying he had been a chronic stutterer for years but had now overcome this humiliating impediment. "The fear and shame in not being able to express myself like a normal person seriously affected my quality of life for years," he told me, which got me thinking about my own crippling fear of maths which had dogged me in the same way for a good part of my life.

As we were talking, he suddenly stopped and said: "Hey, *you're* a latent stutterer."

"A *what?*" I said, thinking I'd missed something.

"There, you're doing it again!" he exclaimed, pointing out a quirky little trip of the tongue I tend to exhibit with certain words.

"Oh that," I said. "I've always had this problem, yet it doesn't seem to interfere with the way I express myself ... and I communicate with people for a living!"

"Well, there's a technical term for it," he said, "and it's called *latent stuttering.*"

Now this insightful revelation was very interesting, and I'll reveal why shortly; but overall I could see a similarity in both of the demoralising situations we'd found ourselves in. Between this businessman's chronic fear of stuttering and my chronic fear of maths, what we'd both been doing for years was telling ourselves how hopeless we were; that the heavy burdens weighing us down were our lot in life; and that this was how things would always be for us. And all this negative reinforcing did was ensure we remained in the debilitating state of mind we kept talking ourselves into!

In contrast, my newly discovered 'latent stuttering' this man had so adroitly pointed out to me was never an issue, just an *occasional trip of the tongue*. Funny how the right voice inside our head can play a big role in how we see things, and even turn a negative potential into something positive. In fact, I'd always find myself smiling – and still do – whenever this imperceptible 'trip' happens, as if I'm saying to myself *oh, there's that thing again*, to the point that it has now become a *positive* part of the natural way I express myself.

Not long after this I was talking to my daughter Felicity in the kitchen when my tongue tripped over one of those *few* words that had bugged me all my life. She laughed and said, "Hey dad, *you've* got a stutter!"

"Ah, that's nothing," I said, "I've done that for years."

"Well, I've never noticed it before," she said. The fact is she hadn't seen it before because I'd never made a big deal about it to myself or anyone else. If only I'd had a similar approach to my terrible fear of maths instead of letting it run my life: a *positive* voice inside my head would have put me in control of what I was thinking; helped me effectively act upon it; and saved me decades of heartache!

Setting others free

What's good about where I'm now at in my life is I'm still *on stage* with my talks and my teachings, for I keep having fun entertaining while teaching, so that side of me is assuaged. The big difference now is I know *when* to stop, step aside, and share the spotlight with others; I know how to encourage *others* to have *their* say and tell *their* stories. When I'm not helping others open their minds in an interesting, entertaining way I no longer feel lonely, or panic, or crave getting back in front of people. Most important of all, I no longer have to go on proving myself to the world that *I matter* and *I exist.* I now *know* that *I matter* and *I'm here* without the need to have this verified by others. *By cutting all of this self-centred worry out of my life I've learnt to accept my imperfect self and help others do the same.* The alternative is to succumb to the pressures of trying to keep up with all the hype and manufactured expectations. That's what I kept doing for decades, and I'm glad I'm free of it.

I share the following story with you *not* to brag and show you how clever I am; at long last I've outgrown my unhealthy urge to always be the entertainer. I'm sharing to illustrate how far I've travelled from the uncertain young factory worker I used to be, to the more rounded person I am now in my exhilarating role as a positive change agent, helping others to shed their fears and have the confidence to speak up and not remain silent when they have every right to speak. And to do this, I've had to sort myself out first and be at peace with who I am and where I've been.

This story is about a remarkable evening that made as big a difference *to me* as it did to the person I was helping. Kayte was twenty-two years old when she first rang me and asked, “Can you help people who are scared of public speaking?”

“Sure I can; in fact, I even help people get *rid* of their fear!”

“Oh … this is not possible with me,” she said. ‘I’m too far gone … mine is more paranoia … I come out in a cold sweat just thinking about it. If you can help me just a little bit that would be a miracle!”

I told her that I stood by what I said. As we were sorting out where this coaching session would take place I found out she lived in St Kilda and I got an idea: “I’m giving a talk called ‘How to Beat the Nerves in a Business Presentation’ this Thursday night for a group at the Australian Institute of Management in St Kilda …… Why don’t you come along as my guest?”

She nearly freaked out! “Oh no!” she said, “I don’t want to speak before groups!”

“I didn’t say that,” I soothed. “All I said was to come along as my guest; I won’t even acknowledge you. You’ll be nice and safe. But I promise you you’ll learn a lot to help you get over this awful fear you’ve been living with for so long.”

The night of the presentation, there were about 150 corporate-type people milling around before we started, and while I was organising my table at the front of the room a young, well-dressed woman came over and said, “Hi, I’m Kayte”. (I learned later that she’d bought her clothes at a secondhand shop to look the part!)

To be honest I was taken aback because I didn’t expect a young student like Kayte to turn up at such a daunting venue, even though I had invited her. But I was impressed because she had taken that first courageous step to simply be there! That was enough for me to know I could help her.

“Great to see you Kayte,” I said. “Just grab a coffee and find someone to talk to. I promise you are in safe hands … I won’t even look your way.”

Not empty vessels

Now the first thing I covered was getting my listeners to see they weren't empty vessels; they'd all lived a life and they all had the right to make insightful comment about the journey they'd travelled and the things they'd learned. Sometimes we don't take stock of this and we sell ourselves short. I got them to see that as speakers we are the sum total of where we've been and who we are; the good, the bad, the laughter and the tears. This is the *believable* vehicle on which our ideas are conveyed, our *self-acceptance* – this vehicle is *our presence*. Here I shared the short version of my story and how I had to learn to believe in myself.

While we were exploring everyone's accumulated experience, out the corner of my eye I could see young Kayte sit up that little bit taller; maybe for the first time in her life she had a sense of her real self-worth, and not the negative image of being a 'lowly student' with little of life's experience and nothing to say. In the space of half an hour she was beginning to see herself in a whole new light: an *authority* on what it's like to be a young person in today's fast-moving world. She certainly had something to say about that!

So now that every person in that room was thinking of themselves as a *believable* conveyance of *interesting* experiences, we moved on to *how* to speak before groups in a liberating way – by obeying none of the rules! When I asked this audience what they thought about that they said, "Sounds great!"

"Well, let's explore this a little," I said. I got them to stand, find a partner and share a recent everyday 'happening' from their life and make some point with it. Well, the room erupted into this warm and animated exchange of experiences and ideas. Everyone was involved. Everyone was engaged. And everyone found the other person *interesting*.

When they sat down I told them what I'd just witnessed ... a group of confident people effectively communicating with one another. And I asked them, "What happens to all that warmth and naturalness I saw down there in the safety of numbers, and where does it go when you're up here all alone? Wouldn't it be great if we could transfer what you just did down there up here to the stage and have your listeners respond in the same engaging way?" They all nodded in agreement.

"I'll tell you what I'll do," I said. "I'm after a courageous volunteer to come up here and do nothing more than what you just did down there … Share your little 'happening' with us as the natural human being you are and make a point." There was no movement, no stampede for the stage. So I asked, "Who's afraid of a large audience?" A sea of hands went up. I then went on to state the obvious; that not one of them had turned up with the intention of doing anyone any harm or making them feel bad. "The truth is," I told them, "you've all come here tonight because you *want* to learn and *encourage* each other to grow … So, I couldn't think of a nicer audience to speak in front of … and I'm still looking for that volunteer."

Moment of truth

I was very patient. By this time my listeners had learned to trust me, for I had not embarrassed or made fun of anyone. Everything had been positive. Then, over to my right, I saw the faintest movement of a hand. And I couldn't believe it … it was Kayte!

Before she could change her mind I said to that audience, "We have our courageous volunteer … will you please join with me in a warm round of encouragement as she makes her way to the stage." This was Kayte's moment of truth. She could either hurry out of that room in tears or face her greatest fear head on. Buoyed by the warmth of the applause, yet filled with great trepidation, she made her way to the microphone. As she did this, I gently left the stage and sat in the front row. To keep the momentum going I announced: "Would you please welcome Kayte!"

Kayte's speech was one of the most inspirational talks I've ever heard. Not so much because of the content, but because she was up there doing it! I can see her now standing on that stage before that room full of businesspeople, her hands shaking and her knees knocking. But she remembered that I'd said get straight into the story and these things would go away. With great courage she began to speak.

"Not too long back," she began, "I went for my first job interview after 18 years at school. And I remember a man walking me down a long corridor to a big table covered in stacks of files and bits of paper. 'These things,' the man said, 'are very important, so don't mix them up with those sheets over there.'"

Kayte said he called them some name she didn't understand, but she didn't have the confidence to say, "I'm sorry, but I don't understand what that means." And the man just kept talking and Kayte didn't have a clue what he was on about. She began to feel faint and came out in a cold sweat. She had to hold on to the edge of the table to stop herself from falling over ... but still he went on. In the end he said, "Now, if you need any help my office is down the end of the corridor ... don't hesitate to ask." Then he left her.

At this point I looked at the audience out of the corner of my eye and the room was absolutely still ... you could have heard a pin drop. Even more remarkable, Kayte's hands and knees were no longer shaking, for she was totally involved in what she was saying.

Kayte's story continued: fighting hysteria, Kayte somehow made it to the ladies room and closed the door. On the wall she saw a stainless steel hand rail; she grabbed it with both hands and banged her head against her clenched fists. Kayte stared at the wall for what seemed like an eternity, until she had the courage to slowly open the door and venture out. But all the lights were out and everyone had gone home! Now openly hysterical, she grabbed her bag and ran out of there as fast as she could ... she was laughing, she was crying, she was shaking all over. When she arrived home she threw herself into the comfort of her mother's arms and said, "I've just had the most horrible experience in my whole life, and I'm never going back there again!"

And her mother said, "You've got to go back, because if you don't, every time you come across a similar thing in your life it will come back to haunt you. I'm going to get you to bed early tonight, give you a nice breakfast in the morning and you'll be just fine."

Kayte explained that climbing those stairs the following morning was like walking to the executioner; but then two remarkable things happened: "First," Kayte explained, "that man turned out to be a very patient person who sat down with me and went through it all again. And when I said I didn't understand some of the things, he explained them to me, and when he left, I had enough fundamental knowledge to make a start. The second thing is, I've now been there for two years … and I love it!"

Kayte's focus changes from 'her' to 'them'

Then Kayte did something she'd never done before in her whole life, because up until then it had been *all about her* and *her* worries and *her* fears. It was as if she stepped out of this prison that had dogged her for so long, for now her focus was on others. With outstretched arms this young woman implored her listeners: "If you're afraid of something, don't just run away, have the courage to face it one more time and you might get a pleasant surprise like I did." The applause was prolonged and heartfelt, and because of her story I'm sure many people in that audience were moved to act on negative things in their lives they'd been harbouring for years.

Those two hours, with a group of people Kayte didn't normally mingle with, changed her life. Kayte discovered that effective public speaking has little to do with set 'rules' and presentation 'technicalities'. It's simply being proud of who you are and making the most of this person. It's knowing you've earned the right to have something to say. It's knowing that using vivid examples people can relate to connects with people. And it's knowing being imperfect and your natural self is okay when speaking before groups.

That night the inspirer drove home inspired! But Kayte wasn't finished with me yet …

Kayte takes control

Two years later I went back to the Australian Institute of Management as a guest speaker, and to my great astonishment Kayte was chairing the session! Unbeknown to me, that very night after her talk she'd walked up to the secretary and said, "I'd like to join this group." For the next two years she'd got herself involved in *this* meeting and *that* committee, having something to say *here*, another opinion *there*, until one day she saw a flyer with my name on it as guest speaker and said: "I'd like to chair this meeting." You can imagine the pride I felt when I walked in and saw Kayte sitting at the top table ... Makes it all worthwhile.

Compared with that first frightened phone call, it was great to see her as a warm and friendly host making us all welcome, dealing with a few housekeeping things, drawing a raffle, introducing me as someone who had made a difference to her life, and at the end of the evening bidding us all goodnight and a safe journey home ... All as the natural, imperfect human being she is ... No big deal.

* * *

Eleanor Roosevelt's words sum up Kayte's enormous courage beautifully:

> "You gain strength, courage and confidence by every experience in which you must stop and look fear in the face ... you must do the thing you think you cannot do."

This example of *real* transformation from *fear* to *freedom* reminds me of the key role I play in the life-changing shift in so many people's thinking. It also reminds me that I had to wait years before I could do this because I had to be happy in my own skin *first*. I keep this example in mind so I don't forget the brave courage of Kayte, who stepped out of her darkness and into the light of *self-acceptance* and a positive frame of thinking, without trying to be perfect. Instead of her own misgivings, she learned to focus on others and *theirs*.

Kayte is now a top advertising executive in England. Even though I acted as her agent of change, I continue to draw inspiration from her and the many other courageous people I have helped as I move forward in my own life.

Let Kayte be your inspiration too!

CHAPTER 29

My mother's other side

So far the picture I've painted of my mother is one that highlights her rough-and-ready eccentricities as well as a loving aspect to her nature when I was very young. But there was another more *refined* side to her we didn't know about, although we'd had glimpses of it throughout the years. We simply couldn't believe it because it didn't fit the rough-edged mother we knew.

As I said in my earliest memories of Donald, I distinctly remember my youthful young mother playing a vigorous game of tennis in her pretty white tennis dress. We three boys were sitting on the grass nearby so she could keep an eye on us. Today I ask myself: *where did she learn to play with such energy and confidence?* Although I must have been only three-and-a-half, I recall the raw energy she radiated on that hot summer day quite clearly. It was only in later years that I realised there was more to my mother than met the eye.

Grandma Florrie

I only ever remember visiting my grandmother Florrie's house, the place where my mother grew up, on two occasions. It was a solid red-brick home and full of polished wooden furniture in Murrumbeena, one of Melbourne's well-to-do suburbs. It was worlds away from where I grew up with my mother, and in no way related to who my mum was or what she stood for. So for us kids Grandma Florrie's place was a bit strange and unwelcoming.

Once every few years she would make a pilgrimage to her wayward daughter's house full of unruly children in a big black car. She could afford this as Grandma Florrie was well off; she had wisely invested in the local brickworks. She was always done up in her fancy clothes and accessories while we three urchins would be running around as she found us. Never did she hug us as a loving grandma would. Grandma Florrie was more a stern and distant figure than a loving grandparent. I hate to think how she would have coped if one of these visits had coincided with the time we were skinning eels nailed to the kitchen table.

During the last few years of Grandma Florrie's life, my mum would travel to Murrumbeena on the train to look after her, which was no mean feat, for as well as looking after us it was a two-hour journey both ways. Although Grandma Florrie was well aware of how much my mother had sacrificed in bringing up her three children on a widow's pension, when she died not a penny was left to her struggling daughter.

Mac.Robertson Girls' High

Our mother was an only child, and for some reason she spent a lot of her youth on the back verandah, which doesn't make for healthy social interaction in her formative years. She had told us she attended the prestigious Mac.Robertson Girls' High School, but we just waved this away as nonsense when compared to our hands-on mum who could swing an axe, dig a garden, and swear with the best of them. She even told us we were part Jewish. We didn't believe that either, and put it down as more of mum's wild assertions.

One day in her mid 60s my mother wrote me a letter and it had been *typed* … something that had never happened before. *Her arthritis has caught up with her so she's got someone to type her letters for her*, I logically surmised. When I put this to her she said, "Oh no, I've always been able to type … I learnt it at school. I got myself a good old typewriter from the opportunity shop that works quite well." I couldn't believe it. *Where did this come from?* I thought, *and what else has she got up her sleeve!* And as if to prove a point, after this I received a spate of letters all typed out with no mistakes.

A stranger at the door

Not long after this my mother received an unexpected visit from a complete stranger. The visitor was of slight build and in her early eighties. "My name is Eula Robinson," this quaint old lady said, "and I've been trying to find you for ages. I'm a distant relative, and I've been doing a lot of research on our family tree and there are a few questions I need answers to."

My mum just stood there stunned; nothing exciting like this ever came to her door in her sleepy hollow. "Come in and I'll make you a cup of tea," she said. It turns out that my mum was up with a lot of the information that Eula had researched, and it all made sense to her. To my mother's astonishment, Eula had thoughtfully photocopied it all as a gift for mum to study for herself.

The next time I visited my mum I was able to read all of Eula's diligent research. And boy was it an eye opener. Everything my mother had been telling us over the years was confirmed. My mother *did* go to the prestigious Mac.Robertson Girls' High just like she'd been telling us, but what she hadn't told us was she was *dux* of the school (and I don't mean ducks, I mean the true Latin meaning of *leader*), and there was a letter stating this amazing fact among the documents to prove it; star billing as a top-rate touch typist was also mentioned; and it also confirmed that there indeed was a Jewish connection with our family, for a Jewish guy by the name of Davis had jumped ship in Geelong in the 1800s and married a lady who bore our direct descendants. I confirmed this by visiting the Fawkner cemetery and seeing his Jewish headstone – all written in Hebrew. *Sometimes we can live with a person all our lives and never really know them.*

If Eula hadn't made that incredible journey from Toowoomba in Queensland to my mother's door in Maryborough with her revealing research, I would never have had the *fanciful* sides of my mother's story verified. These chance insights have helped change my understanding of her, and my own upbringing.

Years later, the day after my mother died, my sister Leanne emailed the office of the secondary school where I was working as an emergency teacher with an important message for me. Apparently it did the rounds of the whole hundred teaching staff before it found me, and generated quite a lot of mirth. It read:

> You get mum's Moo Moo dress and army boots to put in her coffin …
>
> Lee

My mother had a habit of always having the last say.

CHAPTER 30

Life's biggest challenge

Like any couple, Jan and I had our ups and downs; we had times when we were overjoyed, as with the birth of our children; other times we laughed and cried together; and on occasion we could hurt each other. Yet somehow we found our way through it all.

Little did we know that the biggest challenge of all lay ahead of us.

One day something happened that deeply affected us for the next 14 years. I'd just arrived home and found Jan sitting uncomfortable at the table; she was favouring one side of her body and spoke with a slur as if she was drunk.

"Are you okay?" I asked, concerned.

"I'm all right," she said. I wasn't convinced – she appeared disoriented. She then got up and walked to the sink, and her left leg was dragging. That was enough for me. *Stroke!* I thought, and immediately rang for an ambulance.

"I think my wife has had a stroke!" I said to the operator. When the paramedics arrived a few minutes later I repeated the word 'stroke', for that's what the symptoms indicated. They seemed to agree and rushed her to hospital.

All the signs said 'stroke'

The hospital also ran with this notion of Jan having being afflicted by a 'stroke' and treated her accordingly. For two days they monitored her carefully and put her through every test they could – but nothing! They couldn't find anything wrong with her, and sent her home.

Over the next few days we were worried – something wasn't quite right. So she went to her GP to see what he thought. Her doctor assessed the situation and said, "To me, this has all the hallmarks of multiple sclerosis. I'm sending you to see a specialist friend of mine at the Monash Medical Centre to check things out."

That's what we did – and that's what it turned out to be. We were devastated – overnight our whole world had been turned upside down. Then began the testing journey of coming to terms with it all and trying to make her better.

In time she did stop slurring her words and dragging her leg, but she continued to be a bit wobbly on her feet. Although they didn't completely understand the gravity of the situation, the kids all rallied to help their mum every way they could, and were a great support.

An added challenge was that the bills didn't stop coming in. They put her on a regime of Betaferon, a self-administered treatment by needle which seemed to help, yet doctors are not sure why. Another of her treatments was a watered-down version of the chemotherapy they use for cancer patients; again, they're not sure why this treatment works with multiple sclerosis but it seems to have some benefit. "At least you haven't got cancer like the other poor souls in the ward," I'd say, counting our blessings. As time went by we came to accept that this was how things would be from then on, and we learned to work around it and keep living normally as best we could.

But there was worse to come ...

But then one fearful day we were faced with a challenge that was 1000 times more challenging that Jan's MS ever was; the cancer clinic told her they were concerned with one of her tests and would like to see her.

I went with her, for we had to face this together, and although very fearful, we were hoping for the best. She looked so scared and defenceless sitting there … all I could do was hold her hand. Then her name was called. After a routine greeting the surgeon didn't mince her words: "We've found a cancer in your breast," she said to a petrified Jan. Then she gently reached over and held Jan's arm, "But it's what we do about it that matters," she said, "and we're going to do our utmost to help you." That said, we filled out the necessary paperwork and walked out of that surgery completely and utterly shell-shocked.

Our ten-year fight against cancer had begun.

As we walked to the car we were very quiet. There was a lot to take in and many unknown fears to confront. As fate had it, the radio came on when I started the car, and a newsreader was saying Australian pop icon Kylie Minogue had just been diagnosed with breast cancer and said she was going to fight it. This broke the tension a little, and I said, "We're in good company, for we're gonna fight it too!" Having Kylie in the battle alongside us made us feel a bit better.

A shift in our thinking

When we used to visit the cancer wards in St Vincent's Hospital to get our watered-down MS chemotherapy, we always felt sad for the *real* cancer patients who had to receive a *full* dose of it. We would always thank our lucky stars that we were the ones getting off lightly. Yet when the tables were turned and we were the cancer patients seeking treatment, we saw things in a very different light; far from being fearful places where people were waiting to die, we found they were places of hope where people wanted to get better! Each visit we'd get to know people of all ages and all walks of life who had a story to tell and who dreamed of beating their sickness. We'd always come out uplifted and inspired and never dreaded going there. Our weekly trip to the Austin Hospital for chemotherapy became an integral part of our lives.

The nurses in the cancer wards were a kind breed who knew us all by name and uplifted our spirits. We all became so friendly that one day while Jan was out of earshot I said to Belle, one of our nurses, "Do you ever enquire after the people you meet here?"

"No," she said, "I never follow up my patients … it's too sad … you never know … "

Chemo nurses are just like us, I thought, *they have feelings too.*

Jan never saw herself as courageous. "I'm just doing what I have to do," she would say. But she *was* courageous. She paid a terrible price in her quest to get better so she could see her kids grow into respected adults and hold her grandchildren on her knee. She lost her hair three times; the third time it went from her original dark and curly brunette colour to a thin and wispy pink.

While all this was going on, the rampaging MS didn't let up either, and Jan was getting weaker and weaker and looking more and more fragile. Sometimes life is just not fair. One thing that really hurt me was the day young Richard said to his sisters while they were watching our family video: "I want my *real* mum back."

We did our best to maintain a semblance of normality in our family, although it was a losing battle. And my difficulty in openly expressing the way I feel about those I care about in a loving way didn't help. But I tried as best I could.

All our kids were brought up on Monty Python, so we took them to see the Monty Python musical *Spamalot* at Her Majesty's Theatre as a family group like the old days. They loved it. And Jan's super-special treat from me, although at this stage she was very ill, was a night out with *Jersey Boys*. An evening she never stopped talking about.

Rhine River

Once we were browsing through a travel brochure. Jan was looking at enticing pictures of Rhine River cruises in those long luxurious cruise boats when she said, "Let's go on one of these." Now she'd just came out of hospital from a life-threatening operation of draining fluid from her lungs, so I knew this was impossible. When I ran it past our doctor he said she would not survive the air pressure of the plane, so we decided we'd go on a two-week cruise around Tasmania instead. I hired a mini oxygen machine to help her breathing, for by now she was continuously short of breath. And as a special treat, her sister Yvonne and brother Steven and their spouses would be on board too – which helped make up for her disappointment of not going on a Rhine River cruise.

By this time we had palliative care nurses visiting her at home, helping her shower and dressing her wounds. I was still in denial, for even though these kind souls introduced themselves as *palliative care* nurses, I only heard *nurses*.

I always thought she would get better.

Before our Tasmanian trip they said to me, "You'll have to do all these things on the ship, so to learn how, you can dress and bandage her for the next few days." So under their watchful eye they showed me how to dress her breast, which wasn't easy. The trick was to do it in a matter-of-fact way to get her mind off the gravity of it all.

One thing Jan never did was play the 'woe is me' pity card, even when she had every right to do so.

Pampered like royalty

On the cruise, our routine was to help her shower, bandage her wounds, then make her look as nice as I could for breakfast if she was well enough. For dinner in the opulent dining room, we made a real effort and dressed formally in our evening wear. The waiters treated her as a perfectly healthy woman and pampered her like royalty at the table, which was lovely. And for the evening show

I would dress her in her finest clothes she'd bought especially for the occasion – including her black sequinned shoes! As she wasn't able to go on shore trips with the others, I'd walk her around the ship in her wheelchair exploring the sights from the deck.

Only once, after bandaging her and doing my best to make her feel better, did I nearly lose it. But I knew I couldn't, for *she* was the one on the verge of giving up and *I* was the one who had to be strong. I held back my tears and said, "I'll just see what the others are doing," and left the room.

Magic from the crowd

One magic highlight happened while we were in the middle of hundreds of people listening to the Captain's welcome; a complete stranger came up to my very sick Jan in her wheelchair and gently placed a small silver cross and chain in her hand with the words "God bless you". He then faded back into the crowd. This meant a lot to Jan, for deep down she was a believer and always had been. She cherished that little cross and chain and it stayed around her neck.

All in all we had a wonderful, therapeutic trip.

When we got back we had to go to the hospital to get the latest prognosis from the surgeon who had been looking after her for six years or more. After examining the disease's rapid progress, he told her that the situation was terminal.

"How long have I got?" Jan asked straight out. I saw this hardened surgeon with many years' experience almost beg her … "Do you really want to know?"

"Yes," she quietly said. He hung his head and ran his fingers through his hair, "Two months," he said.

Jan and I walked down that lonely corridor arm in arm, the last time we would do so.

A few short weeks

The next little while was surreal as we both tried to adjust to the fact that Jan was going to die in a few short weeks. One of the social workers told me it would be a good idea to watch a family video together to help her let go … and sad though it was, we did this. But nothing was easy.

Every once in a while Jan would have lucid flashes of her old self with a warm sparkle in her eye. One day she asked me to sit down beside her: "I want to tell you something," she said. "In a little while I'll be gone, and it'll be nice if you remember me, but life goes on and if you meet someone else I want you to know it's okay with me."

But I'd have none of it, and – emotionally blind to the truth – I said, "We're going to make you better so things can go on as they were before!"

"No," she repeated, "I won't be here." I was the only one in denial, and remained so right till the end. Maybe that's why the *reality* of her passing hit me so hard.

Prior to my family life I'd never had a close community to call on; I'd always suffered my trials alone. Knowing our cherished neighbours and friends were not far away helped us.

Hollywood Nails

Jan had always been determined to stay at home till the end, but we couldn't cope with the morphine dosages because I wasn't a trained nurse. When she said she wanted to go to the hospice I knew it was the end.

The day before the ambulance came to take her, we went to Hollywood Nails for a complete foot and nail beauty makeover. We loaded her wheelchair into the car and away we went. I sat next to her while she lay back and luxuriated like the Queen of the castle. Jan fell into conversation with a nice middle-age lady sitting next to her.

"I haven't got long for this world," I heard her say.

The other lady gave her a card and said, "If you need someone to talk to, give me a call." When we later looked at the card, the lady was in The Salvation Army – yet another complete stranger who had discerned Jan's need for comfort.

When the ambulance came to transport her to the hospice, the first thing the paramedics commented on was how beautiful Jan's nails looked. She beamed; she had at least made herself beautiful for her final journey.

Richard returns from Ecuador

Amazingly, Richard returned from his sojourn in Ecuador the day before his mum passed away. It really was one of those incredible cases where the parent holds on to life in time to say goodbye. Felicity drove him straight from the airport to the hospice, and Jan was sitting up in bed very lucid while he unpacked his case with her carefully chosen presents in it … a warm, fluffy pair of traditional Ecuadorian slippers, and an equally warm Inca hat. We were all relieved he had made it in time.

That night I slept on a mattress beside Jan, listening to the sounds of dying emanating from adjacent rooms, which she was oblivious to because of her high dosage of morphine. She did wake up sporadically during the night; I'd lean over to let her know I was there, and she'd tell me she just wanted to die. I'd then call the night nurse and they'd increase her morphine dosage to relieve her pain.

The following morning her brother Steven arrived around 7 am and we arranged to have Jan lifted out of bed and put in a big comfy armchair affair where you neither sit nor lie down but you can observe what's going on. Her long-term friends Velda and Graham were there too.

I rushed out to buy Jan a treat of her favourite avocado salad that we'd had together a few months ago and brought it back for her.

How dumb that was. She couldn't eat. She smiled a little and gently shook her head.

A short time later we knew that the time for her to depart this Earth was nigh. Jan said, "I'm dying," ... I held her hand. Then Steven produced a book, and full of emotion said, "I have a poem I want to read to you," which turned out to be John Donne's *No Man is an Island.* A poem about how we human beings are necessarily dependent on one another, for we can't manage things alone.

With trembling hands Steven began to read, but he got all choked up and couldn't go on. "I'll do it for you," I said, and gently took the book from his hands. Time was of the essence, for Jan's hands were turning blue. I'd never read this poem before in my life. But the words became part of me and seemed perfect for the moment.

When I'd finished I whispered in her ear: "Did you hear Steven's poem I just read for you?" She nodded . She breathed her last, thirty seconds later. The last voice Jan heard was mine, the imperfect guy who stood by her through thick and thin; and the last words she heard were those selected by her loving brother Steven.

Saying our goodbyes

Still numb with Jan at peace in the room beside me, the first person I rang was Linda.

She asked, "Do you want me to ring everyone for you dad?"

"Oh, yes," I said, "that would be wonderful ... I don't think I'd be up to it."

So Linda made the calls, and in what seemed like minutes all three of our kids were there to say goodbye to their mum; the brave, unselfish woman who had brought them into the world. Linda preferred to say goodbye to her mum privately in her own heartfelt way. Richard and Felicity said their goodbyes together as their mum lay peacefully at rest.

At her funeral the church was overflowing, with more than 1200 people wanting to say goodbye to their kindly friend and beloved relative and celebrate what a wonderful person she was – which said it all to me. And our neighbours Franz and Inge put on an equally memorable reception in her honour.

Time is a great healer

When all these heartfelt celebrations and commiserations had subsided, there we were – all alone; all four of us separately adrift on an endless sea with no lighthouse and no land in sight. We were left to flounder around with no purpose or direction in the hope that we would somehow make landfall.

My coping mechanism was to retreat into my watercolour painting for the next seven years – *right when the kids needed me*. I'd unintentionally drifted off ... leaving them to find their own way out of their grief as best they could; which in turn caused its own pain and suffering that is still in the process of healing. This is another heavy burden of guilt I'm trying to make peace with.

I am a great believer in the old adage that 'time heals all wounds.'

But Jan had one last touch of her magic for her family. About a year after her passing, the milestone of Richard's 21st birthday was upon us. That evening we were all in the kitchen having a couple of drinks and finger food to celebrate. We'd just sung *Happy Birthday* when Linda pulled an envelope out of her pocket and gave it to Richard: "Happy 21st ... from mum," she said.

We were all stunned, for none of us knew anything of this. Richard opened the envelope and counted out a thousand dollars! Jan had managed to squirrel this away from her pension over the last year or so, knowing she wouldn't be there to give it to him.

We were all moved beyond words. That night Jan was with us in spirit one last time.

Sitting around the campfire

Around this time Richard made a very astute observation. On our fridge there is a photo of me and Jan sitting beside each other on two camp stools around a campfire. We are both smiling and look like any normal couple enjoying each other's company. Which is true, because I proudly stuck it there. Soon after this photo was taken, the scene around that campfire was a much more animated one. I was doing my usual 'thing', entertaining everyone by swinging a billy can of tea round my head as swaggies and the early pioneers used to do to settle the tea leaves. We then enjoyed a nice mug of this carefully-brewed bushman's tea, accompanied by the scrumptious stockman's damper I'd just baked.

Standing there contemplating this photo, Richard said: "Hey dad, I like this picture on the fridge of you and mum sitting together by the campfire. There's something about it that makes you look like two nervous teenagers on their first date, and it's kinda cute."

I couldn't believe my ears, for he was the first person in my whole life who had ever detected this inner 'shyness' secret of mine. But I took careful note that he'd said, "It's kinda cute", a nice positive way of looking at it, and what's more, it put a permanent spin on the way I now see myself.

This small observation from my very perceptive son has helped me understand why I've always struggled with this uneasy feeling of 'what to do' when nothing much is happening or being said.

His insightful comment really got me thinking. *Maybe it's okay to be the way I am?* It helped me to accept that it's all right if every so often I'm casually doing some little thing, like stoking the campfire, pouring another glass of wine, or striking up a conversation with others. It helped me understand that I can still be the funny man, but I've tempered this somewhat. In fact, I can now even feel comfortable contemplating what's going on around me without the urge to do or say anything!

It really is amazing how a simple comment can have the power to inspire one to dramatically shift a faulty state of mind and make a real difference in a permanent way.

Glimmer of hope through the darkness

Although I was living through my own grief and sadness while trying to make life-changing differences to others in my coaching sessions to pay the bills, I had become blind to what was happening around me. My own grief-filled children were drifting away ... They never shared or asked me anything about how *they* were feeling ... But how could they? They were grieving themselves and thought I didn't care!

Only when it came to the crunch and they sent out a plea for me, as nominal head of the family, to do something did I snap into seeing a glimmer of light and arrange for some family counselling sessions. And it was here they were able to vent about how neglected they all felt.

This revelation of perceived *neglect* shook me like an earthquake. While these painful and empty seven years had been flying by, I had mentally retreated to a *safer* period where everything I did revolved around *my vulnerable little children.* I spent my time painting them as kids. I was living in my past memories with them when everything was fine, as if they were still little. Having retreated to this rear-vision state of mind, I was of little help to my *grown-up* children who were suffering in the present.

Coming to terms with my own depression and unintentional distancing from my kids in a time of their critical need has affected me deeply, for great damage has been done. But there is a positive; the difference now is I'm acutely aware of how *everyone* feels, whereas before I was completely in the dark. With this new awareness, all I can do now is reach out a patient hand of understanding.

CHAPTER 31

A new page is turned

To play a confident part in my new role of being father to young *adults* in place of *all-believing little children*, I had to make sure I was happy and stable within myself first. But Jan was gone, and I was a lost and lonely man. Then Jan's words came back to me; that she didn't want me to be alone when she had gone; and it was okay with her if I met a nice person to share the remainder of my life with. But I did feel guilty to even look at someone else, and what would my kids think, for no one could replace their mother. But Jan's words kept telling me it was okay … that she really wasn't being replaced.

I was very scared about it all, for my shyness in talking to women with the purpose of winning them over was still overwhelming. So I tried the internet, and arranged five 'coffees' with five different women.

Five encounters. One of them asked me why I was wearing a suit. "To look like I'd made an effort," I replied. She just shrugged. The other meetings didn't go much better. In the end I just gave up. It was all too hard.

I was very good at small talk, for that wasn't threatening. *But how do I get past that?* I thought. I had other interests that kept me in contact with other people too. Over the years my learning and teaching Italian for a hobby to groups of friends has given me lots of joy. One group I was sharing my love for Italian with was held in a private home, and every Christmas we'd have a year's end celebration there. One year I was struggling with Jan's battle with cancer and Glynis, the host of the house, shared that a few years prior to this her brother had gone through a similar thing and sadly lost his battle.

"What is sad," she said, "is he'd met a lovely person called Carmel not long before he died and they were so happy together." And as a quirk of the universe, Carmel and Jan met at the next Christmas celebration and got on well. It wasn't long after this that my Jan also passed away.

The following Christmas Carmel joined us for our end-of-year Christmas break up, for she knew us all by now. When I met her this time and got talking to her I thought, "She *is* a nice person." One thing I did learn about her was she was a watercolour artist too.

The following year she was at our Christmas party again … as she was the following Christmas … and the one after that … it wasn't until the *forth* Christmas gathering that I finally felt comfortable enough to ask her out to dinner. I guess it was a combination of letting go of the loss of Jan, mixed with my innate shyness of girls, that made it so hard for me. I remember unceremoniously walking over to her at the self-serve table and blurting out: "Do you want to go out to dinner?"

She looked at me totally surprised, for after four years of Christmas party chit-chat she never saw this coming. "Yes," she said. Relieved, I scurried back to the safety of the others.

Our first date

We went to a little Italian restaurant for our dinner and spent the evening in pleasant small talk, only briefly touching on how we coped with our personal losses. We then went back to her place for coffee and discussed the nuances of watercolour painting for a good two hours, then it was time for me to go. I began to panic: *How do I ask for a follow-up date?* I thought to myself. Carmel told me later: "I went to give you a little thank-you kiss on the cheek for such a lovely evening and you simply ran away into the darkness."

I felt really bad about that – it yet again proved to me just how hopeless I was in courting women. I sent her a little card sincerely thanking her for a lovely evening and mentioning how much we had in common. Although I wanted to, the one thing I didn't do was ask her out again. And that's how it stood for yet another *three years*! That's right, three more bloody years! Oh, we'd continue to meet at our Christmas functions and exchange pleasant small talk, but that was it. However, the third year was different, for it was Carmel who made a move and brought me a Christmas present; a packet of special watercolour painting paper. That was it! *Nothing is going to happen unless you make the next move you weak bastard!* I admonished myself.

Early the next morning while it was still dark I put my plan into action. I grabbed a Christmas card, although Christmas had passed, and hurriedly wrote a little note along the lines of "time we caught up for coffee again to chat about our painting and other things ... " and signed it. I then hurried out the door while it was still dark, crept to her place like a thief in the night and popped it in her letterbox, ever fearful she might see me. I heaved a sigh of relief when I was safely on my way home again.

Two weeks later I got a reply, but not the way I thought. It was an email from her daughter saying how pleased Carmel was to receive my card and that she'd love a coffee with me. Great! But the phone number she'd included had an incorrect digit! After juggling them around and trying three times, I got through to Carmel and we made our long-awaited *second* date. This time I didn't let her go, and told her what I really thought; that after all this time we were meant to be together.

My other fear of the kids not liking her evaporated too. The kids love her, and I know Jan would approve of all this as well.

Isn't it amazing how quickly things happen when you have the courage to do something!

Another wonderful thing happened

Then another joyous thing occurred: my daughter Linda and her fiancé Dominic announced their engagement! On their wedding day, before a packed church of family and friends, only I knew the profound depth of my feelings of pride as I walked her down the aisle to the man she chose to spend her life with; I'd never dreamed this would be something I'd ever do. And later at the reception, I felt equally proud as the bearer of heartfelt wishes from her dearly departed mother for a long and happy life together. How proud I was that, along with Jan, I'd done my best – although falling well short at times – to assist in Linda being the successful young woman she is today.

My fervent wish is that with the healing passage of time the rest of us will find our own peace and happiness too.

* * *

Finally: single-minded obsessions – whether magnificent or not – are not good, for they can be all-consuming to the detriment of everything else dear to you. You must find a balance with the other things you care about as well or you'll run the risk of losing them all.

After all these years I'm now fine with *where* I've been and *what* I've learned about myself. Nowadays, if I get the odd pang of shyness it's not a big deal, for I know it will quickly go away; and my lifelong fear of maths has evaporated for I'm now proficient in the use of an *ordinary* calculator.

I realise I can't have a rerun of my life with what I know now. But what I *can* do is move forward with my hard-gained wisdom that allows me to see myself in a *forgiving* new light; and I *can* confidently move forward knowing not only *what* to do, but more importantly what *not* to do.

The interesting thing is that none of *my search for me* was intentional as such, for we only learn from experience and the wisdom of hindsight. The main reason for writing my story was to help you, the reader, relate *your* journey to some of the pitfalls I've had to face as I've stumbled through life trying to understand why I think and act the way I do. If the 'proverbial hindsights' in this book have helped you in some way to see things more clearly, it will have been worth the time and effort in putting it together. Your 'butterfly' mightn't be adorned with all the colours of the rainbow yet but its wings are now complete and it can fly beautifully!

So whatever you do, be comfortable with yourself: be comfortable with where you've been; be comfortable with where you're at; and be comfortable with where you'd like to be. This in mind, I'll leave you to contemplate Ralph Waldo Emerson's wise and timeless words:

Make the most of who you are
for that is all there is of you.

Now that you're treading a whole new path of *thinking confidence*, why not build on what you've learned, and invest further in your personal growth with my other life-changing products written especially to complement the ideas and inspirations in this mind-opening book. Check them out – and my comprehensive package deal – at www.panicfreepublicspeaking.com.au.

Laurie Smale
Inspirational Speaker, Published Author
and Master Speaking Coach

Lightning Source UK Ltd.
Milton Keynes UK
UKHW051136120920
369747UK00019B/703